Montblanc Writing Time

ACKNOWLEDGMENTS

Montblanc would like to express its gratitude to Henry-John Belmont for being a great advisor on the overall development of the book. We particularly thank Guillaume Picon for his historical research on Nicolas Mathieu Rieussec and Dominique Fléchon for his participation in the creation of this book. We would also like to thank Florence Kirkorian and Gaëlle Jeanrenaud for their tireless support at the *manufacture* Montblanc in le Locle.

EXECUTIVE EDITOR
Suzanne Tise-Isoré

EDITORIAL COORDINATION
Sarah Rozelle

GRAPHIC DESIGN
Alain Bourdon

ADAPTATION
François Chaille

TEXT BY GISBERT BRUNNER, AND THE TEXT ADAPTED
FROM THE ORIGINAL BY LAURENCE MARTI
TRANSLATED FROM THE FRENCH BY
Deke Dusinberre

TEXT BY REINHARD MEIS TRANSLATED
FROM THE GERMAN BY
Datawords

COPYEDITING/PROOFREADING
Helen Woodhall

PRODUCTION
Bénédicte Gaudin

COLOR SEPARATION
Les Artisans du Regard, Paris

PRINTED BY
Musumeci, Italy

Distributed in North America by Rizzoli International Publications, Inc.
Simultaneously published in French as *Écrire le Temps*.

© Flammarion SA, Paris, 2010
© Montblanc, 2010

English-language edition
© Flammarion SA, Paris, 2010

All rights reserved. No part of this publication may be reproduced in any form or by any means, electronic, photocopy, information retrieval system, or otherwise, without a written permission from Flammarion.

Flammarion SA
87, quai Panhard et Levassor
75647 Paris Cedex 13
France
editions.flammarion.com

Dépôt légal: 11/2010
10 11 12 3 2 1
ISBN: 9782080301581
Printed in Italy by Musumeci

Montblanc Writing Time

Franco Cologni   Gisbert Brunner   Reinhard Meis

Photography by
Francis Hammond *and* Éric Sauvage

Flammarion

11 FOREWORD

Franco Cologni

I II III

14 MONTBLANC, WRITING TIME

21	**MONTBLANC, MASTERING PENMANSHIP**	123	**A FEW NOBLE CRAFTS**
21	The birth of Montblanc	123	The guardian of time
26	The *Meisterstück* pen conquers the world	124	The innovator of tradition
28	Montblanc at the summit: The "Artisans' Atelier"	127	The artisans of design
31	Montblanc: An exclusive lifestyle	128	The master of perfect beauty
		130	The queen of hearts
41	**MONTBLANC, MASTERING TIME**	133	The machine whisperer
41	From pens to timepieces: Montblanc at Le Locle		
44	Respecting an identity	135	**A TIME FOR THINGS RARE AND ORIGINAL**
48	Iconic Timewriters	136	A watch, a showcase
		136	Multiple missions
57	**NICOLAS MATHIEU RIEUSSEC (1781-1866)**	138	The Institut Minerva de Recherche en Haute Horlogerie
59	**THE RIEUSSEC CHRONOGRAPH**		
59	Inventing the modern chronograph		*Gisbert Brunner*
60	Perfecting chronographs		
62	In tribute to Rieussec		
70	Montblanc means accuracy		
77	**THE MONTBLANC *MANUFACTURE* AT VILLERET**		
77	The perfect symbiosis of Montblanc and Minerva		
81	The *Collection Montblanc Villeret 1858*		

Contents

II|III

144	**150 YEARS OF WATCHMAKING TRADITION IN VILLERET**
145	**A VALLEY TRADITION**
147	**THE ROBERT FAMILY MAKES A START**
149	**PUTTING WATCHES TOGETHER: THE *ÉTABLISSEUR***
156	**PLAYING A PUBLIC ROLE**
160	**WATCHMAKING**
162	**THE BIRTH OF A *MANUFACTURE***
167	**A FERTILE TRANSITION**
170	**STABILIZING BUSINESS**
171	**OPTING FOR QUALITY**
161	**GOING IT ALONE**
175	**A SINGLE BRAND FOR LOYAL AGENTS**
176	**CAUTION AND THRIFT**
178	**TOWARD THE NEXT STAGE**

*Historical and picture research:
Laurence Marti
Text adapted from the original text
by Laurence Marti*

III|II

180	**THE HISTORY OF MINERVA WATCH MOVEMENTS**
183	**HOROLOGICAL SPECIALTIES IN THE SAINT-IMIER VALLEY**
185	**CHARLES IVAN ROBERT STARTS TO DEVELOP WATCH PRODUCTION AT VILLERET**
197	**THE FIRST *MANUFACTURE* MOVEMENTS**
213	**"EXTRA QUALITY" ANCHOR ESCAPEMENTS**
233	**THE BIRTH OF THE CHRONOGRAPH**
239	**MINERVA CHRONOGRAPH MOVEMENTS**
245	**NEW CHRONOGRAPH BY MINERVA**
253	**THE WRIST-CHRONOGRAPH**
267	**THE AESTHETICS OF MECHANISMS**

Reinhard Meis

Foreword

Franco Cologni, *President of the Fondation de la Haute Horlogerie*

If, as was written by Albert Camus, the ancient gods thought there was no punishment worse than futile and senseless effort, then the opposite is also true: few things bring greater satisfaction than work carried out to the highest standards, effort crowned by success and commitment to a goal.

As a young mountaineer, my climbing companions and I were always filled with surprise, admiration and satisfaction upon crossing a high pass or reaching a difficult summit after a long trek. I felt an even greater sense of pride when I climbed Mont Blanc for the very first time, because it's easy to find oneself, one's role, one's identity in the pure air of Europe's highest peak.

In writing this introduction for the book whose title I suggested, I have not been able to resist thinking that Montblanc's path in the world of fine watchmaking is not dissimilar to that of the conquest of this wonderful summit: a path for those specialising in high-mountain ascents, a gradual approach and a series of necessary steps to establish the right pace and respiration. To finally reach a peak where "one cannot lose oneself", as written by the poet Wislawa Szymborska.

Each serious climbing expedition that takes place, not as an adventure but as a well-defined goal and ambition, requires a base camp and a few mandatory stops and crossings.

The starting point for those wishing to climb to the summit of Mont Blanc is either Chamonix or Courmayeur, where one of several routes can be chosen: from the most spectacular (from Aiguille du Midi) to the most traditional (from Nid d'Aigle), from the longest and least popular (through the Grands Mulets) to the most daring (the direct Walter Bonatti route).

In its journey from the glory of writing to the dizzying heights of fine watchmaking, Montblanc has marked its steps on the basis of a gradual acquisition of expertise and legitimate "levels" (from I to VI), while training for the difficult crossings of the Mont Blanc, something that is considered truly "sacred" by the brand. Ascents are never undertaken without a careful eye on both the hours and the minutes. The first stage of the journey in 1997 led to the base camp at a villa in Le Locle. In this historic Swiss town, selected by the best watchmakers and still an important source of expertise today, Montblanc not only began to write a new chapter of its history, but also began to speak a new language: that of fine watchmaking. A language whose basic rules were already being applied by the brand: patience, dedication, precision, elegance and pride: standards of technical and aesthetic excellence.

Facing page

The *Montblanc Nicolas Rieussec Chronograph*, equipped with the caliber MB R 200 self-winding movement made by the Montblanc *manufacture*. Monopusher chronograph equipped with a column wheel and a vertical clutch. Twin barrels. Power reserve 72 hours. GMT function with day/night display.

But only few are able to master this language with the necessary skills to ascend to the peak, towards the heights of fine watchmaking.

The next step in 2007 was the acquisition of Minerva, one of Switzerland's most respected watchmakers, with a century of success and recognition behind it: from the workshop in Villeret that served as Minerva's head office, the summit of the mountain seemed ever closer and clearer. Thanks to the tireless stops organised with a view to the future by Norbert Platt, the best expedition leader that one could wish for, the summit was finally conquered with the knowledge, pride and – dare I say it – the fitness of true athletes: 2008 saw the launch of the chronograph dedicated to Nicolas Matthieu Rieussec, the historic eighteenth century inventor, master watchmaker and father of the first chronograph.

Chrono-graph: an instrument for "writing" time. An instrument of rare style and precision that, just like the masterpieces designed in the Montblanc pen workshops, encompasses an entire universe: beauty and invention, history and time, moments to be measured and instants to be recorded. These instants are recorded by the pen of memory, as watches are ink-free. Or learning to read the time as well as record it, in the light of the passion and pleasure that are experienced each time a difficult target is achieved.

Minerva's gifts, or rather its methods and skills, are those that the Swiss company brought to the craftsmanship, planning and perfection of Montblanc. Just like the ancient goddess of wisdom and intelligence, the history of Swiss watchmaking is symbolic of the wise decision of he who ventures into a fascinating world equipped with all the right tools. This decision is presented and explained in the book using a triple perspective: a true triptych, albeit conceptual and non-pictorial, held together by an identity founded on inspiration and foresight, which passes from the history of Montblanc as the creator of magnificent pens to the relationship between these instruments and the watches, and from the historic origins of their "heart" (i.e. the inventions and complications of the watchmakers in Villeret) to descriptions of the elements, details and enigmatic and scientific mechanisms that make Montblanc timepieces truly distinctive. Thanks to the authors of the triptych and their specific expertise, Montblanc can thus be included in historical texts that focus on fine watchmaking.

In less than fifteen years, Montblanc has conquered one of the highest and most inaccessible peaks: the heights of fine watchmaking. An ascent that only a few, well-trained mountaineers have attempted and successfully conquered.

Taking the mountain route is an ambition born from true passion, unquestionable will and genuine expertise. But now it is today's youth who must try their hand at this ascent, to discover all that our eyes are unable to capture, cast as they are towards scrutinising the past to provide an understanding of the present. The base camps and the route are in place: but as the saying goes, if the bridge is God's, then the advances are Man's.

To provide an incentive for these advances, Montblanc has set up a foundation for the development of research and innovation: because tomorrow cannot do without today's resources or yesterday's conquests. This book is dedicated to all those who are not afraid to trace their own steps forwards, who wish to record their time spent on rocks and glaciers, and who are fascinated by beauty and experience, seeing each limitation as a responsible challenge: an ascent on which my mind lingers in a final memory of my mountaineering days, of the summit of Mont Blanc on a bright, sunny day while the shadows dissipate like dark waters.

Gloria in excelsis.

Facing page
Detail of the chronograph bridge
of the chronograph caliber MB M 16–29.

Montblanc Writing Time

Gisbert Brunner

IIIIII

Montblanc: a name that inspires reverie for anyone who is passionate about writing. Simply uttering the name conjures up the incomparable majesty of the king of fountain pens, the legendary fountain pen *Meisterstück 149*. So perfect and timelessly elegant was this pen that it has become one of the undisputed wonders of modern writing instruments. To cradle a black resin barrel crowned with a mountain peak or snow flake; to glide a platinum-inlaid, 18-karat gold nib across a sheet of vellum; and to allow a pen to respond to ideas with amazing fluidity: such are the pleasures of extreme refinement and sensuality for which many writers have sold their souls since 1924. Once the company realized the extent of writers' passionate attachment to the *Meisterstück 149* fountain pen, it designed fairy-tale variations on the original model, producing treasures straight out of the Arabian Nights in a workshop in Hamburg, Germany. These highly limited editions were made by virtuoso craftsmen and featured, for example, caps of hand-painted Meissen porcelain, barrels of resin adorned with fine cut-out motifs of solid gold, clips decorated with a fragment of a meteorite, and hand-carved nibs engraved with rosettes and an openwork heart. All were dazzling gems designed for today's aristocrats.

Into this exclusive world where words of love are still expressed in writing (as are adventure novels and thoughts both frivolous and profound), Montblanc made an entrance one day in 1997, wanting to address the subject of time. It did so through watches that breathe the same pure air of the heights of refinement. Having made its name in writing instruments—without which there would be no civilization—Montblanc naturally wanted to leave its mark on that other milestone of human accomplishment, the measurement of time, without which there would be no progress. The company's first watches, in black and gold and bearing its trademark star, inevitably evoked the nobility of the writing instrument *Meisterstück*. A new legend was thus born in Le Locle, a town in the Swiss mountains where the finest watchmakers originated and still live. Because Montblanc watches embodied the same sense of eternity, there were soon as many Montblancs on wrists as there were between thumb and forefinger, instantly recognizable by growing numbers of enthusiasts thanks to the snowy star on winding crown or cap. 2008 marked another important milestone for Montblanc watches. That year, Montblanc introduced the *Montblanc Nicolas Rieussec Chronograph* to the public in an homage to Nicolas Mathieu Rieussec, the inventor of the chronograph.

Yet the spirit of the hundred-year-old company remained unchanged. Montblanc retained the "white knight" attitude that had enabled it to accomplish fabulous deeds in the realm of writing instruments. In 2007 it seized the opportunity to enrich its line of watches with lavish timepieces that contain—and often display—the finest and most subtle mechanisms ever invented: hundreds of tiny hand-tooled, hand-decorated, and hand-assembled parts, weighing just a few dozen grams and encased in precious metal, which together drive a beating heart that tells not only the accurate time but also other useful ways of measuring time. Montblanc's wonderful opportunity, a means of offering bliss to a few select individuals, came in the form of a traditional maker—or *manufacture*—of extremely fine timepieces—*haute horlogerie*—founded one hundred and fifty years earlier in Villeret in the Jura Mountains of Switzerland. That maker is named Minerva. Just as Montblanc pens had their own crown jewels, so Montblanc watches also boasted masterpieces produced in limited, numbered editions, or occasionally as unique items patiently and meticulously elaborated by horologists highly skilled in the supreme art of watchmaking. By taking over the *manufacture* Minerva in Villeret, Montblanc was acquiring an enchanted pen for writing time.

The innovation of today is the tradition of the future. Minerva's own extraordinary heritage also needed safeguarding. So even as its traditional technical and artistic skills are still being practiced today at Villeret through the making of exclusive chronographs and *tourbillons*, Montblanc set up a foundation to launch the Institut Minerva de Recherche en Haute Horlogerie with the goal of encouraging young watchmakers through training and support for new projects and creative ambitions to secure the tradition of tomorrow.

Preceding page, right

The *Meisterstück 149* fountain pen is one of the best-known and most famous writing instruments of our time. Hand-crafted in the best European tradition since 1924, its 18-karat gold nib with platinum inlay, three gold-plated rings, gold-plated clip, and deep black precious resin barrel make this luxurious writing instrument a legend among fountain pens.

Right

The famous Montblanc Star emblem representing the snowy peak of Europe's highest mountain, the Mont Blanc, symbolizes high craftsmanship and perfect quality. It adorns all Montblanc products.

Facing page

The year 2006 confirmed Montblanc's skills in the arcane science of horology. For its hundredth anniversary, the company launched its *Montblanc Star Chrono GMT Perpetual Calendar* watch, limited to just one hundred copies in each of the three versions in white, yellow, or pink gold. Its perpetual calendar movement based on the Gregorian calendar should require no manual adjustment until the year 2100, assuming that it is wound regularly. The letters GMT refer to the display of a second time zone governed by an improved automatic caliber ETA 7754 movement; this complication model was also endowed with a special safety crown capped by a Montblanc Diamond.

Montblanc, Mastering Penmanship

THE BIRTH OF MONTBLANC

Given technical hurdles that long seemed insurmountable, it took many years for the fountain pen to be developed as an item of everyday use. Even though early patents were issued for this type of instrument in England in 1809 and in Germany in 1878, it was not until the early twentieth century that an American manufacturer finally produced a fountain pen with a fairly reliable built-in reservoir. This pen soon found its way to Europe. On both sides of the Atlantic, however, potential customers remained profoundly wary of this new and still fairly crude product—users often found their paper splattered and spotted, since a simple tube served as reservoir, and refilling it inevitably entailed spilling a few drops of ink. The built-in nib, meanwhile, was protected by a cap that was not always watertight.

The appearance of safety screw-top caps represented an important step forward because enclosing the nib in them prevented unfortunate ink spills—more or less. Fountain pens that could be filled directly from a bottle of ink thus became more widespread after the First World War, finally becoming dominant in subsequent decades.

When the company that would soon be known as Montblanc was founded, fountain pens had not reached this degree of perfection. But the concept fascinated a Hamburg businessman keen on technical and industrial progress, Claus Johannes Voss. The true start of the Montblanc legend came about in 1906 when Voss met Alfred Nehemias and August Eberstein, a stationer and an engineer who had already teamed up to make fountain pens. Voss, after completing his business studies, had furthered his professional experience in Great Britain, Spain, and Central America, and later acquired a stake in a wholesale distributor of manufactured goods, so he now had access to the financing essential to launching a project on a major scale.

Nehemias and Eberstein had notably developed a promising fountain pen dubbed *Rouge et Noir* (Red & Black) for which they founded a Berlin-based manufacturing company. But they lacked the capital to insure the growth of their business. Voss, enthusiastic about their products, came to their aid. And yet his resources, though substantial, were not enough to build the new *manufacture* required by the two men's ambitions. Another partner, Max Koch, therefore bought a stake in the venture; a former bank employee, Koch had inherited sufficient wealth to quit his job and realize his dream of going independent. In 1908, the Simplo Filler Pen Co. Ltd—Manufacturers of High Class Gold and Fountain Pens—was founded and registered in the Registry of Trade of Hamburg.

The quartet chose the city of Hamburg as the headquarters for the new firm. Voss and Koch each contributed 50,000 marks of capital

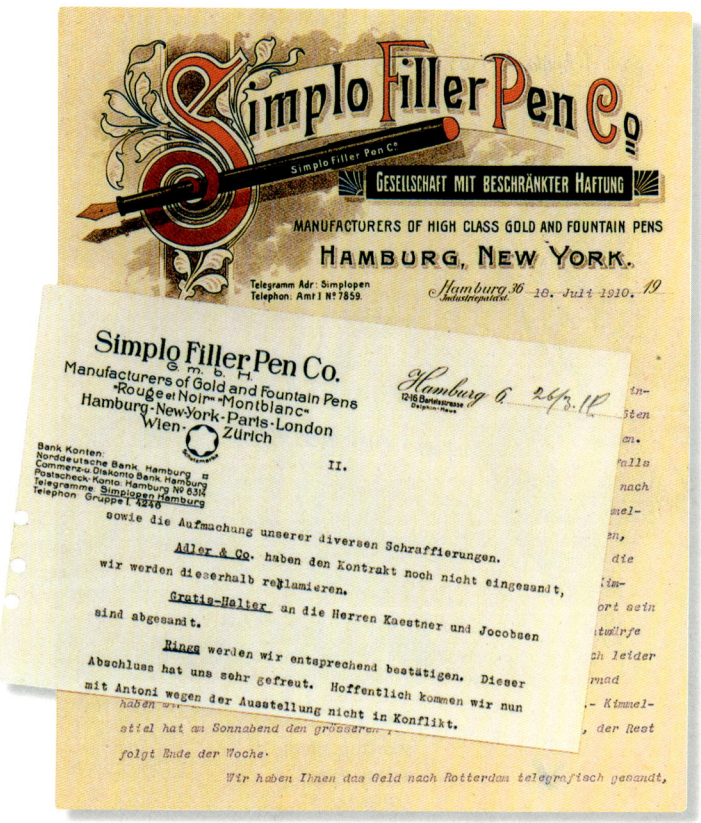

Above

"Manufacturers of High Class Gold and Fountain Pens"—This notice found in the Registry of Trade, allowed Montblanc to enter in history. At the time, the small company was known as the Simplo Filler Pen Company.

Facing page

John F. Kennedy helps the German chancellor Konrad Adenauer out of a predicament by offering him his *Meisterstück 149* fountain pen.

Above
Montblanc advertisement, 1914.

Below
Montblanc's first advertisement, 1910.

whereas Nehemias and Eberstein's contribution consisted of technical equipment, patents, and prototypes under development. The machines remained the sole property of Eberstein, who managed the manufacturing operations. Koch handled administrative affairs while Nehemias headed the marketing side. The agreement also included a silent partner, Wilhem Dziambor, former employee of the Hamburg office-supply firm of Rothschild, Behrens, & Co., soon to play a leading role in the Simplo Filler Pen Co. The corporate name of Montblanc did not yet exist—but everything would happen in good time.

The new company got off to a rough start. Occupying two floors of the Palace of Industry (an imposing building located on Caffamacherreihe), twelve machinists and ten female workers labored under the supervision of a foreman to make "safety pens" of ebonite, marketed under the names of *Diplomat* and *Rouge et Noir* (with a red cap). These products were sufficiently successful for the company to open offices in Paris, London, and Barcelona. But corporate organization was thrown into chaos due to disputes between partners—resulting in the departure of Koch and Eberstein—and the death of Nehemias. The Simplo Filler Pen Company soon found itself with no partner who had sufficient technical knowledge to run the manufacturing operations; given the emergency situation, one competent employee agreed to fill the void. Named production manager, Georg Illgner safely steered the ship through treacherous reefs until it reached calmer waters. His first invention took the form of a "safety reservoir" in which the nib pivoted in the barrel of the pen, allowing a little silver stud inside the cap to enter the feed tube and thereby block any leakage. Since a white cap lent a discreet elegance to this new writing instrument, it was soon dubbed *Montblanc*.

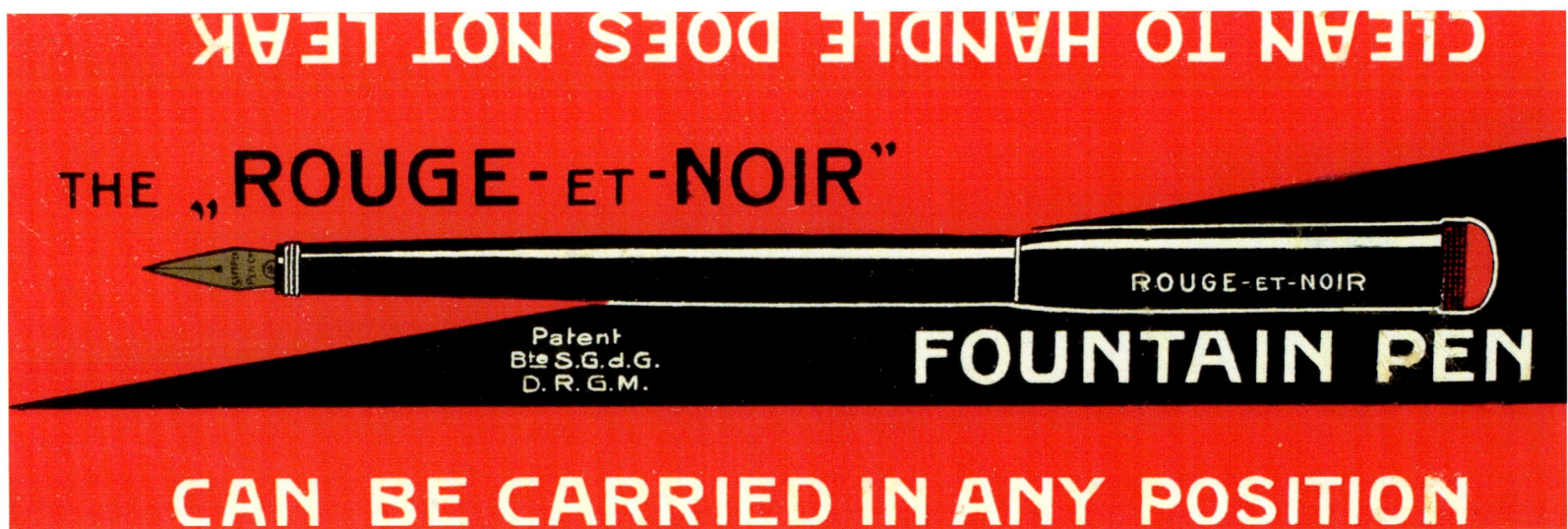

I Montblanc: Writing Time

No one really knows where the name came from. Some people assert that a company salesman on a trip to Geneva (within sight of the real Mont Blanc) came up with it, others cite marketing adviser Carl Schalk who allegedly invented it as the pen was passed from hand to hand during a game of cards. But the name also represents a strong idea that the founders wanted to express: by naming the company after the highest mountain in Europe they expressed their commitment to highest European craftmanship and quality for eternity—like the Montblanc. But one thing is certain: starting in 1910—and for the next two decades—all Simplo writing instruments bore the glorious name of Montblanc, soon accompanied by a symbol of the famous white mountain peak in the form of a triangle.

Further steps were required, however. The white cap merited a more distinguished feature that might also serve as a company trademark. The appearance of the star in 1913, which in fact represents the peak of the Montblanc and its six glaciers, reflected this need for a logo that was easily recognizable and could be registered as a trademark.

Given the popularity of Simplo pens and mechanical pencils, the company soon found itself short of space in the Palace of Industry. So in 1912 it moved into the Dephinhaus in the Schanzen neighborhood, where Montblanc would retain its headquarters until the late 1980s. During the First World War, the company name was changed to Simplo Füllfedergesellschaft. Fortunately, a few years before the war started, manufacturing supplies had been secured through the founding of a subsidiary called Internationale Goldfeder-Fabrik. Shortly afterward, however, stocks of ebonite ran out. And since this special material was made from vulcanized rubber that came from North America, the entry of the United States into the war meant the end of deliveries. Only the Hamburg branch of the New-York-based rubber manufacturer was still able to supply remnants of ebonite, which were sometimes brightly colored. For Simplo, necessity ruled: bright vermilion pens with red and black marbling soon became the latest thing for fashion-conscious consumers.

Montblanc's survival during the dark war years was further assisted by its *Patrone* model, a writing tool often given as a gift to soldiers on the front. The ink came in the form of tiny balls of powder that could be easily diluted in a little water.

Once the war was over Simplo quickly recovered its previous operating levels despite increasing international competition. In fact, such rivalry had its advantages—in the mid 1920s Simplo took advantage of a new material discovered in the United States of America for fountain pens, by adopting the use of celluloid. Unlike ebonite, celluloid could be made in a wide range of colors and was practically indestructible under normal use. Simplo Füllfedergesellschaft also learned from the

Above

In 1909 the company's first fountain pen, *Rouge et Noir*, was released. According to technical standards of the time, it was made of black hard rubber (ebonite) and had a red cap. The name was deliberately chosen to appeal to educated classes and intellectuals.

Following pages

Montblanc outdoor advertisement at the Leipzig Trade Fair, 1922.

23

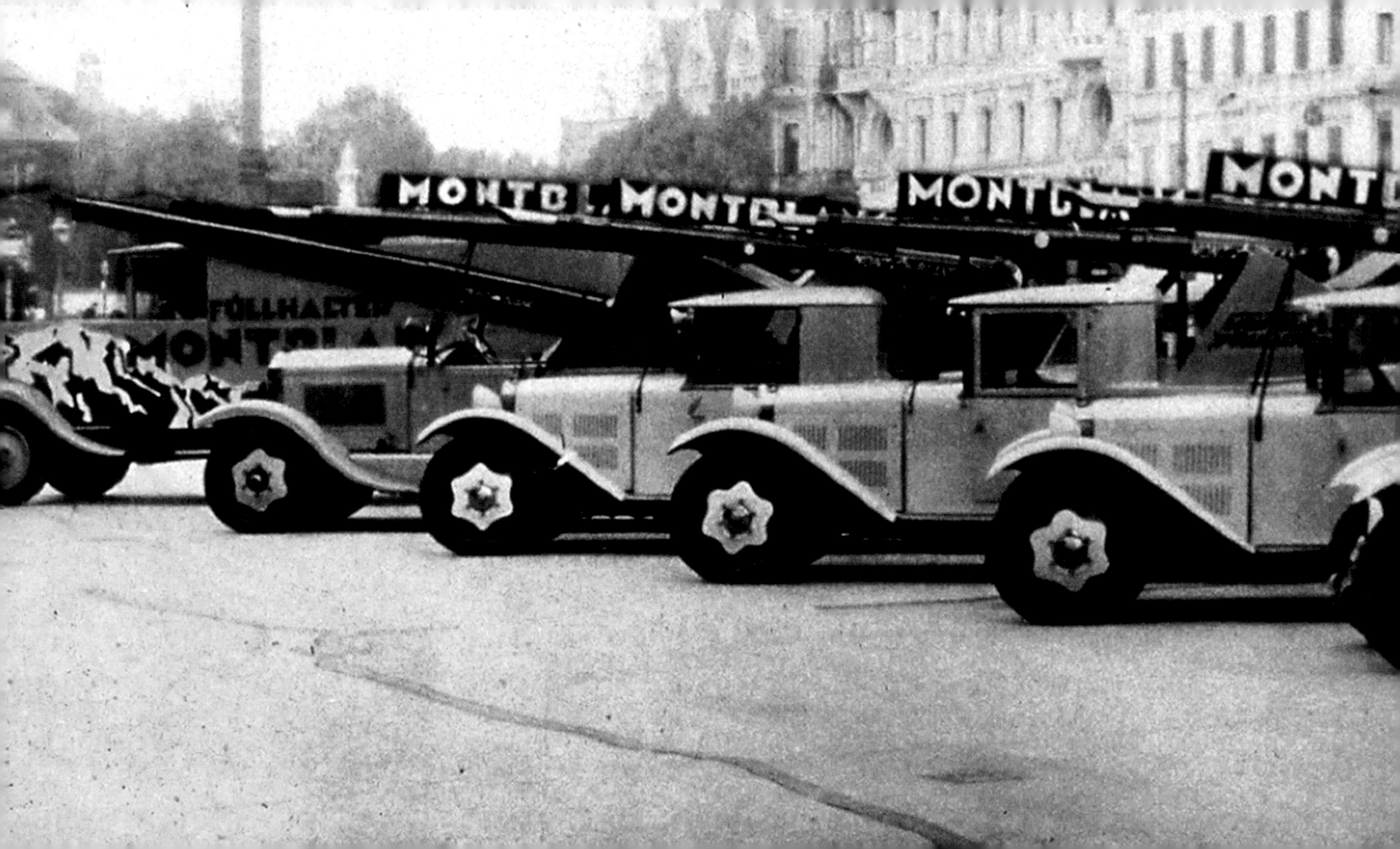
MONTB

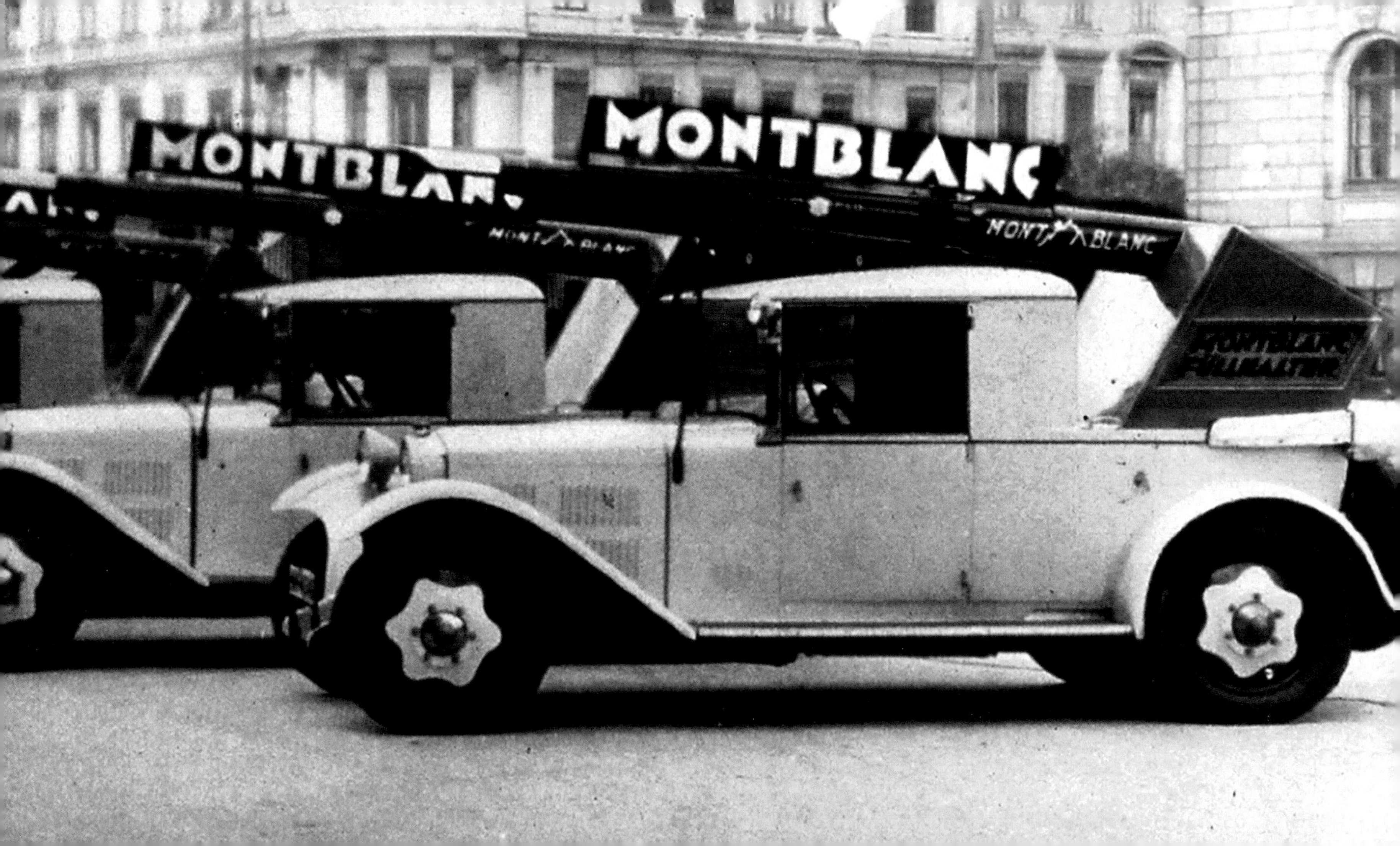
MONTBLANC
MONT BLANC

Above

The Montblanc house in the Schanzenviertel district of Hamburg was the center of production of high quality writing instruments until the fall of 1989.

Below

One of the first Montblanc outdoor advertising campaign banners hanging above Parisian streets in the late 1920s (1926–27).

Americans the value of high-profile advertising. Despite recurring financial difficulties, the now medium-sized family firm invested considerable sums in press advertising, which was the only way to make the public aware—in an imaginative, fanciful way—of the new products it was offering at a time of economic downturn.

At the same time, industrial manufacturing methods increasingly replaced artisanal techniques. The firm attained greater independence by building its own machine tools and by setting up its own galvanization workshop and foundry. By the mid 1930s, Montblanc could afford to buy the entire building in the Schanzen district of Hamburg, thus guaranteeing itself sufficient space. One of the architects of this expansion, from 1919 onward, was Ernst Rösler. For five decades Rösler made a strong mark on the firm. The labor force grew steadily, soon numbering five hundred employees. And the company began opening stores under its own brand name, first in Hamburg (1919), then in Berlin, Leipzig, Wroclaw, Hanover, and Bremen.

THE *MEISTERSTÜCK* PEN CONQUERS THE WORLD

One of the highpoints in the company's history came in 1924 when it unveiled its legendary *Meisterstück* pen. It was an instant hit. From 1929 onward, all nibs of the fountain pens were engraved with the figure 4810, which is the precise altitude, in meters, of the highest peak in Europe: Mont Blanc. In 1934 the firm changed its name to Montblanc–Simplo GmbH and began manufacturing its own ink. The following year it founded a leather-goods factory in Lämmerspiel, near Offenbach. It was also in 1935 that new partner Klaus Voss, Jr., the son of the founding partner who died that year, took over the advertising department and, later, Europe-wide marketing operations. Wilhelm Dziambor retired at that point, appointing his son Wolfram Dziambor as associate director in charge of non-European exports; thanks to Wolfram's efforts, Montblanc managed to conquer major far-eastern markets such as Japan.

As Montblanc's reach extended to over sixty countries, the Hamburg headquarters began seriously considering questions related to the psychology of sales. The training and motivating of staff was identified as a top priority. A manual supplied the sales force with valuable advice, stressing the importance of dealing with customers on a personal level, speaking to them in their own language, and vaunting products that fulfilled their specific needs. When it came to needs, the firm's vast range of writing instruments could meet almost any requirement; and if it failed to do so, the company's lavish leather goods would do the trick. This diversification enabled Montblanc to weather various crises. When pen sales went into decline, accessories made in Offenbach

I | Montblanc: Writing Time

could tide the company over. Furthermore, an image that privileged quality over price helped to sustain the firm's reputation. Montblanc offered a lifetime guarantee to repair all its *Meisterstück* pen models, so that consumers knew they were buying the best. A prominently placed fountain in the store allowed customers to rinse their pens themselves should they so desire; sales staff also used it to check pens for misguided claims of malfunction.

All these rules also applied to the "special" Montblanc outlets whose design had to meet company standards, although each store was owned by an independent dealer. Montblanc was therefore a pioneer of the franchise marketing system. This fruitful alliance rested on the key pillars of cooperative advertising and the company's financial backing. In areas where Montblanc did not have its own outlet, the firm licensed exclusive marketing rights to dynamic retailers.

Above

This advertisement created a conceptual link between the most modern transport system and the most advanced writing instrument of the time.

Left

The double-decker D17 promoted the *Meisterstück* pen and brought the Montblanc name into the third dimension.

Above and right

The *Prince Rainier III Limited Edition 81* fountain pen

Modeled on the armorial bearings of the Grimaldi family, the cap and body in precious transparent resin are delicately set in a filigree openwork structure of 18-karat white gold paved with brilliants. Skillfully cut lozenge-shaped rubies at the top of the cap, below the mother-of-pearl Montblanc Star emblem, endow this fountain pen with its fascinating, characteristic colors. In another striking feature of this edition, the top of the clip is adorned with an artfully engraved crown representing the Monaco coat of arms. On the rhodium-plated 18-karat gold nib, the monogram of Prince Rainier III is finely engraved and artistically embellished with two rubies to provide the finishing touch to this luxurious limited edition.

MONTBLANC AT THE SUMMIT: THE "ARTISANS' ATELIER"

At the close of the Second World War—during which the company nearly folded—new marketing practices were called for. Montblanc bartered pens for hand-knotted Persian carpets, which were then sold for strong marks once the monetary system was reformed. And loyal customers able to honor their commitments in advance so helped the business that Montblanc was able to buy raw materials again and, as early as 1948, to modernize its production tools. In 1952 the company also began making its own ink once again; this innovative, quick-drying ink was not only perfect for the brand's own pens but displayed properties that would come into their own years later with the development of the *rollerball*. Furthermore, company engineers worked to perfect the flow of ink regardless of the position of the pen. Modern methods of injection molding were also developed in-house and progressively replaced the old lathes.

By the mid-1950s, the remarkable quality of the *Meisterstück* pen with its classic nib and piston filler went without saying. Cautious development had continually improved it in many small details. This constant quest for quality would remain the best way to resist counterfeiting, which not even all the patents filed since 1923 could forestall. In 1959 the *Meisterstück* pen line was joined by the *Noblesse* pen model with its meticulous styling that soon made it one of Montblanc's most stunning successes.

Montblanc was henceforth an internationally famous brand. From the nibs of Montblanc pens flowed initials on documents that sometimes changed the face of the world, not to mention the manuscripts of some of the world's greatest writers. Subsequent development of this historic *Meisterstück* pen model met with unexpected success and variations on luxury lines were extremely popular. Solid gold, sterling silver, and silver-gilt versions of the *Meisterstück Solitaire* pen saw the light of day. Meanwhile, the *Solitaire Royal pen* model, set with 4,810 brilliant-cut diamonds, entered the Guinness Book of Records as the most expensive pen in the world.

This long-standing and still effective policy of focusing on the luxury market—so well conveyed by the Star emblem—requires considerable work. Such items can leave nothing to chance when it comes to absolutely perfect execution, from early design sketches to dispatch of the final product. Thus Hamburg is the home of a highly skilled craftsmen's workshop known as the "Artisans' Atelier" where limited editions—indeed, highly limited editions or even unique items—slowly take shape through meticulous manual execution, free of all time constraints. Splendid pens such as the *Bohème Skeleton* pen and the fascinating *Prince Rainier III Limited Edition 81* automatically exclude industrial manufacturing methods. After parts are machined

28

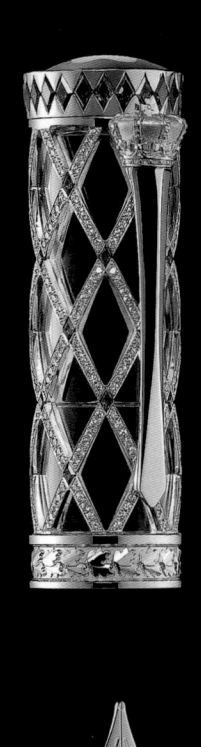

with extreme precision thanks to highly modern production tools, more than fifty percent of the work that goes into each item still calls for skilled craft technique. Jewelers, gem-setters, and precision technicians are needed to execute every detail with the required care. The secret method of setting stones and the final finish on the *Mystery Masterpiece* pen require five hundred hours of intense concentration. Seventy percent of these limited editions are specific to a given country and are impatiently awaited by loyal clients. Some collectors even buy two copies of each item so that they can use the first and carefully conserve the second.

In the new manufacturing premises and office building on Hellgrundweg in Hamburg, where Montblanc moved in 1989, visitors sense this determination to produce items that are exceptional in every way.

MONTBLANC: AN EXCLUSIVE LIFESTYLE

While it is possible to set words to paper with any instrument that leaves a trace on the writing surface, the authentic art of writing—one of human civilization's most important accomplishments—can today only be practiced with a true fountain pen. Letters and documents written with a fountain pen have a special value because they are unique, because they indicate particular consideration shown toward the addressee, and because they convey a personality.

Not all fountain pens are equal in the eyes of God, however: there is no comparison between a mass-produced pen with cheap nib that yields little more than dreadful scratches, and a *Meisterstück 149* pen for example, dubbed a *Diplomat* in its reservoir version. The latter's patient manufacture in the Hamburg company's workshop takes place at a deliberately slow pace. The tasks done by hand, from the careful polishing of the barrel to the meticulous insertion of the gold nib, turn the plant into a veritable craft workshop. If the Montblanc name is seen on the outside, Montblanc quality is guaranteed inside. The reputation of a firm that defends and promotes intangible values depends on maintaining them, whatever the vagaries of economic and social upheavals. Montblanc takes the time necessary to make a writing instrument for the same reasons that the pen's future owner will take the time to write by hand on high-quality paper.

And yet there is nothing in the world that cannot be bettered. Given the brand's extraordinary skills and worldwide reputation in the sphere of the manufacture of traditional pens, in the 1990s Montblanc decided to produce the *Meisterstück* pen in exclusive and limited editions. The first "Patron of Art Limited Edition," created in honor of *Lorenzo de' Medici*, evoked the memory of a great Renaissance art patron even as

Above

The nib is the heart of every Montblanc fountain pen. It is made of hand-crafted rhodium-plated 18-karat solid gold and gives handwriting style and unmistakable character.

Facing page

Representing the six glaciers of the Mont Blanc mountain, the white Montblanc Star adorning the cap of each writing instrument became the brand's emblem and trademark in 1913 and remains a symbol for high aspiration and commitment to superb quality. Inspired by the height of Europe's highest mountain, the number 4.810 was added to the nib of each *Meisterstück* pen in 1929. For decades, the *Meisterstück* pen has been famed for its timeless and fascinating design. The writing instrument has obtained a permanent place in the New York Museum of Modern Art and plays a significant role in politics, business, and culture.

Above and facing page

Montblanc's "Artisans' Atelier" is a hotbed of creativity, inspired by the beauty of the precious materials used during the creation of writing instruments and *haute joaillerie*. The studio also contains albums and sketches illustrating previous works and expertise. Montblanc offers its customers the opportunity of possessing a tailor-made writing instrument of the highest quality.

it paid tribute to a grand pen of the Roaring Twenties. It goes without saying that such a noble instrument could be produced in a limited edition only—one pen for every meter of the altitude of the Mont Blanc mountain.

The striking popularity of this first limited edition encouraged Montblanc to present other exclusive models from time to time. Since such pens are far too costly to risk getting mislaid during some trip or other, the company acknowledged its globetrotting clientele by producing a convenient pocket model, named in honor of Wolfgang Amadeus Mozart.

People drawn to the "Writers Edition" can savor the pleasure of finding themselves in the company of great writers who produced their masterpieces with a traditional pen, such as Voltaire, Dostoyevsky, Edgar Allan Poe, Oscar Wilde, and Agatha Christie, incarnating various types of inspiration depending on personal inclination. The art of writing, as celebrated by Montblanc's flawless craftsmanship, thus becomes a lofty pleasure that combines a superlative touch with obvious intellectual delights.

Montblanc's creations are therefore particularly appreciated by connoisseurs who feel that refined perfection in all things is an essential value. They know that the white Montblanc Star emblem on the cap of a pen, the buckle of a belt, or the winding crown of a watch is the mark of an exclusive lifestyle. Not to be confused with the expression of showy luxury, the image of the snow-white Montblanc Star emblem embodies the discreet charm of timeless objects valued by a cultured elite with a strong identity, far from the fleeting phenomena of fashion trends.

Although anchored in tradition, Montblanc looks to the future, pursuing a long-term evolution based on thoughtful development and principles that reflect the art of writing. There is perhaps no better example of wisdom and serenity than the gliding movement across paper of a pen guided by thoughtful reflection, establishing a wonderfully harmonious balance between the pace of ideas and the rhythm of writing. Many people today seem more comfortable with speed than with slowness, which means—alas—that time slips between their fingers forever. This shortcoming does not apply to individuals convinced of the importance of taking their time, even in today's frantic era, because they realize that time is on their side.

These comments apply not only to fountain pens but also to Montblanc's refined watches. Writing instruments and timepieces are a perfect match, so it is not surprising that people with a sure sense of taste will write with a Montblanc pen and opt for a Montblanc watch. The affinities between a Montblanc watch and the legendary *Meisterstück* pen are obvious. The highly valued perfection of writing instruments made in the "Artisans' Atelier" resurfaces in the luxury line of watches dubbed *Collection Montblanc Villeret 1858*: a unique convergence of priceless cultural tools displaying total perfection down to the tiniest detail, requiring hundreds of hours of loving work—and hence extremely rare.

The links are many between craft and art, between love for a perfect object and love of artworks, between writing and the other major symbols of civilized culture; that is why, since 1987, Montblanc has been an active sponsor in the fields of literature, dance, and music. Awarded since 1992, the Montblanc de la Culture Arts Patronage Award has become a well-known honor bestowed on individuals and institutions for their contribution to culture. Notable winners include Dominique de Menil, the Rockefeller Foundation, Madame Georges Pompidou, James D. Wolfensohn, Walter Carsen, Lila Wallace-Reader's Digest Fund, Sir Run Run Shaw, Lincoln Kirstein, Simon Rattle, Keizo Saji, Alan Ayckbourn, Susan Sontag, Ikuo Hirayama, Gian Carlo Menotti, Jane Alexander, Susan Sarandon, Francesca von Habsburg and Michelle Yeoh.

Among the company's other cultural activities, it is worth mentioning the 1994 founding of the Philharmonia of the Nations, conducted by Professor Justus Franz and placed under the aegis of Montblanc. Four years later the Montblanc Cultural Foundation was launched in close collaboration with the Hamburg Gallery of Contemporary Art; every two years Montblanc donates to the gallery contemporary artworks that reflect the firm's philosophy in the broadest sense. These works are exhibited at the Montblanc art gallery for two years before being permanently handed over to the Hamburg Gallery of Contemporary Art.

Pages 38–39

The limited edition *Mystery Masterpiece* was issued for Montblanc and Van Cleef & Arpels' hundredth anniversary in 2006. This first collaboration marks the beginning of their next hundred years as progressive leading edge luxury companies. This limited edition was released in three variations, set either with rubies, sapphires, or emeralds, and diamonds. The Van Cleef & Arpels famous "Mystery Setting" adorns the meticulously crafted Montblanc skeleton body in delicate white gold. Only three pieces of each design exist worldwide.

The *Montblanc Taipei 101 Limited Edition* fountain pen.

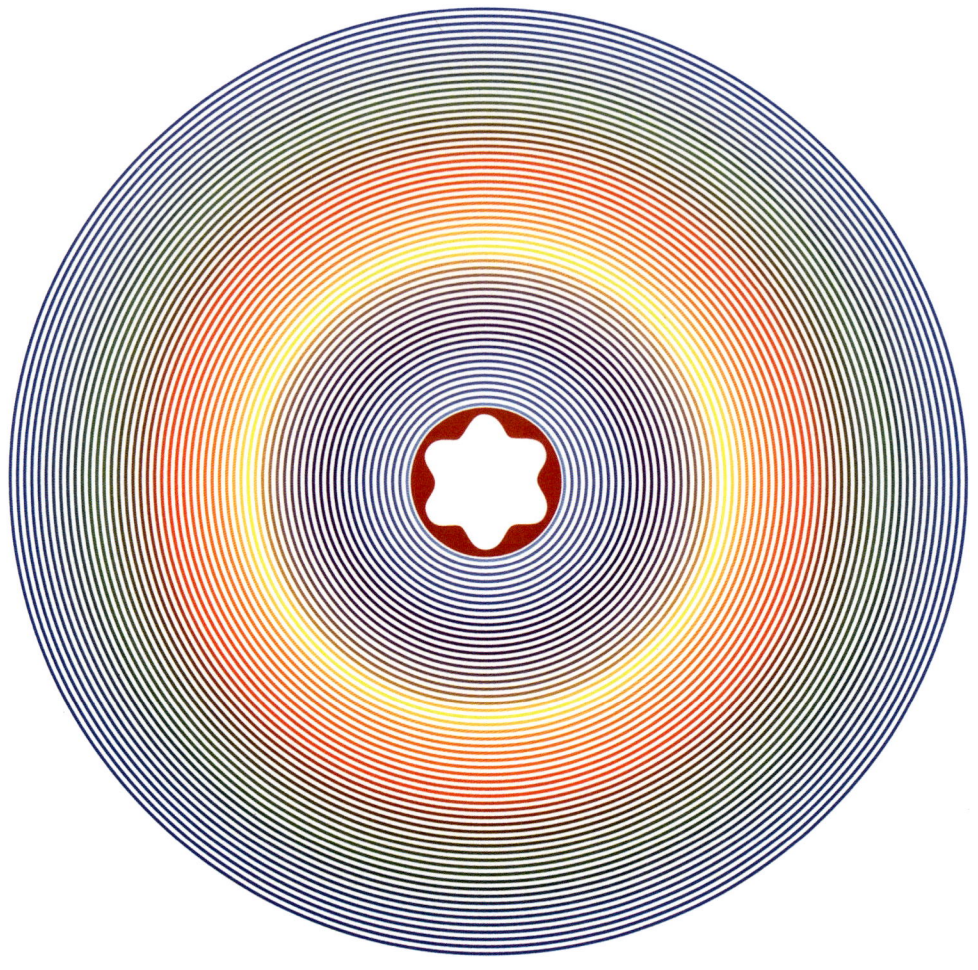

Mikio Taka

The œuvre of Japanese artist Mikio Taka (1978) includes minimalist ink drawings of geometric shapes and complex patterns, watercolors of surreal landscapes and vividly colored photographs that have been painted over. The influence of Japanese manga comics is perceptible in his pictures of mysterious figures with distended heads and bodies covered in tattoos, which the artist draws freehand with incredible precision, and also in his detailed repeated structures and geometric figures. Mikio Taka studied at the Hokkaido Art Vocational School from 1997 to 1999 and won the Sapporo Contemporary Art Award in 1998. In his picture *Wonderful Montblanc* the artist, who lives in Hokkaido, surrounded the Montblanc Star emblem with an aureole of individual rings in all colors of the rainbow which appear to merge and create the illusion of a pulsating, energetic glow.

CAI Contemporary Art International
www.cai-hamburg.de

Stephen Craig

The œuvre of Stephen Craig, who was born in 1960 in Larne, Northern Ireland, spans three different artistic genres: architecture, sculpture, and painting. Following technical training, Craig started studying art in 1982, first at Sydney College of the Arts, then at the College of Applied Arts in Hamburg and, finally, at the Rijksakademie van beeldende Kunsten in Amsterdam. Influenced by Giacometti's sculptures and Mies van der Rohe's architectural vision, the boundaries between functional architecture and autonomous sculpture are blurred in Craig's work. Since showing at Documenta 10 and Skulptur Projekte Münster 1997, the Hamburg-based artist has gained international recognition for his work; in 2001 he took up a teaching position at the faculty of architecture at the University of Karlsruhe. For the past few years the funfair has been a key motif for Craig. "The fair is a metaphor for the city as a whole," the artist explains. "What instantly appealed to me was the handcrafted, self-made aspect of many of the traveling stalls and rides, and the brightness of the colors." As well as exploring mobile architecture, Craig is inspired by the specific aesthetics of the funfair to create vibrantly colored pictures and light installations.

www.realace.de

Every nib has to pass over fifty quality control tests in order to be approved fit for the hands of its future owner.

The pen dances across the paper in calm, controlled circles. Every nib creates its own melody, a scarcely audible sound, which can only be interpreted by specialists. Thousands of flowing figures are drawn to ensure that the nib glides smoothly across the paper.

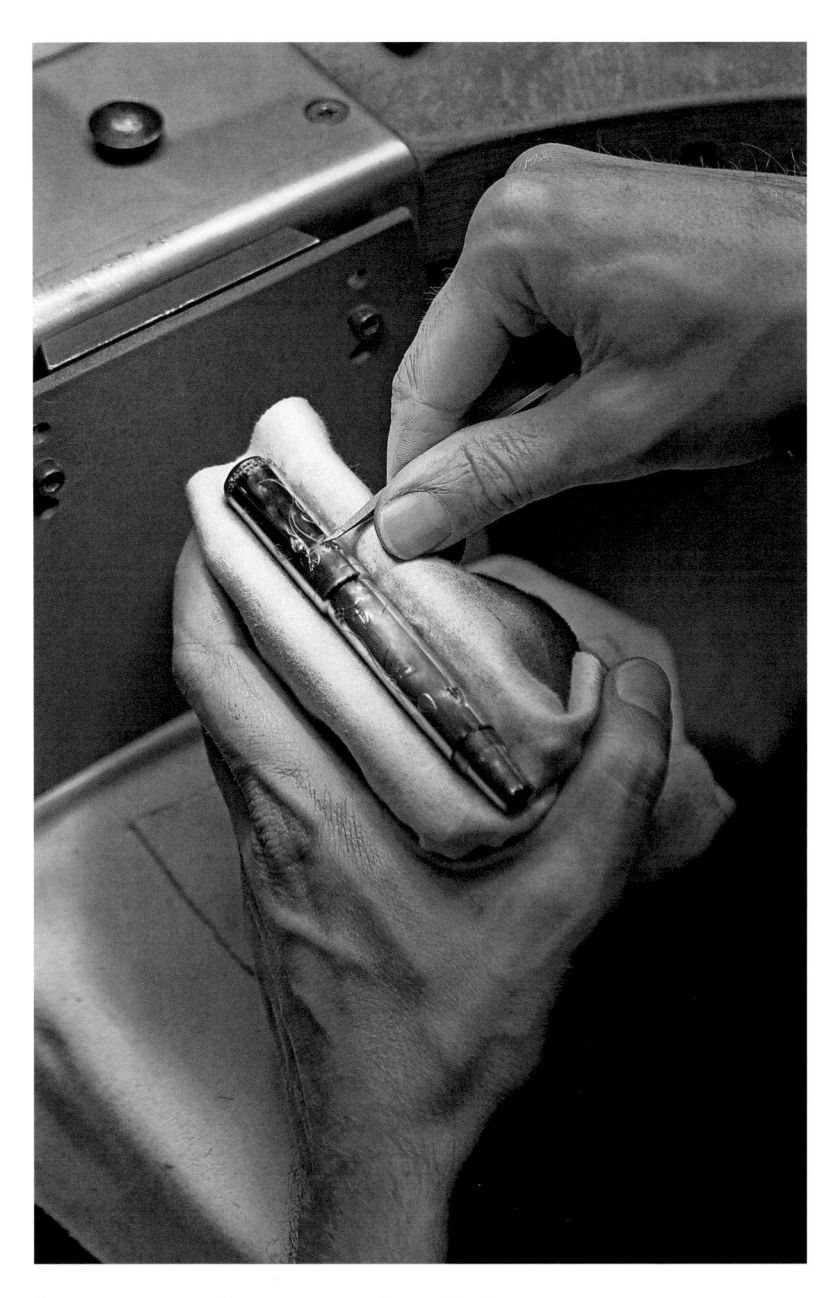

An important production step is the surface's refinement, which is achieved by different engraving, chasing, and guilloche techniques.

In order to resist water and many household chemicals, the individual parts of the fountain pen are hand-polished many times to obtain the required additional luster. Once the writing instrument is completed, it needs to be polished again to give the customer a flawless product.

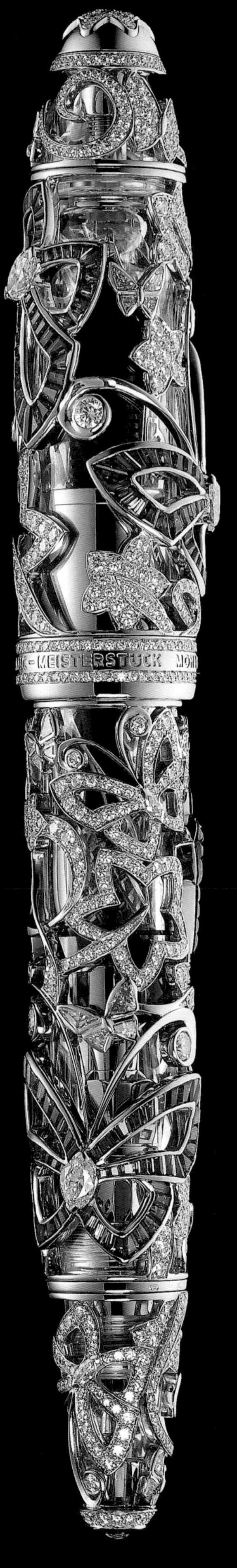
MEISTERSTUCK

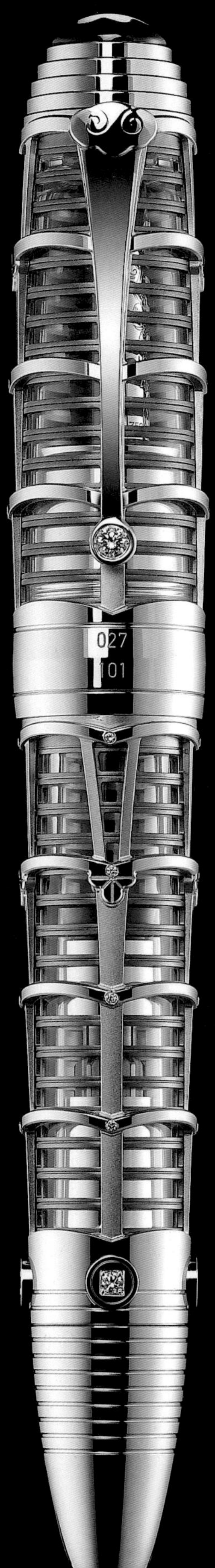
027
101

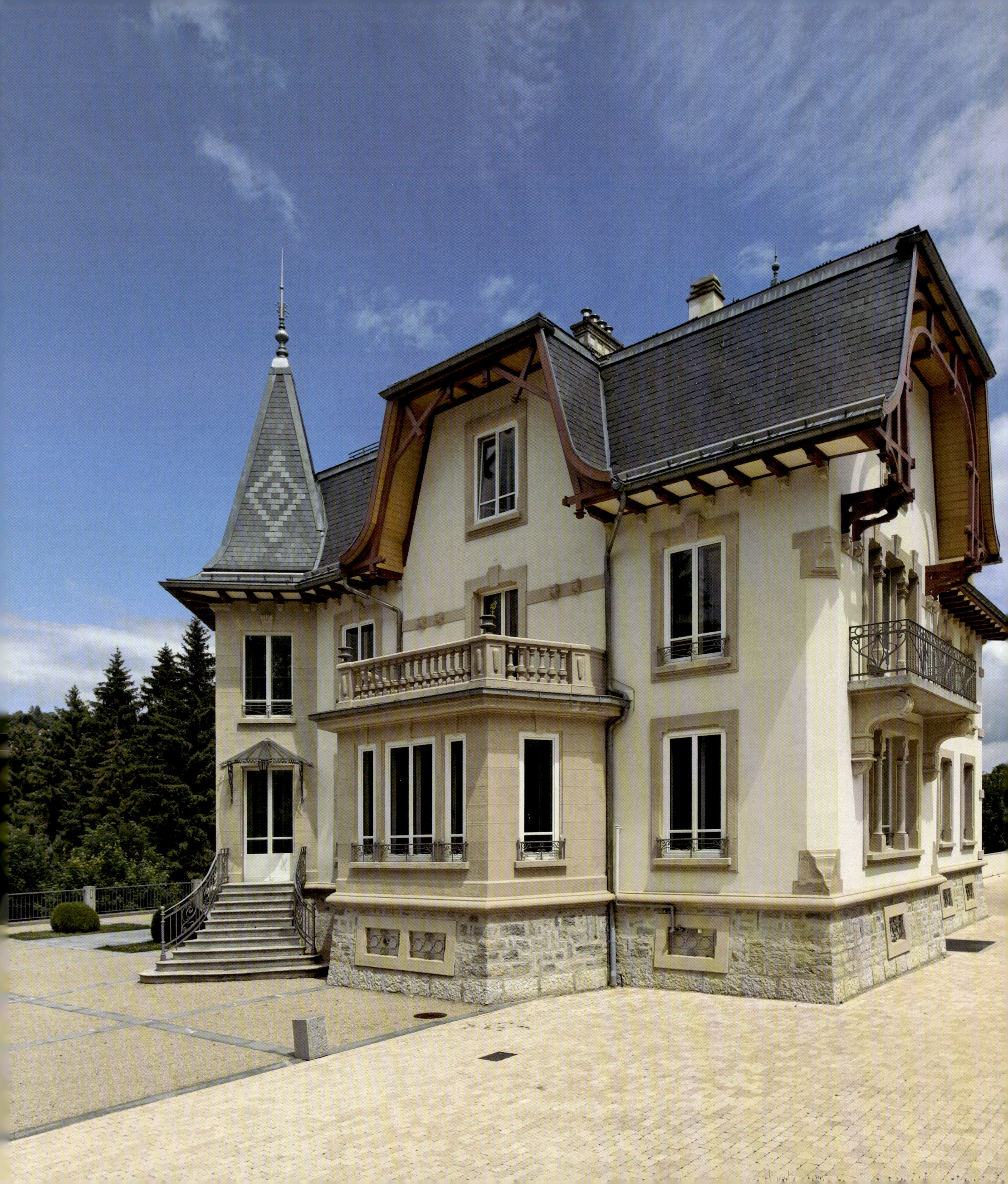

Montblanc, Mastering Time

FROM PENS TO TIMEPIECES: MONTBLANC AT LE LOCLE

Montblanc's decision to start making watches, announced in 1997, provoked both curiosity and astonishment. "But where are you supposed to put the ink?" jokingly asked a journalist of Norbert Platt, then general manager of the company. But Platt believed in the project, and to insure its success he positioned it firmly in line with the firm's key product: "Right from the start, Montblanc has remained faithful to an emblematic item, our *Meisterstück*—black, gold, sensual. We have therefore decided to endow the firm's first watches with black dials and gold cases, in order to cultivate the resemblance." Thus the original cult object found its natural extension in highly accurate wristwatches that represent remarkable examples of ancestral know-how.

Since that time, Montblanc watches have won international fame and ever-growing popularity. These watches, it should be stressed, are entirely made in-house, in the corporation's two *manufactures* in Le Locle and Villeret.

In Le Locle, a small town nestling at an altitude of 3,000 feet in the hilly landscape of the Swiss Jura Mountains, the origins of watchmaking date all the way back to 1630. It was here that the famous mechanic Abraham Perret allegedly made his first bell-tower clock and thus laid the cornerstone of the industry that would make Le Locle a glamorous center of clock and watch-making.

"We may not have produced extravagant adventurers or geniuses," the people of Le Locle used to say, "but we have among us many men of good will who like order and work." For eight hundred years the town held out against the vagaries of history thanks to its citizens' tenacity, zeal, inventiveness, and love of freedom. It is notably worth mentioning Le Locle's subjection to the kingdom of Prussia, which ran—with a few interludes—from 1707 to 1848. Only the revolution of March 1, 1848 and the adoption of a republican constitution finally put an end to the Prussian regime.

Since all the land around the town was composed either of poor soil, damp meadow, or of rocky crags, the residents devoted their time to hunting and raising livestock. Thanks to Daniel Jean Richard, in the first half of the eighteenth century the watchmaking industry began to prosper. By 1750 the "Black Hills" of the Neuchâtel region already boasted nearly five hundred watchmakers. During subsequent decades the industry underwent rapid specialization, with workshops focusing on making ebauches, springs, hands, cases, and chains or concentrating on finishing, gilding, or enameling. Most of them ran their little businesses from a workbench at home. As relative prosperity began to draw jobseekers into the area, the people of Le Locle slowly gave up their farming activities and devoted themselves entirely to the watch industry.

Above

Final assembly of a Montblanc watch from the *Montblanc Star* watch collection, decorated with the Montblanc Star emblem.

Facing page

Montblanc Montre S.A., founded in 1997, at 10, chemin des Tourelles, Le Locle. Villa built in 1906, the same year as the foundation of Montblanc in Hamburg.

Above

Entrance hall of the Montblanc Montre villa in Le Locle, decorated with magnificent, hand-made art nouveau-style stained-glass windows by the Hamburg craftsman Dickmann.

Right

The Montblanc Montre villa, adorned with a majestic turret, which gave its name to the road, the "chemin des Tourelles."

Facing page

The panoramic workshops of Montblanc Montre, built in 2003. A marriage of tradition and modernity.

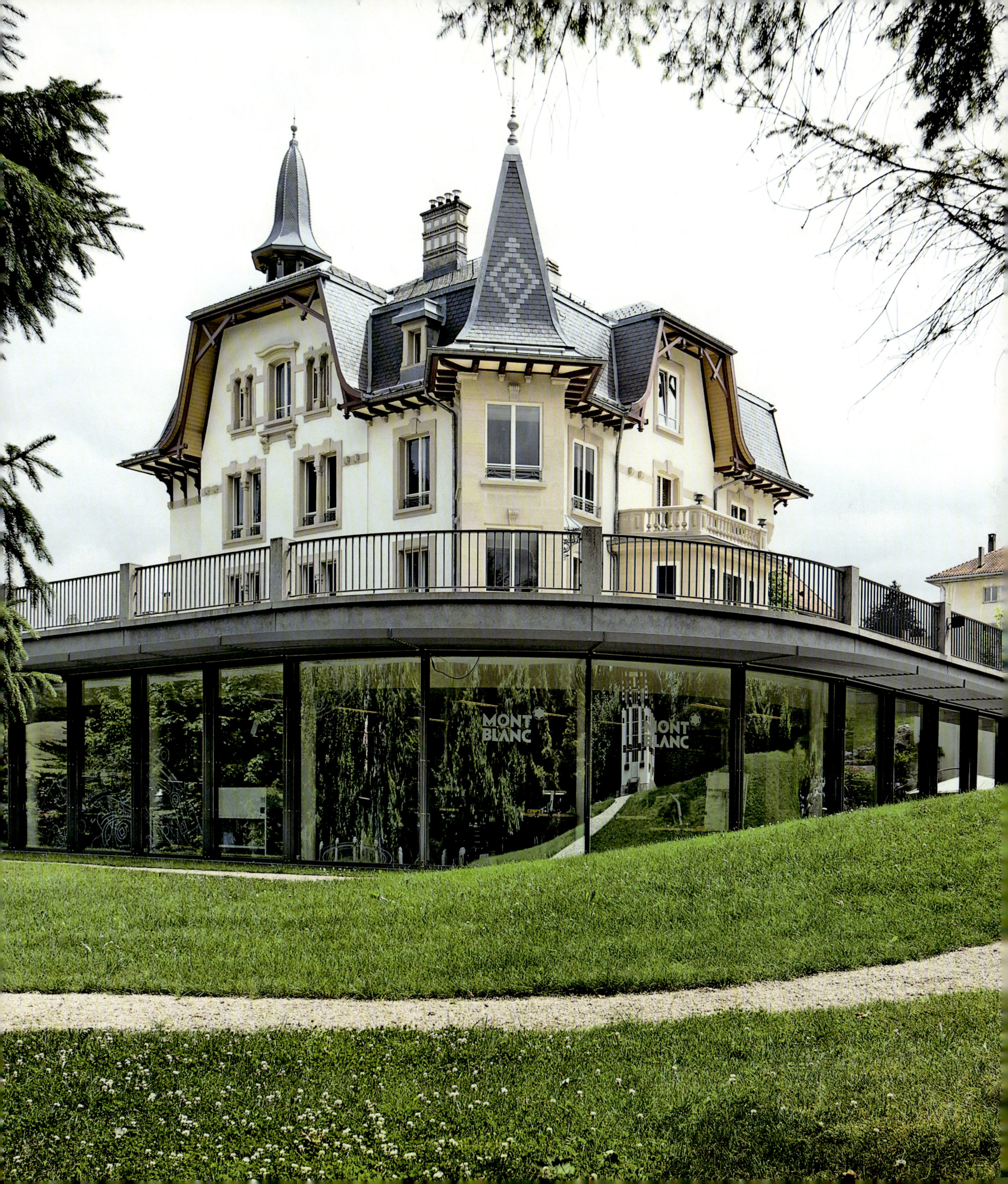
MONT
BLANC
MONT
BLANC

Around 1840, life in Le Locle was already totally dominated by watches and their components. Prussian monarchs, delighted with the artisanal accomplishments of Jura watchmakers, regularly summoned craftsmen to court in order to make timepieces and to spread their knowledge to distant lands.

The histories of several major watchmakers are thus indissolubly linked to the town of Le Locle. In 1997, Montblanc Montres, S.A., opened its headquarters in this prestigious home of watchmakers, in order to produce its own timepieces crafted by the abundant, highly qualified labor force trained in the finest tradition. The company moved into a magnificent art nouveau villa built in 1906—the same year Montblanc was founded—and set in over two acres of grounds. In 2003, the base of the villa was enlarged with a vast, ultramodern atrium perfectly suited to the meticulous work of watchmakers who produce tens of thousands of watches per year. A large north-facing window provides constant lighting conditions for watchmakers bent over a movement (south-facing windows would produce blinding sunlight and shifting shadows disruptive to concentration over microscopic mechanisms). The importance of lighting conditions, already known to the earliest watchmakers, has never lost its relevance.

RESPECTING AN IDENTITY

As part of the Richemont Group, which already owned famous brands such as Cartier, Piaget, Vacheron Constantin, Jaeger-LeCoultre, IWC, and Panerai, Montblanc was able to count on solid support from corporate partners with exceptional skills. Montblanc nevertheless insisted on a good deal of autonomy when it came to the design and positioning of their watches, understandably directed toward the desires of the pen-maker's own faithful clientele. At first, that clientele was mainly composed of enlightened connoisseurs who particularly liked writing instruments marked with the famous white star, which initiates recognized from a distance. Such customers were thus drawn to the first "*Meisterstück* watches" that featured Montblanc's characteristic attributes. Indeed, these watches were instantly popular: the rich black color of the legendary pen appeared on the dial, while the warm gold of its nib, clip, and cap appeared in the cases, hands, and raised Arabic numerals of the watches. The numerals, for that matter, deliberately evoked the period when Montblanc's first writing instruments were made. The company's famous signature, placed on the middle case, was another determining feature. An individual serial number gave the owner the feeling of wearing a truly unique object on his or her wrist. The legendary white Montblanc Star, finally, adorned the winding crown or the clasp of the hand-sewn leather strap, and also served as a perfectly functional counterweight to the central second hand.

Attention to all those tiny details, the goal of total perfection, and a determination to give a strong identity to the watches were the keys to the immediate success of the launch.

Little by little, Montblanc expanded its range, as exemplified by the *Montblanc Star Lady* line of women's watches available with dazzling diamonds and mechanical movements. For women who like to own several watches, Montblanc also proposed the practicality and accuracy of quartz movements. Such movements make it easier to change from one timepiece to another because the hands continue to tell the right time imperturbably, even when not worn for weeks on end. The *Montblanc Profile Lady* range of watches, meanwhile, was designed for women with a strong sense of style who want to sport a watch that expresses refinement through the combination of classic stylistic features with lavish gems and costly materials.

When it comes to outdoor activities, both men and women are attracted to Montblanc's *Sport* watches with their strong lines. The black, self-winding chronograph, for example, has a handsome case forty-four-millimeters in diameter, which is water-resistant to a depth of two hundred meters. Furthermore, the case's extremely tough surface can stand up to occasional knocks: a "diamond-like carbon" layer covers the material in order to protect it from scratches and rubbing; its hardness rating is greater than 5,000 Vickers, that is to say seven times harder than stainless steel, the basic material. The time and money required for this surface treatment affect the sale price, of course, but they also promise an extremely long life to the watch.

Deliberately turning its back on ostentation is Montblanc's *TimeWalker* watch collection. This range is characterized by pure lines, clean formal appearance, self-evident architecture, easy readability, and, depending on personal taste, additional functions such as a chronograph or second time-zone.

Facing page

The first Montblanc watches in 18-karat yellow gold, introduced in 1997.

Left: watch with a self-winding mechanical movement and a power reserve at twelve o'clock.

Center: the first automatic chronograph developed by Montblanc with day/date display.

Right: the first automatic watch with date display.

MONTBLANC
TACHYMETER
MON 8
AUTOMATIC
RESERVE DE MARCHE
MONTBLANC
SWISS MADE
MONTBLANC
AUTOMATIC
SWISS MADE

Montblanc Montre's watchmaking workshops, where master watchmakers execute their work by creating Montblanc watches with care and accuracy.

Caliber MB R 200 self-winding movement made by the Montblanc *manufacture*. Monopusher chronograph equipped with a column wheel and a vertical clutch. Skeletonized oscillating weight decorated with the Montblanc Star emblem.

At Montblanc Montre's watchmaking workshop, a watchmaker carefully verifies the estheticism and good condition of the *Montblanc Nicolas Rieussec Chronograph Silicon Escapement* equipped with the caliber MB R 120 made by the Montblanc *manufacture* with an escapement in non-magnetic silicon.

ICONIC TIMEWRITERS

The *Montblanc Star Chronograph Automatic* watch in stainless steel with a black dial and a stainless steel bracelet with a triple-folding clasp. It has an automatic movement with chronograph functions: rhodium-plated hour, minute, and continuous seconds hands and a date/day display. It features a sapphire crystal case back and a domed sapphire crystal with anti-reflective coating.

Timekeeping Masterpieces

Like every single *Meisterstück* fountain pen, the *Montblanc Star* watch collection is handcrafted with the utmost care and precision. It was originally introduced in 1997 as the perfect matching watch family to the Montblanc writing instruments. It combines Montblanc's values with genuine Swiss watchmaking precision and thus harmonizes perfectly with the company's high expectations concerning craftsmanship and quality standards. The classic circular case has eye-catching horns, curving gracefully downward and the stamped hallmark "Meisterstück 4810" which brings to mind Montblanc's iconic *Meisterstück 149* fountain pen.

The 42-mm *Montblanc Star Chronograph GMT Automatic* watch is one of Montblanc's all-time favorites with its Roman figures and classic design. Its case is made of stainless steel with a fixed bezel and black alligator strap with a triple-folding clasp. It has an automatic movement with chronograph functions: red gold-plated "feuille" hour, minute and continuous seconds hands, a date display, and a 24-hour display with a second time zone. It features a sapphire crystal case back and a domed sapphire crystal with anti-reflective coating.

Montblanc Star 4810 watch collection

With this line, Montblanc's watchmakers offer the ideal combination of perfect functionality and eye-catching design. The collection embodies the "less is more" principle of design which distinguishes all of the timepieces in the *Montblanc Star 4810* collection. A noble guilloche decor forms Montblanc's familiar emblem at the "3 o'clock" position on every watch of the *Montblanc Star 4810* collection. Its concentric waves spread across the dial from the "6 o'clock" epicenter, elegantly reiterating the logo's stellar contours.

The *Montblanc Star 4810 Red Gold Chronograph Automatic* watch stops time with its: 12 hour and 30 minutes totalizers and a central stop second. The watch was officially certified "chronometer" by the Swiss Chronometer Testing Institut (COSC). The 18-karat red gold case has a sapphire crystal case back, and a narrow, high-gloss-polished, 44-mm bezel surrounds an arced, doubly antireflective pane of sapphire crystal. A trio of hands sweep their arcs above the anthracite guilloché dial: the chronograph's elapsed-seconds hand has a red tip at one end and a pierced Montblanc Star emblem serving as a counterweight at the other end, while the hour hand and minute hand are designed in classical dauphine shape.

Montblanc Sport Collection

The *Montblanc Sport* collection is made for dynamic yet elegant people. It embodies the sporting spirit and enhances the casual outdoor look. The Montblanc logotype on the side of the case guarantees the ruggedness and precision of all the watches in the *Sport* collection. Its crown, is designed to function perfectly in any conditions and under all circumstances, protected by the case. Like the back of the case, it screws in and is absolutely water-resistant to 300 meters. The unidirectional turning bezel—a must-have for a real sports watch—turns to the left only for security reasons.

The 44-mm case of the *Montblanc Sport DLC Chronograph Automatic* watch is made of stainless steel is covered with a special coating called DLC (Diamond-like-Carbon). This coating makes the watch almost immune to scratches and makes it much harder than normal steel. It features an automatic movement with chronograph functions: hour, minute, and continuous seconds hands and a date display with magnifying glass.

Montblanc TimeWalker watch Collection

The *Montblanc TimeWalker* watch collection is a combination of traditional craftsmanship and modern aesthetics—especially in terms of using new and innovative materials. Its clear and architecturally inspired contours symbolize the future of watchmaking design. The skeletonized horns on the cases and the links in the bracelet are curved. The slim Arabic numerals and incised hands underpin the overall lightness of the design. The *Montblanc TimeWalker* collection stands for the innovative potential of Montblanc and has become an icon of modern watchmaking design.

The *Montblanc TimeWalker Red Gold Ceramic Chronograph Automatic* watch is the result of combining innovative and classic materials in watchmaking design. While most parts of the case and the pin buckle are made of 18-karat red gold, the bezel is made of shiny black ceramic which gives the watch a very elegant look. It has an automatic movement with chronograph functions: red gold-plated hour, minute, and small second hands. The watch has been officially certified by the Swiss Official Chronometer Testing Institute (COSC), and features sapphire crystal with double anti-reflex coating, a sapphire crystal case back, and is water-resistant to 3 bar (30m).

Montblanc Star Lady watch Collection

For a lady, a watch is more than just a device to check the time. It is a piece of master craftsmanship as well as a piece of jewelry. It is an accessory—not only indicating her taste and style but also representing her personality and character. Nothing is more inspiring than being surrounded by objects of beauty, things that exude sensuality and elegance while also appealing to the intellect. The ladies' watches in the *Montblanc Star* collection transcend the limits of technology. In addition to being perfect timekeepers they are lavish gems that reflect their wearer's sense of beauty and personal style.

The *Montblanc Star Pluie d'Étoiles Automatic* combines the skills of traditional Swiss watchmakers and master jewelers. This watch has been designed with a love of perfection and detail. A sparkling cascade of 298 precious diamonds flows across the mother-of-pearl dial, the bezel is set with 80 baguette-cut diamonds and the 18-karat white gold crown is decorated with a beautiful Montblanc diamond. Its 36-mm case and the pin buckle are made of 18-karat white gold.

The *Montblanc Star Éternel Lady Moonphase* is the perfect blend of technical precision and stunning looks. 275 Top Wesselton diamonds adorn the 18-karat white gold case and horns while another 112 Top Wesselton diamonds are set around the date and across the mother-of-pearl dial. The white gold crown is adorned by the Montblanc signet in natural mother-of-pearl. The precious timepiece features a high precision automatic movement with moonphase display.

Le très humble et très Obeissant
Serviteur.

[signature]

horloger chargé de l'Entretien des pendules
du Ministère de la Maison du Roi.

Nicolas Mathieu Rieussec (1781–1866)

Nicolas Mathieu Rieussec was born in Paris in 1781, several years before the outbreak of a revolution that was to upset France and Europe. To say we know little about his childhood and his years of learning is an understatement. One of his biographers shows him in Paris, under the Consulate, in 1802. While still a minor, the citizen Rieussec was already installed as a watchmaker at 14, rue du Marché-Palu on the Ile de la Cité. The "Almanach du commerce de Paris pour l'an XIII" (Almanac of Commerce of Paris for the Year XIII), that is to say the year 1805, listed 190 famous watchmakers including Breguet. Rieussec was not among them. However, five years later, Rieussec was listed among 222 Parisian watchmakers as being at rue Marché-Palu. By this time, he was married with a son, Joseph Ferdinand, born on December 15, 1804, some days after the coronation of Napoleon as Emperor. The years went by, and after Waterloo and the defeat of Napoleon and his empire in 1815, the monarchy was restored, and the throne once more occupied by a Bourbon, Louis XVIII, brother of Louis XVI who had been guillotined in 1793. The new king does not seem to have considered Rieussec as having been a follower of Napoleon, since the year 1817 saw the beginning of Rieussec's rise, with his nomination as watchmaker to the king. The position was not as glamorous as it might sound; it did not ensure regular orders or a fixed income, especially since this distinction was attributed to several watchmakers. Rieussec, an ambitious man, did not stop there. Hardly had he obtained the position of watchmaker to the king than he was in the running for the status of watchmaker to the "Garde-Meuble de la Couronne." (The Crown Wardrobe). Created in the early seventeenth century, this administration was responsible for the management of furniture and art items for the decoration of royal residences. He was appointed to the post in 1818, by which time he had already been operating out of 13, rue Notre-Dame-des-Petits-Champs for a year. Curiously, he also, for a time at least, ran a currency exchange office.

The young Nicolas was trained as a watchmaker in Paris among the greatest watchmakers of the time. The 1820s was a prosperous decade for Nicolas Rieussec. It certainly started on a high note. On September 1, 1821, he used his new chronograph to time a horse race held on the Champ de Mars in Paris.

Less than a year later, in March 1822, Rieussec obtained a five-year patent for a "timekeeper, or counter, called chronograph with seconds, indicating the length of several successive events without necessitating the attention of the observer."

But Rieussec's work was not only confined to the field of measuring instruments for use by the Navy or by scientists. His appointment of watchmaker to the Garde-Meuble gave him the opportunity to work on movements for clocks ordered to decorate parts of the royal residences. In 1821, he delivered a clock, "Iris rattachant ses ailes," (Iris Reattaching her Wings) for the bedroom of the Duke of Bordeaux, grandson of the Comte d'Artois, brother of Louis XVIII. Between 1820 and 1825 Rieussec worked on a movement for a clock depicting St. Vincent de Paul. This object entered the chateau of Saint-Cloud in early 1826. More active than ever, in 1821 Rieussec delivered a superb clock representing "Sappho inspirée par l'Amour," (Sappho Inspired by Love), and another, "Homère chantant sur les ruines de Troyes," (Homer Singing in the Ruins of Troy), for the Garde-Meuble, the same year. Some time during the last years of the Restoration (1815–30) or at the beginning of the July Monarchy (1830–48), Rieussec produced a pendulum representing the shepherd Bélisaire inspired by a painting by Gerard, which was presented at the Salon in 1795.

These few examples are a reflection of the great activity displayed by Nicolas Rieussec between 1820 and the end of the Restoration. If the inventories established today suggest a slowdown of activity during the July Monarchy, this is not necessarily the case. Watchmaker to Louis XVIII (1815–24) and then to his brother Charles X (1824–30), he retained the position under the government that followed. Louis Philippe, king from 1830 to 1848, liked his work enough to keep his services.

The movements and clocks that Rieussec made for the Garde-Meuble did not preclude research and industrial innovation. In fall 1837, he filed a patent for "Improvements to Chronographs." In early 1838, he obtained a patent for a period of ten years. These new works earned Rieussec a bronze medal at the exhibition of products of French industry of Paris (1839). It renewed and confirmed the one he had been awarded at the exhibition of 1823.

After a dispute over the intellectual property of the chronograph in 1850, Nicolas Mathieu Rieussec died in Paris in 1866.

Facing page

The signature of Nicolas Mathieu Rieussec, taken from a letter written January 10, 1817 addressed to Count de Pradel, Director-General of the Ministry of the King's House, concerning the request for a watchmaking patent from the king.

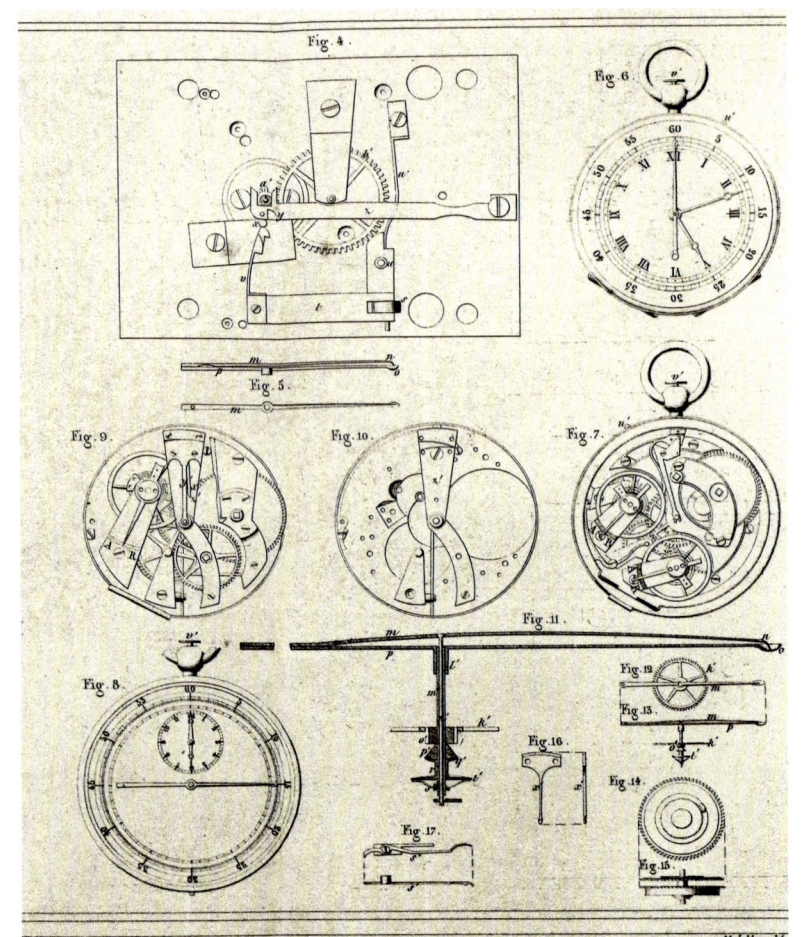

Above

Technical drawing by Nicolas Mathieu Rieussec of a timepiece, or timer, called a chronograph. It showed the duration of several successive events, without the intervention of the observer.

One of the most amazing chapters in the history of watchmaking harks back to a period of lively growth in many fields, notably industry and technology. It was also a time when sports, once reserved for an elite, were becoming spectacularly popular. While men, horses, or dogs also struggled to best one another at highly select events, highrollers bitten by the gambling bug tried to predict the outcome as accurately as possible. Keen interest thus no longer resided solely on the field where the contest took place, but in the stands where the spectators watched. The standard gambler would be equipped not only with money, pencil, and notebook, but also an instrument designed to measure short lapses of time so that results could be recorded. At the end of the day, gatherings were held where winners and losers, active participants and keen spectators, could meet.

On September 1, 1821, the four horse races that were held daily on the Champs de Mars in Paris offered Nicolas Mathieu Rieussec his moment of glory. He had long been working on an invention that would record the time, accurate to one second, required by the various horses to do one lap around the track. On that day in September he took his device along to the track and successfully demonstrated it, dazzling onlookers. A highly laudatory report by two specialists—the famous horologist Antoine-Louis Breguet and the engineer and mathematician Gaspard de Prony, who was also a member of the longitude commission—convinced France's Académie Royale des Sciences to officially acknowledge Rieussec's invention—which he called a *chronographe*—on October 15, 1821. "[It] records the duration of several successive events without obliging the observer to turn his eyes to the dial or to concentrate on an audible signal or the swing of a pendulum…. A chronograph with these properties will certainly constitute a precious aid to physicists, engineers, and all other people who wish to measure events that take place in time." Rieussec's name for his device came from the Greek words *chronos* (time) and *graphein* (write).

Rieussec nevertheless had to wait until March 9, 1822, to be issued a five-year patent for his invention. The description of his mechanism referred to "a timepiece called a 'seconds chronograph,' which records the elapsed time of several successive events without requiring the observer to look at it." Concretely, the new instrument was endowed with a dial bearing a 60-second scale that rotated on its axis once per minute. When a button was pressed, a pointer would leave a drop of colored ink on the enamel disk. Obviously, the device had to be thoroughly cleaned after each use, and dial and pointer had to be kept perfectly horizontal and stable. The chronograph was also equipped with a 10-minute digital totalizer, which could be seen through a small window. The movement with lever escapement measured 112 × 85 × 58-millimeters, and was set in an elegant mahogany case.

The Rieussec Chronograph

The issuing of this first chronograph patent to Rieussec spurred the inventiveness of his fellow horologists. Thus Frederick Louis Fatton in London presented a pocket version of this inking chronograph, while Breguet and Perrelet in Paris made mechanisms equipped with inking hands. Rieussec, meanwhile, perfected his invention. In order to mark the sixty minutes of an hour, he made a second model with two rotating dials and twin inking hands able to record both seconds and minutes. A later version took the form of a pocket watch whose inking hands rotated around a fixed white dial.

INVENTING THE MODERN CHRONOGRAPH

In the realm of measuring tiny intervals of time, Rieussec was preceded by Jean Moïse Pouzait. Back in 1777 already, Pouzait had demonstrated a pocket watch with independent seconds hand, driven by a specific mechanism, which could be stopped, looked at, and restarted at will. But the instrument did not allow for instant reset to zero. This timepiece nevertheless stood out for one specific feature: even when the seconds hand was halted, the minute and hour hands would continue to advance.

It was not until 1844, however, that the history of modern chronographs truly got underway, thanks to a Jura horologist working in London, Adolphe Nicole. High society in London, like Paris, was mad about betting. With the help of instruments to measure brief lapses in time, people wanted to establish which competitor covered a specific distance in a given time. In those days, the founding of clubs and associations meant that sports were slowly losing their character of enjoyable aristocratic pastime—the general public was becoming avid of knowledge of spectacular victories and performances. There was great interest in breaking speed records on foot, on horseback, or by carriage. In this respect the hands of chronographs spurred competitors onward—new competitive sports called for timers that were easy to handle, endowed with the rapid stopping and resetting mechanisms that were essential to swift use of the device for timing events. And that was precisely the advantage offered by the heart-shaped disk invented by Nicole, which returned the chronograph hand to the 12-o'clock position instantly. This talented watchmaker also invented the reset lever. His patent for this device, numbered 10348, was dated October 14, 1844. And yet the first chronograph actually fitted with this inspired mechanism would only see the light of day eighteen years later.

In 1862 London hosted a Universal Exhibition that featured the first chronograph fitted with a real reset function. It was made by Henri Féréol Piguet, who worked for the Nicole & Capt company, also based in the Joux Valley. Adolphe Nicole, one of the company's owners, filed that same year for a patent in Britain; a second patent, issued by the French government, followed on November 13, 1862.

On these timepieces, the chronograph mechanism was still placed beneath the dial, for reasons of simplicity. This placement was shrewd, because it allowed the makers to pay only marginal attention to the overall geometry of the movement. However, this arrangement required the complete disassembly of the hands and dial for any repair or adjustment. Another hero thus entered the history of chronographs, namely Auguste Baud, who managed to incorporate this additional mechanism on the movement side. By the time this development brought the long gestation period of chronographs to a close, calendars were displaying the year 1868. As is often the case in horology, however, chronographs continued to be perfected.

Below

The ink recording chronograph with double disk invented by Nicolas Mathieu Rieussec, watchmaker to King Louis XVIII.

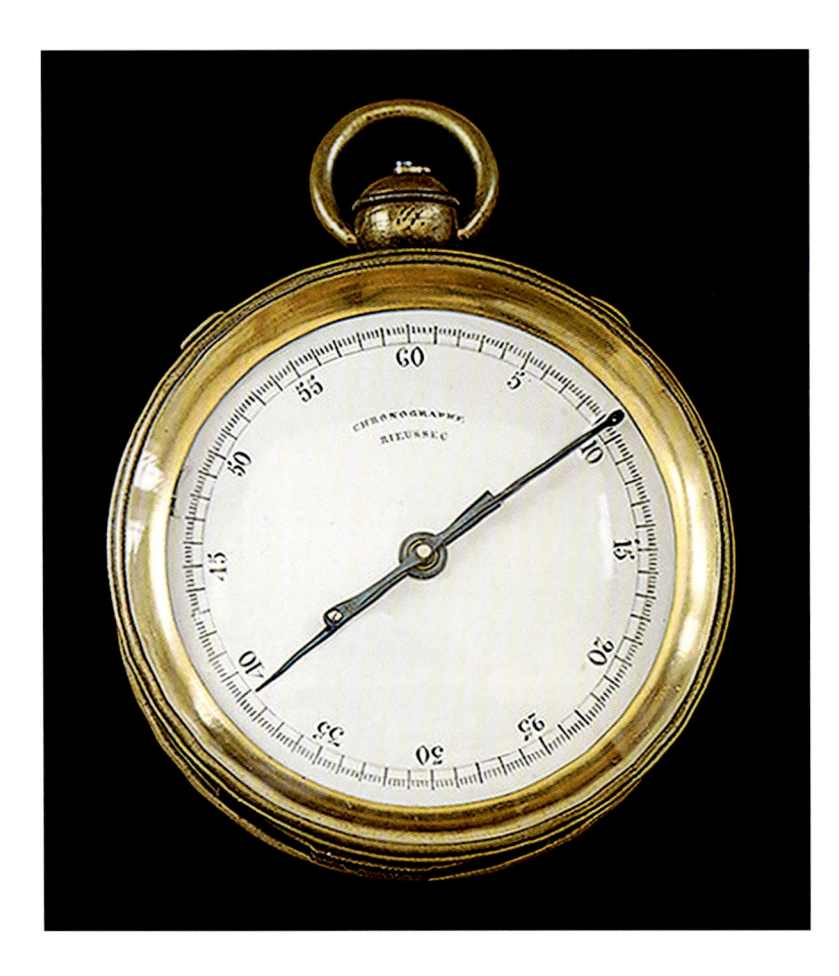

Above

Pocket chronograph with tracing point by Nicolas Rieussec in which the hand turned and the dial was stationary.

Facing page

In the movement assembly workshop of Montblanc Montre, a watchmaker performs a meticulous check on the swing of the balance wheel in order to ensure that the movement is perfectly regulated.

PERFECTING CHRONOGRAPHS

By their very nature and the large dimensions they require, these complementary functions did not generally appeal to women. Yet every imaginable path toward the miniaturization of chronographs was explored. In the early twentieth century wristwatches began to appear in hesitant but steady fashion until they became a standard item. As early as 1910, certain wristwatches were endowed with a chronograph mechanism. Until the early 1930s, a single push-button activated the three functions one after another: start, stop, reset. No intermediate pause was possible. Only the invention of a two-pusher system made it possible to halt the timing process whenever desired, then add the elapsed times. Furthermore, technicians struggled to resolve another weakness in the original mechanisms. In most cases the totalizer could cumulate only thirty minutes, which limited the potential uses of a chronograph. Although the first patent for an hour totalizer was filed in 1892, it was not until 1937 that a truly practical solution to this problem was found.

The system for controlling the various functions was also the object of continuous development or, to be more precise, of simplification. The start was marked by a component that has now become synonymous with upmarket chronographs, namely the column wheel that drives the mechanism of levers and hooks at a precisely defined angle when the pusher is pressed. Like an electronic control based solely on 1s and 0s, this component knows only the positions "in" or "out." The chronograph mechanism reacts differently depending on whether the tip of the lever in operation meets one of the columns on the wheel or slides into the gap between them. Depending on its origin and caliber, a column wheel may have five, six, seven, eight, or even nine columns. During the troubled decade of the 1930s, watchmakers sought less costly alternatives. Their ébauche-making partners developed chronographs in which shrewdly shaped cams, which could be oriented and endowed with reset levers, performed the functions traditionally assigned to the column wheel. In contrast to the complex and therefore relatively costly column wheel, these new cams could be machined simply; furthermore, they could be replaced if necessary without a good deal of work. From 1940 onward these movements swiftly became popular, elbowing out the good old column wheel in a matter of decades.

The year 1969 was when automatic—or self-winding—chronographs became an instant hit. Two companies simultaneously launched models equipped with a self-winding rotor. The unrivaled bestselling movement in this sphere, which since 1997 has also been at the heart of many Montblanc timepieces, was introduced in 1973—the ETA/Valjoux caliber 7750 with coulisse-lever and tilting pinion drive engagement.

Without this movement, highly appreciated for its stunning reliability, chronographs would occupy a much smaller part of the landscape of contemporary timepieces.

When it comes to the engagement system, it should be pointed out that this is as crucial to a chronograph as the command system, because such timepieces include a perfectly normal watch as well as the additional mechanism to measure brief lapses of time. The combination of both elements may be done in additive, hence modular, fashion, or through careful integration into a single ensemble of smaller size, like the entity formed by the motor and gearbox of an automobile. In both instances, a system of engagement—clutch or coupling—is what connects them. In its classic horological version, it is notably found in chronographs bearing the famous double Montblanc–Minerva signature, composed of a horizontal directional lever and a toothed wheel. When the pusher is pressed, this wheel engages the movement's seconds wheel (which makes one revolution per minute) with the chronograph's center wheel. Once coupled, these wheels logically turn at the same speed, so the same is true of their various hands. For technical reasons, the chronograph's center wheel cannot move with total freedom; in order to assure the regular progression of the chronograph hand, watchmakers use a friction spring, which results in a certain loss of energy for which the movement must compensate.

For the ETA/Valjoux caliber 7750's tilting pinion drive, patented in 1968, a similar but markedly more simple construction employs a rotating shank with two pinions. One pinion is continuously engaged with the movement's seconds wheel, while the other is brought into engagement with the chronograph center wheel only once the pusher is pressed, thereby starting the chronograph. Another press of the pusher withdraws the tilting pinion and halts the chronograph.

The third variation, also used by Montblanc, was patented by a certain Henri-Jacot Burmann in 1892. His novel engagement system was based on a vertical clutch. In 1936 it first appeared in wristwatches, yet its instrumentation remained somewhat fragile. The modern friction version dates from 1969. This construction has the uncontested advantages of sapping almost no energy from the movement and of triggering the chronograph hand with none of the jerkiness that might affect accuracy. It therefore seems like an ideal solution.

Facing page
*Montblanc Nicolas Rieussec
Monopusher Chronograph*

Limited edition of 125 pieces in red gold

Case 18-karat red gold convex sapphire glass antireflective

Dial beige, "*Côtes de Genève*" decoration between 4 and 8 o'clock

Crown 18-karat red gold with inlaid Montblanc Star in mother-of-pearl

Strap brown alligator with double folding clasp in 18-karat red gold

Manufacture caliber MB R 100

Hand-wound movement, monopusher chronograph function with column wheel control and vertical disc clutch, twin barrels and stop balance wheel

Dimension diameter 43 mm ; height 14.8 mm

Number of components 286

Number of jewels 33

Power reserve 72 hours with twin barrels

Screw balance wheel Ø 9.7 mm, 12 mg/cm^2

Frequency 28'800 semi-oscillations per hour (4 hertz)

Spring flat

Plates rhodium-plated and circular-grained

Bridges rhodium-plated with "*Côtes de Genève*" decoration

Going train special toothing for more efficient power transmission

IN TRIBUTE TO RIEUSSEC

Montblanc, famous throughout the world for high quality writing instruments, had been in the watchmaking business for a decade when it decided to pay a tribute to Nicolas Rieussec's double disk chronograph. Although the inking function has now been universally replaced by display hands, the use of two rotating dials inspired Montblanc's engineers and horologists in Le Locle to design a novel chronograph mechanism, which entailed developing a movement that could drive a double-disk display—no easy task. The initial ideas on how to design this new family of watches emerged in 2005.

Scarcely three years later, in early 2008, Montblanc unveiled a chronograph with entirely new features, equipped with the *manufacture*'s own specially developed movement. It was presented at that year's Salon Internationale de la Haute Horlogerie (SIHH).

Montblanc Nicolas Rieussec Chronograph

The first model of this new chronograph design was produced in a strictly limited edition of twenty-five watches in platinum 950, seventy-five in white gold, seventy-five in yellow gold, and 125 in 18-karat pink gold. The new case had a single pusher at 8 o'clock, which successively triggered three functions: start, stop, and reset to zero. The dial was unique in the world of watchmaking: the upper part was reserved for the hand-display of hour, minutes, and date, whereas the lower part featured two small rotating disks marked with numerals that indicated the chronograph's seconds and minutes, anchored by a bridge in the shape of a wide smile. On each disk, the elapsed time was read from a fixed vertical pointer.

Two crucial aspects of the design of this manual caliber MB R 100 movement are worth considering: the measurement of elapsed time via two disks, and the presence, underneath the bridges of the movement, of a vertical coupling mechanism for the chronograph. These requirements led engineers down new paths. The use of heart-shaped cams for the reset function had to be entirely reconceived given the distance separating them. Montblanc's watchmakers came up with a technical solution for placing wheels and levers and the visual-design team coordinated the traditional "*Côtes de Genève*" decoration, polishing, and beveling of the bridges and levers. Furthermore, a 72-hour power-reserve indicator had to be incorporated into the movement (read through a transparent sapphire caseback). Right from the start of the development process, the design of the movement entertained the future possibility of a self-winding caliber.

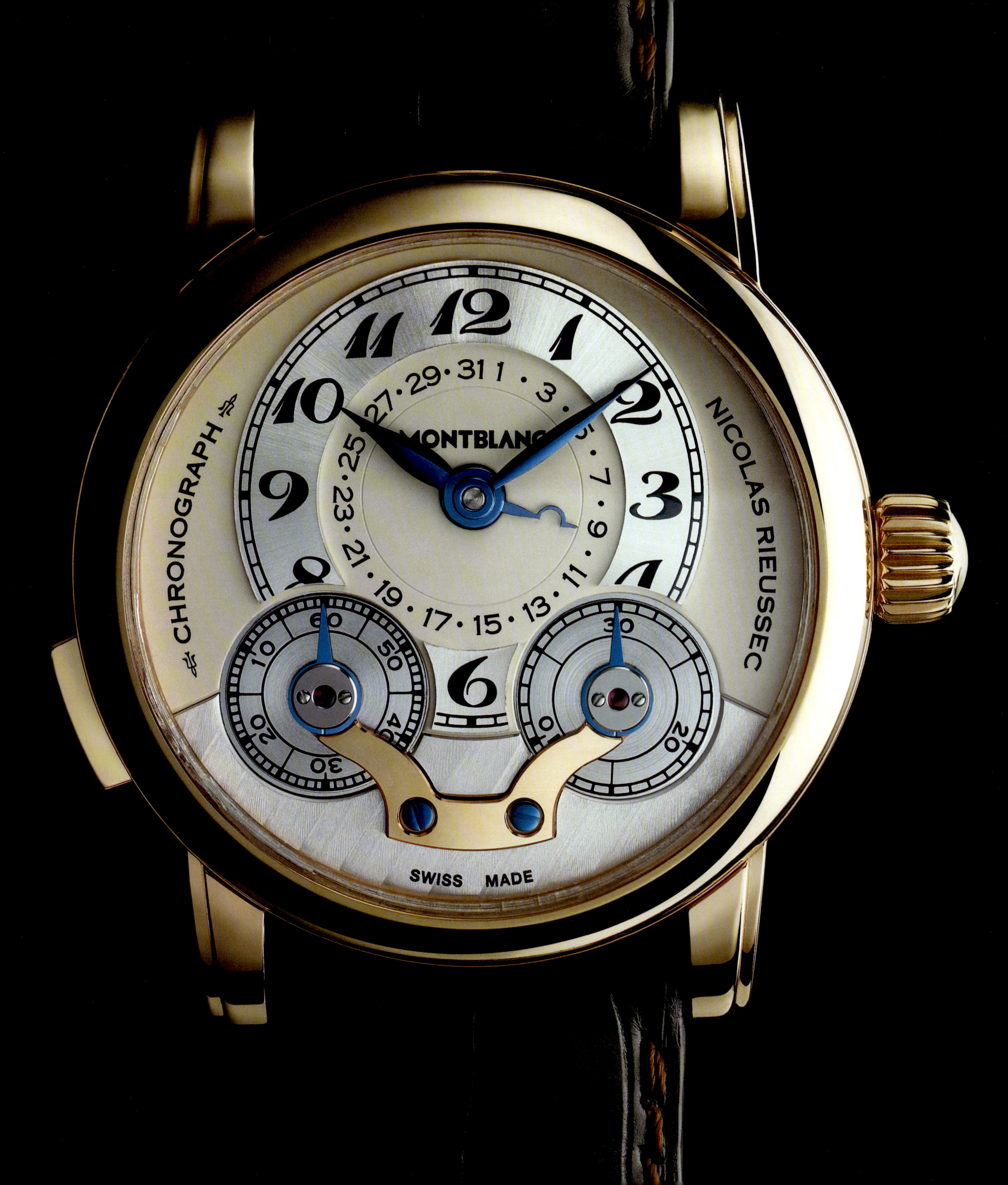
MONTBLANC
CHRONOGRAPH
NICOLAS RIEUSSEC
SWISS MADE

Each Montblanc watch is created by the expert hands of designers. First comes the sketch, the artistic interpretation of the values of Montblanc which will define the appearance of the watch. Then comes the digital design which will give the watch its shape. This is how the *Montblanc Nicolas Rieussec* chronographs are created.

In the workshop where the movement is assembled, each watchmaker exercises his craft to breathe something special into each timepiece that he makes: its soul. The balance wheel with its spiral spring is the organ that gives life to the movement. It is fixed to the balance wheel bridge with meticulous care, an operation that demands great skill.

Every movement, including the chronograph system of the Montblanc *manufacture* caliber MB R 200, in the *Montblanc Nicolas Rieussec* collection, is meticulously assembled in the workshops of Montblanc Montre by the expert hands of the watchmakers.

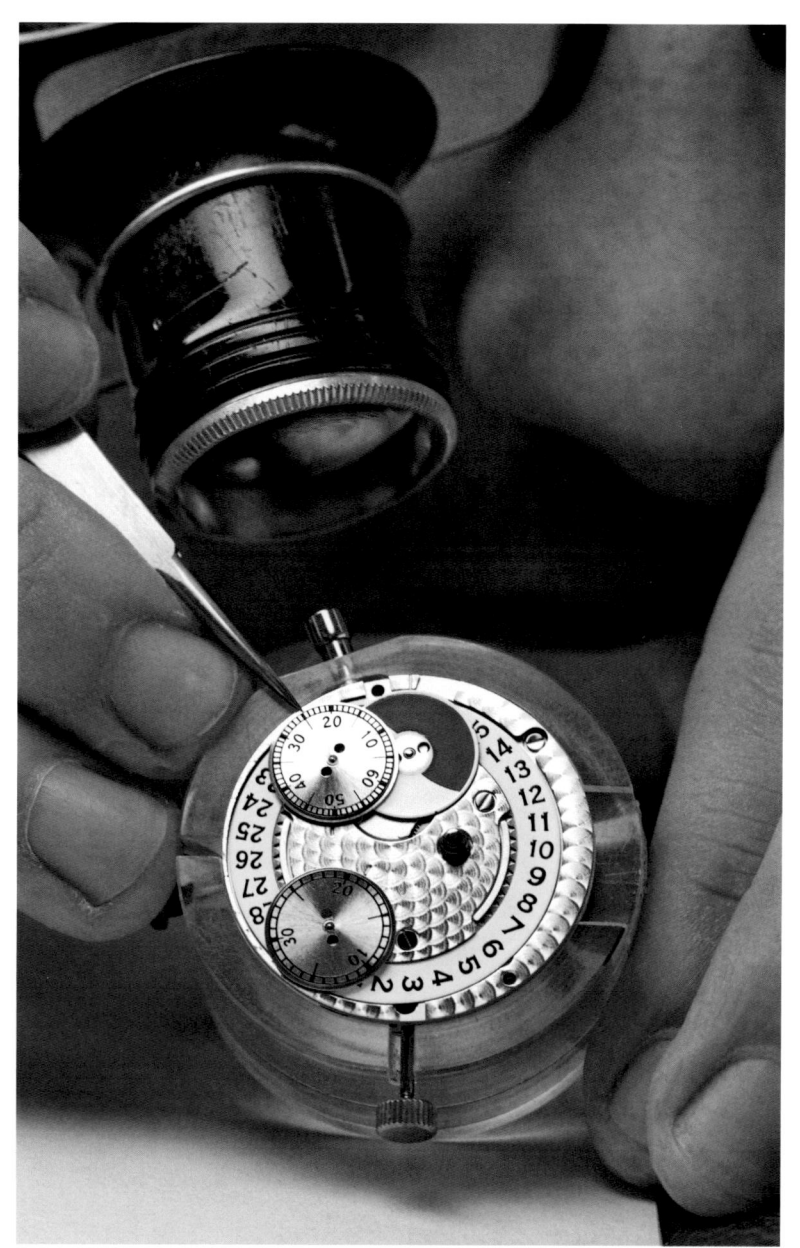

Assembly of the rotating disks of the chronograph and the day/night display. The distances between the date disk, the day/night disk and the chronograph disks measure a few tenths of a millimeter. A rigorous control of flatness and rotation is necessary for this exceptionnal chronograph.

Presented in 2009, the *Montblanc Nicolas Rieussec Chronograph* watch was awarded at the "Watch of the Year" Award presented by the Swiss watch magazine *Montres Passion* and was nominated for the Grand Prix d'Horlogerie in Geneva. The appearance was somewhat modified from the manual wound model by moving the date indicator toward the exterior, in a window at 3 o'clock. Its place was taken by another hand indicating "home time" plus a day/night indicator at 9 o'clock.

Also unveiled in 2009, in a manual version, was the *Montblanc Nicolas Rieussec Chronograph Open Date* watch. Its openwork date disk and skeleton chronograph disks offer a view of the movement through the dial, revealing how the various components of the mechanism function. The newly perfected version of the caliber MB R 100, the MB R 110, is a manual movement with hour display against an off-center minute track, on which the date disk turns. The rotating second and minute disks of the chronograph—endowed with a classic column wheel but a novel disk-coupling mechanism—remained in their standard place. The novelty was a red triangular pointer to indicate the date. The chronograph is triggered by a monopusher at 8 o'clock with successive functions: start, stop, reset to zero. The movement is driven by two barrels that provide a power reserve of seventy-two hours.

The 2010 SIHH was the setting for the presentation of the limited-edition *Montblanc Nicolas Rieussec Chronograph Silicon Escapement* watch. This model is endowed with a newly developed caliber MB R 120 that employs innovative materials in the escapement, in particular totally non-magnetic silicon. Silicon is seventy percent lighter than steel yet sixty percent harder. Corrosion-and-scratch resistant, silicon makes it possible to obtain perfectly flat surfaces. The dial also underwent some modification—the date disk appears in curved windows—whereas the chronograph disks still feature skeletalized execution.

From left to right
1 *Montblanc Nicolas Rieussec Chronograph Automatic*
2 *Montblanc Nicolas Rieussec Chronograph Open Date*
3 *Montblanc Nicolas Rieussec Chronograph Silicon Escapement*

I Montblanc: Writing Time

67

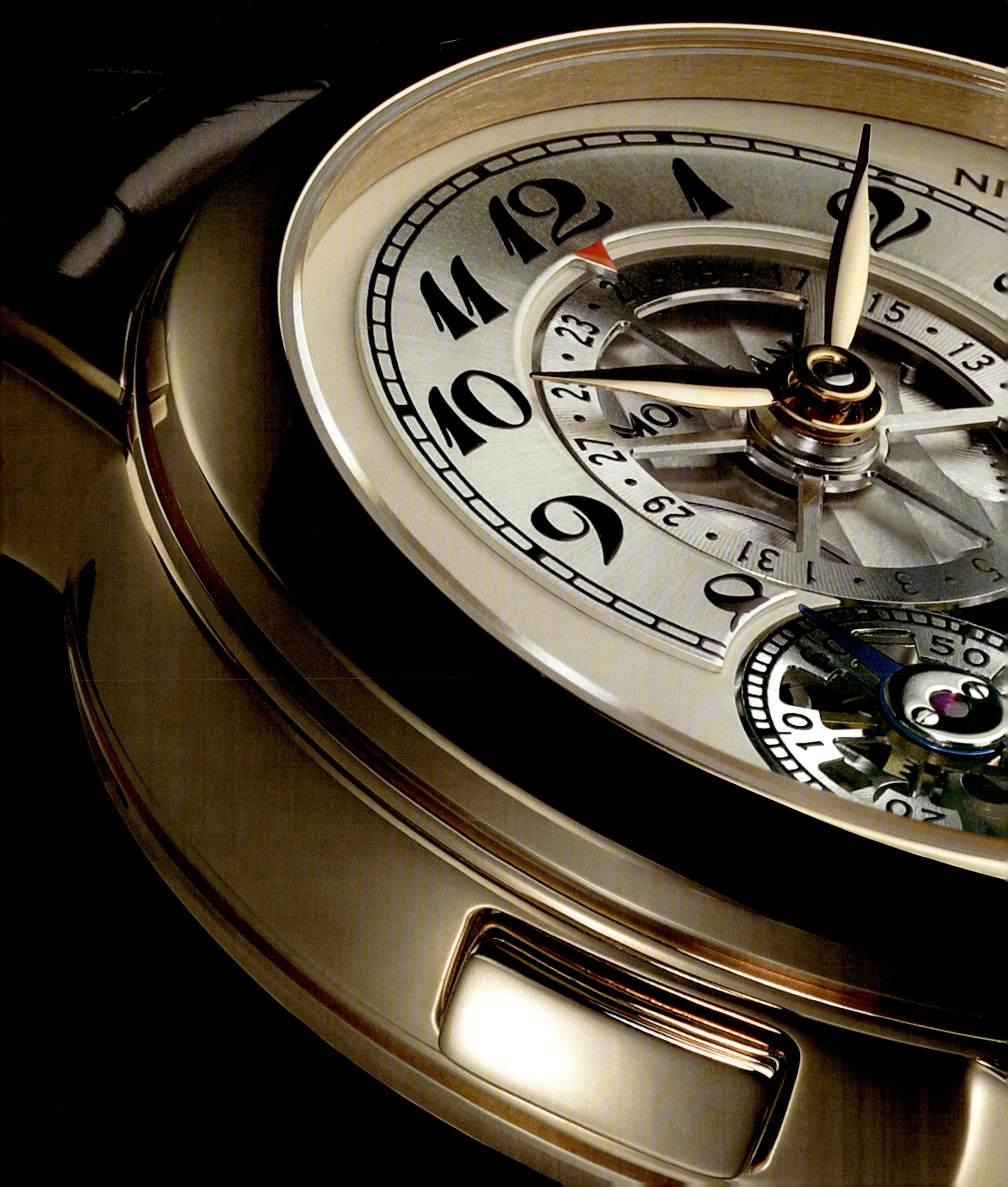

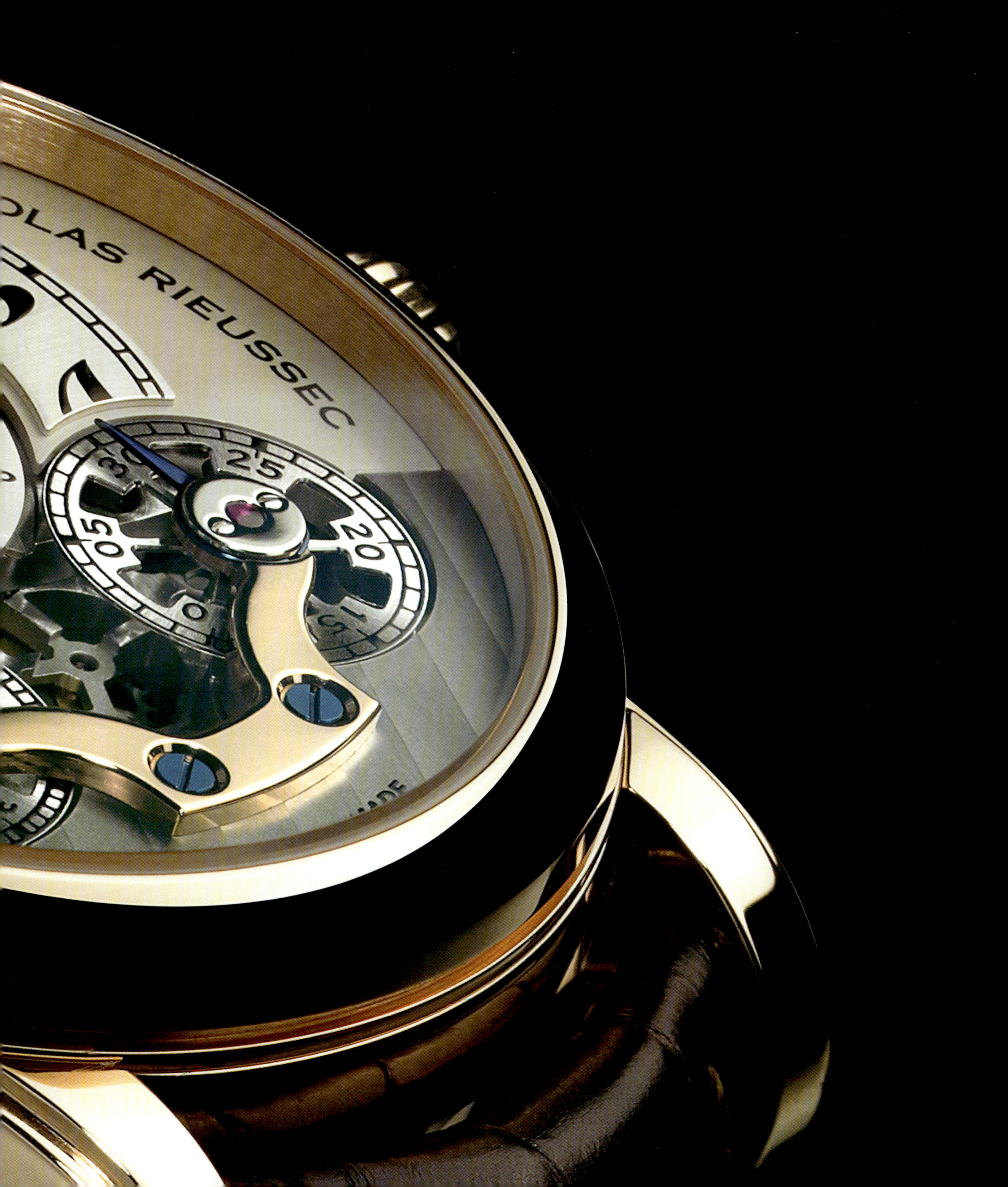
RIEUSSEC

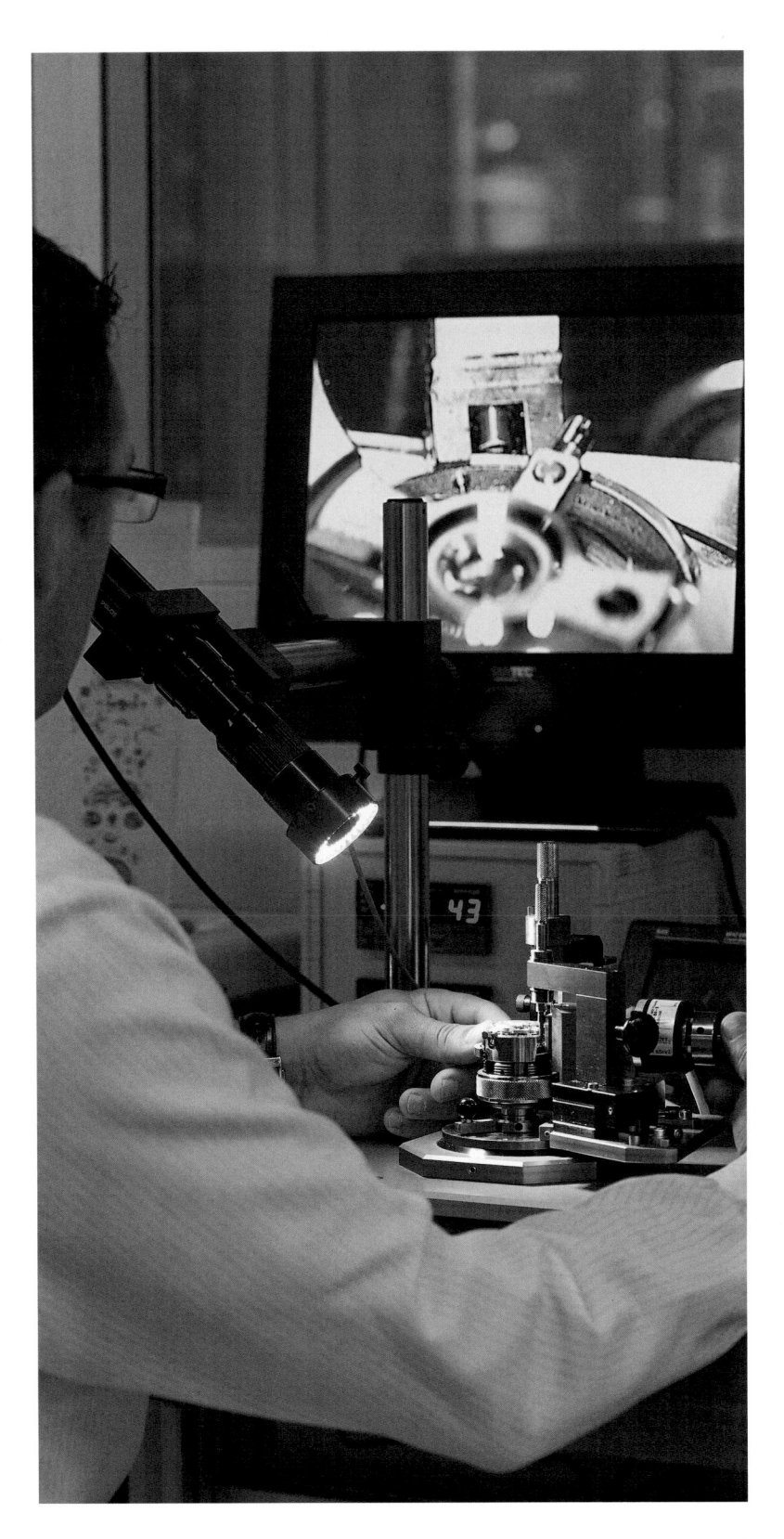

MONTBLANC MEANS ACCURACY

In a brand new workshop carefully trained horologists assemble the various calibers that go into the *Montblanc Nicolas Rieussec* chronographs—the MB R 100, MB R 110, MB R 120, and MB R 200. Step by step, the complicated movements, which require over 280 parts, take shape. Regular quality-control checks prevent errors during the manufacturing process, because the subsequent search and correction of any fault would be long and difficult. The men and women who work here are assisted by modern, sophisticated tools, some of which have been specially developed for Montblanc. Long hours are required before a final push finally brings to life this complex device that is able to divide time into strictly defined intervals. Other team members are responsible for regulating the ideal frequency to 28,800 beats per hour. They know that customer satisfaction is not just a question of sturdiness, but of accuracy. Thus the timepieces must function within a narrow window of plus or minus six seconds per day. From the standpoint of the 86,400 seconds that elapse in the average solar day, these six seconds are insignificant, and margin of error for wristwatches driven by the movement turns out to be less than one percent.

Certain self-winding watches are subjected to official verification of their extraordinary accuracy of over 99.99 percent. Their movements must take a little trip across town before they are finally set in the watchcase. Indeed, the official certifying agency, known as the Contrôle Officiel Suisse des Chronometres (COSC) is located downtown, where all movements that are submitted to it will be verified with total objectivity. Submission criteria notably include Swiss origin of manufacture, a condition easily met by all of Montblanc's movements, plus respect for stipulated dimensions. Verification procedures are based on Swiss norms SN/ISO 3159, in which each movement—endowed with an individual serial number to prevent confusion—is placed in a transparent synthetic case; additional test conditions include a special dial and a standardized seconds hand.

The process begins by winding the movement with an electric motor. Then everything follows according to a precise plan: the movement is left for twenty-four hours in a horizontal position, with winding crown on the left, at a temperature of 23°C (73°F); its performance is measured, then the movement is re-wound by motor and left for another twenty-four hours in a horizontal position, winding crown to the left, at 23°C, followed by another measurement of performance, then another re-winding, and so on. The COSC records the results using the most modern techniques, which naturally include computerized technology. A camera monitors all the important features, and by employing a time signal broadcast from Mainflingen, near Frankfurt, Germany, it measures

I Montblanc: Writing Time

the tiny differences of fractions of a second. The various data are then sent to a computer that stores them in its memory. Thus the final results can be instantly accessed at the end of the fifteen-day trial. Movements that either stopped at some point or did not meet the strict performance criteria are returned to the maker without comment.

The movements that successfully pass the test must display an average functional accuracy within a precisely defined range of minus four to plus six seconds per day at temperatures ranging between 8° and 38°C (46° and 100°F). They are returned to their maker with a report, called the Grand Bulletin de Marche, that scrupulously details their recorded performance. All Montblanc's certified movements are then given a dial that bears the word "chronometer," plus their permanent hands, cases, and straps, before being subjected to a final, pitiless check that verifies total adherence to the performance certified by the COSC. The *Montblanc Nicolas Rieussec Chronograph* watch, which features a rotating dial to indicate the seconds, is too particular to pass these tests. The in-house tests it undergoes are no less rigorous. Whereas the tests of the COSC are performed on the movement before it is encased, all the *Montblanc Nicolas Rieussec* chronographs are exhaustively tested on the movement as well as on the complete watch. This is done to respect the Montblanc commitment of more than 100 years old, which is perfect craftsmanship and quality for every Montblanc product—symbolized by the Montblanc emblem.

Preceding pages

The *Montblanc Nicolas Rieussec Chronograph Open Date* watch with skeleted chronograph disks and an openwork date disk.

Facing page

In order to ensure perfect operation, the watchmakers of Montblanc Montre carry out precise regulation of the balance wheel and balance spring of the Montblanc *manufacture* caliber MB R 200 movement, an operation demanding the most modern techniques combined with manual skill.

Above

The movement is placed delicately in the case. Dial and hand are fitted with the most meticulous care, then the functions are checked. Once assembled, the watch will undergo the numerous checks and tests that Montblanc imposes on every one of its timepieces.

Right

Montblanc *manufacture* caliber MB R 100 movement, with manual winding. Silicon escapement. Monopusher chronograph equipped with a column wheel and a vertical clutch. Twin barrels. 72-hour power reserve display on the back of the watch.

Following pages

Some of the many tools present on the watchmaker's workbench to assemble movements: tweezers, buffs, chucks, screwdrivers, files, etc.

FIVE (5) POSITIONS — D'N – POWER RESERVE – UP — THIRTY-ONE (31) JEWELS

MONTBLANC
LE LOCLE

Cal. MB R 100

100011

Au750

MONTBLANC

SWISS MADE

24 48 72

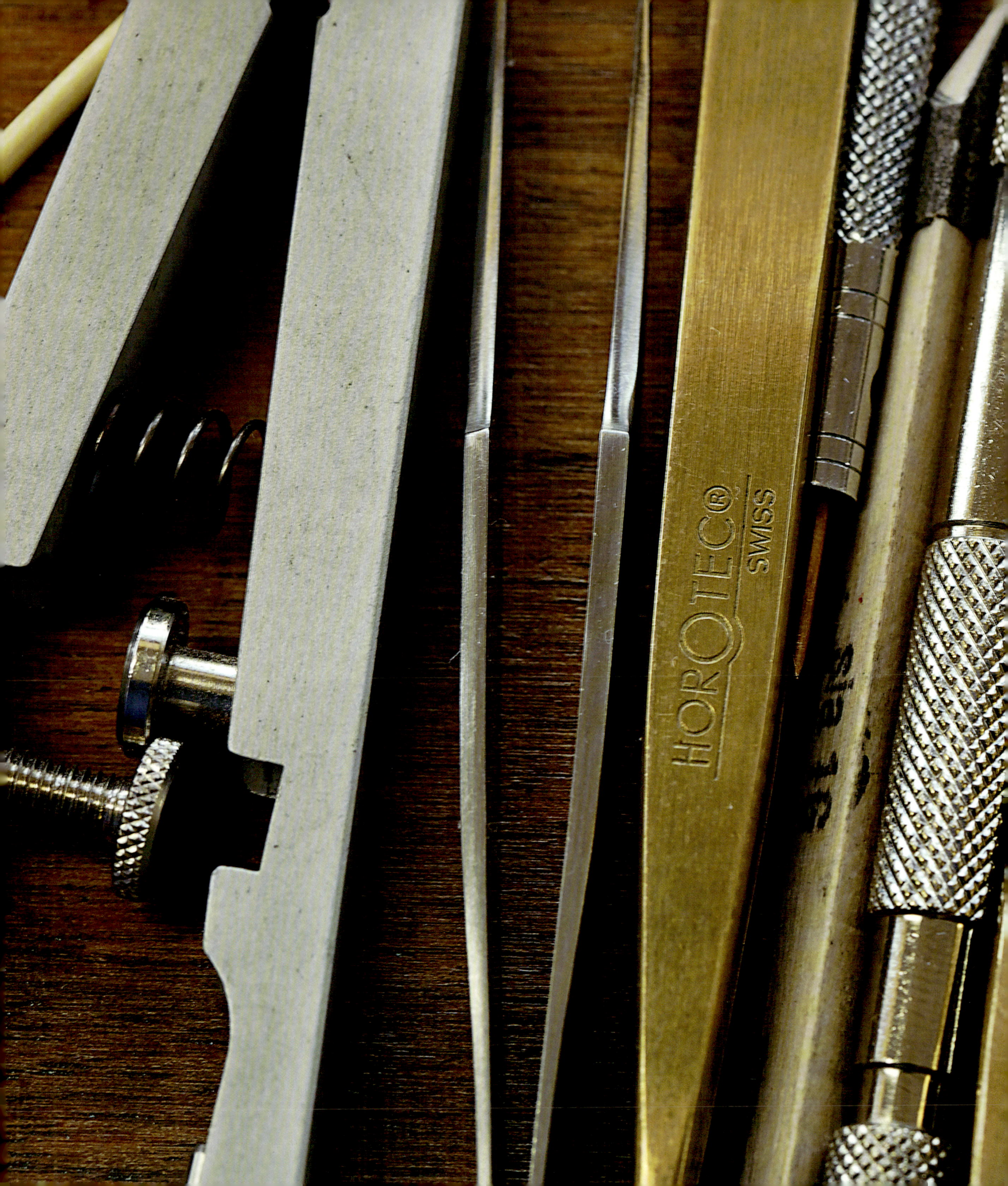
HOROTEC®
SWISS

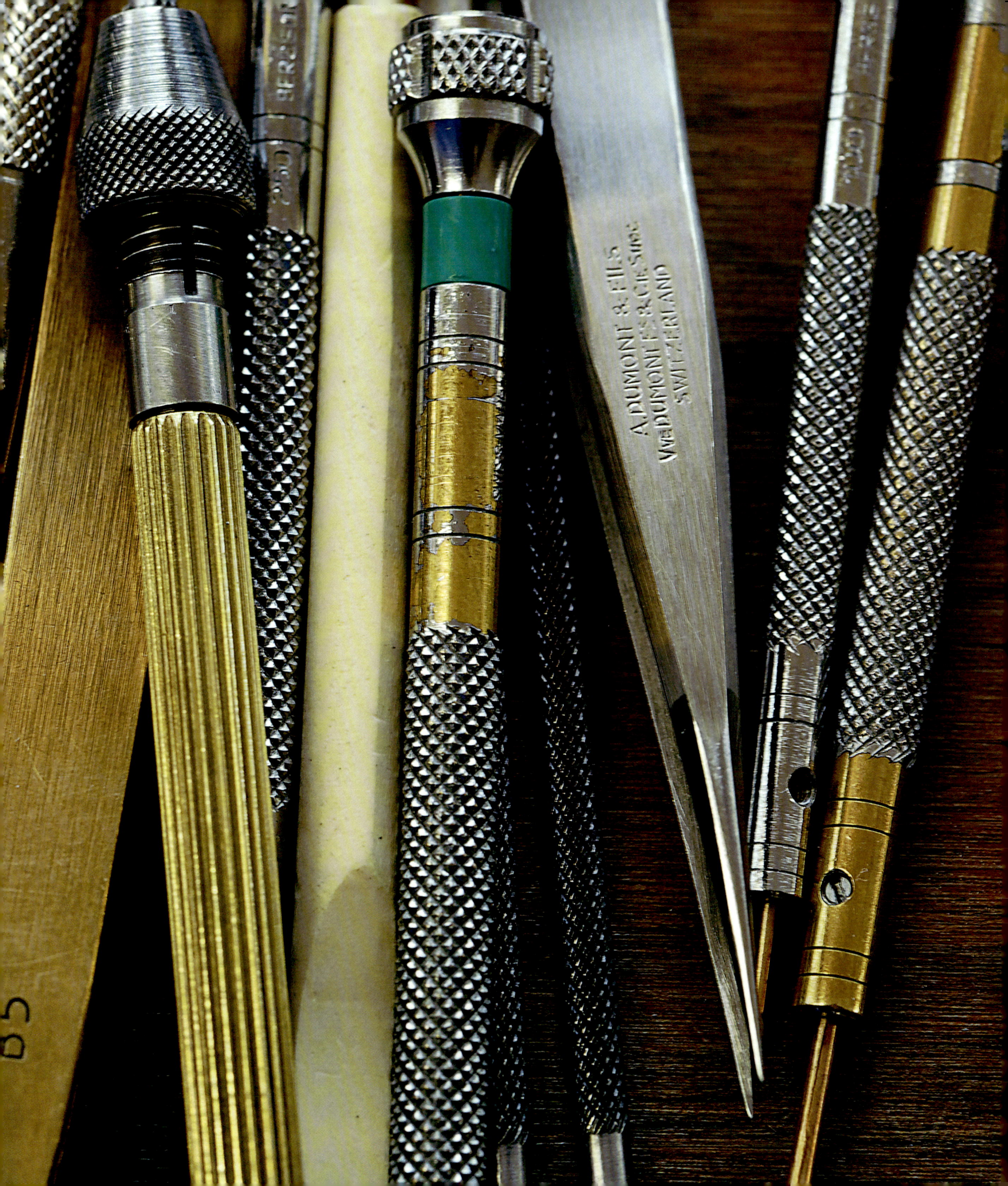
A.DUMONT & FILS
SWITZERLAND

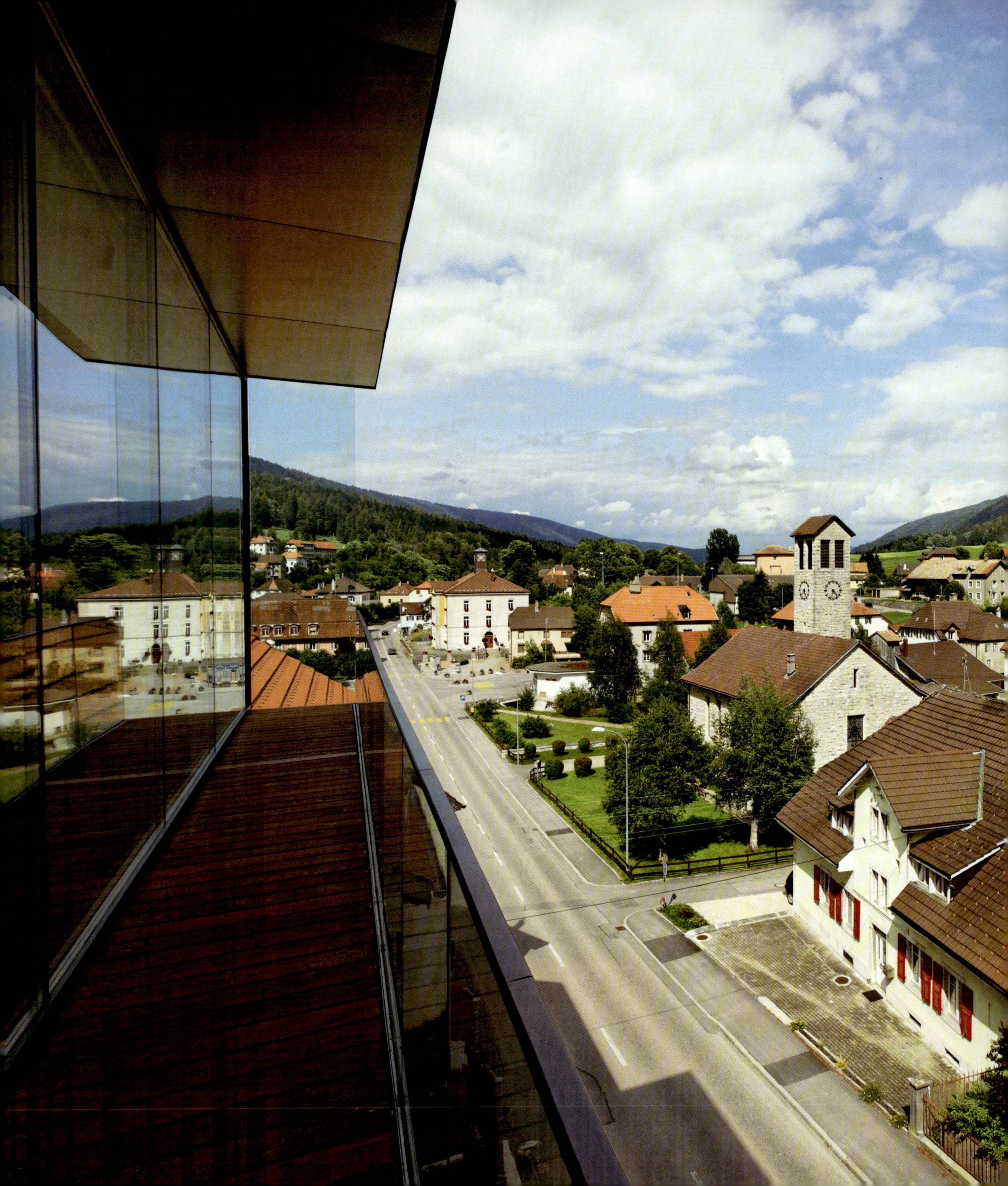

The Montblanc *manufacture* at Villeret

THE PERFECT SYMBIOSIS OF MONTBLANC AND MINERVA

In the fall of 2006, the Richemont Group, which focuses on luxury watchmaking, bought the small but highly prestigious *manufacture* Minerva at Villeret. Although the watchmaking world was surprised by this acquisition of a 150-year-old *manufacture*—which included unlimited rights on all calibers, an impressive stock of movements at the ébauche stage, and an emblematic building in the town of Villeret, not to mention machines, tools, and a workshop stocked with spare parts—the deal immediately proved to be shrewd as Minerva was a perfect fit for Richemont's portfolio. Indeed, almost no other firm in the corporation's fairly wide group of brands had such extensive experience in the realm of mechanical chronographs. The families who owned Minerva were passionate watchmakers and had handed down their unique skills from generation to generation. Each new generation made a point of honor not just of respecting this valuable heritage but also of enhancing it through careful development. Although revolution and war changed the face of France from 1789 to 1799 and that of Germany in 1848 and 1919, no violent upheaval ever threatened the destiny of Minerva, which constantly sought steady, lasting change. That is why the *manufacture*'s remarkable calibers have been the mark of reliability for decades. The purchase of a Minerva watch was never the product of chance or passing fancy, but the outcome of a thought process that resulted in the choice of a very particular item. Minerva therefore had a core of faithful clients, as attested by the carefully handwritten ledgers now conserved in the company archives. Some rival brands even bought ébauches from Minerva, considered to be unbeatable.

The formula for success developed in all modesty in Switzerland's Jura mountains is not unlike a great culinary recipe: use of the finest ingredients, insistence on quality for a limited number of customers, know-how based on long experience, a creative bent that nevertheless avoids foolish risks, and a profound love of one's craft—in this case, watchmaking. The Richemont Group had no intention of sacrificing any of these principles.

Following the acquisition, the simplest path to corporate integration would have been to invite Minerva to play as independent soloist within the Richemont orchestra. Other possibilities included the instrumentation of a partnership with mutual, synergistic advantages, an approach perfectly described as a "win–win" situation. But this possibility required the choice of a partner from the group known for its defense of tradition and respect for timeless values. It then emerged that the principle of cautious yet steady change strictly monitored over a period of decades was perfectly suited to Montblanc, admittedly

Above

Chronograph with two push-pieces. Stainless steel case. Black dial with luminous numerals, tachymeter scale from 60 to 700 km/h and telemeter scale from 1 to 20 (1950s).

Facing page

The village of Villeret as seen from the fourth floor of the *manufacture*, a meeting place for the young and old generations of watchmakers.

a relatively young player of the watchmaking scene but with long experience in the world of luxury writing instruments under its belt. There were clear similarities between Montblanc's "Artisans' Atelier" in Hamburg, where limited editions of extremely luxurious pens are made by hand, and Minerva's chronograph workshop in Villeret. These two workshops were never interested in designing complicated items that corresponded to no real demand. Their interest rather lay in forging useful products that stemmed from traditional values. From a technical and craft standpoint, they illustrated the crucial principles of a manufacture, in which excellence went hand-in-hand with exclusiveness.

Bridges were soon built between the two firms as Montblanc took over responsibility for Minerva to continue its tradition under the name of the Montblanc *manufacture* Villeret—a solid symbiosis grew up between two apparently distinct worlds.

The missions assigned to Montblanc's *manufacture* at Villeret include making watches of outstanding quality, but also encouraging creativity among young members of the profession. As independent associates, young horologists can come to Villeret with their innovative ideas and seek financial backing to concretize them.

Above

Stop watch 100th second. Chromed case, white dial with 100th second scale and 30 seconds counter. Balance wheel, 360 000 variations per hour. 1950s.

Right

Pocket watch, case in German silver (maillechort). Black dial with luminous figures. 30 minutes counter and small second. White luminous hands. Caliber 19/9 CH. 1940s.

Facing page

Cooper printing plates used in the 1950s to advertise in newspaper. They are saved in the wooden drawers like most of the historical pieces in Minerva.

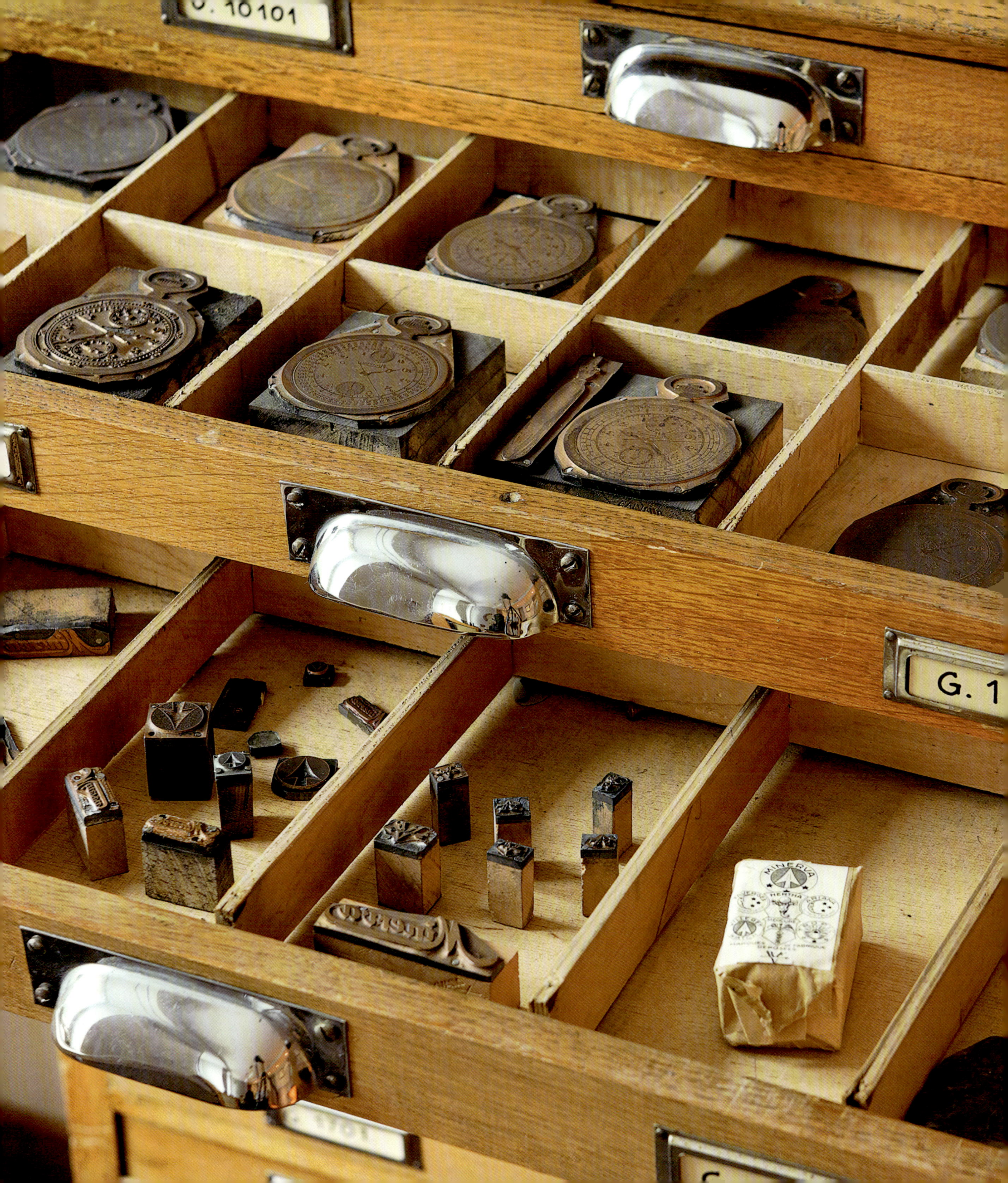
G. 1
MINERVA

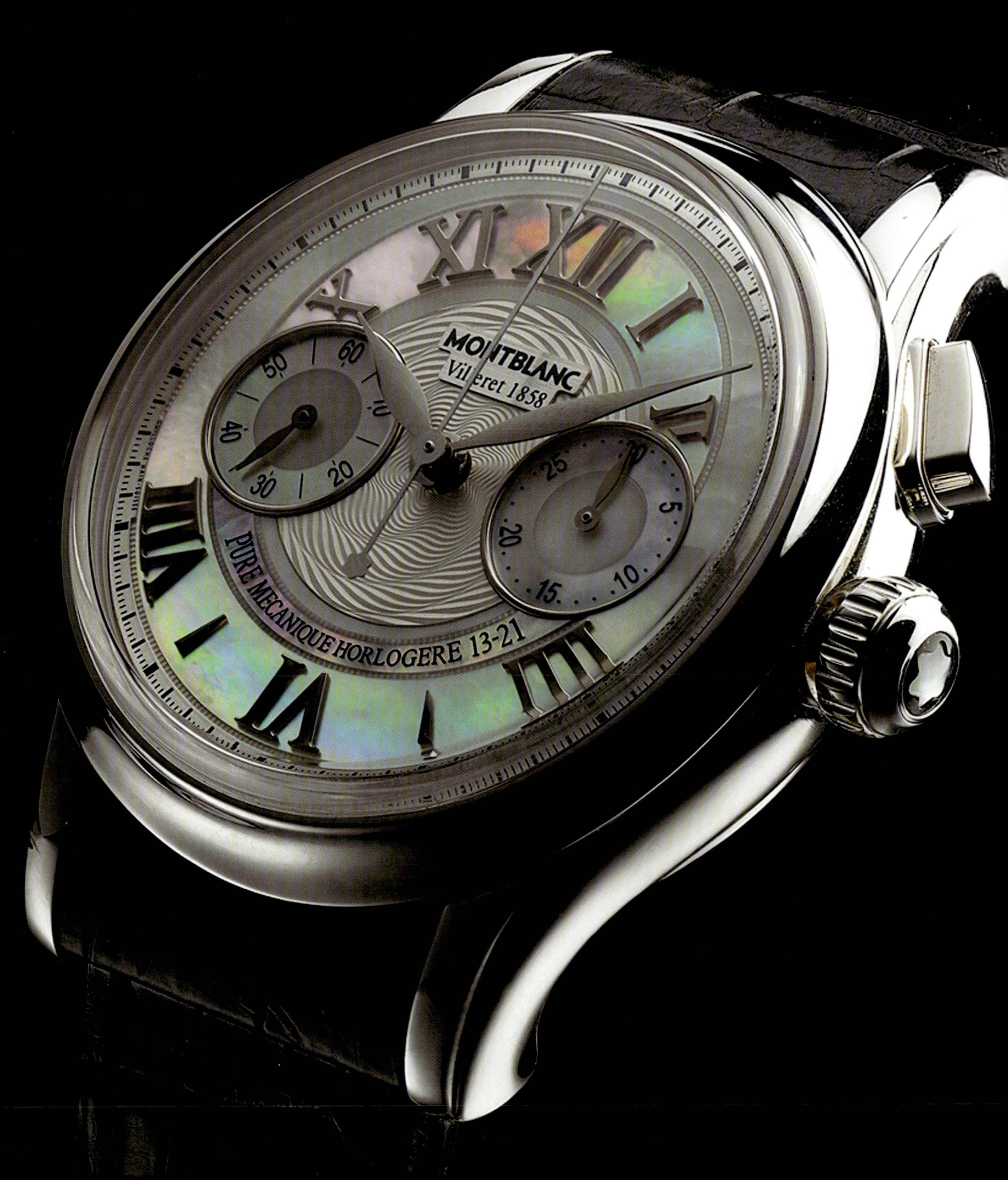
MONTBLANC
PURE MECANIQUE HORLOGERE 13-21

I Montblanc: Writing Time

THE *COLLECTION MONTBLANC VILLERET 1858*

Movements

The first fruit of the marriage of Montblanc and Minerva was the line of watches dubbed *Collection Montblanc Villeret 1858*, referring to the year that Minerva was founded. Introduced in 2007, this line represented the pinnacle of an art known to connoisseurs as *haute horlogerie,* or fine watchmaking, which demands exceptional levels of craft and technique, features complex additional functions, favors classic design, and insists on strict limits on output. Firm determination is required to scale these heights of watchmaking, for no compromise is tolerated and comparisons are all the easier to establish since competitors are few and customers are particularly critical. Yet this is precisely the world in which both Montblanc and Minerva are most comfortable.

In order to understand the context in which the Montblanc *manufacture* in Villeret developed its first watches, a little history would be useful. Minerva produced its first in-house caliber for a pocket watch in 1902. By 1910, the company was already making a range of a dozen or so attractive ébauches, along with chronographs and stopwatches endowed with a column wheel. The 19-*ligne* "No. 3" movement was the object of special attention and led to several further developments. By 1923 the company's own movements were being set in wristwatches. The remarkably robust caliber MB M 13–20 CH, which was 29.33-millimeters in diameter, constituted a new chapter in the history of chronographs.

This historical background represents not just a priceless treasure of experience but also underpins a present largely devoted to chronographs. Faithful to a long tradition, Minerva has retained the classic construction principles of manual wind, column wheel, lateral coupling system, single pusher, and stately frequency of 18,000 beats. It is the only one that can accurately halt a fifth of a second and that uses standard scales on the dials. Critics might complain that modern chronograph technology with faster balance frequencies and vertical clutch system has various advantages. Such a viewpoint is highly pertinent, but there are several counter-arguments. For instance, the traditional horizontal coupling is very pleasant to view, because the full mechanism is visible to the eye; it alone can offer the visual splendor of beveled parts with spectacular polish whose movements imbue the chronograph with life. It also allows the eye to observe the various stages of coupling and uncoupling. That is why each watch in the *Collection Montblanc Villeret 1858* has a transparent, if deliberately discreet, sapphire caseback. Simple observation of the various processes triggered by starting, stopping, and resetting the

Facing page

Chronographe Authentique
Unique piece
Case 41mm in 950 platinum
Dial 18-karat gold hand guilloche with mother-of-pearl inlays
Indexes and hands 18-karat gold, sweep-second in Pfinodal®
Movement MB M 13–21

Facing page

Caliber MB M 16–29

Type of movement hand-wound movement with chronograph and small seconds

Chronograph monopusher chronograph mechanism with column-wheel and horizontal coupling

Dimensions diameter 38.4 mm; height 6.3 mm

Number of components 252 (complete movement)

Number of jewels 22 (hemispherical, domed, olive-cut)

Power reserve 55 hours

Balance screw balance, Ø 14.5 mm; 59 mg/cm^2

Frequency 18'000 semi-oscillations per hour (2.5 hertz)

Balance-spring with Phillips terminal curve

Plate German silver (maillechort), rhodium-plated with circular graining on both faces

Bridges German silver (maillechort), rhodium-plated with *"Côtes de Genève"* decoration

Going-train gold-plated wheels, faceted arms, diamond polished hubs

Following pages

Assembly workshop at Villeret. At these traditional workbenches, each watchmaker meticulously assembles the components of the movement—an operation that requires many years of experience.

stopwatch reveals why chronographs are considered to be among the most important of horological complications. The successive, multi-leveled rotation of the column wheel and the engagement of a swarm of levers dazzle connoisseurs of precision mechanics.

"Such beauty exists in the refined movement of a watch, or an electric motor, or the sparkling machinery of a ship," wrote Carl Ludwig Schleich in the early twentieth century. "What is remarkable is attaining one's goal through the simplest of means—the most direct path, like the purest line, becomes the symbol of the idea.... A guardian angel always presides over the practical needs of technology, namely the guardian of beauty! If matter dominates the idea, ugliness enters; if the idea is superior to the matter, beauty reigns."

It is hard not to recall this vibrant profession of faith when studying the various calibers that equip the watches in the *Collection Montblanc Villeret 1858*.

The relatively low frequency of the balance wheel perhaps calls for an explanation here. Nowadays, the rate of 28,800 beats per hour (4 Hz) has become standard for good reasons. When modern movements are being timed, the four-hertz frequency has clear advantages because it insures remarkably accurate operation in the mid and long term, thanks to partially automated procedures. Conversely, slower frequencies call for incomparably more work. In Villeret, this takes the form of a large balance wheel of classical design and almost majestic appearance. During a time-consuming process, each wheel is matched with the balance spring that best suits it, then is meticulously balanced by hand. The negative effects of the earth's gravity can thereby be minimized, attaining outstanding performance despite the relative slowness of the frequency. It should be pointed out here that mass-produced calibers almost always require higher frequency, so those that can function at the traditional 2.5 Hz—or 18,000 bph—represent a veritable luxury in the eyes of connoisseurs. Such movements have more soul: the slow but constant oscillation of the balance wheel, the steady pulse of the balance spring with its terminal curve—not unlike the beating of a human heart—and the accurate yet elegant swan-neck regulator all add up to the most beautiful way to measure time mechanically. The *Collection Montblanc Villeret 1858* pays watchmaking tradition the tribute it deserves. Of course, such watches are designed for a limited number of connoisseurs who always insist on exceptional features.

Another profession of faith is embodied by the *Grand Chronographe Authentique* watch, an impressive and imposing, yet also functional timepiece. Its large, 47-millimeter case houses a prestigious movement fully 38.4-millimeters in diameter and 6.3-millimeters high. As the dial claims, everything is pure horological mechanics.

MINERVA Villeret

122034

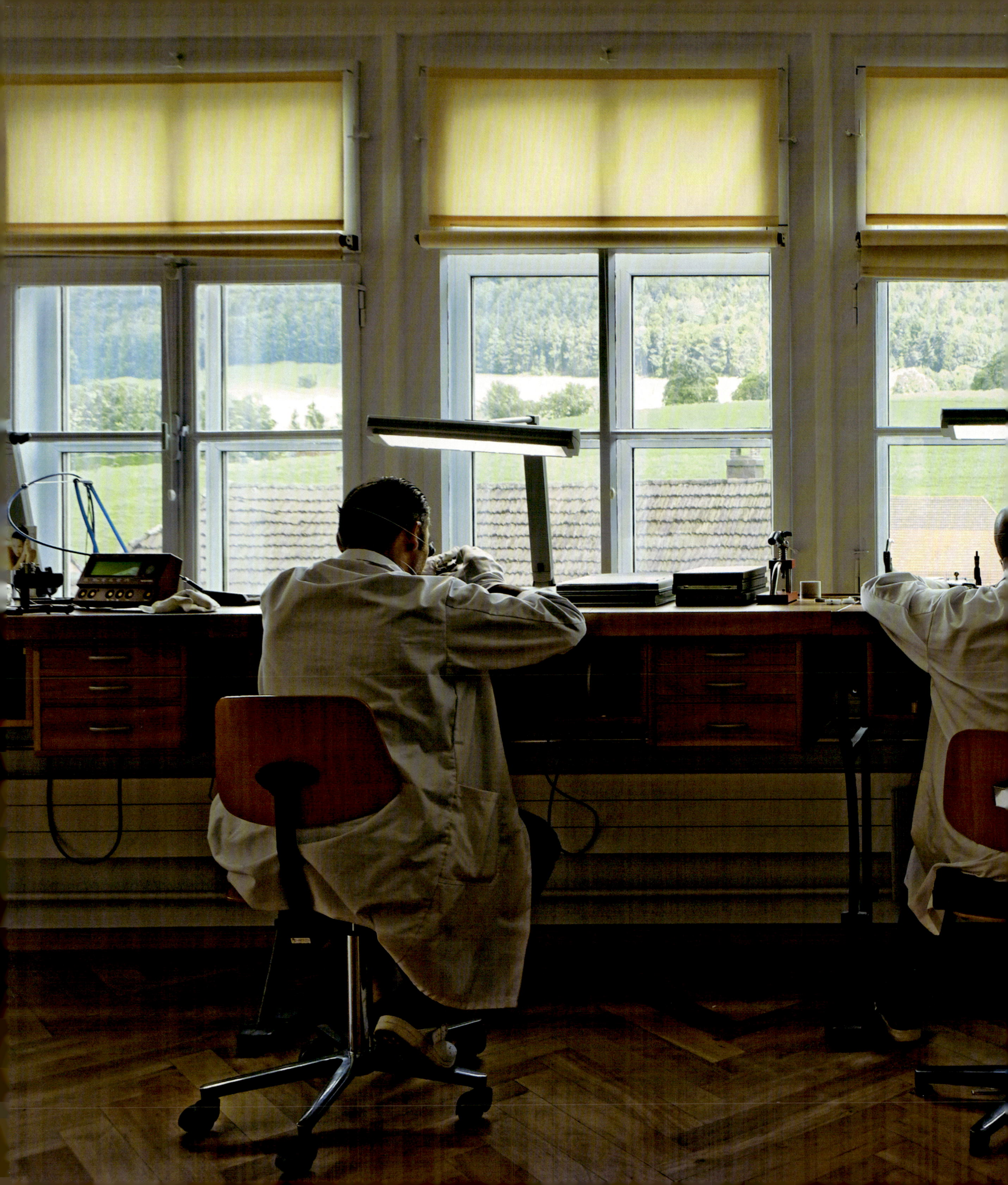

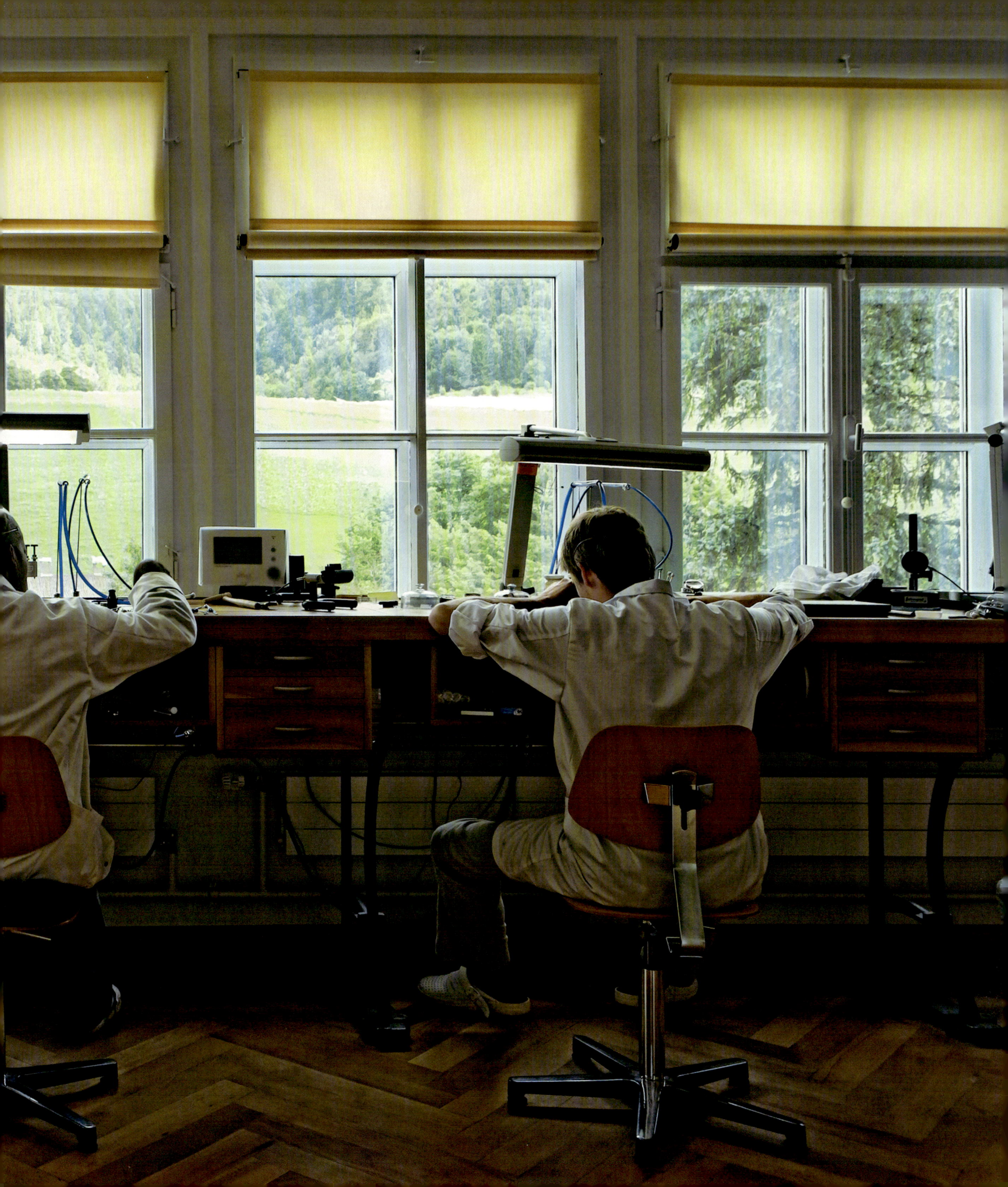

Above

Chronographe Authentique watch with patented system of opening of the back and view of caliber MB M 13–21

Facing page

Chronographe Authentique

Limited edition of 58 pieces

Case 41 mm in 18-karat red gold domed sapphire crystal (forme chevée), transparent pane of sapphire crystal inset into screwed back beneath hinged cover

Dial 18-karat gold silver hand guilloche

Index and hands 18-karat gold, sweep-second in Pfinodal®

Wristband hand-sewn alligator-leather

Caliber MB M 13–21

Type of movement hand-wound movement with chronograph and small seconds

Chronograph monopusher chronograph mechanism with column-wheel and horizontal coupling

Dimensions diameter 29.50 mm; height 6.4 mm

Number of components 239 (complete movement)

Number of jewels 22 (hemispherical, domed, olive-cut)

Power reserve 60 hours

Balance screw balance, Ø 11.4 mm; 26 mg/cm^2

Frequency 18'000 semi-oscillations per hour (2.5 hertz)

Balance-spring with Phillips terminal curve

Plate German silver (maillechort), rhodium-plated with circular graining on both faces

Bridges German silver (maillechort), rhodium-plated with "*Côtes de Genève*" decoration

Going-train gold-plated wheels, faceted arms, diamond polished hubs

Endowed with a column wheel and superbly polished levers, a 14.5-millimeter screw balance, a balance spring with terminal curve (respecting the designs published in 1861 by Professor Édouard Phillips from France), and an elegant classic design, the chronograph's mechanism is particularly well suited to the respectable size of the manual caliber MB M 16–29, composed of 252 meticulously decorated parts. To position and time the Glucydur® balance wheel using five adjustments, watchmakers employ inertia blocks and little screws of gold or platinum. The twenty-two jewels, three of which are set in chatons (or bezel rings), are all of peerless quality.

The mainspring can run for fifty-five hours before it needs a boost in energy, so the power reserve is more than two days. The delightful sensation of winding by hand only has to be experienced once to appreciate the amazing smoothness of the manual mechanism—wearers may find themselves fingering the winding crown more often than necessary. The crown incorporates the chronograph pusher that triggers the three functions of start, stop, and reset-to-zero in sequential order. A 30-minute totalizer at 3 o'clock records the sweeps completed by the chronograph's slender hand.

Since not all wrists can cope with such size, and since tastes vary, Montblanc produced a somewhat smaller version, the *Chronographe Authentique*, with a diameter of 41-millimeters. It is equipped with the in-house manual caliber MB M 13–21 that boasts a power reserve of sixty hours. The movement, featuring a column wheel, is 29.5-millimeters in diameter and 6.4-millimeters high; the dimension of the balance has therefore been reduced to 11.12-millimeters. Beating at 2.5 Hz, a balance spring with Phillips-type terminal curve and a sensitive swan-neck regulator seem like obvious choices. However, it would be a mistake to suppose that smaller size means the watchmakers have spent less care on the finish of the 239 parts, including the twenty-two jewels. The criteria established by master watchmaker Demetrio Cabiddu, technical director of the Villeret *manufacture*, are applied to all movements regardless of size or complexity.

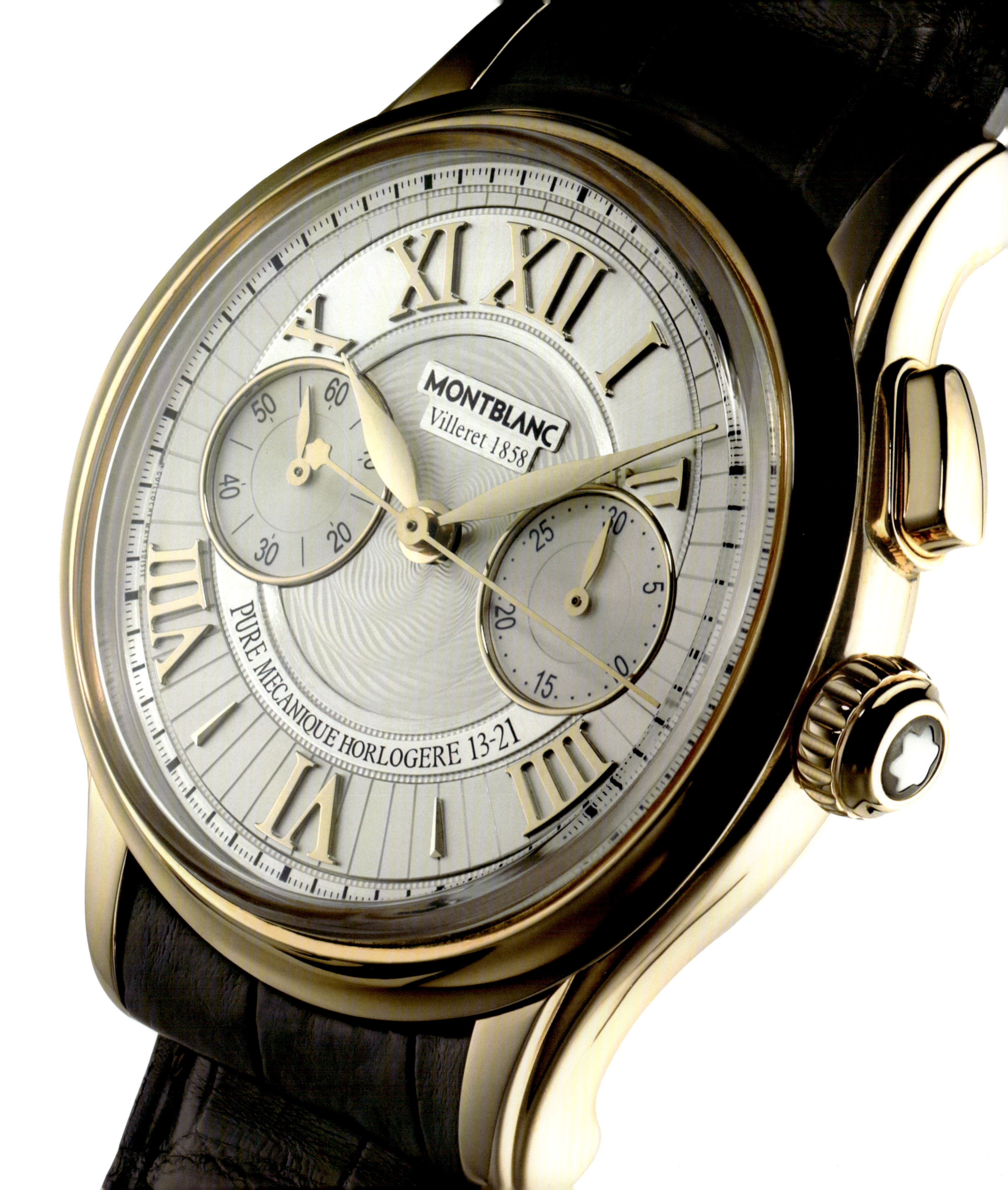
MONTBLANC
Villeret 1858
PURE MECANIQUE HORLOGERE 13-21

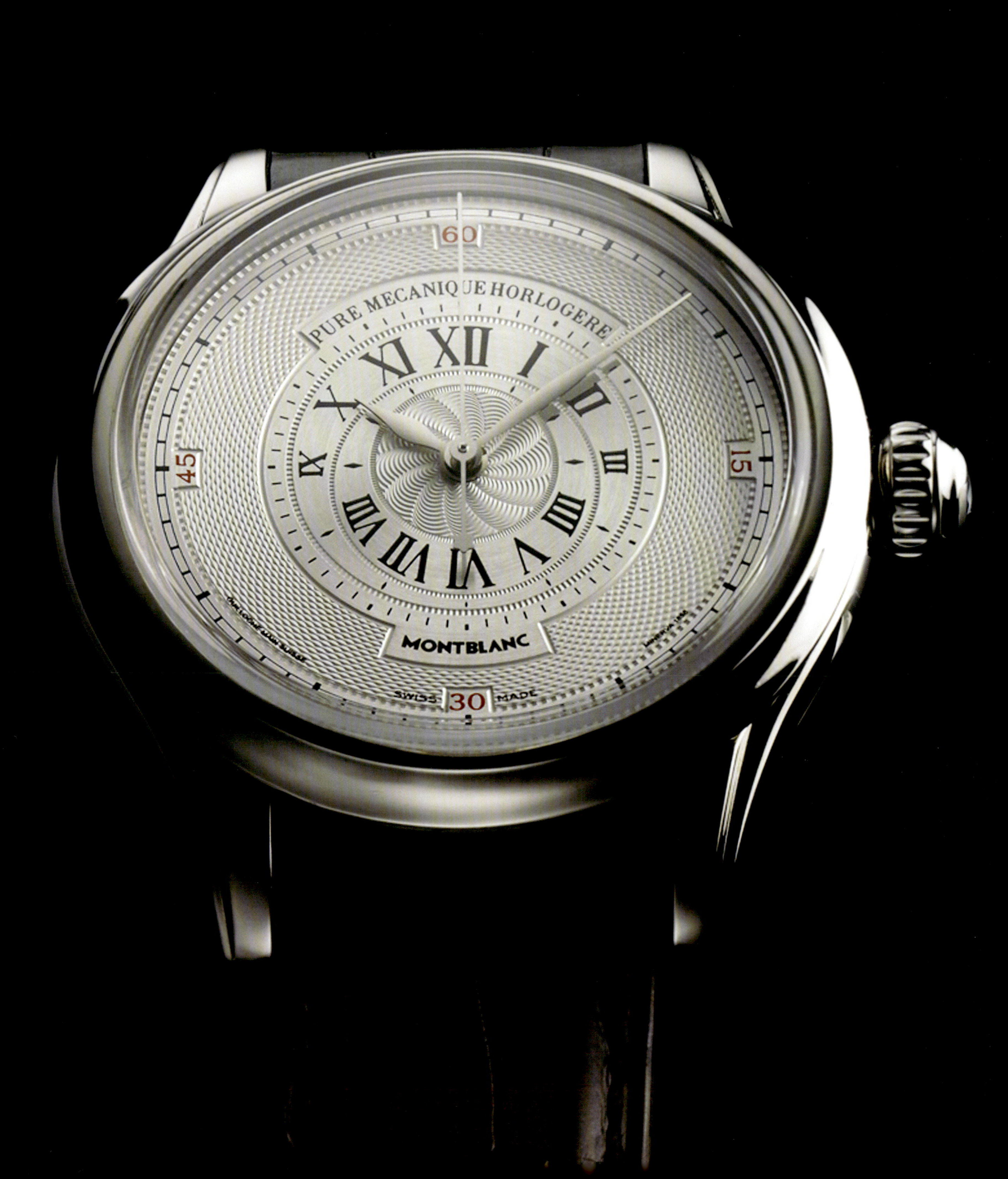
60
PURE MECANIQUE HORLOGERE
45
15
MONTBLANC
SWISS
30
MADE

External appearance
Meticulous artisanal skills are applied not only to the watch movement, but also to the case, which is always polished on every side. A curved bezel holds an equally curved crystal. The transparent back is screwed on, then protected with a hinged cover, or cuvette, which opens thanks to a discreet, patented mechanism; the cuvette also attests to the authenticity of the watch, being inscribed not only with an individual serial number but also with "Montblanc Villeret 1858," "Édition Limitée," and "Fait main à Villeret" (Hand made in Villeret). Inside is yet another, equally important, inscription: "Demetrio Cabiddu, Maître-horloger" (Master Watchmaker). In fact, as technical director of the Montblanc *manufacture* at Villeret, Cabiddu personally guarantees the outstanding quality of all movements that bear the *Collection Montblanc Villeret 1858* name. Finally, there is Montblanc's own characteristic logo—a silhouette of Europe's highest peak with its six glacier tongues, depicted in real mother-of-pearl, which adorns the winding crown or chronograph pusher on these watches.

Dials are said to account for eighty percent of the overall impression made by a watch. Given their size and the importance of the information they display, this assertion seems well founded. Furthermore, it is probable that most men and women look at their watches more often during the day than they look in a mirror. Montblanc therefore pays special attention to the decoration of dials, using the full range of traditional techniques such as cloisonné and champlevé enameling and manual guilloche.

Manual guilloche—also known as guilloche work—is a fastidious technique done by a skilled craftsperson who hand-guides a special engraving machine. This particularly demanding decorative process was probably first used on a wide scale by Abraham-Louis Breguet when making his metallic dials. The variety of engine-turned decoration is practically unlimited. However, artisans who still know how to use these old, capricious engraving engines are even rarer than the copies in a limited edition of the *Collection Montblanc Villeret 1858*. Just fixing and centering the dial calls for special patience, while the subsequent stages demand exceptional skill. The machinist must engrave countless lines, one after another, maintaining an equal distance between each line. From this standpoint, the choice of a model calls for serious thought, and the degree of difficulty increases with the number of structures. Decorating a Montblanc dial thus requires a painstaking series of operations: apply the graver, lift the graver, apply the graver, and so on. The endless patience required for such work is a wonderful embodiment of the expression "to give it time" as well as a perfect illustration of the methods used to make wristwatches in the *Collection Montblanc Villeret 1858*.

Facing page
Grande Seconde au Centre Retour-à-zéro
Limited edition of 8 pieces
Case 47 mm 18-karat white gold with palladium 210
Dial 18-karat gold silver hand guilloche
Hands 18-karat gold, sweep-second in Pfinodal®
Caliber MB M 16–18

Facing page
Grand Chronographe Émail Grand Feu
Limited edition of 8 pieces
Case 47 mm 18-karat white gold with palladium 210
Dial champlevé, émail grand feu blanc in 18-karat gold
Hands 18-karat gold, sweep-second in Pfinodal®
Wristband hand-sewn alligator-leather

Caliber MB M 16–29

Montblanc has taken ornamental considerations to an extreme for these unique dials. Engine-turned decoration is even complemented by lavish mother-of-pearl inlays on certain watches, while Roman numerals and indices are applied by hand, one by one. Each dial thus becomes a setting worthy of receiving the leaf-shaped, minutely curved hands of time. In order to achieve the right balance, the hand of the chronograph is amazingly slender, and is capped by a stylized Montblanc star that serves as counterweight.

The extent of the limited editions is based on the figures in the year 1858, the founding year of the *manufacture* Minerva: 1, 8, 58. For each model, a single example is made in that most noble of metals, platinum; eight others are made in white gold, that mark of well-heeled discretion; and fifty-eight are produced in the warm, delicate tones of pink gold. The major investment made in hand-crafting, independently of the nature of the case, inevitably results in the creation of incomparable, unique watches—whose price is inevitably substantially higher than mass-produced models.

Exclusive collector's items
A regrettable, if inevitable, result of this strict limitation was that the magnificent chronograph edition sold out quickly. In 2008, Montblanc gave these spectacular movements a new face: chronograph calibers MB M 16–29 and MB M 13–21. Montblanc combined the occasion with the 150th anniversary of the founding of the *manufacture* Minerva to forge a perfect synthesis of horological tradition—the final timepieces equipped with this edition's two little mechanical marvels are endowed with enameled dials of unequaled lavishness.

The enameling process refers to the technique of applying colored glass to metal as a decorative and protective layer. From a chemical standpoint, enamel is composed of a special glass that can notably be colored by the addition of antimony, zirconium oxide, or titanium oxide. The glass must be fused, or melted, at a temperature of 1,200°C (2,200°F) and then cooled. The granular product is then mixed with coloring additives and crushed to a powder. The metallic support is first thoroughly cleaned, and then the enamel is applied by immersion, by spraying, or applied with a brush. The item must then be fired in a special kiln at a temperature of 800° to 900°C (1,500–1,650°F).

In the mid seventeenth century, clock and watchmakers realized that they could use this age-old technique. The hands of many high quality timepieces began to sweep across sparkling white enamel dials. This fashion lasted into the 1920s. A curtain then came down upon the relatively costly and extremely delicate art,

PURE MECANIQUE HORLOGERE
EMAIL GRAND FEU SUISSE
MONTBLANC
MINERVA 1858
SWISS
MADE

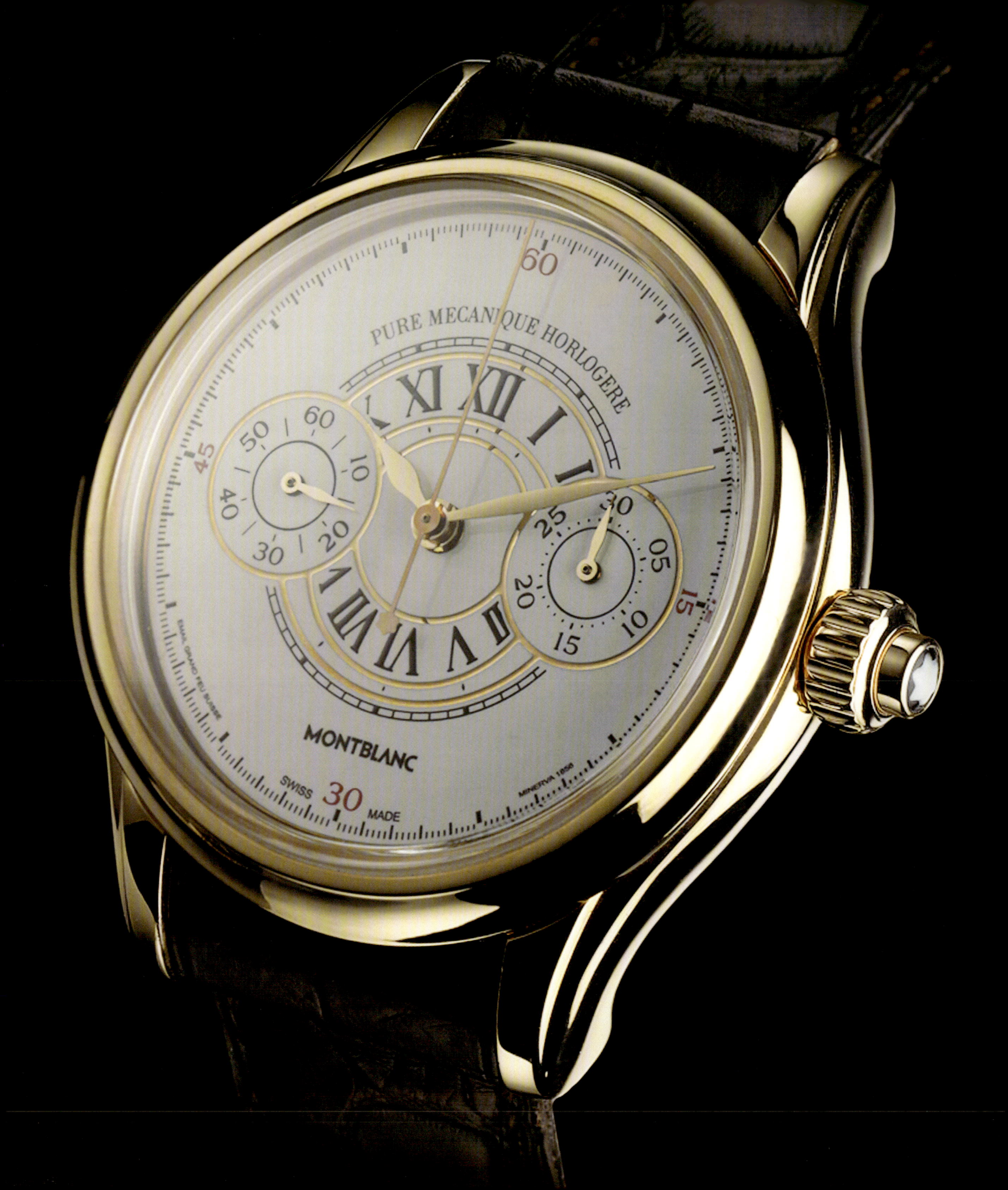
PURE MECANIQUE HORLOGERE
MONTBLANC
SWISS
MADE

I Montblanc: Writing Time

which Montblanc nevertheless continues to practice in a traditional manner.

One of the specific techniques used by Montblanc is called champlevé; with the aid of a graver, specialist artisans carve little depressions. These hollows are then filled with powered enamel, the chosen color being specific to a given model. (On the exclusive *Grand Chronographe Émail Grand Feu* model, the metallic plate is not the usual copper, but solid gold, as befits the philosophy behind these exclusive timepieces.) The future dials are then fired in the kiln, where the miniscule particles fuse together and take on the desired color, white or black. Since the gold support and the enamel have very different expansion and contraction rates during firing and cooling, the back is also enameled—this "counter enamel" prevents the dial from deforming and the enamel from shattering during the cooling process, a stage that must be conducted very slowly and progressively to reduce these tensions. An initial inspection then verifies the quality of the result obtained. Any pieces with imperfections, however minor, will be pitilessly rejected. Only absolutely perfect pieces will then be diamond-polished in order to give a uniform sheen to the surface of enamel and metal. Another layer of colorless enamel is then added to the dial, and a final firing transforms this flux into a transparent, protective cover. The last step involves inscribing the dial with the indication "Émail Grand Feu Suisse" (Swiss High-Fired Enamel). But should this work of art fail its final inspection, the artisans will have to begin the entire process from the start. Montblanc accepts only flawless quality, which is the sole way to guarantee that its chronographs with "Grand Feu" enamel will become true collector's items of ever-increasing value over the years.

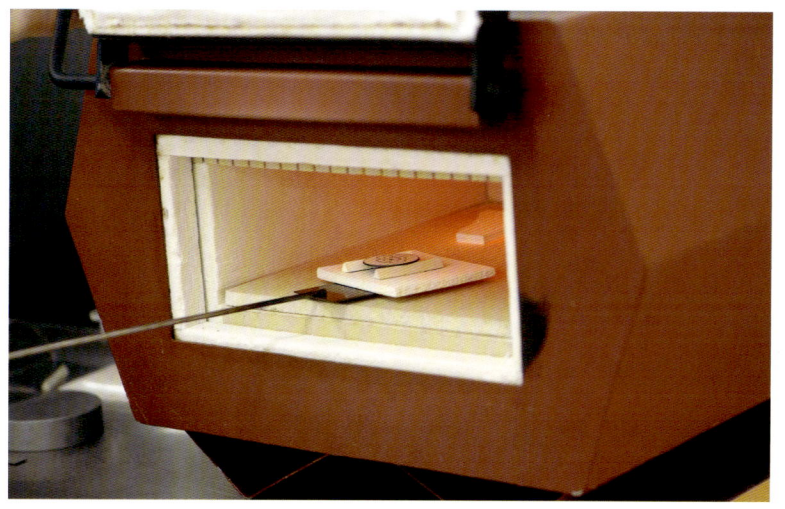

Above

Production of a Montblanc champlevé "Grand Feu" enamel dial.

Facing page

Grand Chronographe Émail Grand Feu
Limited edition of 58 pieces
Case 47 mm 18-karat red gold
Dial champlevé, émail grand feu blanc in 18-karat gold
Hands 18-karat gold, sweep-second in Pfinodal®
Wristband hand-sewn alligator-leather

Caliber MB M 16–29

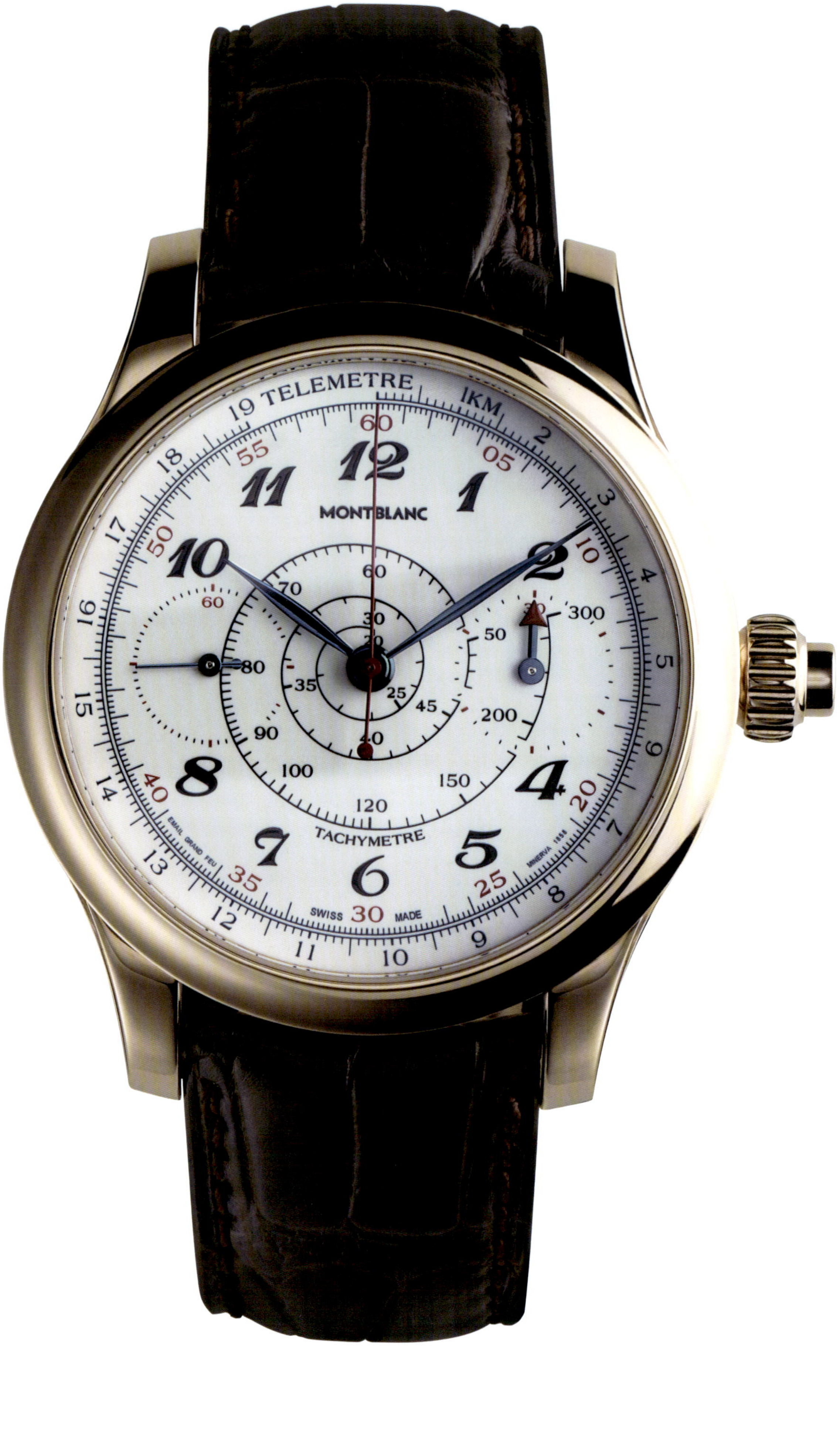

TELEMETRE
1KM
MONTBLANC
TACHYMETRE
SWISS
MADE

Chronographe Vintage

Some innovations have become legendary, and they take on a second life when revived in a "vintage" manner. Such is the case with a limited edition model in the *Collection Montblanc Villeret 1858*, unveiled in 2010, endowed with a characteristic spiral tachymeter scale in the middle of the dial, just like the legendary Minerva chronographs made between 1910 and 1930. The firm's archives still contain many enamel dials from that period, whose scales with their specific divisions were designed for particular types of timing: race timers, pulsometers, part counters or instruments devised for precision timing down to one-hundredth of a second. Thanks to high-precision movements designed for a wide range of applications, the Villeret watchmakers earned a worldwide reputation for the quality of their chronographs, which are still admired by connoisseurs today.

Since the rim of the dial was reserved for a range finder, the tachymeter scale was shifted to the center and given a spiral shape long enough to calculate speed over a three-minute period. Such timepieces were therefore multipurpose instruments, which combined remarkable functions with outstanding mastery of the watchmaker's art. Like those venerable instruments, the watches in the *Collection Montblanc Villeret 1858* have a dial decorated with traditional high-fired enamel, made from a solid gold plate covered with layers of enamel fused at a temperature of roughly 800°C (1,500°F) in successive firings.

The novelty of the *Chronographe Vintage* resides in its 43.5-millimeter case, which lends it a modern elegance. In order to preserve its historic proportions, all the parameters of the case had to be reconceived, including the lugs. The result of such work is a timepiece that splendidly displays its glamorous heritage even as it conveys a sporty, high-tech feel.

Accurate beauty

A little brother to the chronograph is a watch with a "return-to-zero" function. Pulling the crown triggers the instant return of the central seconds hand to its vertical position. People keen on accuracy are delighted with the feature when setting the time, because they can set the watch going—by lightly pressing the crown—at the precise instant they hear a time signal. Over the centuries, innovative horologists have designed a whole series of mechanisms to perform this function. Montblanc's *manufacture* in Villeret has chosen the most complex—and clearly most beautiful—version, whose resemblance to a chronograph mechanism is obvious. The slender seconds hand, set very visibly in the center of the dial, is thus fixed to the axle of the center wheel of the chronograph. Lateral coupling makes constant contact possible with the seconds wheel. The situation becomes

I Montblanc: Writing Time

Above

Large wrist-chronograph, caliber 19/9CH in steel case from the 1940s. The dial with telemeter and spiral tachymeter was reused by the designers of the model *Chronographe Vintage*.

Facing page

Chronographe Vintage

Limited edition of 58 pieces

Case 43.50 mm in 18-karat red gold

Dial émail grand feu blanc in 18-karat gold

Tachymeter scale in the center of the dial with colimaçon form

Telemeter scale on the exterior of the dial

Caliber MB M 16–29

Type of movement hand-wound movement with chronograph and small seconds

Chronograph monopusher chronograph mechanism with column-wheel and horizontal coupling

Dimensions diameter 38.4 mm; height 6.3 mm

Number of components 252 (complete movement)

Number of jewels 22 (hemispherical, domed, olive-cut)

Power reserve 55 hours

Balance screw balance, Ø 14.5 mm; 59 mg/cm^2

Frequency 18'000 semi-oscillations per hour (2.5 hertz)

Balance-spring with Phillips terminal curve

Plate German silver (maillechort), rhodium-plated with circular graining on both faces

Bridges German silver (maillechort), rhodium-plated with "*Côtes de Genève*" decoration

Going-train gold-plated wheels, faceted arms, diamond polished hubs

Facing page

Grande Seconde au Centre Retour-à-zéro

Limited edition of 8 pieces

Case 47 mm in 18-karat white gold with palladium 210

Dial 18-karat gold anthracite hand guilloche

Hands 18-karat gold, sweep-second in Pfinodal®

Wristband hand-sewn alligator-leather

Caliber MB M 16–18

Type of movement hand-wound movement with retour-à-zéro function

Dimensions diameter 38.4 mm; height 6.3 mm

Number of components 209 (complete movement)

Number of jewels 21 (hemispherical, domed, olive-cut)

Power reserve 52 hours

Balance screw balance, Ø 14.5 mm; 59 mg/cm²

Frequency 18'000 semi-oscillations per hour (2.5 hertz)

Balance-spring with Phillips terminal curve

Plate German silver (maillechort), rhodium-plated with circular graining on both faces

Bridges German silver (maillechort), rhodium-plated with "*Côtes de Genève*" decoration

Going-train gold-plated wheels, faceted arms, diamond polished hubs

Following pages

Caliber MB M 13–18

Type of movement hand-wound movement with retour-à-zéro function

Dimensions diameter 29.5 mm; height 6.4 mm

Number of components 199 (complete movement)

Number of jewels 21 (hemispherical, domed, olive-cut)

Power reserve 55 hours

Balance screw balance, Ø 11.4 mm; 26 mg/cm²

Frequency 18'000 semi-oscillations per hour (2.5 hertz)

Balance-spring with Phillips terminal curve

Plate German silver (maillechort), rhodium-plated with circular graining on both faces

Bridges German silver (maillechort), rhodium-plated with "*Côtes de Genève*" decoration

Going-train gold-plated wheels, faceted arms, diamond polished hubs

somewhat more complicated when the time is being set. Pulling out the crown first interrupts the contact and then presses the heart-piece lever against the return-to-zero heart piece. The seconds hand returns with lightning speed to the top of the dial, where it remains motionless. When the crown is pressed, the events recur in reverse order: the lever is withdrawn from heart piece and the coupling wheel is re-engaged. The engagement of the winding shaft with the chronograph levers called for great creativity from the technicians. The results of their research are the calibers MB M 16–18 and MB M 13–18. The former movement is placed in the watch called *Grande Seconde au Centre-Retour-à-zéro*, whose case measures 47-millimeters. The smaller MB M 13–18 confers a serene pace on the *Seconde au Centre Retour-à-zéro*. The large Glucydur® balance wheels with their impressive mass comfortably maintain their stately 2.5 Hz frequency in all circumstances. Thus the long hand of the *secunda diminutiva pars* (i.e., seconds) advances in distinctly visible leaps of one-fifth of a second. As is generally the case with movements of the Montblanc *manufacture* at Villeret, both the circular-grained plates and bridges are made of rhodium-plated German silver (maillechort). The level of finish applied to all parts by Cabiddu and his teams is identical to their work on chronographs.

Making it essential

"Perfection," wrote Antoine de Saint-Exupéry, "is apparently reached not when there is nothing more to add, but when there is nothing left to subtract." Such is the case with the two *Seconde Authentique* models in the *Collection Montblanc Villeret 1858*. They are designed for upholders of watchmaking purity, who wish to tell time from a dial by noting the position of superbly curved hands, to the exclusion of all other displays. Such purism masks stylish discretion, because behind the apparent minimalism lies a refined mechanism that can be viewed by simply and silently opening the hinged cover on the back. Through the transparent caseback will be seen a classic manual movement—caliber MB M 16–15 or MB M 62–00—whose bridges reveal its traditional construction. The central bridge over the gear train is appealing for its elegant curve and characteristic shape; from a technical standpoint, this elegance is not the reflection of a particular constraint, because straight lines would have fulfilled the same function. However, such lines would have betrayed the higher principles of fine watchmaking. In both the design and execution of a simple mechanism that merely measures and displays the time, Montblanc's watchmakers always include proof of their remarkable skills—the full repertoire of beveling, graining, polishing, and satin-finishing is found on these movements. Circular graining is done by

PURE MECANIQUE HORLOGERE
60
15
30
45
MONTBLANC
SWISS
MADE
GUILLOCHE MAIN SUISSE
MINERVA 1858

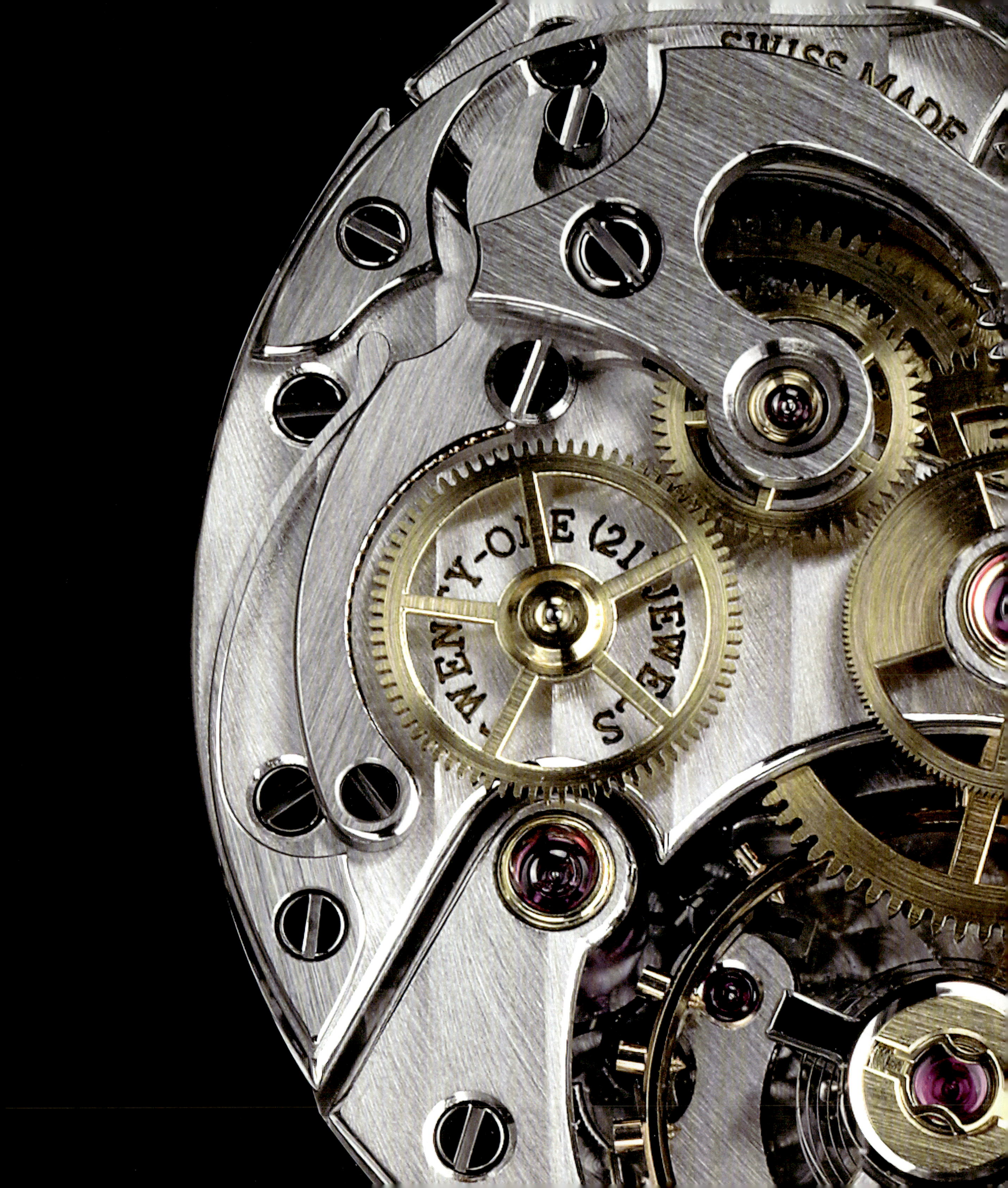
SWISS MADE

MINERVA

Facing page
Seconde Authentique
Limited edition of 58 pieces
Case 41 mm in 18-karat red gold domed sapphire crystal (forme chevée), transparent pane of sapphire crystal inset into screwed back beneath hinged cover
Dial 18-karat gold silver-colored hand guilloche
Index and hands 18-karat gold
Wristband hand-sewn alligator-leather

Caliber MB M 62–00
Hand-wound movement with small second at 6 o'clock
Dimensions diameter 24.00 mm; height 3.90 mm
Number of components 162 (complete movement)
Number of jewels 19 (hemispherical, domed, olive-cut)
Power reserve 50 hours
Balance screw balance, Ø 9.7 mm; 15 mg/cm²
Frequency 18'000 semi-oscillations per hour (2.5 hertz)
Balance-spring flat
Plate German silver (maillechort), rhodium-plated with circular graining on both faces
Bridges German silver (maillechort), rhodium-plated with "*Côtes de Genève*" decoration
Going-train gold-plated wheels, faceted arms, diamond polished hubs

hand even on the inside of the barrel, which is never seen by anyone other than watchmakers; formerly, before airtight cases existed, this pattern of tight concentric circles had a specific function, because the miniscule lines would trap dust that entered the case. Nowadays, such finesse attests to a profound respect for tradition. The caliber MB M 16–15, which is 38.4-millimeters in diameter and 5.05-millimeters thick, has 158 parts. Four of its eighteen jewels are set in chatons. The central stone for the minutes wheel is screwed to the main bridge, thereby harking back to bygone days before synthetic rubies came along with their remarkable precision and sturdiness, like the system that made precision push-fitting possible. The large Glucydur® balance wheel, an imposing 14.5-millimeters in diameter, swings at 18,000 beats per hour. The balance spring that drives the return action is made in-house, with a terminal curve that points upward in true Phillips tradition. A regulator can adjust the effective length so that the balance swings at the optimum frequency; its index can be moved thanks to a precision system based on a micrometric screw and spring whose free end adorns the tip of the Minerva arrow.

Its smaller companion, the caliber MB M 62–00 (24-millimeters in diameter), is composed of 162 parts, including nineteen jewels. The screw balance measures 9.7-millimeters.

Both models—*Grande Seconde Authentique* and *Seconde Authentique*—feature dials of outstanding quality with gold hands whose upper surface has been rounded by hand. The large model is wound manually and boasts a power reserve of fifty-five hours. The small version has a barrel with a power reserve of two days. Connoisseurs never wait that long, however, because they perform the winding ritual every day, thereby avoiding any risk of damaging the delicate winding stem.

The glamor of the *Grand Chronographe Régulateur*
"What never improves will soon no longer be good." It was to respect this proverb that the Montblanc *manufacture* in Villeret developed a masterwork of complication watches, the *Grand Chronographe Régulateur* model, for its *Collection Montblanc Villeret 1858*. Unveiled in 2008, this large regulator chronograph was equipped with a new 38.4-millimeter caliber, MB M 16–30, whose 304 parts are packed into a height of 7.9-millimeters.

A simple glance at this chronograph convinces the beholder of its quality, just as the special display of the hour hand reveals its function as a regulator. The term "regulator" requires some preliminary explanation: around 1770, early precision clocks driven by pendulums appeared in astronomical observatories, where they played a key role in the accurate measurement of time. In those days, the second was

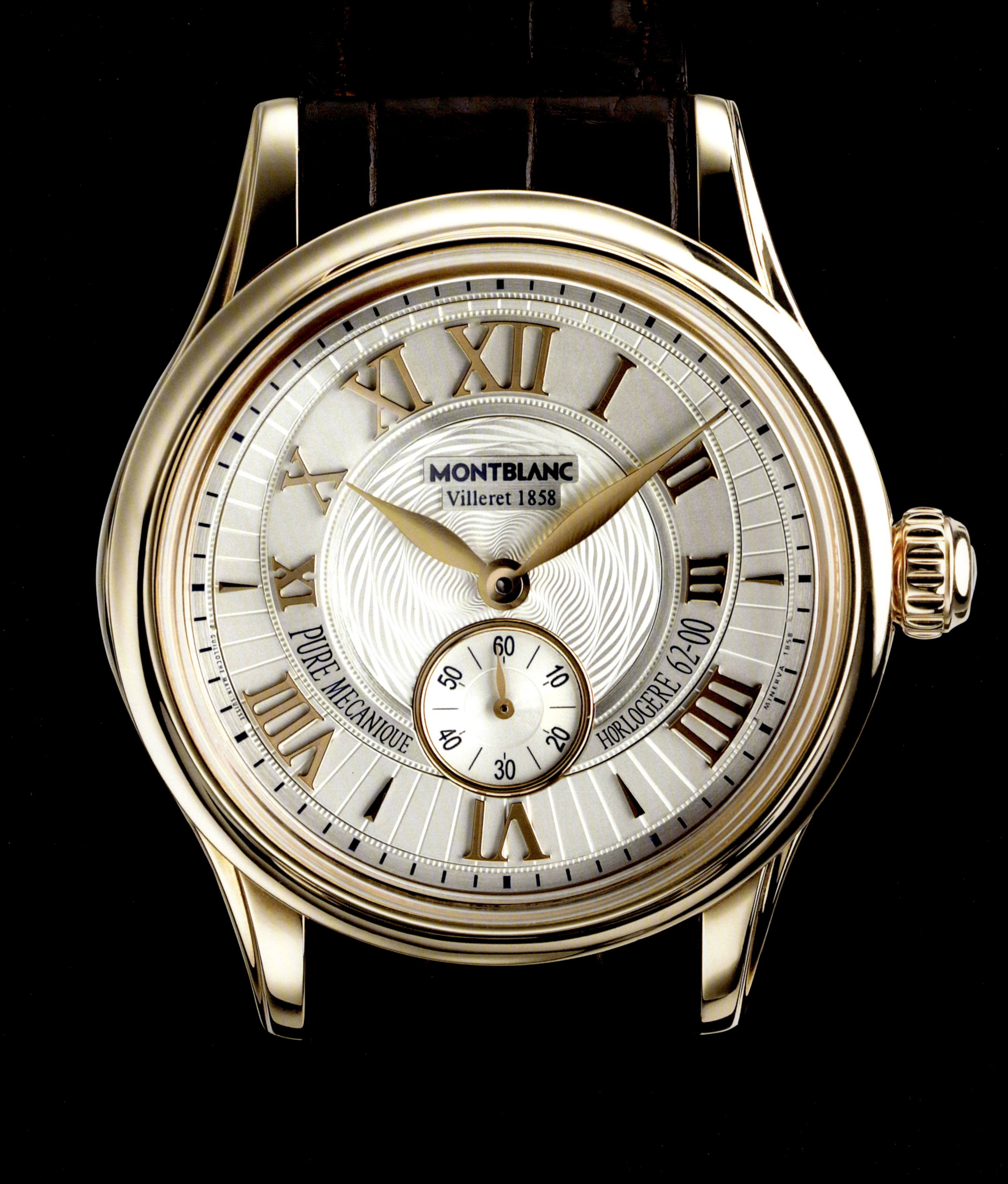
MONTBLANC
Villeret 1858
PURE MECANIQUE
HORLOGERE 62-00

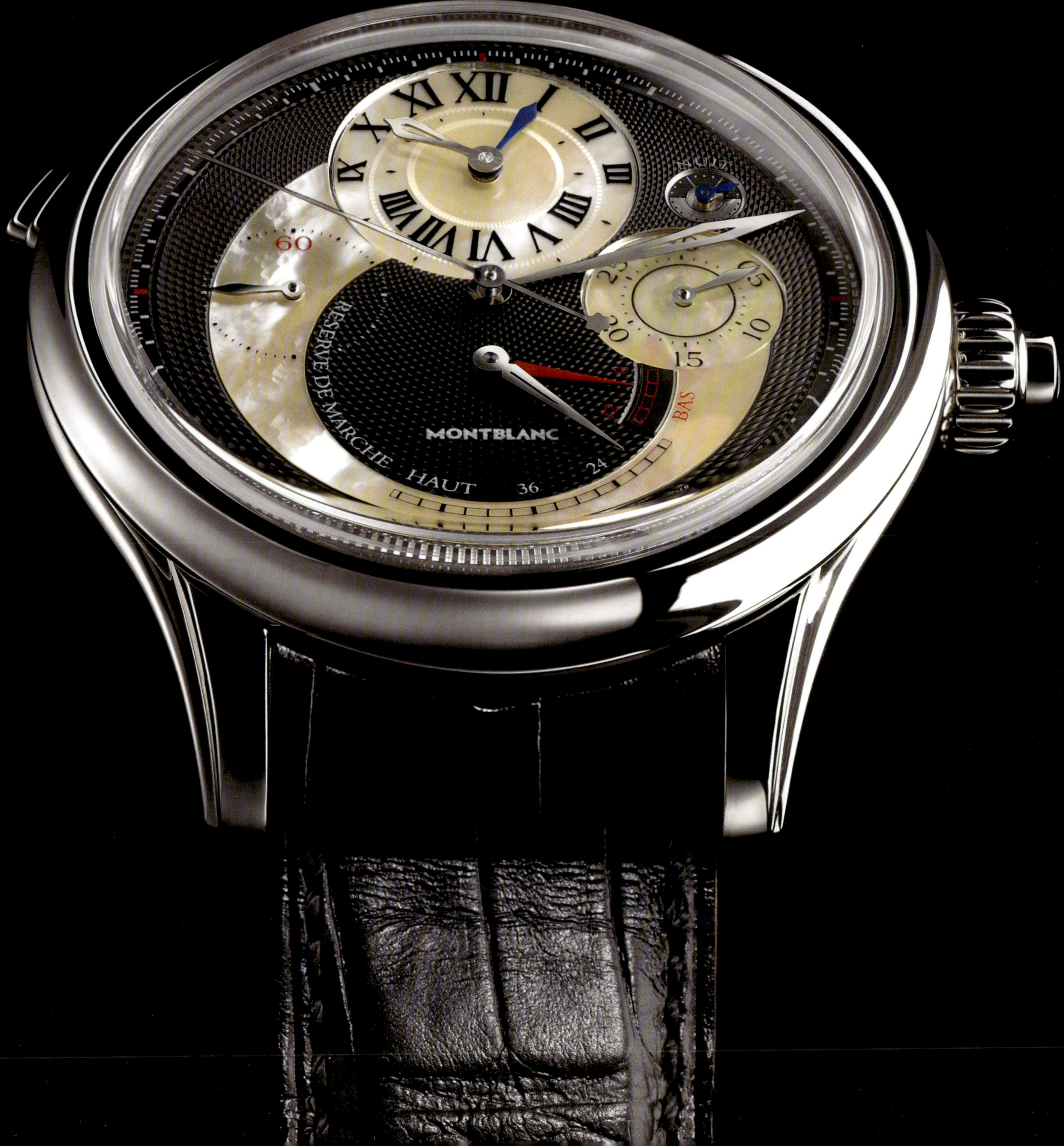
MONTBLANC
RESERVE DE MARCHE
HAUT
BAS
36
24
60
15
10
20

the yardstick of accuracy for these fine instruments. But the hand responsible for that stunning accuracy was too often covered by the slow-moving hour hand. In order to avoid this drawback, clockmakers invented the "regulator dial," which involved an off-center subdial for the hour hand. This arrangement is endowed with a double function on Montblanc's *Grand Chronographe Régulateur* watch. Indeed, travelers who arrive at their destination with an ordinary watch are confronted with a difficulty: in resetting their watch to the local hour, they lose the exact position of the minute hand, which does not really require adjustment. This is precisely the problem solved by the Montblanc *manufacture* in Villeret in the *Grand Chronographe Régulateur* watch, which has two hands for the hour. One, gilded, can be set to the local time—say, in San Francisco—advancing one hour at a time, while the other, in blued steel, retains the normal home time. An additional day/night display indicates the daily cycle on distant parts of the globe in order to avoid waking someone in the middle of the night. On returning home, the two hands advance in perfect unison, one covering the other, to avoid any mistake in telling the time.

But Montblanc's watchmakers didn't stop at this complication. To insure that the movement is rewound at the right time despite a time-zone shift—and despite its fifty-five hour power reserve—the technicians devised an entirely new display for which Montblanc has filed a patent. The lower part of the dial, superbly finished by hand with manual guillochage, is devoted to this display. It entails a small planetary gear train that transmits the mainspring's energy to two hands, which constitute its exceptional feature: when the fifty-five-hour power reserve has more than twelve hours of power left, only the gilded hand is visible; but when the reserve falls below twelve hours, a small red hand appears, emerging slowly from behind the larger hand in order to remind the wearer that the movement is drawing on its last resources of energy. Although such energy would suffice to drive the watch for another twelve hours or so, the diminution in inertial momentum affects the amplitude of the 14.5-millimeter screw balance, oscillating at 2.5 Hz, which undermines the accuracy of the time-keeping. Hence the watch should be rewound as soon as possible—which means that the wearer can enjoy the wonderfully smooth action of the winding mechanism.

Above

Caliber MB M 16–15

Hand-wound movement with small second at 6 o'clock

Dimensions diameter 38.40 mm; height 5.05 mm

Number of components 158 (complete movement)

Number of jewels 18 (hemispherical, domed, olive-cut)

Power reserve 55 hours

Balance screw balance, Ø 14.50 mm; 59 mg/cm^2

Frequency 18'000 semi-oscillations per hour (2.5 hertz)

Balance-spring with Phillips terminal curve

Plate German silver (maillechort), rhodium-plated with circular graining on both faces

Bridges German silver (maillechort), rhodium-plated with *"Côtes de Genève"* decoration

Going-train gold-plated wheels, faceted arms, diamond polished hubs

Preceding page, left

Grand Chronographe Régulateur

Unique piece

Case 47mm in 950 platinium

Dial 18-karat gold hand guilloche with mother-of-pearl inlays

Index and hands 18-karat gold, sweep-second in Pfinodal®

Caliber MB M 16–30

Hand-wound *Régulateur* movement home-time linked to a day/night display, patented power reserve with « emergency indication » monopusher chronograph mechanism with column-wheel and horizontal coupling

Dimensions diameter 38.4 mm; height 7.90 mm

Number of components 353 (complete movement)

Number of jewels 34 (hemispherical, domed, olive-cut)

Power reserve 55 hours

Balance screw balance, Ø 14.5 mm; 59 mg/cm^2

Frequency 18'000 semi-oscillations per hour (2.5 hertz)

Balance-spring with Phillips terminal curve

Plate German silver (maillechort), rhodium-plated with circular graining on both faces

Bridges German silver (maillechort), rhodium-plated with *"Côtes de Genève"* decoration

Going-train gold-plated wheels, faceted arms, diamond polished hubs

Facing page

"Grand Tourbillon Heures Mystérieuses"

Limited edition of 8 pieces, made for the 150 years anniversary of Minerva

Case 47 mm in 18-karat white gold with palladium 210

Dial 18-karat gold, sliver and anthracite colored hand guilloche

Caliber MB M 65–60

Tourbillons

In Paris, on the 24th day of the month of Floréal in the French Revolutionary year IX—otherwise known as April 14, 1801—the inspired Swiss watchmaker Abraham-Louis Breguet took up his finest pen to write to France's minister of the interior. "Dear Citizen Minister, I am pleased to present here a report concerning the registration of a new invention for timekeeping devices, which I call a *Régulateur à Tourbillon*; I am applying for the privilege of being sole maker of these regulators for a period of ten years. Through this invention I have managed to eliminate, through compensation, the anomalies created by the different positions of the center of gravity when a regulator moves…. Finally, I have determined many other sources of error that more or less affect the accuracy of a movement, which the [watchmaker's] art could attain up to now only with infinite groping of uncertain success. After consideration of all these advantages, and the perfected manufacturing methods that are now in my grasp and the considerable expense to which I was put to procure these methods, I have decided to seek a privilege to establish the date of my invention and assure myself the financial rewards of my sacrifices."

Prior to Breguet, many horologists had tried to improve the functional accuracy of mechanical watches. They understood the factors that could affect the precision of a timepiece, such as changes in temperature that made metals expand or contract. In this respect, bi-metallic compensating balances provided one efficient solution—the first pocket watches made by Minerva were equipped with such balances. Nowadays, a monometallic Glucydur® balance combined with a self-compensating Nivarox® balance spring provides efficient protection from temperature swings. The staunchest enemy of portable timepieces, however, is undoubtedly earth's gravity. Ideally, the center of gravity of the unit composed of balance wheel and balance spring should be located precisely in the middle of the balance shaft. In that way no part of the oscillating system struggles against the earth's gravity. From a theoretical angle, this subtle equilibrium is not an insoluble problem—and in practice it can be resolved, as demonstrated every day by the timers in the Villeret workshops. However, the pleasure of obtaining a perfect equilibrium is short-lived, because gravity-induced errors reappear at one point or another. These effects slow or speed the movement of the balance wheel and therefore undermine accuracy. The effects of the earth's gravity are particularly pernicious when it comes to pocket watches, which are usually carried in a vertical position.

The *tourbillon* therefore sought a solution to this problem by compensating for the unequal effects of gravity. The practical

GUILLOCHE MAIN SUISSE
MINERVA 1858
TOURBILLON HEURES MYSTERIEUSES
MONTBLANC

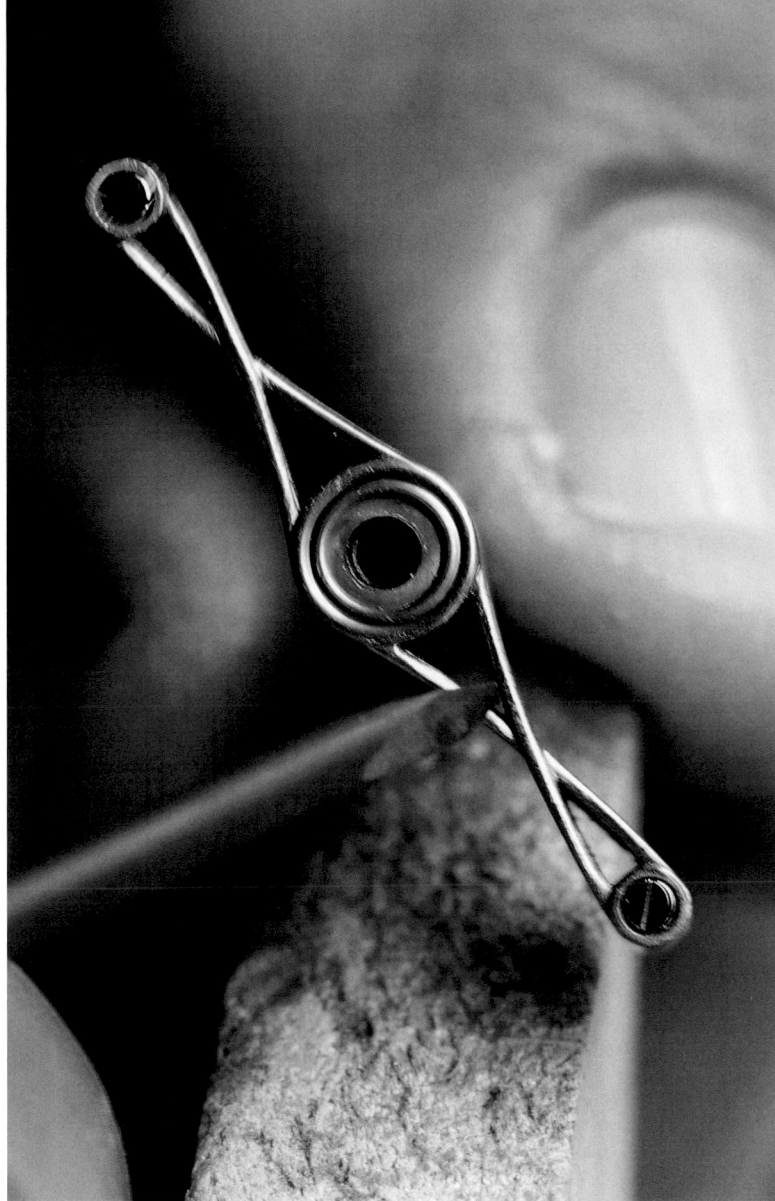

Burnishing and finishing the tip of a pivot in the "*Grand Tourbillon Heures Mystérieuses.*" The watchmaker uses a small lathe fixed in a vise on his bench. With one hand he turns the pivot shank with a bow, and with the other he uses a buff to polish the pivot.

Manually beveling a bridge of the Montblanc "*Grand Tourbillon Heures Mystérieuses.*" The art is to make each stroke of the file identical to the preceding one because no correction is possible.

Assembling the components of the *tourbillon* and screwing the fixed seconds wheel. This 18.4 mm *tourbillon* contains 95 parts yet it weighs no more than 0.96 g.

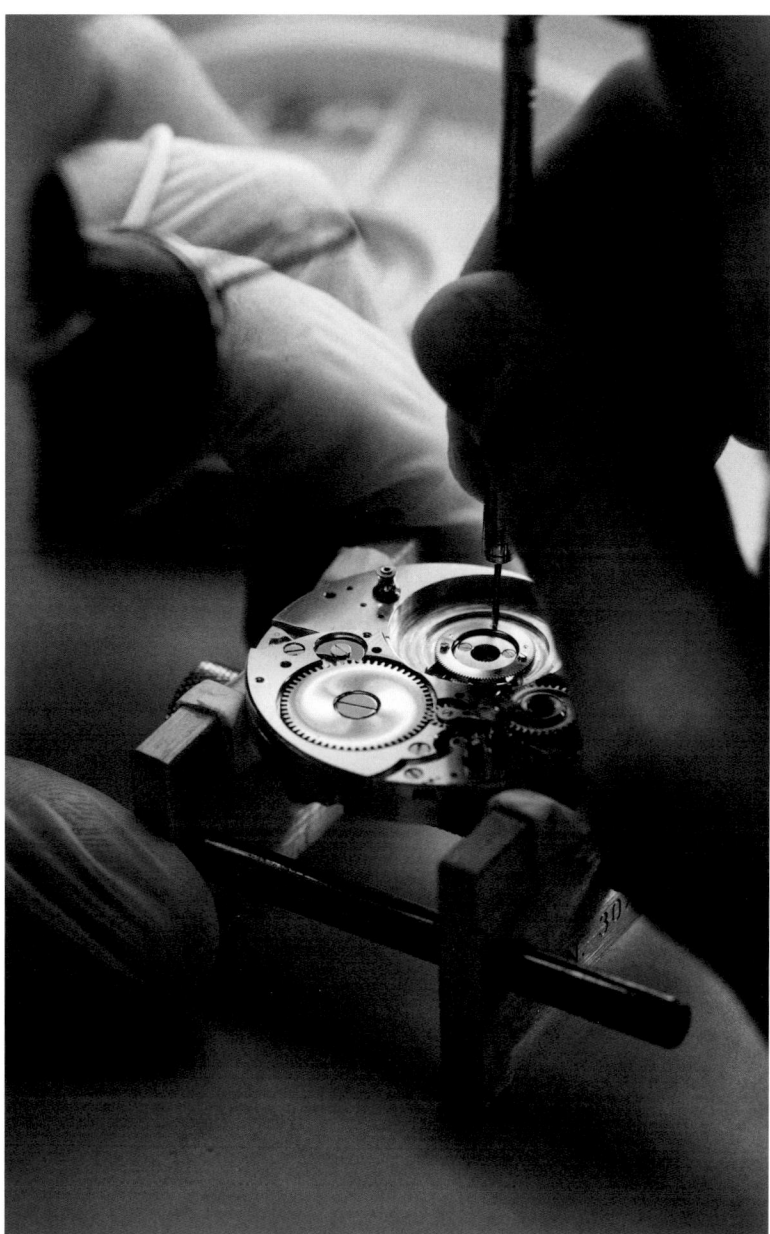

Fitting the *tourbillon* cage into its movement. The generous size of this cage provides enough space for a solid Glucydur® balance.

TOURBILLON HEURES MYSTE

application of this apparently straightforward principle nevertheless required colossal effort. In order to succeed the entire oscillating system and escapement had to be placed—that is to say, the balance wheel, balance spring, escape wheel, and escape lever—in a little housing, or cage, that turned on its own axis once every minute. In this way, any errors of gravity also went through a 360-displacement with wonderful regularity, thereby canceling themselves out.

Hence the accelerating and slowing effects on the movement of the pocket watch, carried in a vertical position, were effectively neutralized thanks to this system of constant compensation. Breguet could blithely ignore the horizontal position, in which gravity naturally had no angle of attack.

Making a standard watch fitted with a rotating cage was—and remains—a technical feat reserved for the finest professionals due to its incredible complexity. A high quality *tourbillon* calls for a fine, filigree cage, as light as possible and perfectly balanced, traditionally made of steel. On either side it has pivots that allow it to be set, and rotate, within the movement. The cage must have enough room for the swinging balance wheel, balance spring, and escapement. The escape wheel and pinion extend slightly below the lower edge of the cage, on the movement side. The pinion for the seconds wheel also passes through its center. The seconds wheel is set and screwed to the plate in a concentric fashion, which means that the center wheel, in its quality as the final moving gear of an ordinary train, drives the seconds pinion and consequently the entire rotating cage. The leaves of the escape pinion mesh with the teeth of the seconds wheel. Given the rotation of the cage, these leaves have no option other than to advance continuously, turning the escape wheel and maintaining the swing of the balance wheel constant through the usual means of pallet lever and pallet fork. The steady rotation of the balance and escapement is as understandable as the extreme rarity of such *tourbillons* prior to the invention of computer-controlled tools for machining the hundred parts. This complication was probably produced no more than a few thousand times in versions small enough to fit in a wristwatch, until the first, limited "line" of *tourbillon* wristwatches was unveiled in 1986.

"*Grand Tourbillon Heures Mystérieuses*"

When the Montblanc *manufacture* at Villeret decides to take up a new challenge, its commitment is total. Such was the case with this *tourbillon* built according to time-honored tradition yet also enhanced with numerous technical refinements. The master watchmakers spent many years studying the thorny question of mechanisms endowed with a rotating cage, and the Montblanc *manufacture* in Villeret was finally able to put their ideas into practice.

Facing page

"*Grand Tourbillon Heures Mystérieuses*"

Limited edition of 8 pieces, made for the 150 years anniversary of Minerva

Case 47 mm in 18-karat white gold with palladium 210

Dial 18-karat gold, sliver and anthracite colored hand guilloche

Mysterious indication of hours and minutes

Caliber MB M 65–60

Hand-wound movement 16'" ¾ tourbillon with a revolution in one minute

Dimensions diameter 38.4 mm; height 9.70 mm

Number of components 284 (complete movement)

Number of jewels 28 (hemispherical, domed, olive-cut)

Power reserve 45 hours

Balance screw balance, Ø 14.5 mm; 59 mg/cm^2

Frequency 18'000 semi-oscillations per hour (2.5 hertz)

Balance-spring with Phillips terminal curve

Plate German silver (maillechort), rhodium-plated with circular graining on both faces

Bridges German silver (maillechort), rhodium-plated with "*Côtes de Genève*" decoration

Going-train gold-plated wheels, faceted arms, diamond polished hubs

Like the large chronograph calibers, the pure German silver plate boasts a respectable diameter of 38.4-millimeters. The substantial dimensions are no luxury, because they are required for the inclusion of an almost monumental *tourbillon* measuring 18.4-millimeters and containing no fewer than ninety-five parts. Yet it weighs less than one gram—96 centigrams, to be exact. The ample size of the cage provides sufficient space for a massive Glucydur® balance with a rotational inertia of 59 mg/cm². As a diameter of 14.6-millimeters is not compatible with the current fashion for rapid frequencies, the watchmakers had their work cut out for them when they opted for a frequency of 2.5 hertz: this relatively low rate calls for additional work during timing. Since the philosophy adopted by the Montblanc *manufacture* in Villeret excluded the purchase of an oscillating system from an outside supplier, the balance wheel, fine balance spring with Phillips terminal curve, escape wheel, and lateral lever were all entirely made in the company's own workshop. The three inertia blocks that make it possible to adjust the left/right equilibrium of the large steel cage are adorned with the Minerva arrow, becoming irresistible objects of visual contemplation. Meanwhile, the *tourbillon* bridge of steel symbolizes the infinity of that precious fourth dimension, time, by adopting the shape of a horizontal, intertwining double-eight.

Even without its movement, every cage constitutes a micromechanical work of art requiring three weeks of intense, painstaking labor by a team of masters of their craft.

While the beholder is understandably entranced by a *tourbillon*, it constitutes just one part—albeit a crucial one—of an ensemble. In contrast to the *tourbillon*, the time display assumes a genuinely discreet form: the hour and minute hands move, apparently weightless, in front of a mirror. The Montblanc *manufacture* in Villeret has managed to transpose the fascinating "mystery clock" technology to a wristwatch. The hands are etched onto very thin disks of transparent sapphire that have toothed outer rims. These toothed gears are driven in conventional manner by a manual movement with a power reserve of fifty hours.

The incredible work required to make this majestic *tourbillon*, which embodies a return to the very essence of measuring time, fully justifies the decision to produce it in tiny quantities only. The case features an original tear-drop bulge at 6 o'clock and is 47-millimeters in diameter, a size that matches many of the early pocket watches with *tourbillon*. The conscious decision to "go big" stems from this classic interpretation of a complication invented over two hundred years ago.

The Montblanc *manufacture* at Villeret has deliberately left the field of rapid-frequency *tourbillons* of high-tech materials to the competition. Instead, the *manufacture* decided to stress its link with

Facing page

The revolutionary four-minute *tourbillon* in the *ExoTourbillon Chronographe* watch. The turning cage is smaller than the balance which oscillates outside it on a level above. This arrangement makes it possible to use a balance in solid Glucydur® with an impressive moment of inertia of 59 mg/cm².

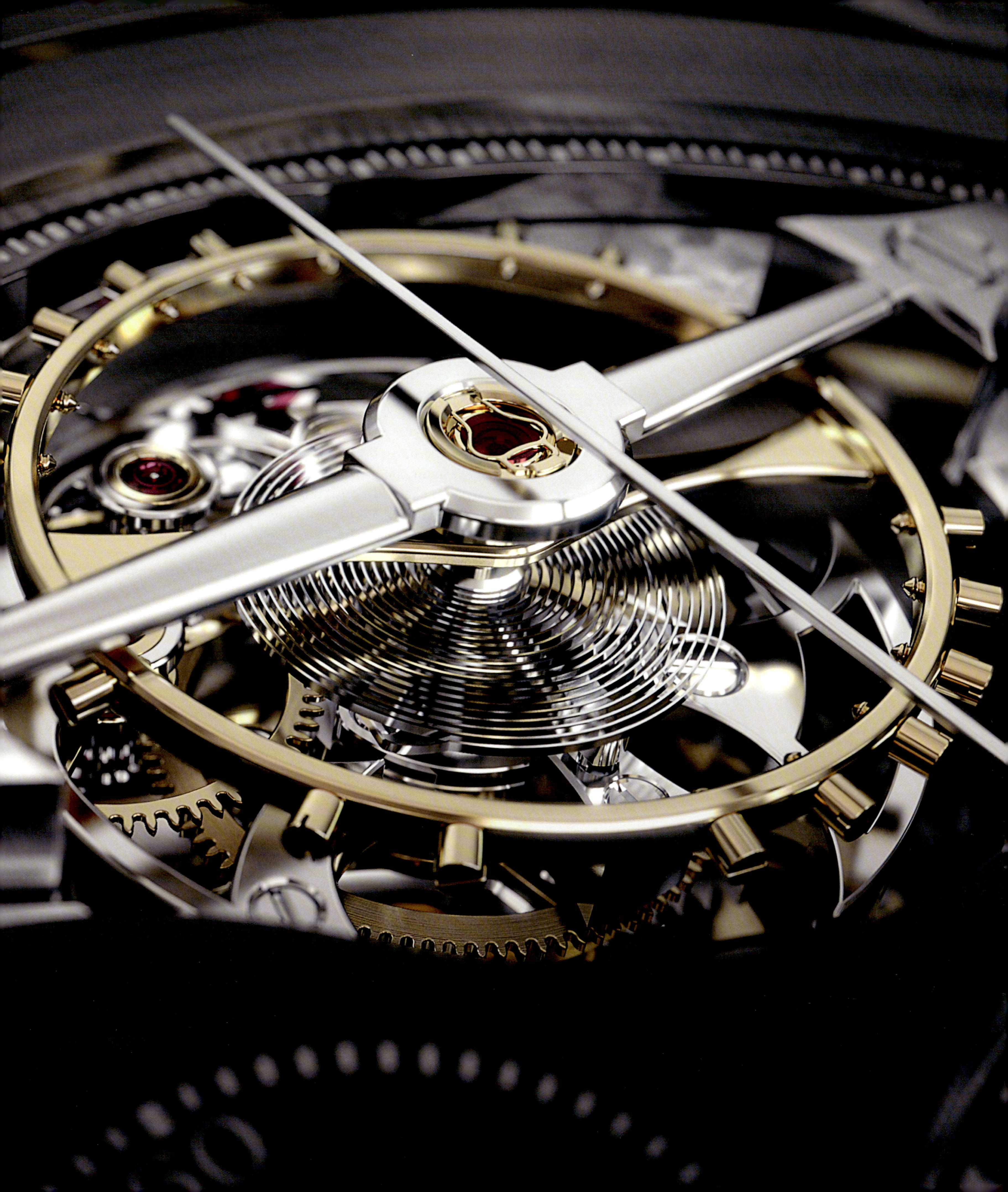

tradition. Indeed, when making chronographs, *tourbillons*, and other complications, the forerunners of Villeret's virtuoso watchmakers strove above all to find a harmony and equilibrium that set just the right tone.

ExoTourbillon Chronographe

The *ExoTourbillon Chronographe* was the first model in the *Collection Montblanc Villeret 1858* to combine two of the most valued complications, a chronograph and a *tourbillon*. The mastery of these extreme refinements thereby became one of the trademark technical feats of Montblanc's *manufacture* in Villeret, especially since the *manufacture* simultaneously wed the classically noble appearance of a chronograph (with column wheel and lateral clutch) to the revolutionary design of a four-minute *tourbillon*. Since the invention of the *tourbillon* in 1801, this innovation represents a major change in the way a *tourbillon* is constructed. Indeed, the balance wheel was placed outside the rotating cage in order to isolate the movements that perturbed the escapement. This separation made it possible to design the world's first *tourbillon* whose cage is smaller than the balance wheel, which oscillates outside the cage. Hence the name of this watch, from the Greek word *exo* for exterior. In this unusual configuration, the balance wheel swings between its own shock-absorbing bearings while the cage rotates independently between two jewels.

The considerations that led to the choice of this complex architecture involve the conventionally large size and mass of the balance wheel, which would have required an equally large cage. A smaller cage, meanwhile, has a smaller mass and therefore requires less energy to drive its rotation. Furthermore, the rotating cage no longer contains the weight of the balance wheel, an advantage that results in further reduction in energy requirements—compared to conventional designs, there is a gain in energy of roughly thirty percent, which can then be usefully allocated to the chronograph's other functions. And once placed outside the rotating cage, the balance wheel is no longer influenced by the inertia of the cage, which lends greater accuracy to the amplitude of its swing.

Through a window at 12 o'clock, above a meticulously hand-grained plate, the *ExoTourbillon* movement offers the wonderful sight of a large screw balance wheel that swings freely in all its splendor, spinning on its shaft unhindered by the narrow restrictions of a *tourbillon* cage. A patent has obviously been filed for this fundamental innovation, found exclusively on timepieces in the *Collection Montblanc Villeret 1858*.

The dial of this chronograph reflects the configuration specific to regulator timepieces, with the minute hand and seconds hand sharing a shaft in the middle of the watch whereas the hour has its own off-center display in the lower part of the dial. The other indicators evoke a miniature solar system, with a gold sun (the *tourbillon*) at 12 o'clock, the Earth at 6 o'clock, the Moon as a 24-hour subdial located between 4 and 5 o'clock (with day/night indicator for second time zone). Two other heavenly bodies, represented by the seconds subdial at 9 o'clock and the 30-minute totalizer at 3 o'clock, complete this special solar system. The 30-minute totalizer comes in the form of a half-moon with two differently hued scales, 0 to 15 and 15 to 30 minutes, indicated in turn by the two distinctly colored ends of the hand. The caliber MB M 16–60 is a chronograph movement with large central seconds, a 30-minute totalizer, and a classic column wheel and lateral clutch. The steel parts are meticulously finished by hand. The movement is also "set in motion" by hand, using a microscope to observe the successive coupling of levers with the column wheel and reset heart piece, in a step-by-step process that coordinates the functions of the chronograph with an accuracy down to one-hundredth of a millimeter. The steel parts and Minerva's special V-shaped chronograph bridge are all carefully hand beveled and polished. The levers are smoothed with a fine-grained stone and the bridges are adorned with *"Côtes de Genève"* decoration. The large screw balance wheel with Phillips-curve balance spring oscillates at the classic frequency of 18,000 beats per hour (2.5 Hz), which makes it possible to measure time down to one-fifth of a second. The chronograph is activated by a pusher on the crown that successively triggers the functions of start, stop, and reset to zero.

Frequent travelers will appreciate the inclusion of a second time zone; a blue hand indicates home time, while a skeleton hand above it indicates the local time. When at home, both hands are perfectly aligned one above the other, but as soon as the time zone changes, the local time can be set by a pusher located at 8 o'clock, which advances the local hand in one-hour leaps. The small 24-hour dial with its blued hand and day/night indicator will continue to tell home time, however far away.

Like every model in the *Collection Montblanc Villeret 1858*, the *ExoTourbillon Chronographe* will be produced in limited editions only. The white-and pink-gold models have solid gold dials with meticulous hand-guilloche decoration. The unique piece to be made of platinum will have certain parts of the dial set with mother-of-pearl. The impressive 47-millimeter cases are mirror polished and feature a curved bezel that holds the straight sides of a domed sapphire crystal (hollowed form). The sapphire caseback is protected by a hinged cover that opens through a patented mechanism hidden beneath the lugs holding the strap. The outside is engraved with "Edition limitée," "Montblanc," and "Fait main à Villeret" (Hand made in Villeret). The inside of the cover is inscribed with the master watchmaker's signature, "Demetrio Cabiddu Maître Horloger" while the movement bears the gilded inscription "Minerva Villeret," which can be seen through the sapphire caseback.

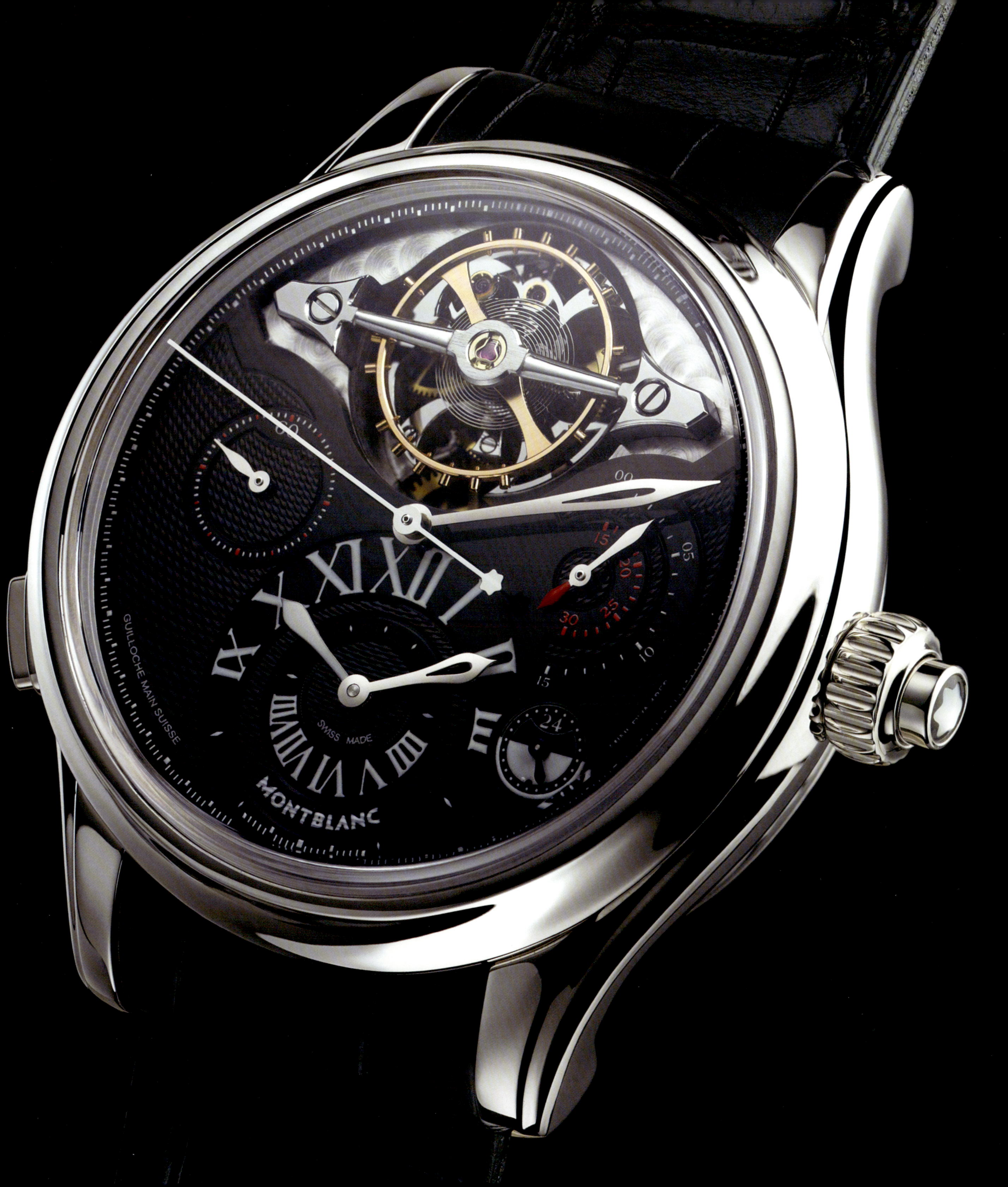
GUILLOCHE MAIN SUISSE
SWISS MADE
MONTBLANC

Preceding page, right

ExoTourbillon Chronographe

Limited edition of 8 pieces

Case 47 mm in 18-karat white gold with palladium 210

Dial 18-karat gold anthracite hand guilloche

Caliber MB M 16–60

Hand-wound movement *Régulateur* home-time linked to a day/night display. *ExoTourbillon* movement with a revolution in four minutes.

Chronograph monopusher chronograph mechanism with column-wheel and horizontal coupling

Dimensions diameter 38.4 mm; height 10.34 mm

Number of components 341 (complete movement)

Number of jewels 32 (hemispherical, domed, olive-cut)

Power reserve 55 hours

Balance screw balance, Ø 14.5 mm; 59 mg/cm^2

Frequency 18'000 semi-oscillations per hour (2.5 hertz)

Tourbillon 1 revolution in 4 minutes

Balance-spring with Phillips terminal curve

Plate German silver (maillechort), rhodium-plated with circular graining on both faces

Bridges German silver (maillechort), rhodium-plated with *"Côtes de Genève"* decoration

Going-train gold-plated wheels, faceted arms, diamond polished hubs

Right

The *reprise* workshop where old machines are lovingly preserved. They are still used today in conjunction with the latest digital automatic equipment.

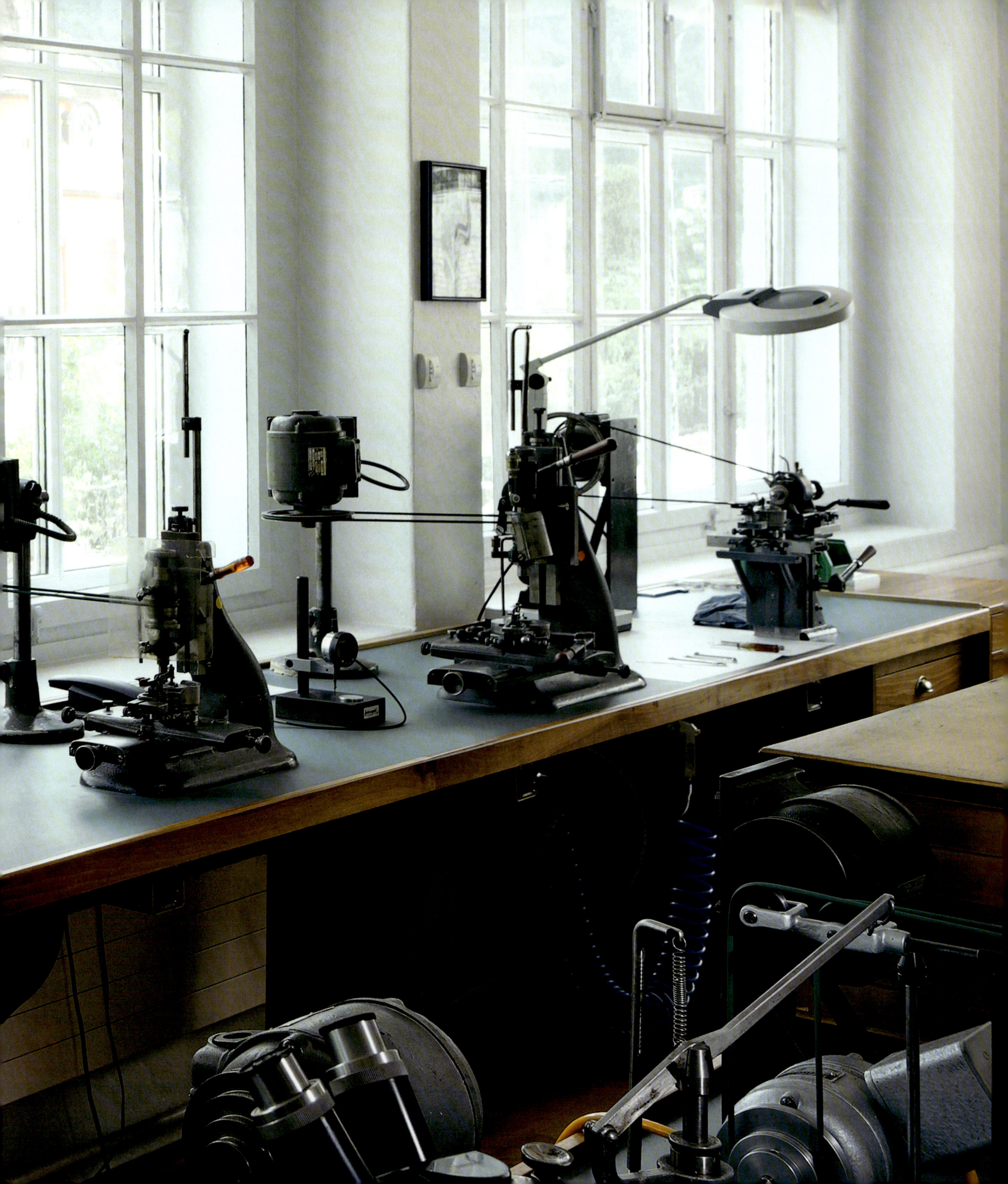

Above

Small *reprise* press used to adjust the sides of chronograph hearts.

From initial idea to finished watch

When the idea of designing an original new watch is raised in Villeret, the range of possibilities initially seems infinite. But early feasibility studies soon define certain constraints. Which design features are functional, which are not? Which aspects meet customers' desires? Even ideas that originally seemed the best may be eliminated if their implementation would result in an unacceptably steep cost.

The next stage involves drawing up product specifications, designed to establish the precise technical character of the product; take, for example the caliber MB M 16–30 that drives the *Grand Chronographe Régulateur* watch. A large role in the specifications document is played by the requirements of *haute horlogerie,* or luxury-watchmaking standards, which are crucial to the *Collection Montblanc Villeret 1858*. The V-shaped bridges, later engraved with the gilded inscription "Minerva Villeret" convey the aesthetic appearance specific to a chronograph. The symbol of the arrow, immediately apparent to the beholder's eye, makes a significant contribution to the image and identity of Minerva calibers. Symbolizing the spearhead of the former Minerva logo, it imparts inimitable character to the free end of the blocking lever or swan-neck regulator.

Based on these specifications, the various ideas are then steadily transformed into sketches. Technicians masterfully employ graphic processors and specially made software to compute parameters at blinding speed. Enlarging, diminishing, rotating, measuring, weighing, applying, animating—everything is possible. Engineer and computer function in wonderful tandem, ultimately getting the screen to display perfectly functioning mechanisms that provide the foundation of subsequent manufacturing processes. Naturally, in order to carry out this development in a reasonable time frame, various technicians work on a new movement simultaneously, focusing on one of the several groups of functions.

In another office, graphic designers study the proposal's visual attractiveness, which is equally crucial. If a watch doesn't appeal to the eye, the most innovative and ingenious mechanism will fail to attract interest.

The moment finally arrives when the virtual stage is wrapped up by a complete theoretical presentation of the caliber. Once the time has come to concretize things, prototype makers enter the scene. Following indications supplied by the construction department, they make several hundred different parts, with which the watchmakers put together the very first prototype. The value of preliminary work now becomes fully apparent. Computers can calculate structures in a detailed way, perfectly simulating not only the functioning but also the real load placed on certain parts, which may already produce some unpleasant surprises. If necessary, the computers can ignore tolerances, but material constraints make these tolerances crucial to the way a watch movement actually functions.

A dialogue is thus embarked upon—on a constantly upbeat note—between technicians and designers, the manufacturing department, prototype makers, and watchmakers. This is an important step in the long path toward a finished product (which usually lasts several years at Montblanc's Villeret *manufacture*). Watchmakers at their workbenches receive visits from theorists in the manufacturing department, who provide valuable advice and also bring the watchmakers back down to earth if their ideas ultimately prove to be overly bold. The key concept here is always perfection, whether technical or aesthetic.

When making a movement, past and present converge. Old stamping machines, which accomplish their task to the din of the thump of several tons of pressure, cohabit with digitally controlled equipment. Milling machines shape plates and bridges in nickel silver, a material more expensive but incomparably more stable than the usual brass. Depending on the caliber, making a plate may require as many as fifty milling operations. Heat treatment increases the resilience of parts subjected to great stress during machining. Finally, both sides of the plate are hand decorated. Bridges and balance cocks are given circular graining on the under side, and classic *"Côtes de Genève"* decoration on the upper side.

The *manufacture* also relies on a versatile process called electrical discharge machining (EDM), which uses sparks to slowly cut steel chronograph parts placed in a dielectric liquid. Using specially prepared sheets of metal, the parts can be accurately machined down to a few thousandths of a millimeter.

Although confidence in computer-aided technology is high, quality-control inspection is still more important. Specialists regularly check the precision of parts produced in this way. To this end they use not only micrometric calipers but also state-of-the-art laser measuring devices. No detail escapes them. For the base plate alone—on which the movement will be placed—Montblanc carries out roughly thirty checks on the dial side and sixty to eighty on the movement side. This inspection procedure alone requires three to four hours of painstaking work. If any discrepancies are too high, that is to say over a few thousandths of a millimeter, production is immediately halted until the proper adjustments have been made and everything can begin again from scratch.

Stamped and milled parts have sharp edges. They are trimmed and filed by hand when it comes to watches made in limited numbers, which is an everyday affair at the company.

Top

Old cutting tools carefully maintained for use in after-sales service.

Above

Different stages of machining a bottom plate in German silver.

Without an experienced toolmaker, the production department and the watchmaking workshops would be at a loss. A toolmaker is crucial when it comes to the production of miniscule levers and Lilliputian balance springs. The toolmaker is responsible for the milling, boring, and engraving tools that have to be the right size and quality for the given task. The toolmaker's versatile talent also makes it possible to devise special equipment or production methods.

Once all the parts have been made, the watchmakers go to work. They must hand-decorate the parts using meticulous craft techniques developed by their distant ancestors. These artists are familiar with every form of ornamentation, which is also applied to hidden parts such as gears, pinions, pivots, and screws. No part is overlooked. The gilded gears in the back are given a linear polish and faceted stripes, while the hubs receive a mirror polish. The shafts and leaves of all pinions are also polished, an operation that reduces friction and hence wear on the parts.

Screws make a special contribution to the appearance of a watch movement, which is why their heads are flat, and why their slot edges and outer edges are very carefully beveled, then all surfaces polished. A mirror polish may be given to the exposed edges of various parts; burnishing enhances the sloping sides of the precisely drilled hole, or *découverture,* in which ruby-red jewels are set. Depending on the caliber, three or four of the jewels may be set in a special bezel called a chaton.

When it comes to chronographs, which are the clear area of expertise of the Montblanc *manufacture* in Villeret, the watchmakers polish all levers and springs by hand. Also standard is the beveling and satin-finishing of sides, while functional edges receive particular attention. All surfaces that come into contact with the column wheel or the reset heart piece are adjusted with great precision by hand and meticulously polished to conform with the relevant counter-part.

Personalized timing is also characteristic of models in the *Collection Montblanc Villeret 1858* when they are majestically "brought to life." This dramatic stage in the life of a chronograph is a solemn ritual during which all its operations—the various interactions of the column wheel, levers, springs, and gears—are carefully and lengthily observed with a magnifying glass known as a loupe. Each stage is subject to meticulous inspection: what happens when the chronograph pusher is triggered once, then a second time, and then a third? How accurately does the clutch lever fit between the five columns on the column wheel? How exactly does the braking edge of the blocking lever sit once the fine teeth of the chronograph's center gear have come to a halt? How do the levers and heart-pieces interact when the hand is reset to zero? Any imperfection, however tiny, requires the complete disassembly of the movement and the checking of all parts. Once reassembled, the movement goes through the same inspection process until absolutely flawless results are obtained.

Above

In the spiral workshop, the *régleuse* makes the "Philips" terminal curve of the "Minervir" hairspring, entirely developed and produced at the Montblanc *manufacture* in Villeret. To become a *régleur*, one must possess unique craftsmanship and a rare know-how, which Montblanc wishes to preserve and perpetuate.

I Montblanc: Writing Time

Equally strict criteria are applied to the final adjustment and timing of the oscillating system. Made in-house, the oscillating mechanism is composed of the balance wheel, balance spring, escape lever, and escape wheel. The greatest possible accuracy must be attained. An important feature of the Montblanc *manufacture* at Villeret is its mastery of spiral production. The ability to make this minuscule, yet essential, component is very rare in watchmaking. While no mechanical watch could function without it, very few *manufactures* still possess the know-how required for the fabrication of this unique component. Until recently, its complex production led watchmaking brands to focus on a sole supplier. Today, the spirals used by luxury watchmaking have become more and more complex. The capacity to produce them allows Montblanc to develop and create movements with exceptional balance wheels and balance springs, worthy of the most precious timepieces of the past. Once the final quality-control test has been completed, the movement is given its splendid hands and dial, then set in a case of precious metal, thereby constituting a whole that, when it comes to the *Collection Montblanc Villeret 1858*, is far more than the sum of its many parts.

Above

A spool of "Minervir" wire after drawing. The wire then passes through a rolling mill that gives it a rectangular cross-section and becomes the raw material for the hairspring.

Following pages

Machine used to reduce the gauge of the "Minervir" wire. The machine is equipped with ten *filières*. The wire will pass through each *filières* in order to reach the desired gauge, usually thinner than a hair: 0.05 mm.

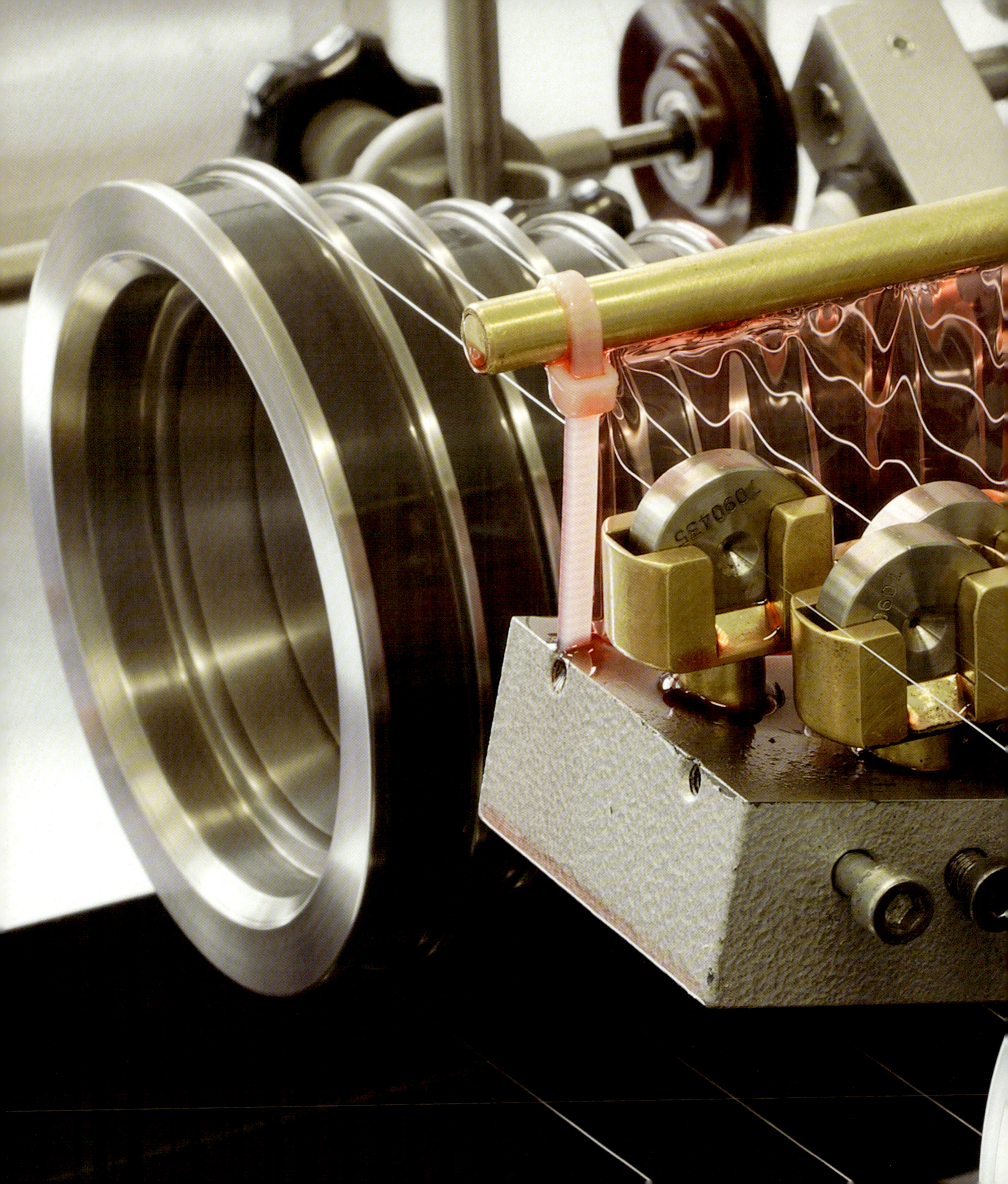

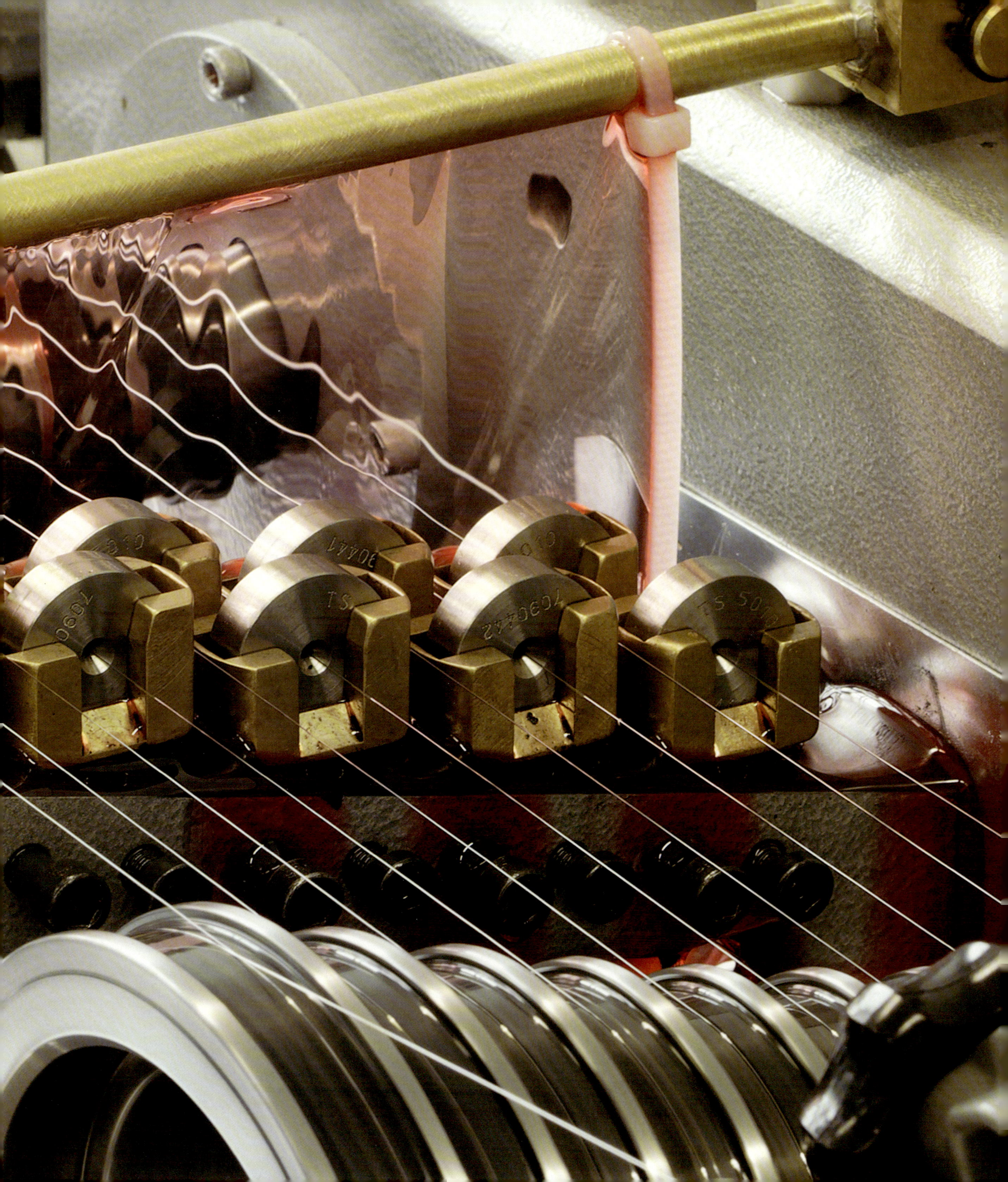

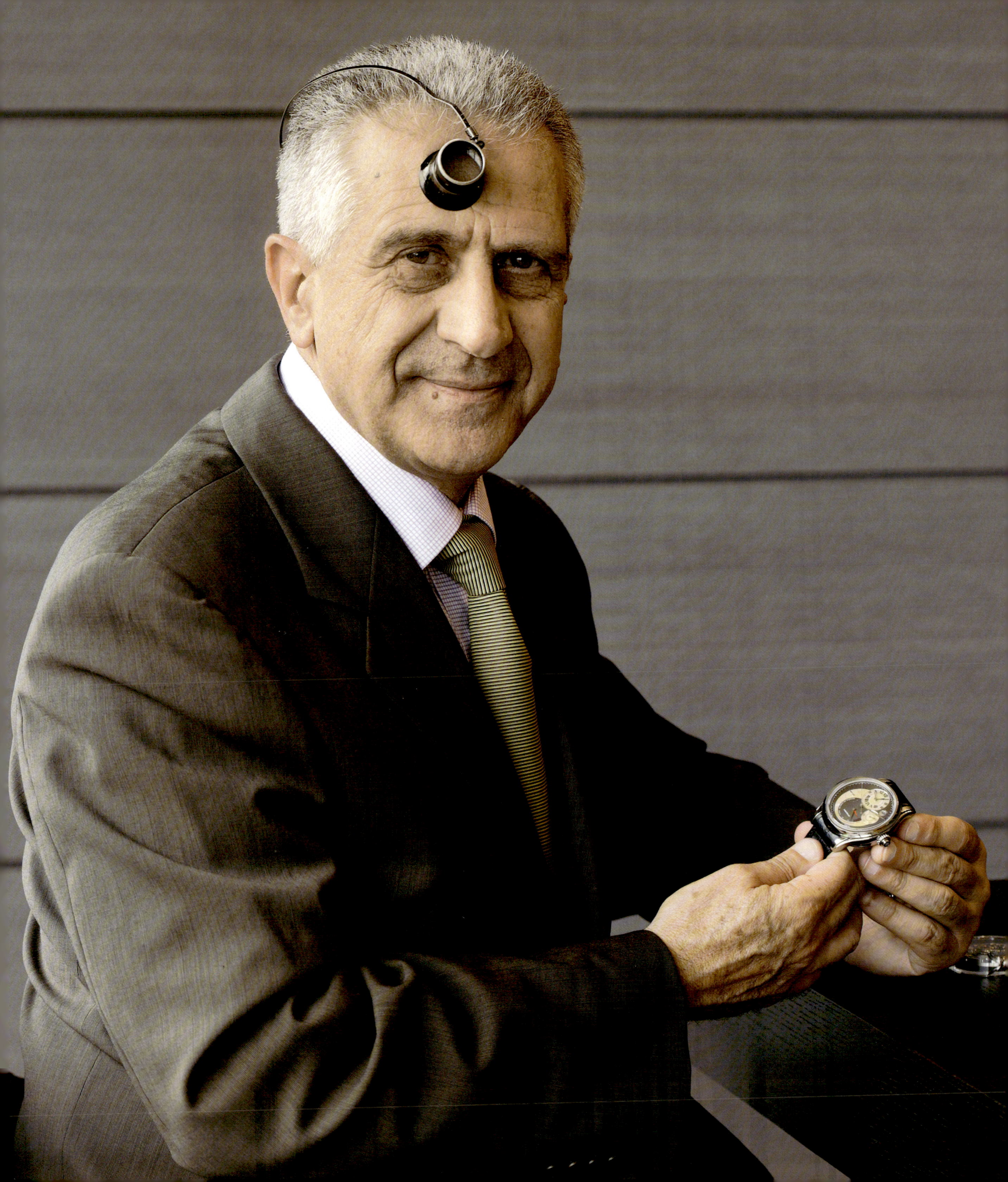

A Few Noble Crafts

THE GUARDIAN OF TIME

Aged only fifteen, Demetrio Cabiddu left the fabulous landscape of his Mediterranean island of Sardinia and headed to Switzerland, or more precisely to Switzerland's Joux Valley, which runs along a lake at altitude of over 1,000 meters. The people who live in this area, most of whom work for one of the many watchmaking companies, are called "Combiers." For centuries this isolated valley had been almost totally cut off from the rest of world during the long winter months. Given this environment, the fifteen-year-old foreigner from Sardinia who said he wanted to become a watchmaker had to overcome a good deal of prejudice. The first manufacturer simply gave him the brush-off: he was too young, *much* too young, claimed the head of human resources. But if you're a member of the Cabiddu family, you don't give up so easily. So Demetrio stubbornly continued to look for work until he was taken on as an apprentice in a firm that made ébauches. Once in Lemania, the company in question, the lad was taken in hand by Jacques Reymond, an excellent apprenticeship mentor who was always available to answer the young Sardinian's questions. Having successfully completed his training, during which he also attended courses at the École d'Horlogerie du Sentier, Cabiddu stayed faithful to Lemania. In all he spent fourteen years with the firm, where he acquired numerous skills in the realm of mechanical complications, including an extraordinary knack when it came to chronographs, which was the specialty of the company founded back in 1884 by Alfred Lugrin. Cabiddu was named head of the assembly workshop of the up-market caliber 27 CHRO C12, which equipped the legendary Moon Watch worn by Neil Armstrong and Buzz Aldrin.

By 1981, the effects of the quartz revolution had led to major changes at Lemania. It was time for Cabiddu to broaden his professional experience. At the École Technique de la Vallée de Joux he worked with professors at the institute on several development projects, including *tourbillons* executed in various ways. Five years later, his career took him back to Lemania—meanwhile renamed Nouvelle Lemania—where he was appointed head of the prototype department. "It was a fascinating but highly demanding job," he says today. The next step on the career ladder came in 1991 when he joined Gérald Genta in Le Brassus. The company founded by the famous designer was then making a large range of complications, notably including repeater wristwatches. As director of this small but famous workshop, Cabiddu coordinated a great number of new techniques relating to the construction and production of mechanical movements. So in 2001 he didn't hesitate to accept the offer to become head of the technical department at the venerable firm of Minerva. Henceforth, the adoptive "Combier" would shuttle back and forth between his home in the Joux Valley and his new place of work in Villeret, where his childhood dream came true: he could design and make watch movements of peerless technical and artisanal quality, in the finest, most venerable horological tradition. Although mass-produced models were always alien to Minerva, the company's new owner wanted to stress its exclusive image even more by strictly focusing on limited editions. To meet that goal, no compromises would be allowed when it came to ébauches or craft labor, which meant that Cabiddu could finally run a largely integrated *manufacture*. But when the new owner decided, just a few years later, to re-sell Minerva, the master watchmaker was worried: would his supreme quality standards be maintained? Cabiddu was one of those people who reckoned that the Richemont Group, one of several potential buyers, would be most likely to preserve—and even enhance—the company's top-of-the-line image. When the desired sale took place in 2006, Cabiddu and his team of specialists were invited to join a partnership based on promoting exclusive craftsmanship. The future suddenly held out the promise of extremely refined chronographs, of exceptional *tourbillons*, and of the original combination of these outstanding complications—with no compromises whatsoever. Named director of Montblanc's *manufacture* in Villeret, Cabiddu had achieved his professional goal. What more could he want? Nothing, except perhaps to focus all his vitality on the challenges of the coming years. He keeps in shape with a daily jog at the end of day, even running in marathons in Berlin, Rome (where he was born), Florence, and New York. During a few weeks of vacation he decided to walk the famous Silk Route from Tibet toward Beijing. "In Villeret, we do everything ourselves and there's almost nothing we can't do," he replies when asked if regrets having left the Joux Valley. "Within the watch industry, our freedom is unique. An opportunity like this only comes along once in a lifetime, and I consider myself very lucky to have been able to seize it."

THE INNOVATOR OF TRADITION

Things start with an idea. And a sketch. It has always been thus ever since the earliest days of mechanical horology, whose history now stretches back seven centuries. Hugo Lopez, who heads Montblanc's technical research-and-development bureau in Villeret, knows this only too well. With a team consisting of two developers and a visual designer, Lopez's job constitutes the indispensable foundation for all further work by the engineers, technicians, and watchmakers employed in operational manufacturing. "The plans for mechanisms that leave our computers for the workshop," he explains, "must work not only in the form of a unique part, but must also be conducive to production in limited series." The formerly crucial hand-drawn sketch now only plays a subsidiary role, given the super-rapid calculations of today's computer software. For example, the new power-reserve indicator on the *Chronographe Régulateur* represents an outstanding accomplishment, which required Lopez and his team to meet, right from the conceptual stage, the challenge of mastering a great number of horological and technical issues. Specifically, the power-reserve indicator called for a differential clutch on the barrel, an idea that comes from the automotive world where fuel gauges display the remaining amount of gas with growing insistence. Since such a gauge had never been incorporated into a mechanical watch, Montblanc obviously patented it.

Once the module functioned properly on the computer screen and the team was convinced that its invention would work down to the tiniest detail, the data from this electronic interface were handed over to the firm's prototype makers. These demanding professionals focus on the concrete aspects of any issue. Questions, critical suggestions, and proposals for improvement spring from every side. Only a constant dialogue between theory and practice, innovation and tradition, marked by several stages of optimization, make it possible to produce a mechanism that will function reliably, to devise a useful innovation that will find its way into certain future models and to build a bridge between innovation and tradition. But the beauty of the movement—and of each single part-remain the common guideline for each new movement. In fact, close discussions between the constructors and the watchmakers who will eventually craft the watch assure that the proud heritage of the exceptional beauty of the Minerva movements is found in every new development.

Facing page
Technical drawing of the *tourbillon* caliber MB M 65-60.

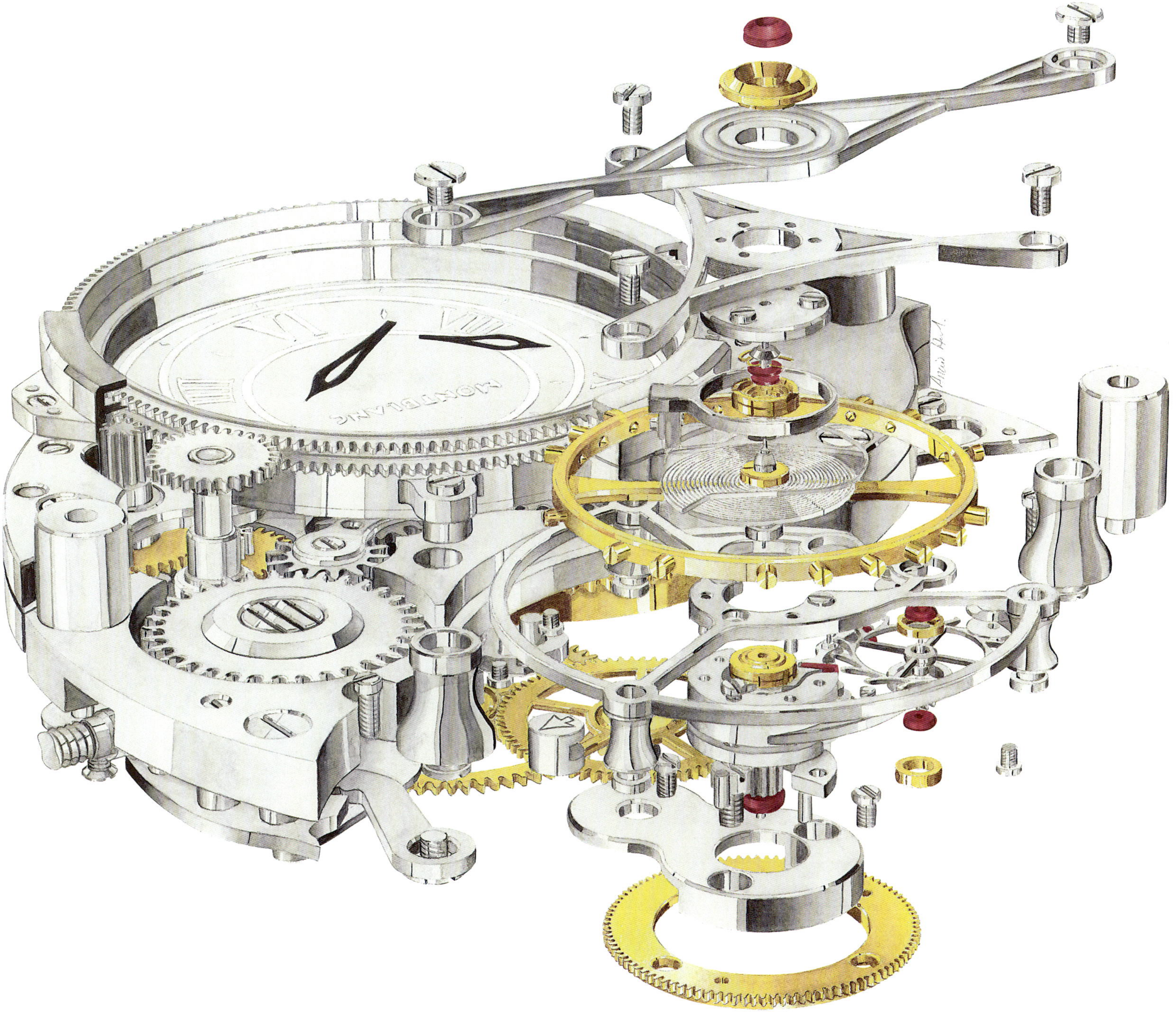
MONTBLANC

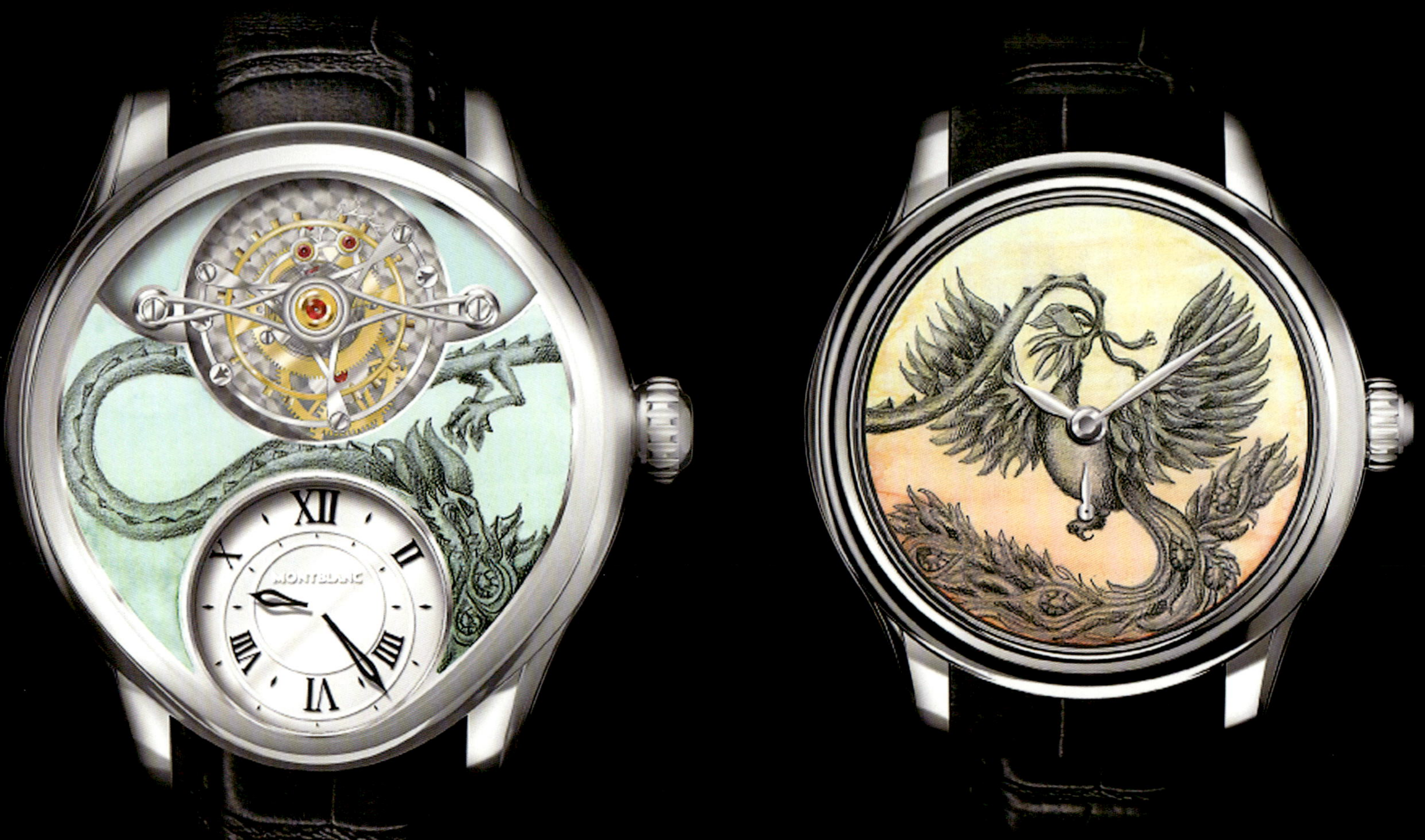
MONTBLANC

THE ARTISANS OF DESIGN

The designers at the Montblanc *manufacture* in Villeret are Anais Hamel and Leila Ruffieux, both of whom studied at the École Supérieure d'Arts Appliqués in La-Chaux-de-Fonds, a watchmaking town where the twentieth-century architect Le Corbusier was born. In this particular sector, spontaneous talent and creativity must constantly be reconciled with the countless constraints imposed by watchmaking. Even the initial artistic impetus comes from the company's strategic sphere, in close collaboration with the master watchmaker.

Starting from that initial input, the designers get down to work. They must try to respond to a request for a watch that reflects a given spirit, or is adapted to a given circumstance, or contains a given complication, through an innovative visual design that respects the brand image and fulfills the clientele's heterogeneous expectations. That is a real design challenge. Sometimes the solution emerges slowly, requiring long maturation, while other times the right idea comes in flash, like a heaven-sent miracle. Once the graphic idea has been established, executing it follows a tried-and-true method. The designers first turn to a large box containing watercolor pencils. Slowly they set their ideas down on paper, giving birth to an artwork that represents a future masterpiece of fine watchmaking.

The designers also fulfill special commissions from certain clients who want to have a watch that has its own very individual look. In this case, *haute horlogerie* has much in common with haute couture. Obviously, a unique, made-to-order artwork comes at a price, which not everyone can afford. In this very exclusive sphere of personalized luxury, the designers sometimes travel to meetings held anywhere on the planet, packing a notebook of sketches and colored pencils in their luggage. In that way the avid watch-lover will come to realize, through discussions with professional designers, the difficulties that their requests often encounter—sometimes a client comes here to exceed the limits of the possible. It is the designer's task to find a way to realize the client's dream. The designers deal not only with artistic and horological constraints, they also have to remain constantly aware of new trends, fashions, styles, and behavior. The basic philosophy at Montblanc Villeret, however, absolutely excludes hasty action. The *manufacture* must remain aloof from fleeting fads. It wholeheartedly embraces the idea attributed to Kierkegaard that, "those who wed the spirit of the times will soon be widowed." Reconciling the fashion of the day with lasting values therefore remains the toughest challenge for the designers in Villeret.

Facing page
Design study for a made-to-order pair of watches.

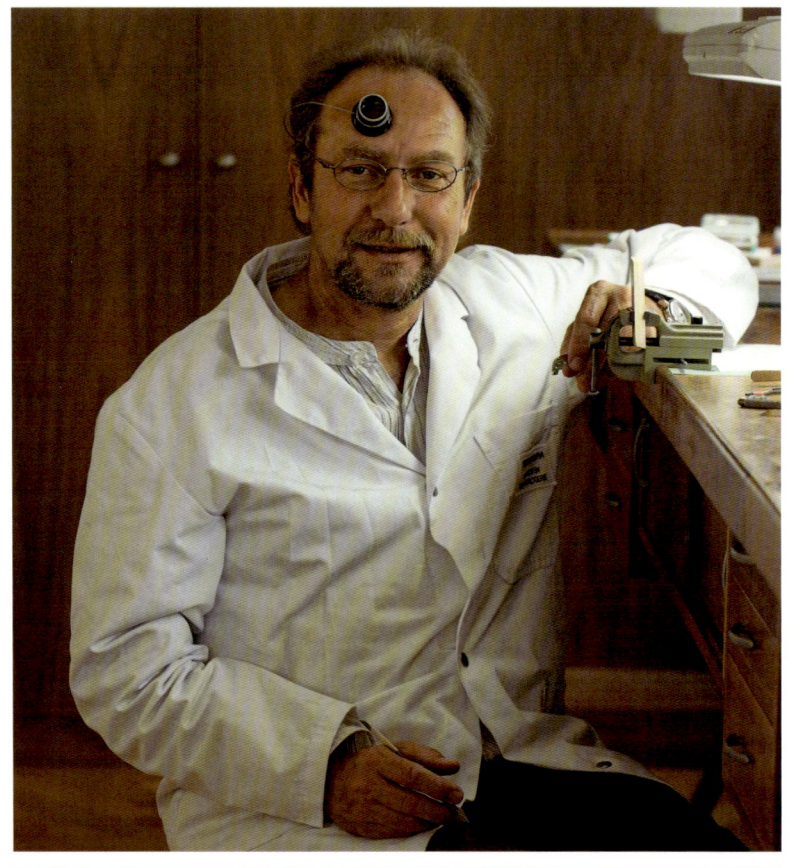

THE MASTER OF PERFECT BEAUTY

"Nobody's perfect. Something can go wrong every now and then. Which means that several hours of work can wind up in the trash," recounts Jean-Paul Goidet, a beveler and polisher. Indeed, in Goidet's line of work no subsequent correction is possible, especially when it entails beveling a tiny steel part by hand. Every stroke of the beveler's file must be confident and perfectly identical to the one that preceded it if the surface is to be uniformly smooth. The absolute rule requires a beveled (or chamfered) edge to have an angle of 45 degrees—no more, no less. To this end, watchmakers traditionally have a range of tools, and long experience is required to choose just the right one for the job. Every move has to be absolutely right. Watchmakers distinguish between straight and round corners, flat and rounded angles. Everything must be done according to very clear rules. All edges must be equal in width and perfectly parallel. On completion of this work, which can require over four hours of intense concentration for a chronograph lever, its silhouette alone identifies a given part. Beveling edges is only one stage—although an important one—in the process of ennobling a movement. Polishing and satin-finishing are other craft secrets. Five or six different operations are required to obtain the specific look of a watch that meets *haute horlogerie* standards. The craftsperson plays on lighting effects through tiny lines that follow the same direction and assume a black, gray, or white appearance depending on the angle from which the part is viewed. At the same time, polishing makes the surface more homogenous and resistant to oxidation. Satin-finishing, also done by hand, lends the sides that soft, velvety look. Here again, precision down to the tiniest details is required, and original dimensions must always be respected. Once the part is finished, it must fit harmoniously into the overall geometry. This requirement forbids the removal of too much metal and guarantees that every function will operate properly.

At Villeret, these tasks are not subject to time constraints. In the end, what counts is the perfect appearance and beauty of parts that are often miniscule, some of which are totally invisible to the eye of the wearer. When it comes to fine watchmaking, perfection and beauty run deep.

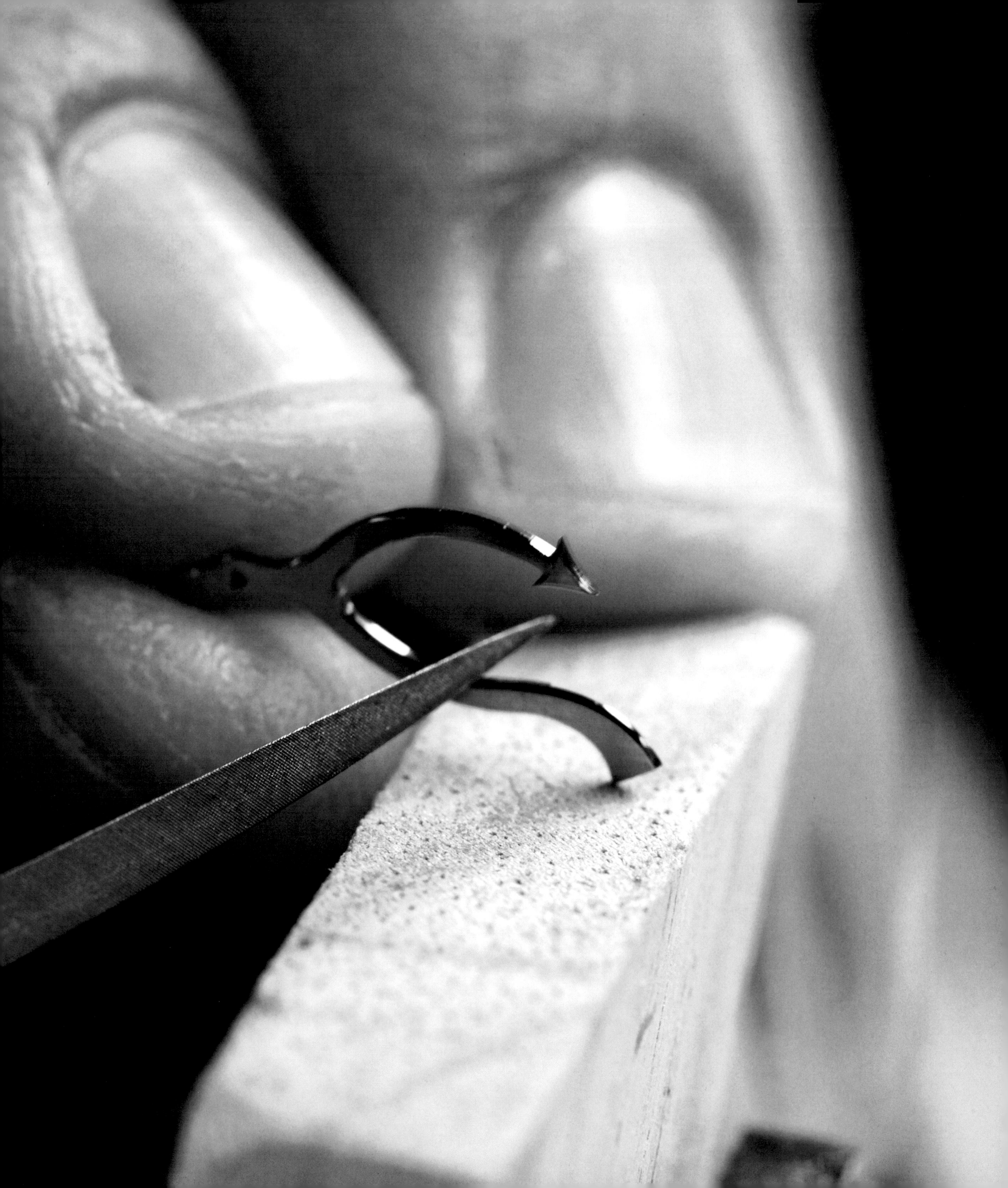

THE QUEEN OF HEARTS

Ever since she trained as a *régleuse*, Monique Wyssmeuller has devoted her life to the souls of mechanical watches. And since 2000 she has been keeping watch over the very special soul of Minerva timepieces. The *régleuse* is responsible for the most important part of every mechanical timepiece, namely the balance wheel and its highly sensitive balance spring. They represent the true heart of a watch. Surprisingly, the balance component has now become one of the most standardized parts in the watch industry—most makers simply buy it from a specialized supplier. But because Montblanc wants to maintain the tradition of a *manufacture* at Villeret, this highly strategic part of the watch is produced entirely in-house. And such a sensitive, crucial component calls for special hands to care for it.

The ultimate job of a *régleuse* is to modify and adapt the component's miniscule parts so that balance wheel action is accurate to within ten seconds per day. To achieve this, she works with tools called "Potence." In a drum below the spring to be adjusted is a master spring and balance wheel oscillating at a steady 18,000 beats per hour. The timer holds the tip of the new spring with tweezers and alters its point of attachment to its own wheel until the two balances are oscillating in a perfectly synchronous manner. Only then has the balance spring found its correct length. This process could be done much more quickly by an electronic device, but without the accuracy and reliability required of *haute horlogerie*.

When balance springs arrive on the *régleuse*'s workbench, they are flat. Yet the finest watchmaking tradition uses only so-called "Phillips" springs, which are given an upward terminal curve that allows for optimal concentric expansion. *Régleuses* who can master this technique have become as rare as diamonds. The best ones do it in a natural way, without really thinking about it—their hands move with a magical agility under the light of the loupe and the first upward curve suddenly appears. Once they've mastered this knack, they never forget. Each balance spring requires a good hour of work, from attaching it to the wheel to applying the raised curve. She will seal a lifetime in a Villeret watch.

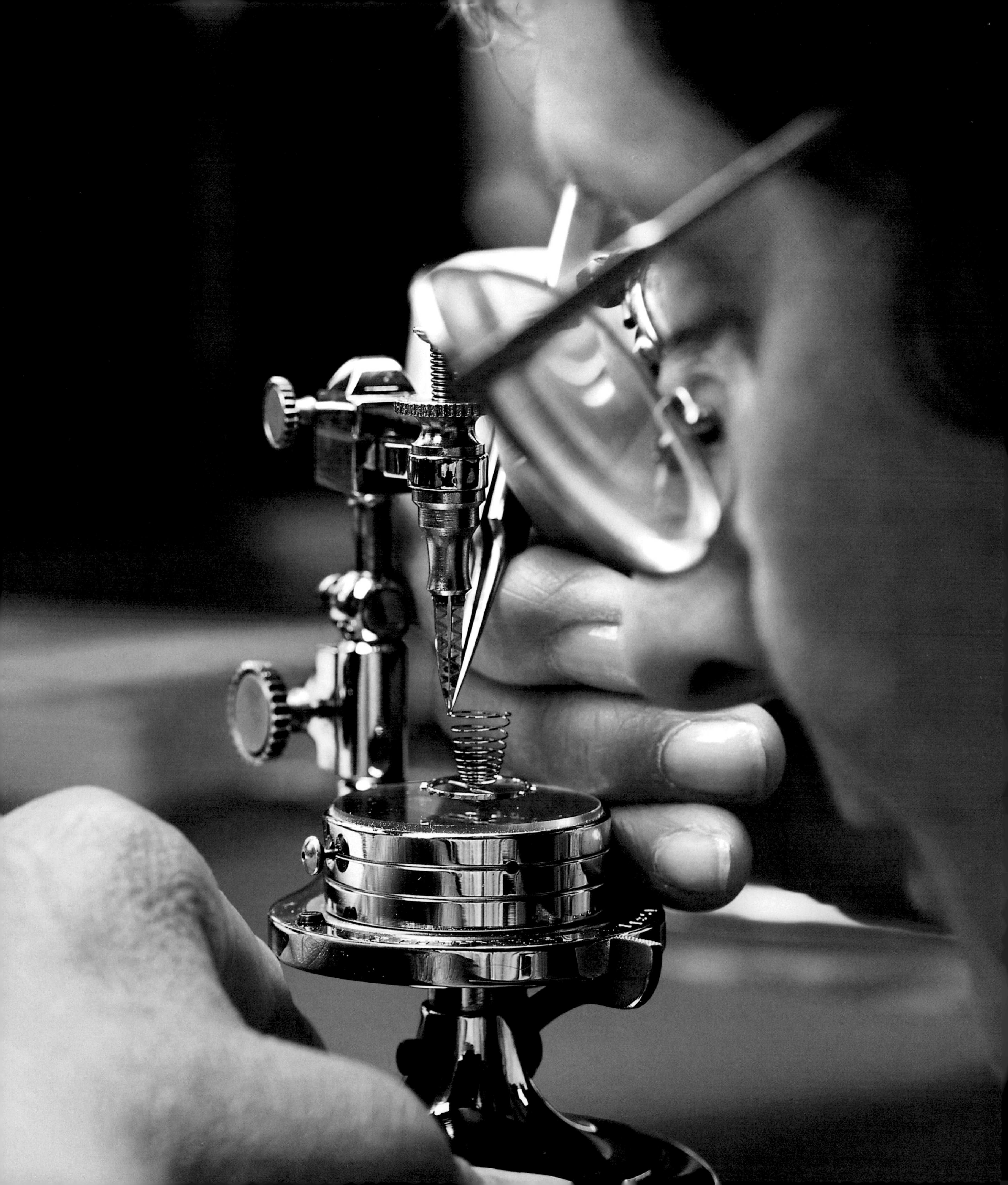

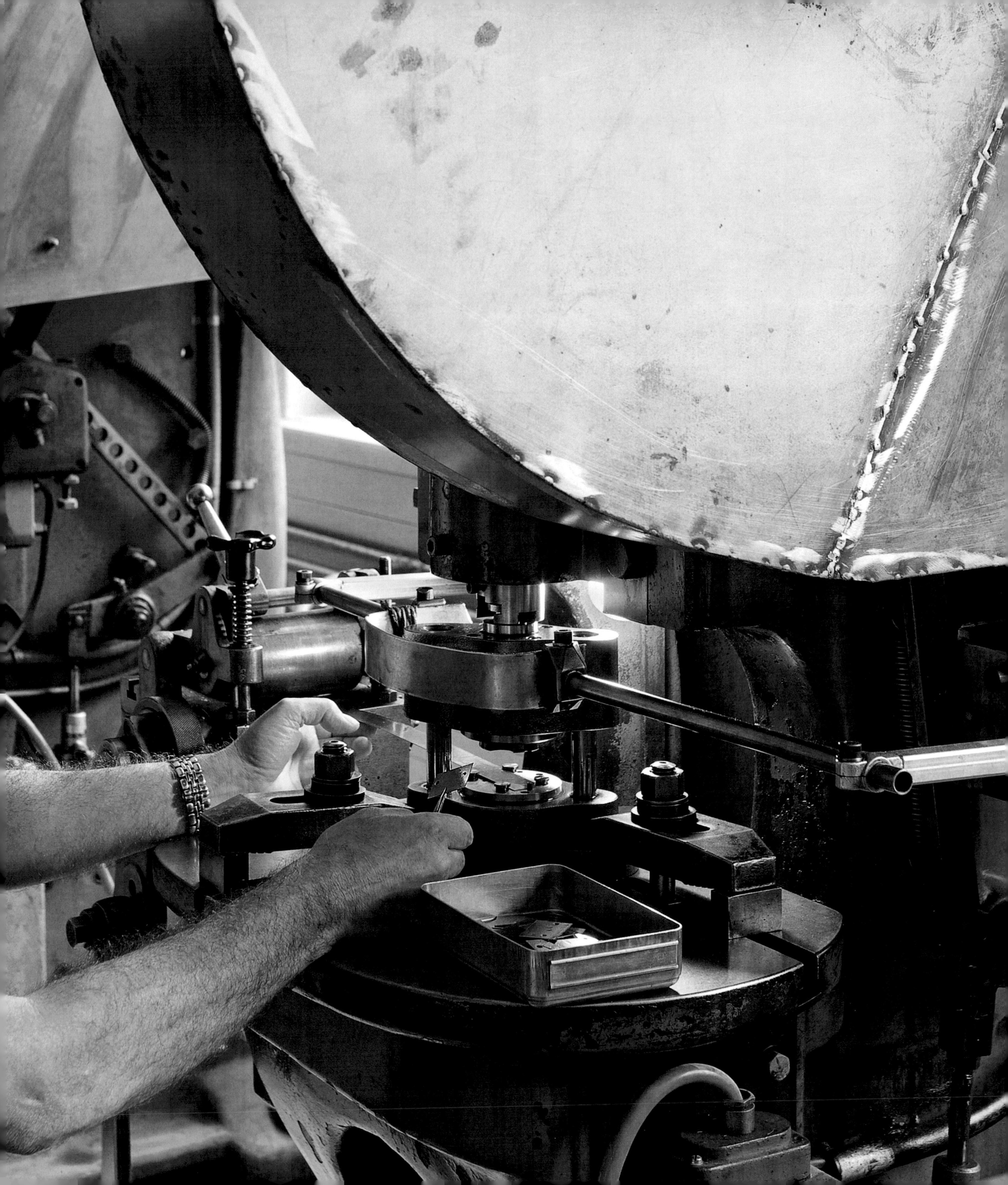

I | Montblanc: Writing Time

THE MACHINE WHISPERER

The work of a toolmaker is highly diverse by nature. He makes the tools with which watchmakers concoct their tiny parts, and he also has to maintain them. This job requires great skill because in fine watchmaking the various machining tasks are never routine. Creativity, an ability to improvise, and mental flexibility are therefore necessary to resolve the ever-evolving problems. At the center of a world populated by some twenty machines of respectable age, Olivier Hadorn proudly performs this job for Montblanc. Every machine has a clearly defined role. Some of them are used only once a month, whereas others display their remarkable qualities every day. Traditional in design, they nevertheless boast remarkable precision and longevity, still unmatched—in this specific sphere—by computer-controlled equipment. With a horizontal drill dating from the 1950s, for example, Hadorn turns a part already in the machine toward himself, then with infinite care sends the tip of the bit into the side of the plate, making a hole of the precisely desired size. Elsewhere, huge gray presses stamp out tiny parts with meticulous accuracy, hammering down several tons in a deafening din. The thousandth part produced by these stamping presses will be perfectly identical to the first one, without the least difference. In contrast, digitally controlled devices require regular checks because the values can change after only twenty parts or so.

Maintenance of such machines is costly, however. Given Minerva's deliberately low output, the cost per part is high. But these machines are a guarantee of perfection.

Above

Reprise machine used for drilling lateral holes.

Facing page

70-ton press used for cutting washers in nickel silver and blanks of steel mechanisms.

133

NUIT
30
05
10
15
20
25
RESERVE DE MARCHE HAUT
MONTBLANC
GUILLOCHE MAIN SUISSE

A Time for Things Rare and Original

As Cicero fittingly asserted, *Omnia praeclara rara:* "All the best things are rare." Montblanc illustrates this principle with its notably precious editions of writing instruments, as well as with the timepieces that emerge from the Villeret workshop. Made in just a few copies, their prestige and rarity are unmatched.

As mentioned above, for the limited editions of the *Collection Montblanc Villeret 1858*, the formula that embodies this profession of faith is based on the figures 1, 8, and 58, commemorating the foundation of Minerva in Villeret in 1858: unique pieces in platinium and in addition, eight watches in gray gold and 58 others in white or red gold. Every watch that emerges from the *manufacture* displays the emblematic signs of perfection: sophisticated construction, exceptionally refined horological mechanisms, and peerless quality of dials, hands, and cases. Strictly limited production is the only way to fulfill such high expectations, along with the choice of the best materials and the skills of the finest craftspeople. The production level at Villeret is now approximately 250 watches per year. And despite the popularity of these watches, no significant increase in production is envisaged for the moment.

This approach has given birth to authentic collector's items that will be passed on from generation to generation, losing none of their value—indeed, they will increase in value. The early editions of Villeret models sold out long ago, and the chances of buying one today are very rare.

All over the world there are people who are fond of exclusive objects, who do not want other people to own the same watch as they do. Montblanc is able to fulfill this wish—a team of highly qualified specialists can make the client's dream come true. Even when requests seem unrealistic, the team will bend over backward to square the circle and produce a unique piece from one of the firm's calibers, satisfying the client's wishes. Dial, hands, case, additional function, and so on: every kind of personalization is envisageable. The client is nevertheless asked to remain patient, for the firm's capacities in this sphere are limited. The development and manufacture of a special order, liaising constantly with the client, takes time: a year or more may go by in the Jura Mountains. Here again, parallels emerge between the Montblanc operations in Villeret and Hamburg. The craftspeople in Hamburg's "Artisans' Atelier" take special pleasure in creating a personalized writing tool for a client with special requirements. Currently five projects of this kind are underway, with others on the books.

Facing page

Grand Chronographe Régulateur
Limited edition of 8 pieces
Case 47 mm in 18-karat white gold with palladium 210
Dial 18-karat anthracite and silver gold hand guilloche
Hands in 18-karat gold, sweep-second in Pfinodal®
Secrets signatures "Minerva 1858" and "guilloche main Suisse"

Caliber MB M 16–30

Following page, right

View from the fouth floor meeting room of the Montblanc *manufacture* in Villeret This is where the younger and older generations of watchmakers meet in order to develop the great watches of tomorrow while respecting the great watchmaking traditions.

A WATCH, A SHOWCASE

When a client finally receives the horological creation he or she has long awaited—whether a unique piece or a limited edition—attention instantly goes to the elegant showcase in which the pure mechanical gem has been set. Furthermore, all watches are accompanied by a set of real prints—a leather portfolio contains a series of splendid lithographs of historic depictions of the old Minerva *manufacture*, impressions of the mountainous Jura landscape, pictures of the *manufacture's* movements, and of course an illustration of the watch just acquired by the owner. In fact, this last print could be considered the highlight of this elegant portfolio. Like the watch itself, it is an exclusive, unique item that bears the watch's individual serial number and the total number of watches in the limited edition. This artwork also bears the signature of Demetrio Cabiddu, who assumes ultimate responsibility for all the timepieces that leave the Montblanc *manufacture* in Villeret. Montblanc feels that this splendid, personalized set of lithographs complements and augments the exceptional rarity of timepieces in its *Collection Montblanc Villeret 1858*.

MULTIPLE MISSIONS

In 2007, the former *manufacture* Minerva became Montblanc's artisanal horological workshop. A year and half later, the historic building on the main street in Villeret displayed a new sparkle thanks to substantial renovation and extension work. Montblanc had charged a team of experienced architects and craftsmen with the job of meticulously restoring all the typical features of a Jura watchmaking workshop. The success of the operation is symbolized by the solid oak flooring that is over a century old. Although ecological considerations dictated replacement of the old windows by double-glazed versions that resulted in significant savings in energy, the carpenters scrupulously reproduced the original frames and crossbars.

Apart from considerations of appearance, a complete revamping of the plumbing, electrical wiring, and even computer cabling was required for safety reasons. In contrast, the entire set of machines, some of which had been in service for decades, was retained. As a rule, such equipment can only be seen today in a museum. Yet in the Montblanc *manufacture* at Villeret they are still in use alongside the most modern electronic equipment. The same is true of the watchmakers' workshop, which retained its original appearance, complete with traditional tools, instruments, and measuring devices. Only the new user-friendly workbenches provide a much-appreciated touch of modern sophistication.

Overall, these measures have created the ideal conditions for Montblanc to accomplish its mission in a manner as authentic as that used by Minerva for the past 150 years. One of the tasks involves promoting

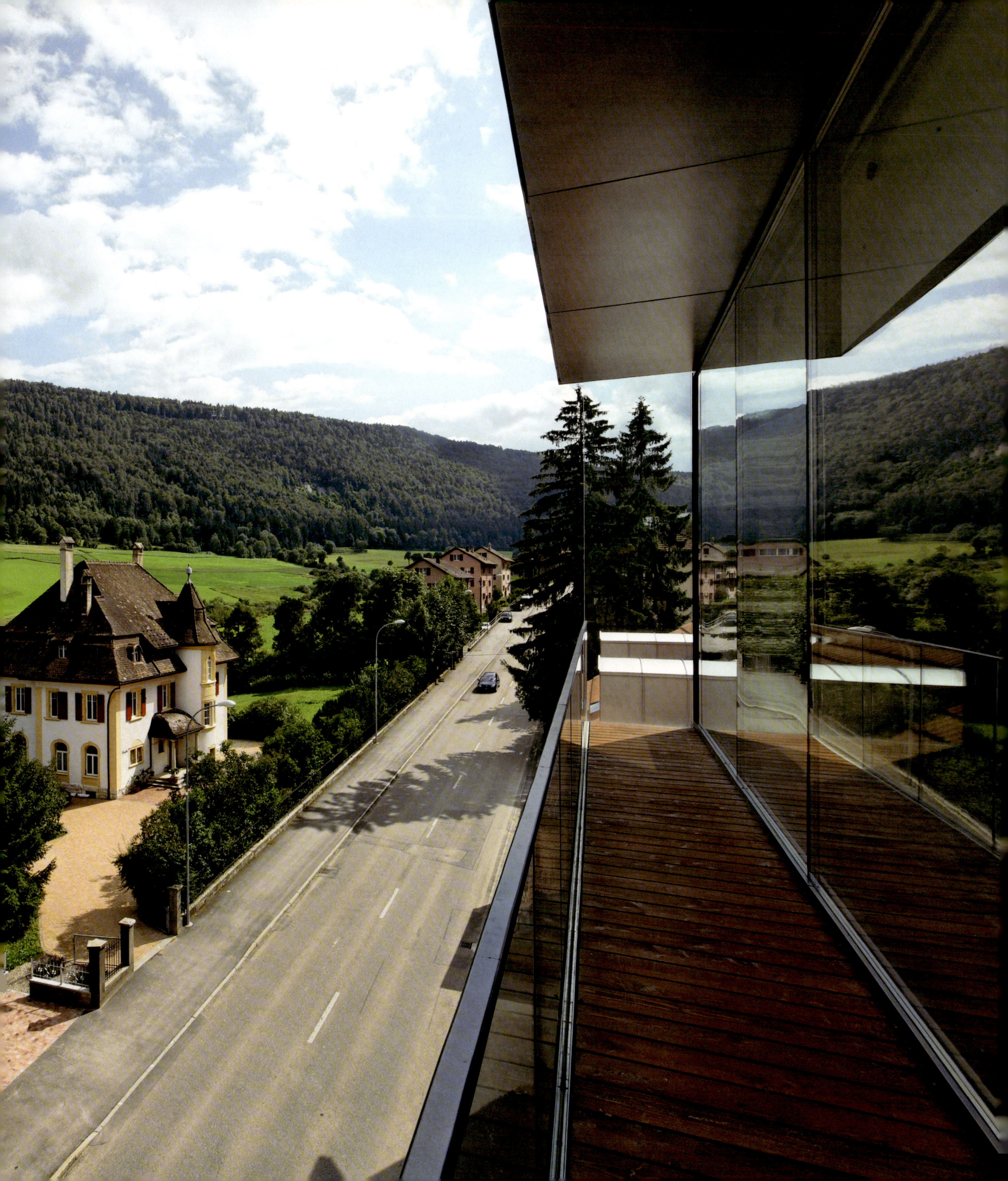

research and development in every field of horology, which naturally includes the making of ébauches, complete movements, and finished watches in a form that favors handcrafted products. Not to be overlooked is the crucial aspect of after-sales service: every mechanical timepiece needs careful maintenance at regular intervals if it is to survive in perfect condition from generation to generation.

However, all watches made in Villeret since 2007 differ from their predecessors in one specific way—they bear the Montblanc name. And for good reason. It is this prestigious firm that provided the necessary security for the Minerva heritage to pursue its ambitious, extremely costly climb to the summit of the art of watchmaking. As history has often shown, without such support the development of chronographs with sophisticated complications (such as the double power-reserve indicator and universal time), not to mention extraordinary *tourbillons*, would have remained an impossible dream.

THE INSTITUT MINERVA DE RECHERCHE EN HAUTE HORLOGERIE

Finally, one of the main missions of the *manufacture* is to preserve and extend the precious horological expertise accumulated over the past century and a half. The education and continuous professional training of young watchmakers, in collaboration with well-known institutions, is therefore of crucial importance. To this end, the attic level of the *manufacture* was remodeled to contain an upper floor with a panoramic vista where young watchmakers can meet with their elders and learn about the age-old techniques and traditions developed by earlier generations. Exhibitions, forums, and seminars are also hosted by Montblanc on its own premises and elsewhere, in order to present the traditions of *haute horlogerie* enthusiasts all around the world.

Furthermore, in 2008 Montblanc set up a foundation called the Institut Minerva de Recherche en Haute Horlogerie, designed to support budding projects by creative young watchmakers to help them realize their dreams.

The Institut Minerva de Recherche en Haute Horlogerie encourages talented young people whose dynamism and innovative spirit will make original contributions to the art of watchmaking. In this context, Montblanc launched the "TimeWriter" concept, through which the company backs creative projects by aspiring independent watchmakers. Indeed, the complexity of the art and technique of watchmaking calls for major investment, often far beyond the limited means of young entrepreneurs. The Institut Minerva de Recherche en Haute Horlogerie, then, with Montblanc's support, seeks to provide both material and intellectual input to ambitious young people setting up on their own. The foundation plans to unveil a new project every two years. The first one has just been announced, two years after its inception: the *TimeWriter 1–Metamorphosis* watch.

Metamorphosis

The *Metamorphosis* watch incarnates a terrifically inventive approach to the challenge of applying traditional watchmaking principles to the design of a timepiece with extraordinary, absolutely original features, ones that highly impressed the Institut Minerva de Recherche en Haute Horlogerie's board of directors. Two young horological specialists, Johnny Girardin and Franck Orny, submitted a plan for a twin-faced watch. At first sight, there is nothing new about a timepiece that employs two dials to display different functions—but the way in which the *Metamorphosis* watch transforms itself is absolutely unique. The wearer merely needs to push a slider up or down to change a standard watch into a chronograph, and vice versa. In order to effect this transformation through purely mechanical means, Girardin and Orny pooled their watchmaking expertise and explored methods used to make automatons—a venerable trade long practiced, like watchmaking, in the Jura Mountains of Switzerland. In a perfect synthesis of tradition and innovation, this revolutionary transformational mechanism is based on the chronograph movement MB M 16–29, made and assembled by hand.

Prior to effecting the transformation, the wearer can appreciate the large drop-shaped case with a dial displaying the usual hour, minutes, and seconds of "civil time." A regulator-style subdial with single hour hand and set of Roman numerals is located at 12 o'clock, while a retrograde hand for minutes moves in an arc in the middle of the dial between 8 and 4 o'clock. A large, central seconds hand makes one turn per minute. A subdial for the date, also indicated by a hand, is placed at 6 o' clock. All these indicators provide the civil time and current date at a glance. However, at any moment the wearer may decide to push the slider on the left side of the case from the 10 o' clock position to 8 o' clock, which triggers a wonderful change of the watch into a chronograph.

Like a sudden change of sets between two scenes in the theater, the speed of this transformation of scenery is startling. Within roughly fifteen seconds four blades in the lower part of the dial slide open and vanish to left and right, below the central bar. Simultaneously, two blades over the regulator subdial at 12 o' clock do the same. At this point, a totalizer disk appears at 6 o' clock and rises upward as though on an elevator—it is the minute totalizer for the chronograph. It contains an opening that "swallows" the date subdial as it ascends. This entirely mechanical system, which functions on the principles of an industrial hoist, inevitably sparks stupefaction and admiration from fans of *haute horlogerie*.

Above

The Montblanc *manufacture* in Villeret, following its renovation in 2008. The old buildings were entirely renovated but kept their original style. Montblanc added the panoramic window in the center of the fourth floor to create a the link between tradition and modernity.

Left

The first young watchmakers supported by the Institut Minerva de Recherche en Haute Horlogerie. Johnny Girardin and Franck Orny stand on either side of Monsieur Cabiddu. Their project, the *Metamorphosis* watch, was presented at the Salon de la Haute Horlogerie in January 2010.

Following pages
Metamorphosis
Left: civil time face
Right: chronograph face
Caliber based on MB M 16–29
Limited edition of 28 pieces
Type of movement hand-wound monopusher chronograph, mechanical transformation of design and function of the watch from simple time indication to chronograph
Chronograph monopusher mechanism, chronograph with column wheel, horizontal clutch
Dimensions 16 Lines (38.40mm); height 11.20mm (with the dial mechanism)
Number of components 567, including 252 components for the basic caliber MB M 16–29
Number of bearing jewels 67
Power reserve 55 hours
Balance screw balance, Ø 14.5 mm; 59 mg/cm^2
Frequency 18'000 semi-oscillations per hour (2.5 hertz)
Balance-spring with Phillips terminal curve
Plate rhodium-plated nickel silver, circular graining on both sides
Bridges rhodium-plated nickel silver, *"Côtes de Genève"* decoration
Going-train gold-plated, faceted arms, hubs with diamond polished surfaces
Classical displays hours in a subdial at 12 o'clock, retrograde minutes, central seconds, date indication at 6 o'clock
Chronograph indications central chronograph seconds, 31 minute counter at 6 o'clock
Features
Case 18-karat white gold; Cambered sapphire crystal, sapphire crystal case back
Dimensions diameter 47 mm; height 14,8 mm
Water-tightness to three bar (30 meters)
Crown 18-karat white gold with Montblanc Star emblem in mother-of-pearl / pusher in the crown
Pusher sliding mechanism in the case's flank at 10 o'clock to start transformation and pusher for date setting at 4 o'clock
Dial titanium, stainless steel, sapphire crystal
Hands date hand in peraluman, hours and minutes hands in brass, chronograph elapsed second hand in steel
Wristband hand-sewn alligator-leather

Following this transformation, the *Metamorphosis* watch presents a face that is entirely devoted to chronograph functions. Whereas the civil-time dial projected a classic elegance based on Roman numerals and a harmonious blend of black and silver hues, the sudden appearance of the chronograph dial is accompanied by Arabic numerals and red indicators that convey the sporty, high-tech appeal of an instrument designed to measure tiny increments of elapsed time. The hour is still displayed at 12 o' clock and the minutes by the retrograde center hand. The central seconds hand henceforth functions as the central hand of the chronograph, while the subdial that appeared at 6 o' clock reveals an unusual feature: it has a chronograph minute track numbered from 1 to 31—a fixed pointer on the central bar of the main dial indicates the minutes that have elapsed. The unusual scale of thirty-one minutes was not chosen for technical reasons, but simply because the inventors wanted to introduce a witty reminder that the date subdial can also occupy this position. Future owners of this unusual timepiece will certainly appreciate the inclusion of such detail, notably once it is realized that the two display systems function totally independently. Whereas the minute disk continues to rotate indefinitely, the date hand moves out of the way in an almost instantaneous fashion.

When the slider that triggers the shift from one function to another is moved, many operations must occur within Montblanc's *Metamorphosis* watch. The mechanisms governing this choreography are so innovative that a patent has been filed for them. Together they constitute a set of wheels and pinions with an integrated transformational role that also drives the cams coordinating the whole process. They alternately open and close the ten wing-like blades that hide or reveal "the scene," they regulate the speed at which this action occurs, and then they anchor all the components once the transformation is complete. Eighty parts make up this mechanism, with a thickness that never exceeds 4.3-millimeters. However, in order to make their plan a reality, the two inventors were obliged to adapt all the components of the *Metamorphosis* watch mechanism—including a separate barrel and a centrifugal force regulator in addition to a large number of tiny, mostly completely original elements—to fit with the construction of the existing caliber MB M 16–29. Even if the structure of the chronograph required little modification from the bridge side, the minute totalizer had to be thoroughly reconceived so that it could occupy a new position at 6 o'clock. The traditional V-shaped chronograph bridge was eliminated and the zero reset lever was extended from the column wheel through the plate, because the heart of the minute totalizer was located on the dial side. Altogether, the *Metamorphosis* watch complication required 315 parts in addition to the 252 components of the caliber MB M 16–29, resulting in the impressive total of 567 parts. Montblanc's *Metamorphosis* watch is therefore one of the most complicated models made today. Needless to say that this development is protected by a patent, which, however, Montblanc deliberately kept under the name of the two inventors. As with every other timepiece in the *Collection Montblanc Villeret 1858*, it goes without saying that every one of these 567 parts meets the strict standards of quality, appearance, and fabrication—largely by hand—that have become emblematic of Switzerland's age-old watchmaking tradition.

At the time of writing, the Institut Minerva de Recherche en Haute Horlogerie and its partners have launched the development of the second TimeWriter project. Montblanc Villeret is therefore looking boldly toward the future by encouraging creative watchmaking in a spirit of refinement and perfection that will certainly yield worthy new symbols of the eternal quest to master time.

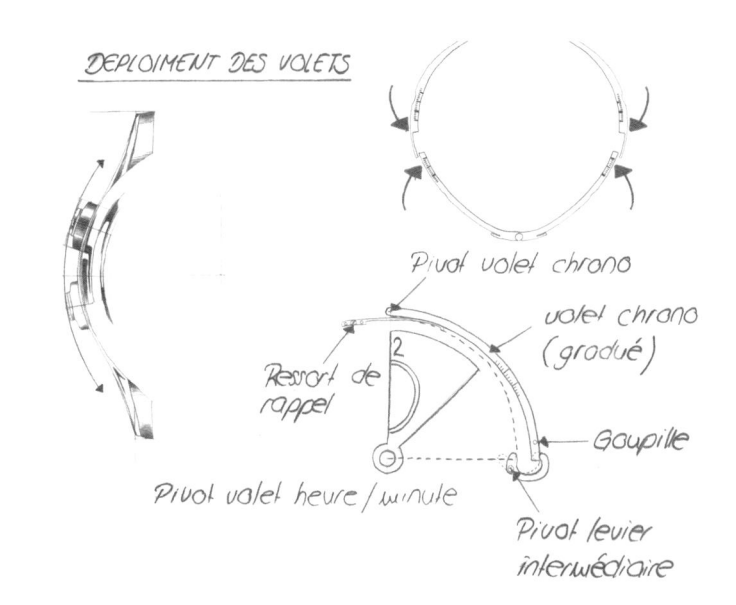

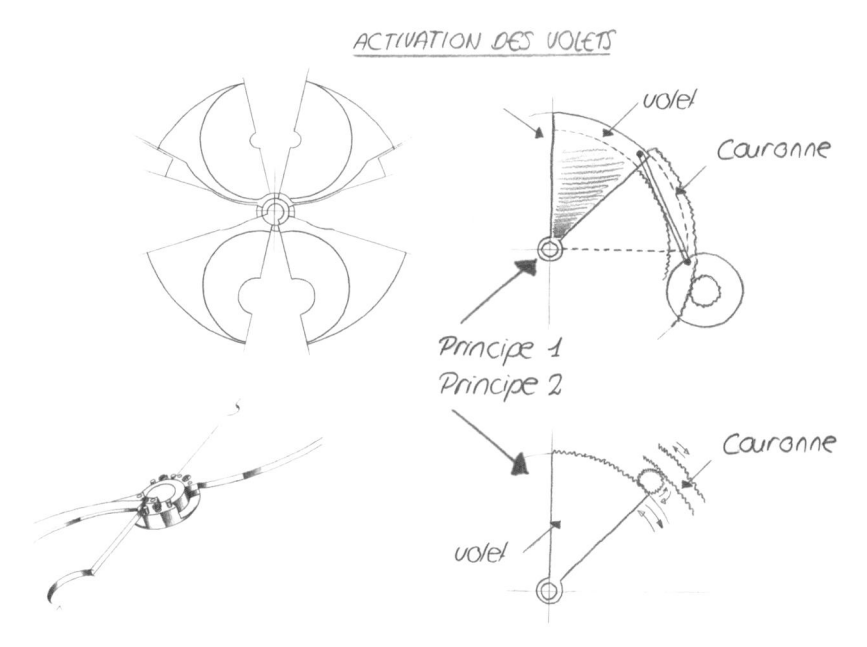

Above

First drawings of the mechanism for turning the hour-minute calendar watch into a chronograph with big seconds and a minute counter.

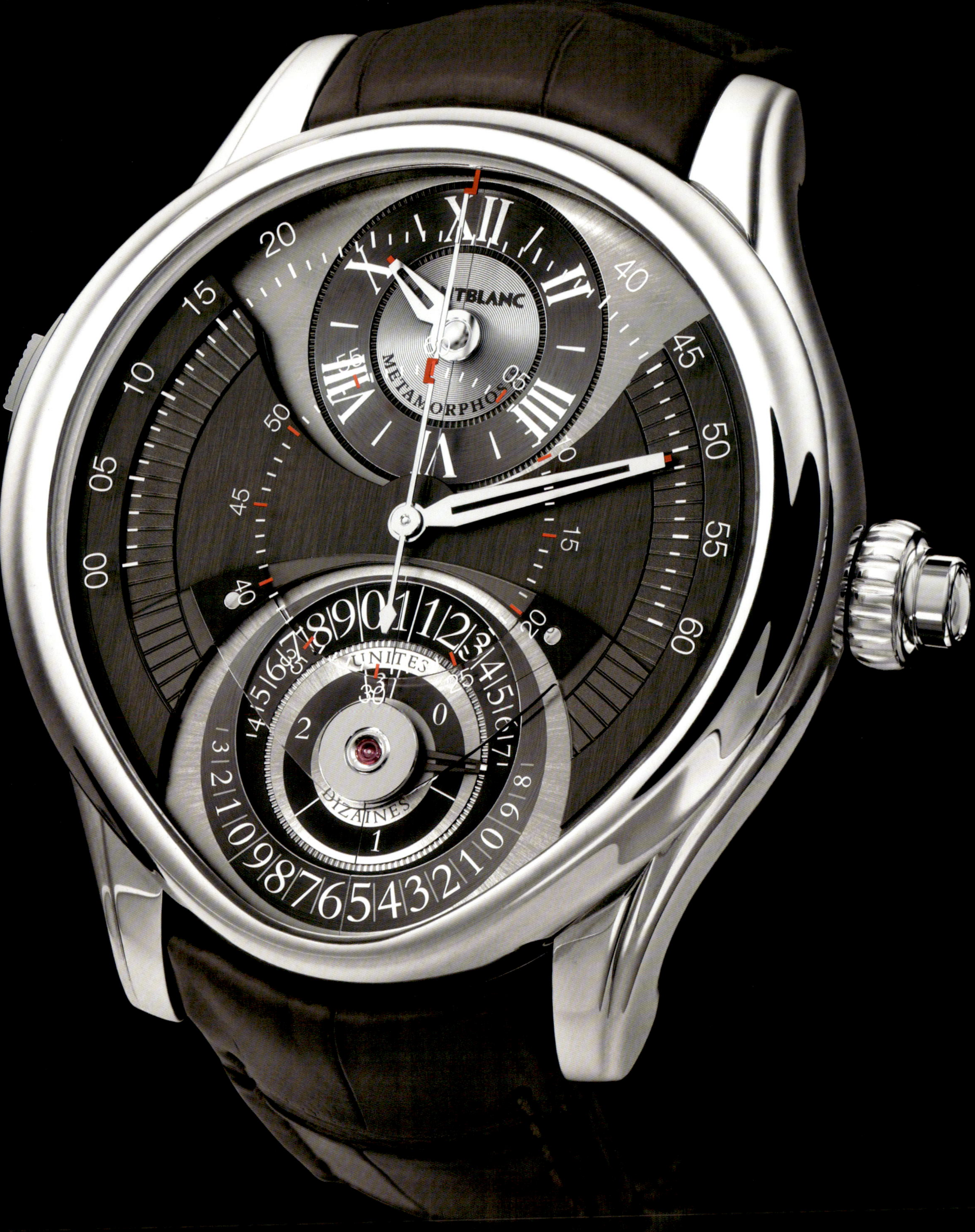
UNITES
DIZAINES

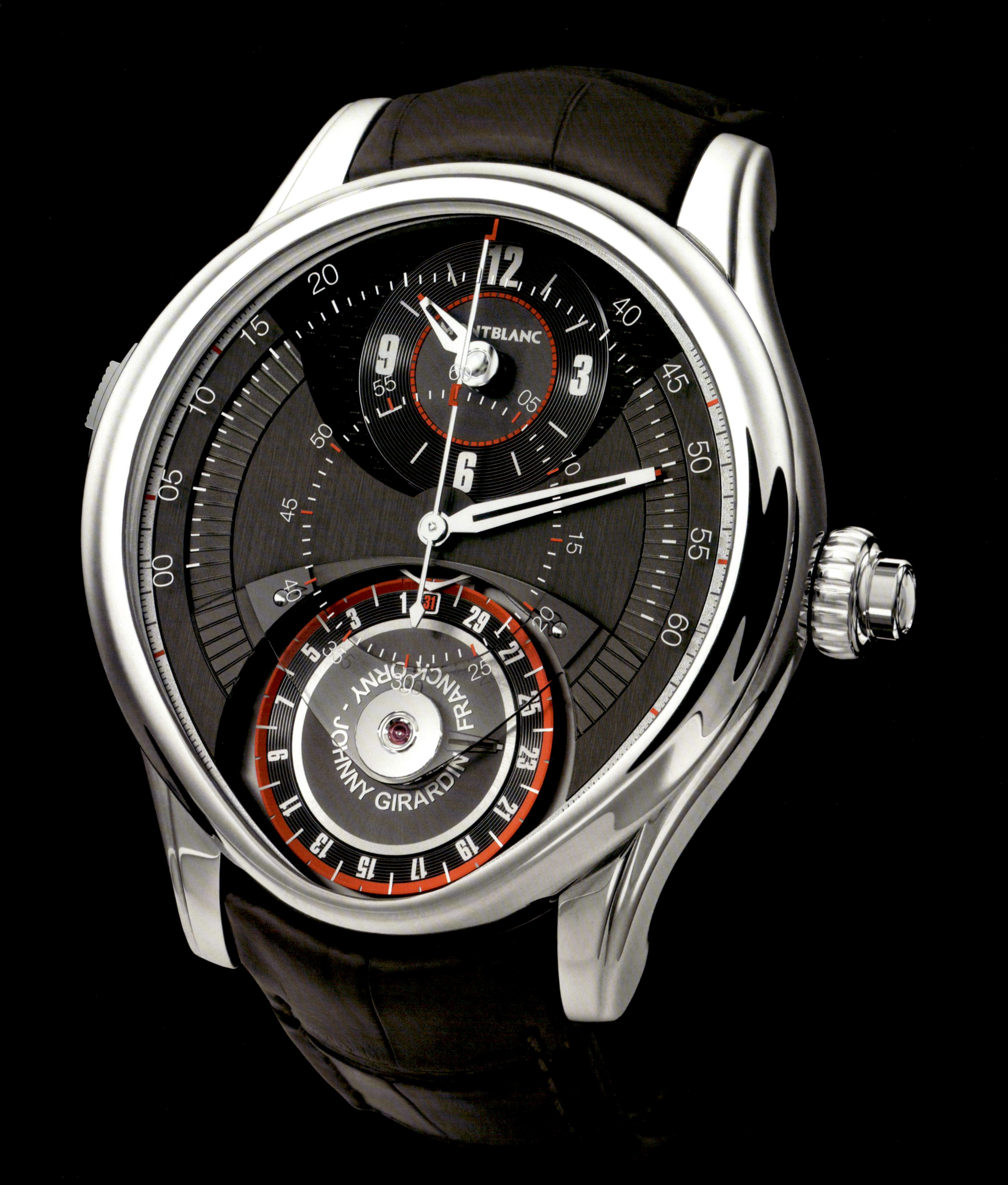
FRANCK ORNY - JOHNNY GIRARDIN

150 Years of Watchmaking Tradition in Villeret

Historical and picture research:
Laurence Marti
Text adapted from the original text
by Laurence Marti

IIIII

A Valley Tradition

The Saint-Imier Valley, where in 1858 Charles Ivan Robert opened what was then called a watchmaking *comptoir* (agency), is just one of the many valleys in Switzerland's Jura Mountains. At each end of this twenty-mile-long valley lying between the Chasseral chain to the south (altitude 5,200 feet) and Mont-Soleil to the north (4,600 feet) there is a major watchmaking town: La Chaux-de-Fonds to the west and Biel (Bienne) to the east. In between, some fifteen villages nestling within the valley boast a distinguished manufacturing tradition that dates back to the seventeenth century or earlier. In those days the presence of a small river, the Suze, with its multiple tributaries, plus the surrounding forests, favored the growth of various production facilities that were first artisanal, then industrial. To these factors should be added the encouragement of the prince-bishops of Basel, who had jurisdiction over the valley prior to the French Revolution.[1] Influenced by Enlightenment philosophy, the successive prince-bishops were favorable to new developments in the arts and crafts. The absence of guild restrictions, an open trade policy, the presence of natural resources, and freedom of action stemming from the valley's remoteness from the center of power all provided a particularly propitious context for experimentation and the rise of numerous industries. Thus at a very early date items made in Erguël, as the region was then called, acquired a certain fame in spheres as varied as milling, metalworking, nail-making, textiles, lace, and, of course, clock- and watchmaking.

The strikingly dynamic Saint-Imier Valley was the birthplace of such internationally known companies as Longines, Heuer, Chopard, Blancpain, and Breitling. Minerva, one of the oldest, has been based in the village of Villeret, in the heart of the valley, for 150 years. In many respects, Minerva's story illustrates the history of every industry in the region. Horology in the Jura Mountains attained a high degree of development by relying on a specific model of industrial organization, *établissage* (component assembly), based not on bringing workers together in a large firm, but on mobilizing an extensive network of small, domestic workshops. Although not very mechanized, the workshops scattered among the villages and surrounding hills were coordinated by the watch-assembling merchants known as *établisseurs*. This production model has constantly interested and intrigued the experts—Karl Marx even referred, with a certain skepticism, to Jura watchmaking as a "heterogeneous" model of manufacturing, while in 1971 Jean-François Gravier pointed out that, "by all appearances, the climate should have discouraged any notable industrial development."[2] Jura watchmaking was one of those historical models—like Sheffield cutlery and Lyon silk manufacture, for instance—that offered an alternative to the large industries associated with Manchester in England. Nor is there anything

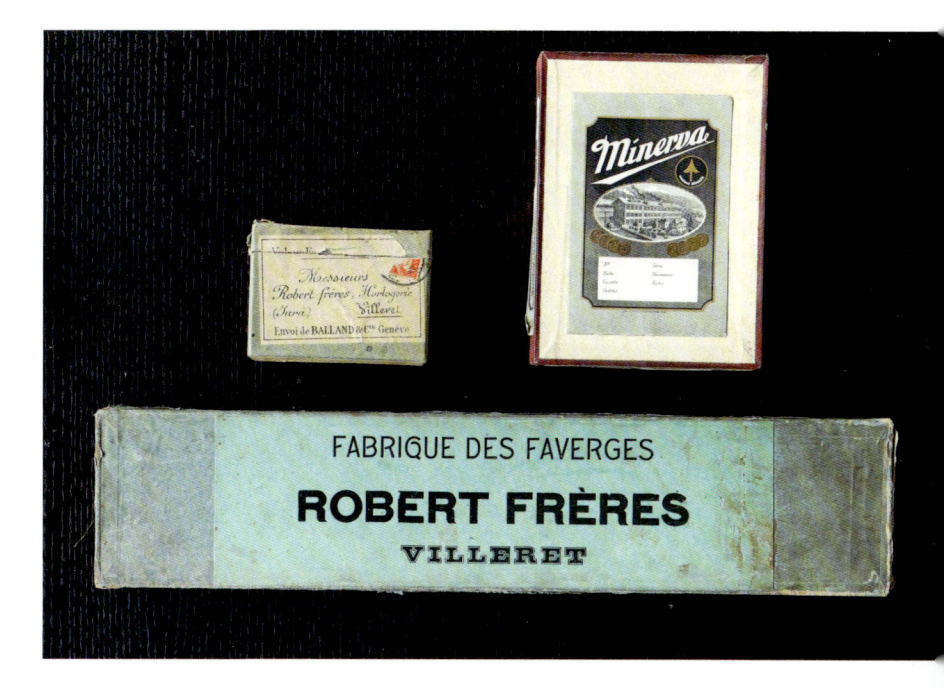

Above

Cartons used by the *établisseurs* to distribute parts to the small home workshops. Each carton contained 10 to 12 sets of movement components (except the escapement and the spring balance).

"archaic" about this model, which has reemerged in the past thirty years in modern forms exemplified by Silicon Valley.

Although the Jura Mountains are not the only place to practice dispersed manufacture, one distinctive feature stands out: this is probably one the few regions in Western Europe that has managed to retain part of its industrial specificity for nearly three hundred years. The original mode of production has of course evolved, adapting to the major industrial trends (mechanization, structural integration, and globalization), but it is still highly marked by its original configuration, notably retaining a higher than average dispersion of production units and a geographic implantation that continues to defy the fully integrated, concentrated model of industrial organization. Minerva is part of that tradition: small in size, it has obviously grown and acquired the status of factory, ultimately becoming part of an international outfit even as family management was succeeded by more distant corporate management. At every stage, products and strategies had to be adapted, as did production tools; but what never died was the determination to maintain a special relationship with specific skills and institutions, with a particular history and environment. For example, "La Minerva"—as the firm is affectionately called in the area—never expanded beyond several dozen employees, and the shift from small workshop to factory occurred progressively, with no social disruption. When mechanization arrived, it was incorporated very gradually, with a view to maintaining original skills and expertise. In this spirit the company has always rejected mass production, staunchly defending its independence and specificity even during the difficult decade of the 1970s. Such concern for tradition even motivated the decision not to make quartz watches at a time when conventional watches seemed doomed to extinction. Despite the ups and downs common to every company, this strong attachment to specific skills, to a special history, and to respect for tradition have always been the bedrock of Minerva's values.

Above

The Montblanc *manufacture* in Villeret today, with its historical entrance door restored in 2008.

Facing page

A map of the windmills, rivers, and streams in Villeret in 1637. At the top is the Faverges stream, the by-channel, and the recently built windmill which would all be bought by Charles-Auguste Robert in 1846.

THE ROBERT FAMILY MAKES A START

By 1780 all the villages in the Erguël area had their own watchmaking activity. In Villeret itself, the first horologists seem to have set up in the years 1720–30. But the true rise of a watchmaking industry in the village only got underway in the 1770s. Some sources claim that the nail-making industry was sufficiently buoyant to slow the growth of watchmaking, a point that paradoxically indicates one of the reasons for the success of the latter activity: watchmaking took over from other businesses either because they were in decline—such as clothmaking and metalworking, which suffered from the effects of increasingly mechanized competition— or because it promised better income. Throughout the eighteenth century, watchmaking nevertheless remained just one industry among others. It only rose to dominance following the French Revolution.

Several watchmaking families in Villeret made their mark right from the eighteenth century. They included the Blancpain family, which founded the now-famous brand. Jehan Jacques Blancpain began watchmaking activity on the family farm no later than 1735, although "he did so as a side business, continuing to farm his land at the same time," wrote his descendant, Claude Blancpain.[3] "Isaac Blancpain, Jehan Jacques' son, soon joined his father and they worked together for a while. Since Isaac was a schoolteacher, watchmaking was a sideline for him, too. But thriving business led to the establishment of a true workshop by David Louis Blancpain (born 1765), son of Isaac and grandson of Jehan Jacques. Another member of the family went to sell these watches abroad."

We can thus see how the watchmaking evolved from a sideline in the early eighteenth century to a full-fledged business fifty years later. The example of the Blancpains also illustrates the freedom enjoyed by these families, who could easily change professions without running foul of guild regulations, as would have been the case in Geneva or Paris. It also exemplifies the model of domestic, family-based production, typical of all watchmaking activity right up to the early twentieth century. Since watchmaking required no heavy infrastructure, it was easy for anyone to set up a workbench with several tools in one room of the house, and begin making watch parts.

The division of labor and dispersion of workshops meant that even in the eighteenth century Villeret already boasted not only watchmakers but case-fitters, ébauche makers, chasers, pinion makers, and other specialists. All these various specializations could be learned either from another horologist or within the family, once again free of guild regulations that might restrict access to such skills. Such freedom favored the rapid spread of watchmaking skills among the residents of the Saint-Imier Valley.

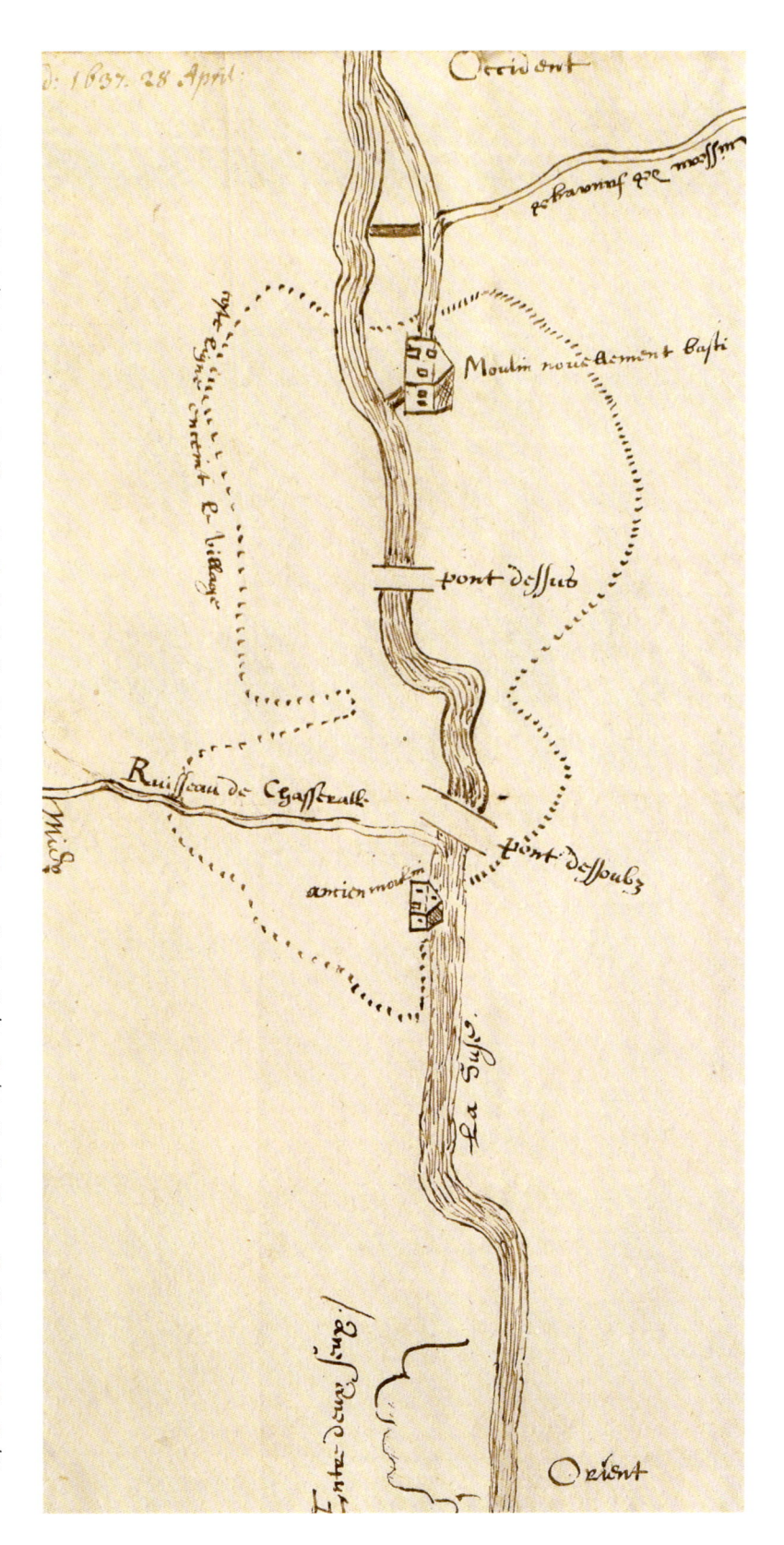

Also by the eighteenth century, several valley watchmakers, including some from Villeret, had made their name in the courts of Europe thanks to their reputable products. In terms of quality and price, the area already competed with the major watchmaking centers of the day—Paris, Geneva, and London—which it ultimately dethroned in the early nineteenth century.

In 1856 Charles Auguste Robert, probably attracted by Villeret's dynamism, bought a few properties and moved there the following year. As a craftsman, traveler, and entrepreneur whose activities ranged from copper engraving to watchmaking, Charles Auguste illustrates the great geographic and professional mobility typical of the early Jura watchmakers. Caught up in the swirl of ideas characteristic of that century, driven by a spirit of discovery and initiative, they nevertheless always maintained a link with their mountain-pasture homeland.

In Villeret Charles Auguste bought the "upper mill-house" somewhat outside the village, at a spot called "Le Pecaut" on the road to Saint-Imier. At the same auction he purchased a nearby orchard and another house. The total acquisitions cost him 10,816 Swiss francs at the time. Because he died shortly afterward, we do not know Charles Auguste's long-term plans for the site. But his son, Charles Ivan, immediately picked up the torch, and at the tender age of eighteen opened his first watchmaking workshop.

There is little documentation concerning Charles Ivan Robert's early years of watchmaking. All we know is that he did not begin all alone—the registers mention the names of "H. and Ce. Robert," whom Jean-Jacques Frey identifies as Hyppolite and Charles Robert.[4] This partner might either have been a relative or the Geneva watchmaker Hyppolite Robert, who was highly active at the time. The partnership only lasted three or four years, until the early 1860s, and was probably designed to allow Charles Ivan to reach the age of majority and stand on his own two feet. The year 1863 appears to have been a pivotal one. On June 15 he married Adèle-Emma Blancpain (born in 1841), daughter of Frédéric Émile Blancpain and sister of Jules Émile Blancpain, the two owners of the Blancpain watchmaking workshop in Villeret. "That is how the close link between the two families was formed," comments Claude Blancpain.[5]

Top

Arms of the Robert family.

Above

The pediment of the Robert family's house (the old windmill) on which appear the letters CARM 1847 (Charles Auguste Robert-Matthey 1847). This house now is the protestant parsonage.

148

PUTTING WATCHES TOGETHER: THE *ÉTABLISSEUR*

Charles Ivan began business as an *établisseur,* or assembly coordinator. There were already ten or so *établisseurs* in the village at the time, rising to twenty in the 1880s. In the eighteenth century, the main job of an *établisseur* was to organize and supervise the multiple to-ings and fro-ings between specialist workshops, to receive the finished products at his *comptoir*, and then to forward the watches to a seller. Starting in the early nineteenth century, *établisseurs* often performed several tasks themselves, for example final assembly or sale. This was probably the case with Charles Ivan, since his *comptoir* included a workshop and office.

Although Charles Ivan already had a small production setup, his main business still involved distributing work and coordinating production among several dozen subcontractors. By the latter half of the nineteenth century Villeret *établisseurs* were at the heart of a complex production network. "The ébauches came from the Robert workshop in Fontainemelon and the Japy workshop in Beaucourt; the pinions were partly made in the local area and the rest came from Montbéliard. Villeret watchmakers had their gears made in Tramelan, Cormoret, Courtelary, and Cortébert, whereas the assembly itself was done in Villeret and Cormoret. The silver cases were made in Les Breuleux and more especially Villeret and Saint-Imier, where there were major case-making workshops. Plain-metal cases came from the Doubs region, notably Damprichard. All the work was done at home, and shipped from one place to another by couriers who operated daily between Villeret, Les Breuleux, and Tramelan, as well as between Villeret and the lower valley."[6] This division of labor led to the implementation of a highly dense network of operations within the same village as well as across the various regions of the Jura Mountains. The subdivision of operations was called *production en parties brisées* (divided-segment production), each "segment" representing a specific operation was assigned to a different worker. "While there were already fifty-four 'divided segments' around 1830, by 1870 they numbered over one hundred. Each worker repeatedly focused on one single segment, thus acquiring great skill in his or her specialty.[7] The increasing subdivision of labor was often due to the introduction of jobs assigned to women, such as timers, dial drillers, and polishers.

During that same period Villeret acquired greater autonomy through the launch of new workshops that specialized in producing escapements, assortiments (the assembled escapement units), and springs, as well as attaching hands. At the same time the village expanded its business in activities such as setting and polishing through an increase in the number of workshops, often employing a largely female workforce. The increasing diversification of tasks and division of labor meant that the number of workshops in Villeret grew from seventy-three in 1858 to 121 in 1900.

Top

Charles Ivan Robert when he began his business.

Above

The family's house enclosing the watchmaking *comptoir* at the end of the 19th century.

LOUIS BURGY, SAINT-IMIER _ 1234

mont le 1ᵉʳ janvier 1902

pour la nouvelle année, L. et E. Roh

By 1880, Charles Ivan's workshop had won repute. The Robert firm was mentioned that year in the Indicateur Suisse de l'Horlogerie (Swiss Horology Guide), which pointed out its specialty of pocket watches of gold, silver, and other metals, featuring winding crowns on the pendant. Robert had clearly made a name for himself by applying the new winding technology introduced by Louis Audemars of Le Brassus in 1837, and which became more widely available around 1875.[8] Robert's watches at that time seem to have had many points in common with Blancpain's, although we don't know whether there were exchanges between the two workshops. Charles Ivan appears to have been both an *établisseur* and a maker of certain specific parts.

He took advantage of the establishment of an official Trade Register to register his company on March 13, 1883 under the name of "C. Robert à Villeret" (C. Robert of Villeret).[9] In 1884 the trademark of "C. Robert, Villeret" was officially registered. The first logo included a caduceus, probably inspired by the neo-classical art trends of the day—references to mythological sources would remain one of the company's distinctive signs.

Charles Ivan Robert first won international recognition in 1885, when his pocket watches and winding mechanisms were awarded a medal at the Universal Exposition hosted in Antwerp, Belgium. He entered the exposition under the name of "Ch. Robert, Villeret, Horlogerie et montres de poche" (Ch. Robert, Villeret, Horology and Pocket Watches).[10] By the mid 1880s the company was turning new corners: two new brand names were registered in 1886 and 1887, Mercur (sometimes spelled Mercure or Merkur) and Minerva. The former referred to the mythological god of commerce, whose emblem was the original caduceus, while the latter was the goddess of arts, the techniques of war, and the sciences, as well as the patron of artisans. Along with the spearhead (or arrowhead) associated with Minerva, the company's logo was born.

These efforts were rewarded in 1889 by a bronze medal at the Universal Exposition held in Paris, where the Eiffel Tower was inaugurated. "Villeret," stated the jury's report, "sent a major exhibitor to the Champ-de-Mars [exhibition grounds], who specialized in lever and cylinder keyless winders, set in a wide range of cases."[11] Charles Ivan was thus pursuing his specialty by adapting his winding mechanisms to lever and cylinder movements, and by paying special attention to his cases.

The catalog for the Exposition provides some further information on the development of Robert's products. In what might be considered one of the firm's first known advertisements, Charles Ivan Robert described himself as a "Maker of Timepieces through Mechanical Methods – Interchangeable Movements – Specializing in Lever and Cylinder Keyless Winders – Anti-magnetic Watches."[12] Clearly, his range of watches had grown and adapted to technical developments then underway. Indeed, lever escapements were beginning to unseat the former cylinder escapements, while the anti-magnetic watch was a novelty, being a timepiece that functioned undisturbed in the presence of magnetic fields, which entailed the use of specific metals for the machining of parts and movements. Several other watchmakers in Switzerland, including Vacheron Constantin and Patek Philippe, were working on this development. A significant breakthrough had been made in 1878 by Charles Auguste Paillard, who developed the first balance springs from an anti-magnetic, rustproof alloy of palladium. Charles Ivan Robert quickly appropriated this novel development, managing to add such watches to his range by the late 1880s. His production methods also evolved, incorporating mechanization and a certain standardization of parts (interchangeable movements). Mentioning this fact was also a precocious move for a Saint-Imier Valley watchmaker, because only a few makers were employing mechanized methods in the 1880s and 1890s. At the 1885 Exposition in Antwerp, the jury report nevertheless noted that, concerning watches exhibited by makers from the Neufchâtel and Jura Mountains, "the problem of interchangeability was indeed nearly resolved."[13]

The novelties were accompanied by ever greater mastery of the production of the component parts of a watch: the Ch. Robert and Mercur brands turned out movements, cases, and cuvettes, while the Minerva brand applied to movements, cases, and dials.

The late 1880s was a period of significant development in Robert's production methods, although this did not entail a brutal shift from one mode to another—the adoption of mechanized processes did not radically alter either the organization of labor or the workshop structure. In fact, the size of the company remained modest, never exceeding seven workers. Rather than a real watch factory, the company was still just an advanced form of *comptoir*.

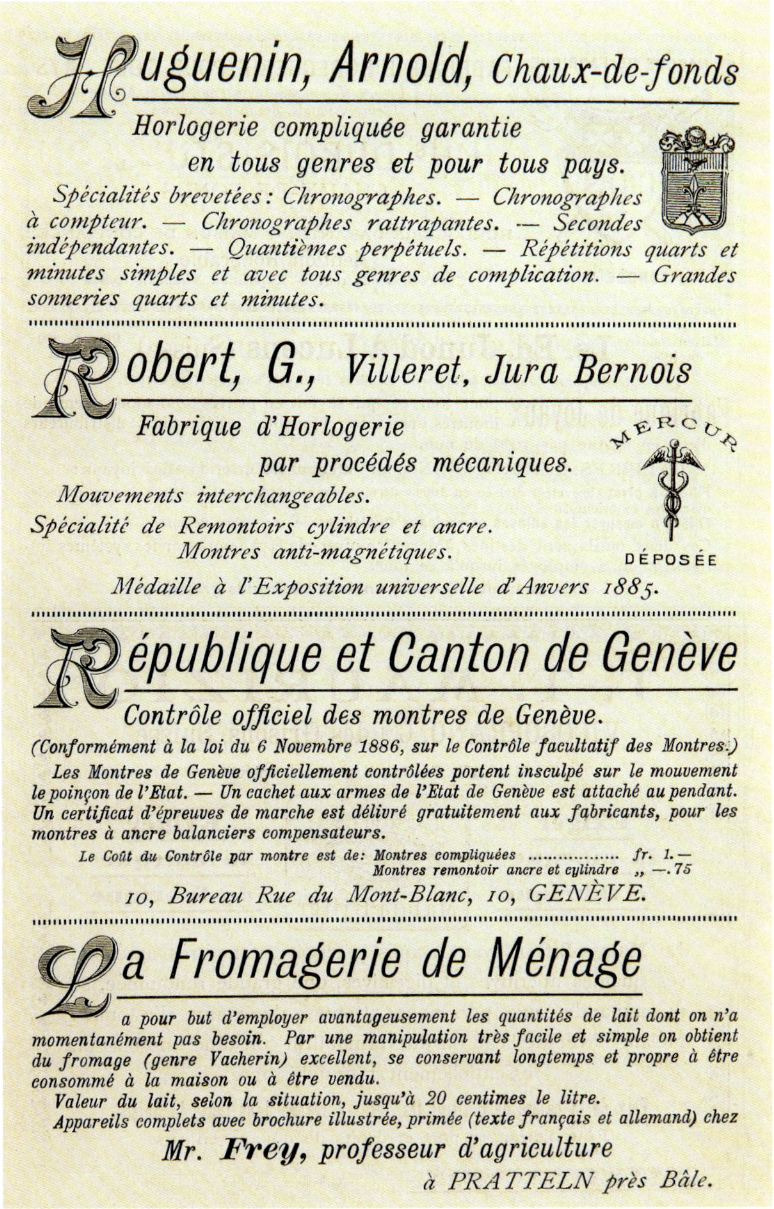

II 150 Years of Watchmaking Tradition in Villeret

Preceding pages

The Corgémont mill in the early twentieth century.

Above

Villeret's main square in 1860, painted by Marc Bourquin.

Left

The first known advertisement of the Robert firm issued in the catalog of the Universal Exposition of 1889 in Paris in 1889. There is a mistake in the initial of the first name.

Following pages

Villeret in 1850.

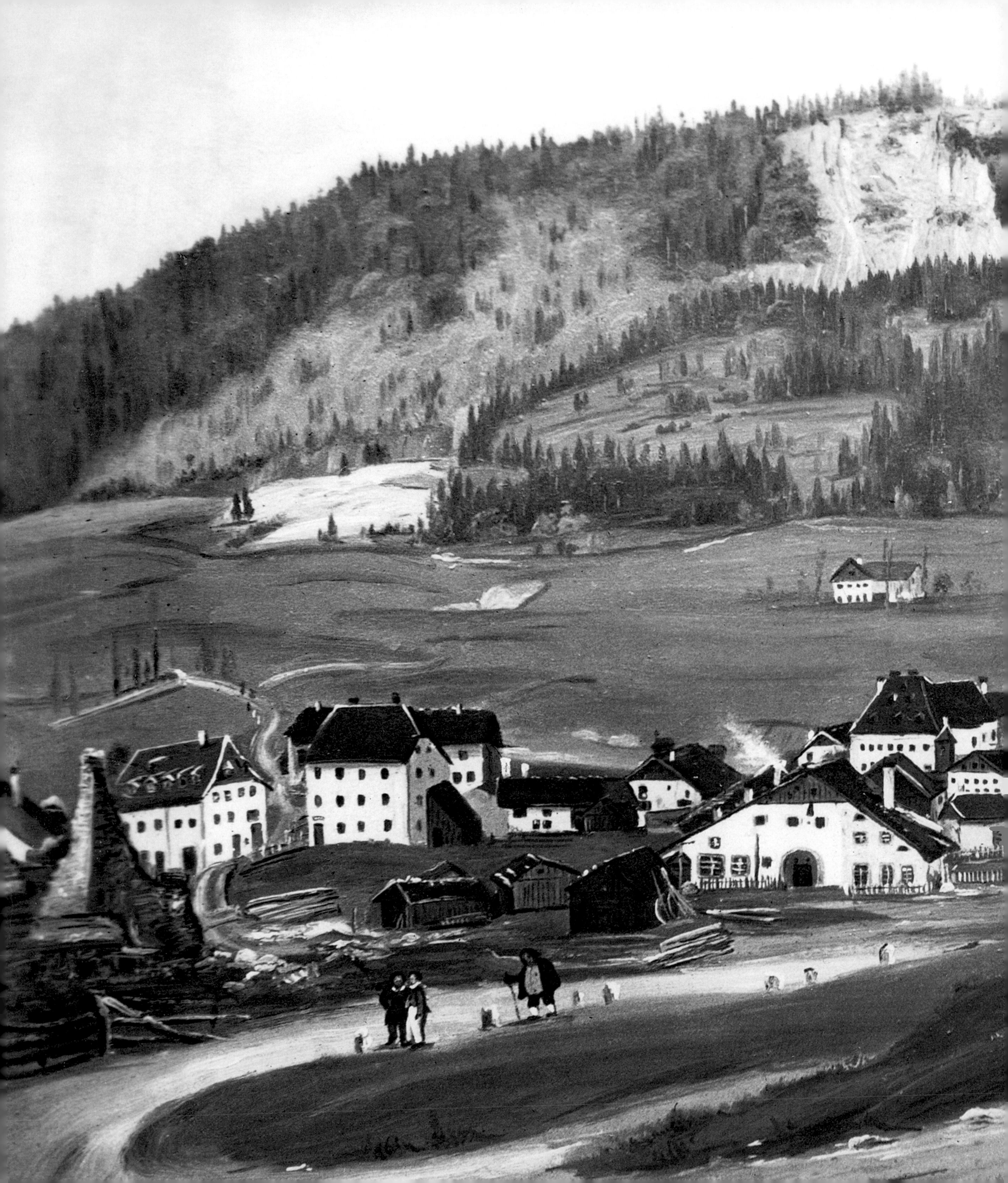

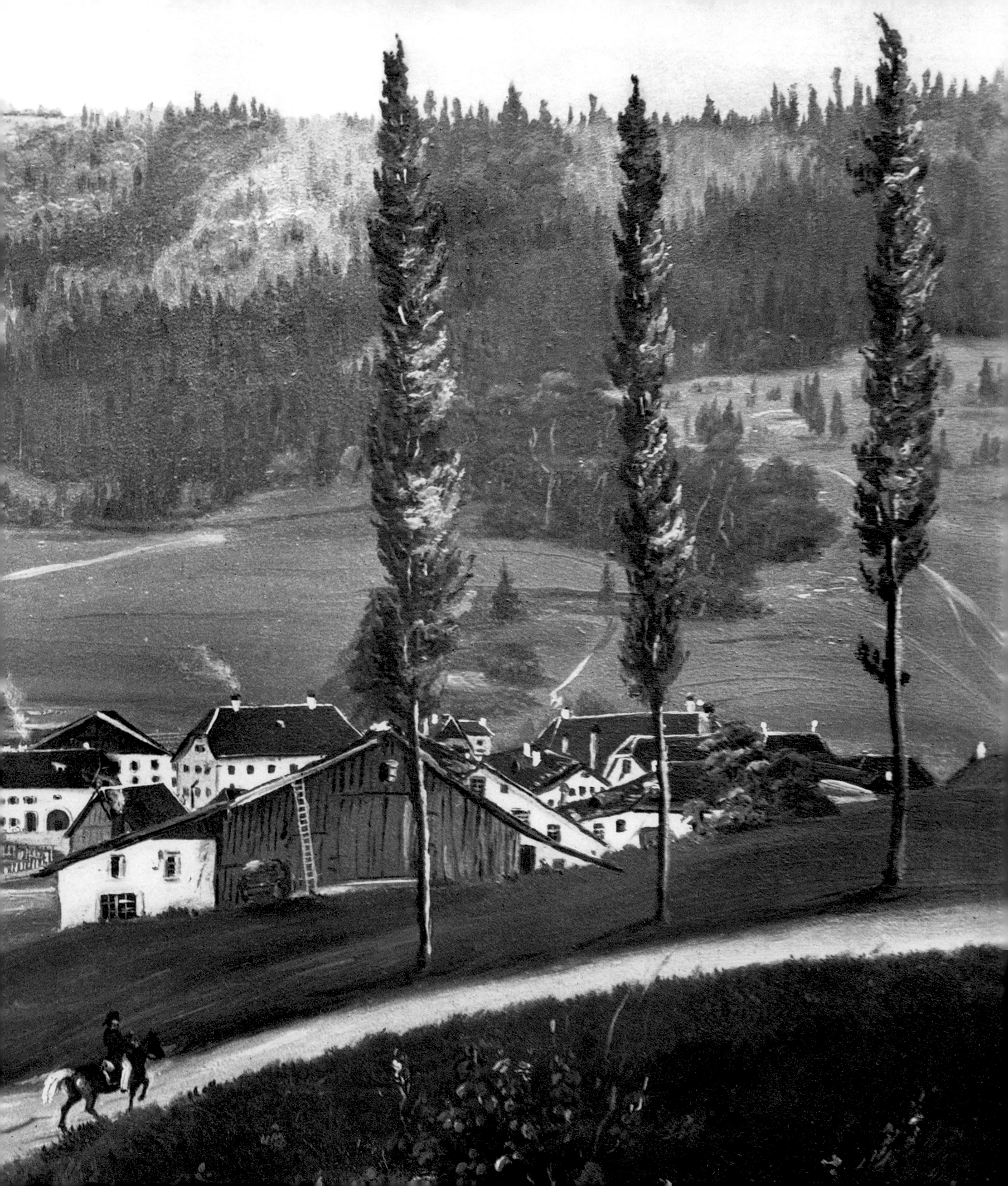

PLAYING A PUBLIC ROLE

In a matter of years, Charles Ivan and Emma Robert's family grew, thanks to the successive births of Charles-Auguste (1865), Cécile (1868), Georges-Louis (1870), Émile (1871), and Ivan (1878). In addition to his status as a well-known watchmaker, head of family, and large landowner (following the death of his mother), Charles Ivan played an increasingly important public role. A member of the city council as early as 1865, in 1873 he became mayor of the town, holding this office until 1889, after which he remained a councilor right up to 1903. His political commitment also extended to the canton level, where he served on the Grand Council for the Canton of Bern from 1875 to 1902. He was apparently a staunch pacifist, in the tradition of Albert Gobat and Élie Ducommun, two Jura men who won the Nobel Peace Prize in 1902. Nor did Charles Ivan Robert ignore social welfare, notably sitting on the board of a hospital in Bern that would later become the cantonal hospital.

Charles Ivan and his family thus reflected the spirit of the new watchmaking bourgeoisie that emerged throughout the region in the latter half of the nineteenth century. This bourgeoisie was active on every level, becoming involved in economic, political, and social issues, assuming decision-making responsibilities in all these spheres, and thus having a real impact on local and regional life.

Right

Charles Ivan Robert and Emma Robert-Blancpain.

Facing page

Family reunion at La Cibourg in 1889.

Following pages

Country picnic in Villeret, 1900.

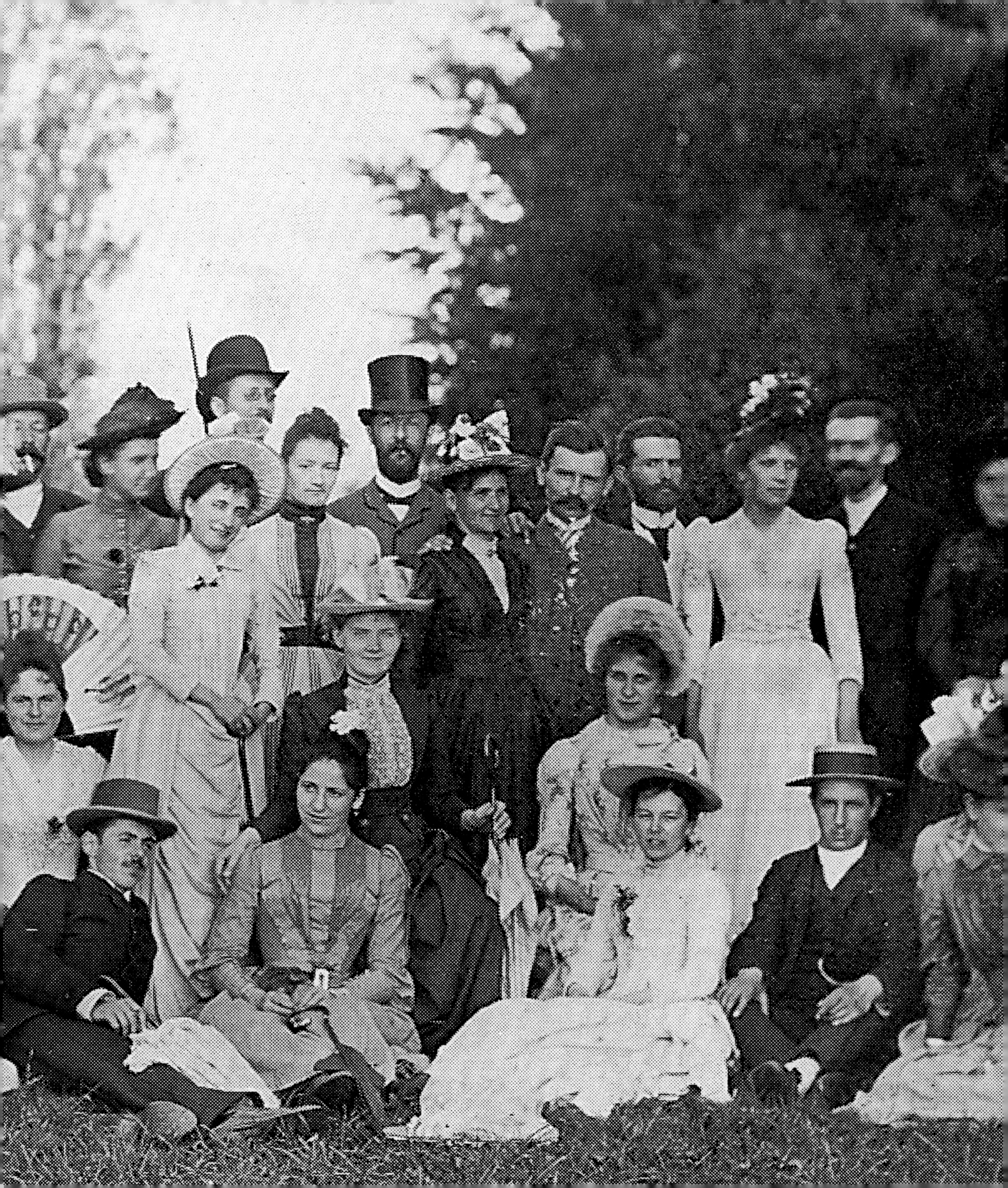

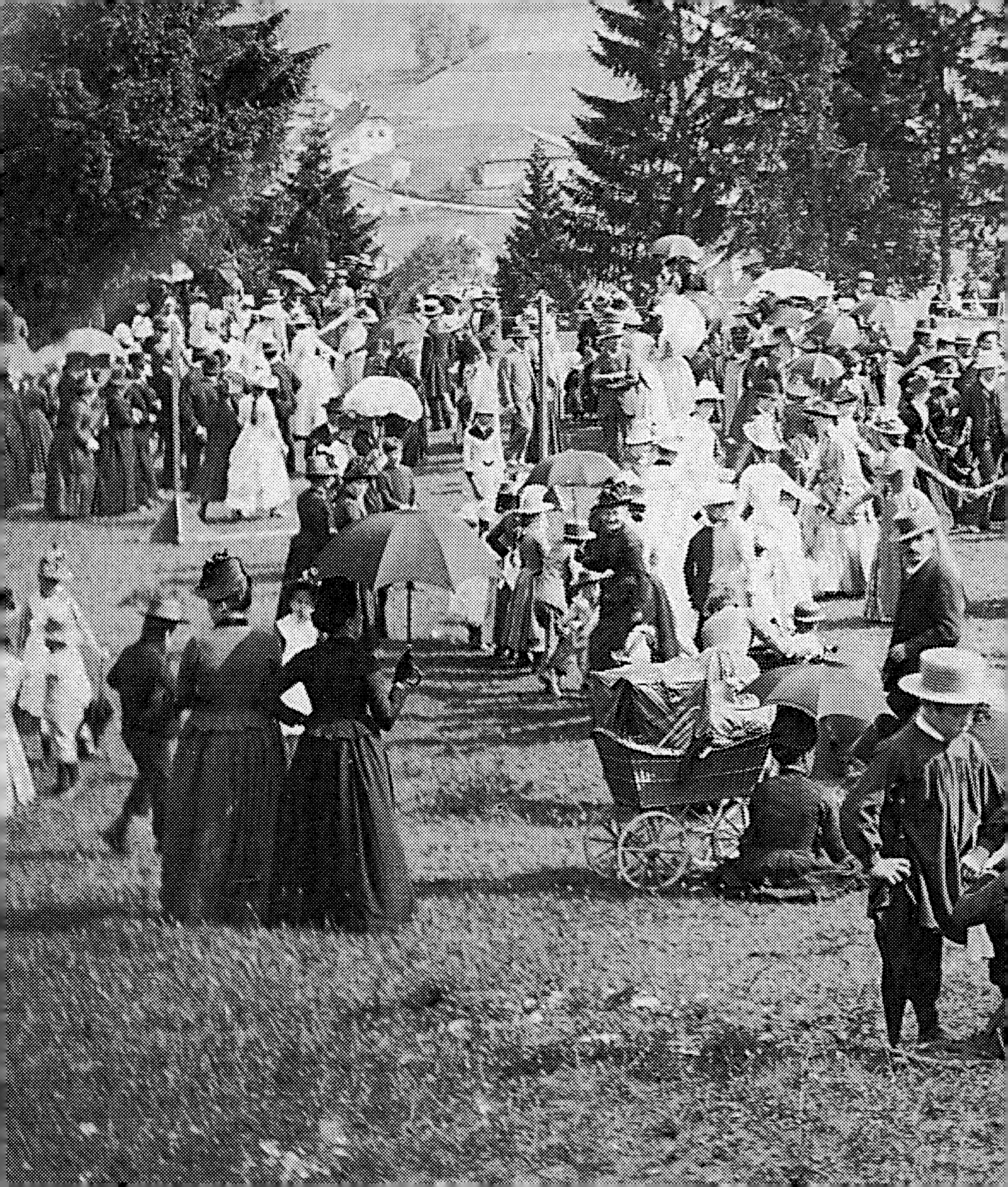

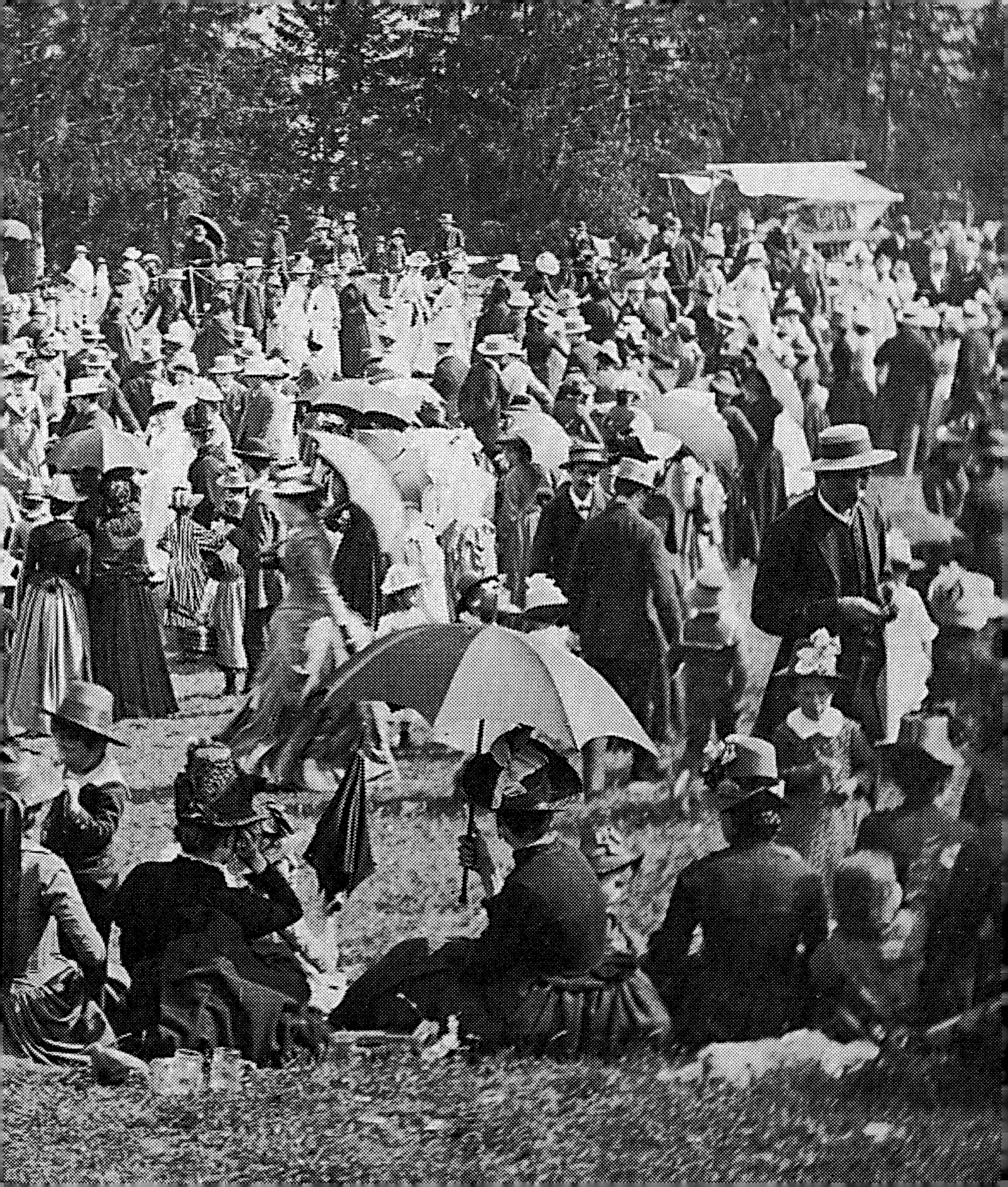

WATCHMAKING

Starting in the late 1890s, the Robert firm was marked by further developments. Charles Ivan's sons officially joined the company, steadily taking over from their father, who nevertheless remained present until his death in 1912. Their stake in the firm was enhanced in two stages: first with the transformation of the company into a collective identity, "Robert Frères" (Robert Brothers), on February 1, 1898, when Charles Auguste and Georges Louis assumed its management; and then in 1902 when Ivan, the youngest brother, was taken on board and the name was changed once again to "Fabrique des Faverges Robert Frères" (Robert Brothers Manufacturing, Les Faverges).[14]

The official handing over of the firm to the next generation included, in 1901, Charles Ivan's sale to the company of the houses built in 1875 with their accompanying land, Charles Ivan himself having bought up all the land from Eugène Vuilleumier in 1893. The changes of company name and the sale of properties henceforth made the company independent of the private family estate and endowed it with the potential for growth.

Since Charles-Auguste remained a bachelor, Georges-Louis seemed to be his father's natural successor on both the corporate and social levels. He married Lucie Fanny L'Épée (whose possible connection with the L'Épée factory in Sainte-Suzanne, Franche Comté, has not been authenticated). In 1914, two years after his father died, Georges-Louis followed in his footsteps by running for a place on the Villeret town council.

Above

The Robert brothers motoring along the hills of the Mont-Soleil in 1905.

Right

Ivan Robert in 1900, two years before he joined the company, and Georges-Louis Robert.

Facing page

The three Robert brothers on Villeret's main square in 1909 (behind the wheel, Georges-Louis, on his right Charles-Auguste, on his left Ivan).

160

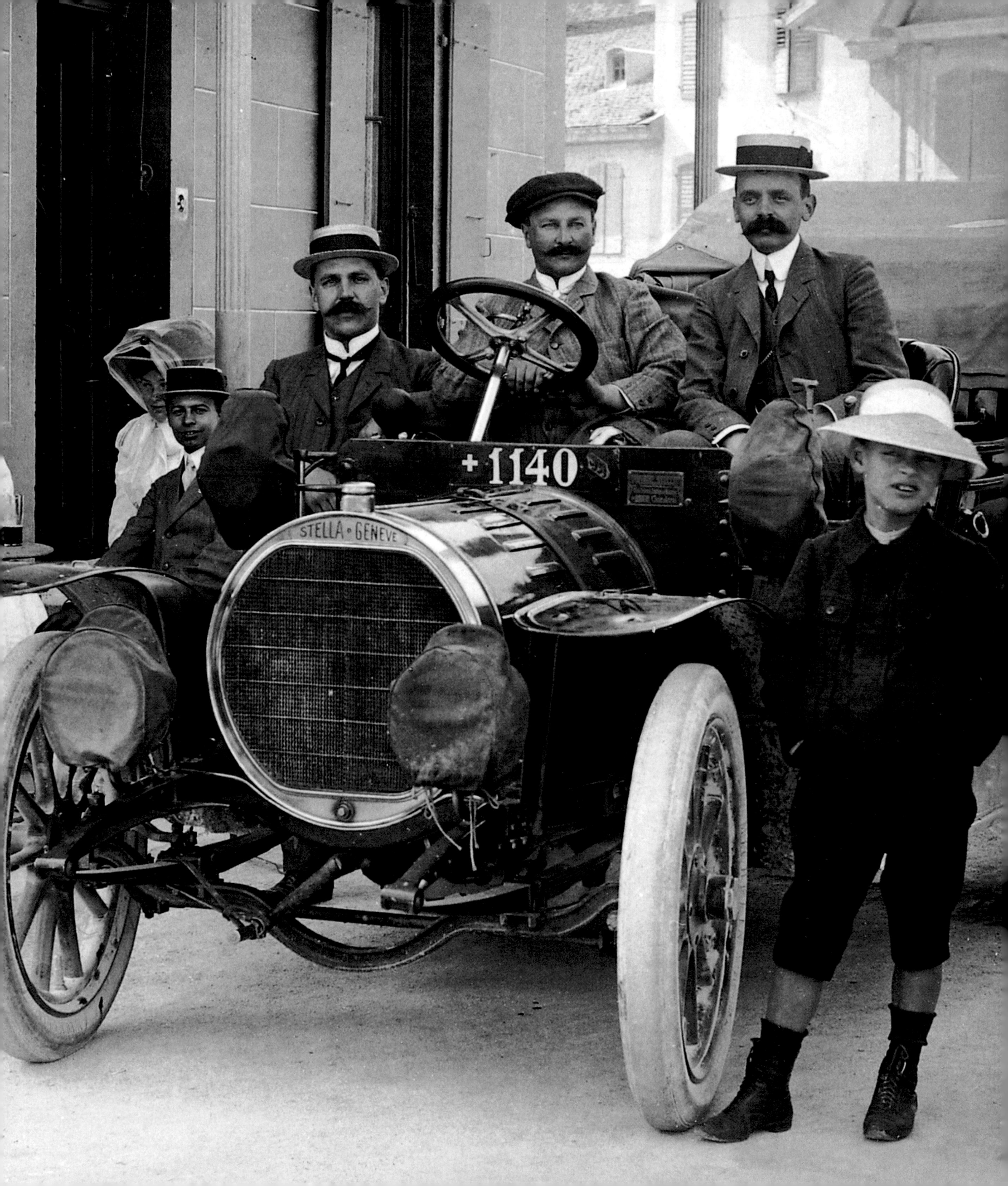
+1140
STELLA GENEVE

THE BIRTH OF A *MANUFACTURE*

The accession of the third generation to positions of management marked a key turning point for the company. First of all, the most striking change was probably the Robert brothers' development of their first in-house movement, an 18-*ligne* caliber movement with cylinder escapement, designed for a pocket watch. Official production of the caliber began in 1902, which gave the firm the glamorous status of a *manufacture,* a term in the Swiss watch industry referring to a company that makes watches almost in their entirety, as opposed to the dispersed, specialized workshops that supply an *établisseur*. The Robert firm has retained this status right up to the present, which furthermore enabled it to remain independent of the consolidation underway in the making of ébauches, which ultimately resulted in the founding of the company called Ébauches, S.A., in 1926.

The change in name also clearly pointed to another major transformation of the company: Charles Ivan's sons completed the step he had tentatively begun, namely turning the commercial agency (*comptoir*) into a factory. This transformation entailed both the addition of new operations (notably the making of ébauches) and the mechanization of various processes. The plant henceforth included workshops for making ébauches and cases as well as setting and gilding the movements.[15]

The transition to a factory operation required a complete renovation of the buildings. In 1902 a new extension was built eastward, very soon followed by a second one, westward. The plant then acquired the overall appearance it retains today, divided into three parts: a central building that houses offices and residences, with two wings that contain the respective workshops.

Even if the company was still a long way from effecting every single stage of production in-house, the Robert brothers' company was clearly no longer a *comptoir*. In 1902, for the first time, an employees' ledger was begun, a sign that production had outstripped the family context. The first worker listed in the ledger had been hired in 1895. Watchmaking in Villeret, as in the rest of the valley, was undergoing consolidation, marked by the closure of many workshops and *comptoirs*. By 1913, the village hosted just six watchmakers (three of which were factory operations) and forty-three specialist workshops,[16] less than half the number there in 1900. Consolidation did not affect every stage of production equally, however. Small or home workshops still remained the rule for a certain number of jobs that escaped mechanization: the workshops listed in 1913 notably included six steel and screw polishers, six timers, and four assemblers. The extremely dense network typical of the late nineteenth century had thinned, but had not been completely replaced by factories. These latter, in fact, generally remained small—Robert Frères had scarcely more than twenty employees at first, which hardly led to a complete revolution in working methods. Instead, it was more a question of centralizing the main tasks in a single plant, rather than altering the tasks themselves. The Robert Brothers' plant in Les Faverges was a typical feature of the industrial landscape of the Jura Mountains at the time: a factory on a human scale, whose emergence was part of a progressive evolution from the original infrastructures.

These transformations were accompanied by the development of new products. The decision to make ébauches in-house triggered an extremely fertile period in terms of technical creativity. Once the first movement was developed, another ten or so followed in the years 1902–08, including a series of calibers for chronographs and stopwatches that heralded the firm's future specialty. The main research still bore on pocket watches with cylinder or lever escapements, in Lépine and hunter models of varying quality. One of the most meticulously made timepieces of that period, which led to a whole series of other calibers, was the number 3 pocket watch with lever escapement and 19-*ligne* caliber movement.[17] But Robert Frères also moved into another type of product—as early as 1909 (the same time as Longines) the firm developed its first caliber for wristwatches, which were just then coming into widespread use.

Finally, Robert Frères attempted to protect the knowledge on which they had built the firm's reputation by filing several patents, including one for a winding and time-setting mechanism in 1903, and others for dials in 1905 and 1906.

These technical innovations were matched by several marketing moves, including the launch of new brand names. In 1898 the Hertha brand was registered (sometimes spelled Herta), alluding to a fertility goddess in Germanic mythology. That same year, two non-mythological brand names were registered in the name of the fourth Robert brother, Émile: Ariana and Tropic, the former alluding to the moon, the latter to the sun, both being translated into Chinese. The planets and geography thus entered the company's expanding frames of reference.

In 1902, the Ariana brand was bought by Robert Frères, which also added the Faverges & Villeret Watch name to its list, not to mention new versions of its Mercur and Minerva lines. In 1905 the Faverges and Ariana brands were merged when a moon was added to the Faverges logo. The following year, Robert Frères registered the Rhenus brand (Latin for Rhine). In 1909 the company took over the Tropic brand and in 1911 launched the RFV line (Robert Frères Villeret), whose logo once again featured Minerva's arrowhead. Finally, in 1909 and 1912 two further brands were registered, Adler and Bahnzeit. The firm thus boasted over a dozen brand lines covering not only watches themselves but also watch parts, cases, and packaging.

II 150 Years of Watchmaking Tradition in Villeret

Above

The new neighbourhood of the Rue Neuve (left). Picture taken in 1965.

Following pages

The Minerva *manufacture* 1905 with the Suze in the foreground, the family house, the garden and annexes behind the trees, and the *manufacture* in the background.

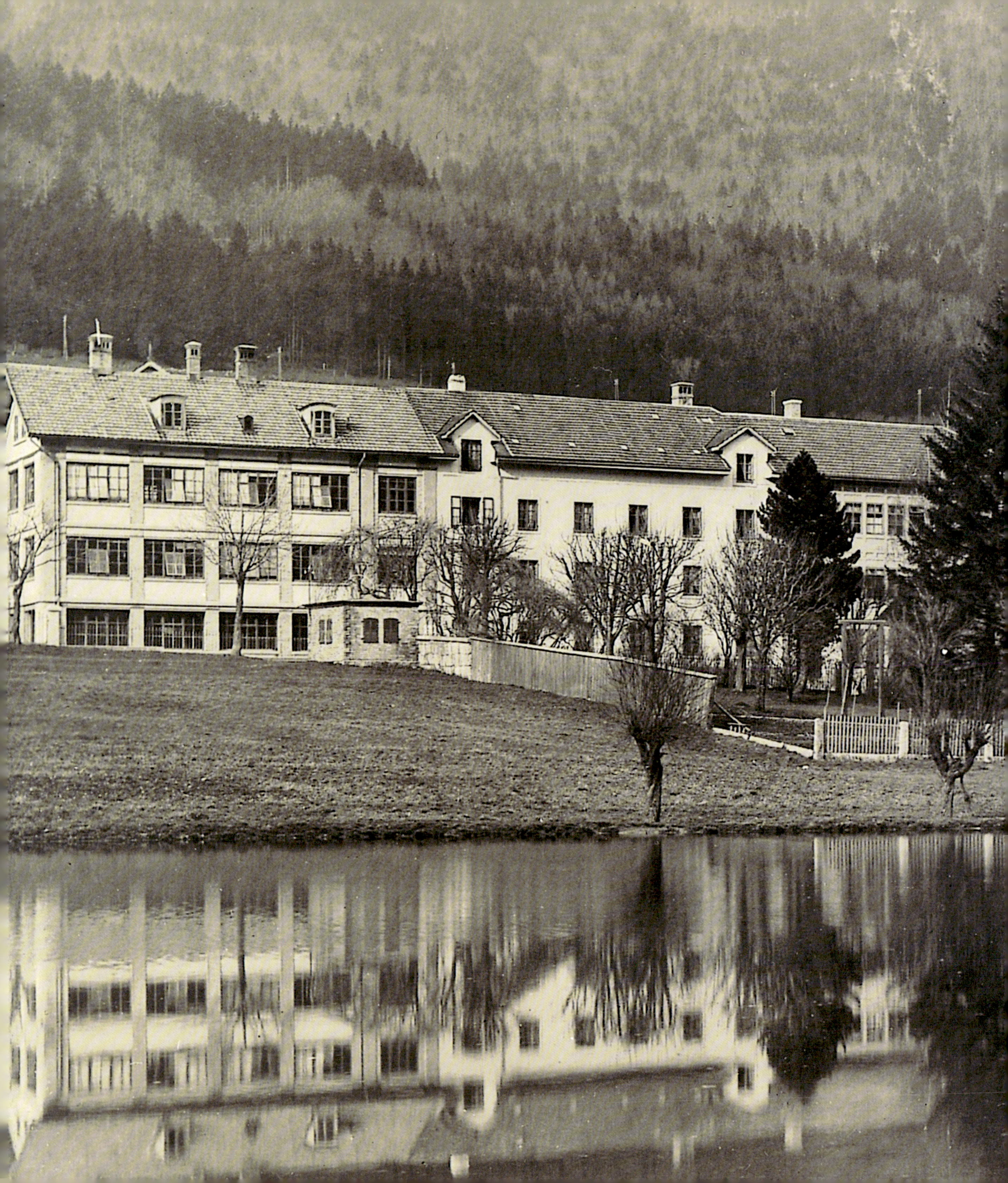

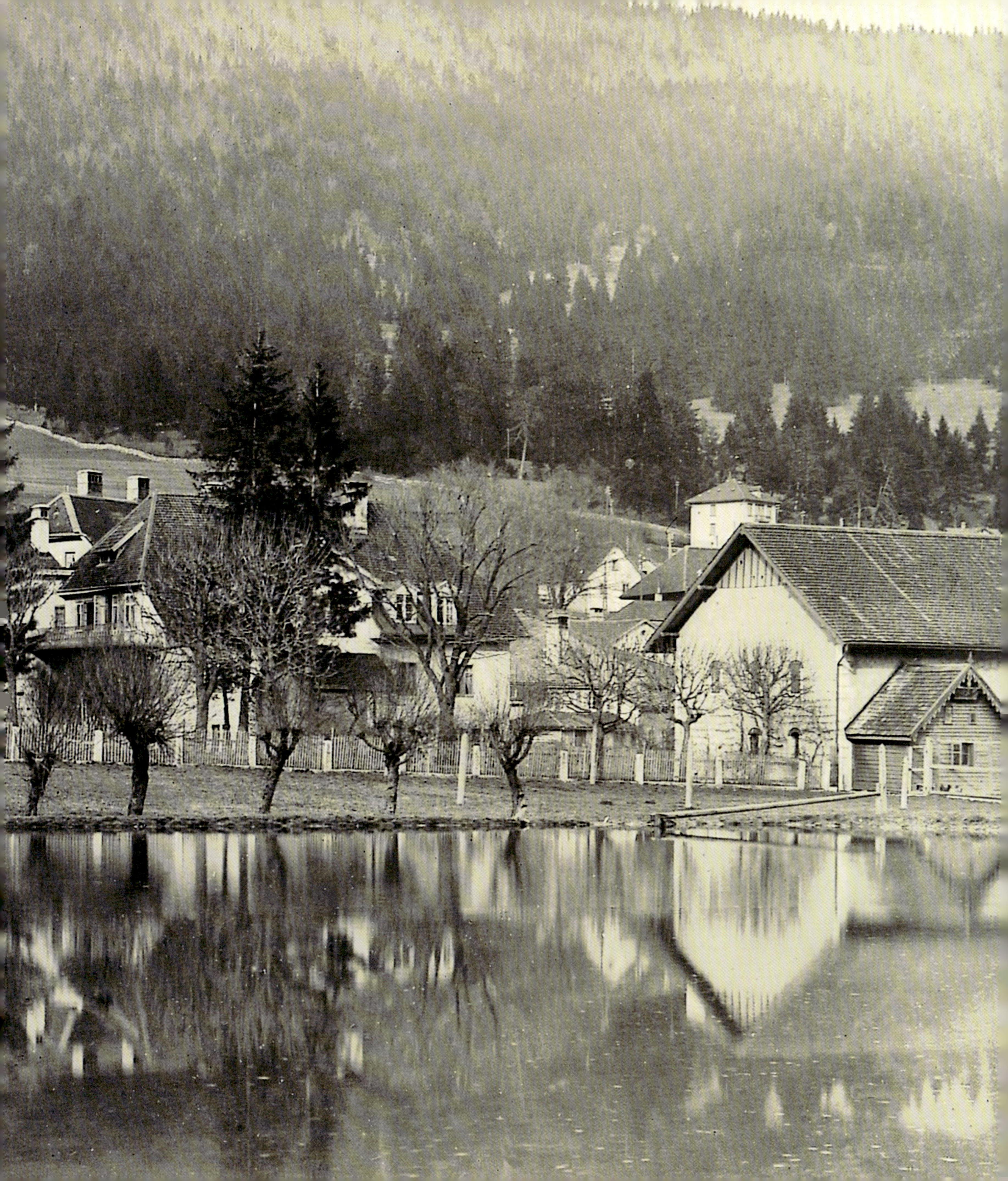

This plethora of brand names—which did not have the image impact they enjoy today—was typical of watchmaking at the time. Multiplying the number of brands made it possible to adapt to different markets and to underscore the variety of models available. In this instance, the brands behind the models produced by Robert Frères were above all aimed at one market, Germany, which explains their Germanic overtones. An advertisement of 1900 confirms this policy by referring to the firm's "German-style specialties in gold and silver. Merkur, Hertha, and Minerva brands." A question nevertheless still exists over the Adler and Bahnzeit brand names, which already belonged to famous businesses, namely the Adler jewelry shop in Istanbul and the Bahnzeit watchmaker. Were the Robert brothers making watches for these firms? The answer remains unclear. But ads for the year 1915 referred to the making of "special calibers for monopolies," which suggests that Robert Frères was exploiting what would be called the "private label" sector today, namely producing movements for other brands.

The company prospected for new markets in addition to Germany, its leading customer base. For several years Émile Robert served as Robert Frères' agent in Singapore, the launching pad for the Asian market. The registering of brand names in Chinese testifies to these efforts, which appear to have met with mixed results. According to Kathleen H. Pritschard, the New York-based company A. Wittnauer, the main American distributor of the Longines brand, also carried Robert watches from the early years of the twentieth century.[18] This move probably explains the emergence of a brand name with an English ring, Villeret Watch. Although such deliveries clearly testify to a desire to expand the client base beyond Europe, it would be several years before these early efforts made a significant impact on the company.

166

A FERTILE TRANSITION

Even as the Robert Frères company changed dramatically between 1900 and 1910, the foundations for even more significant developments were apparently being laid.

Charles-Auguste, the eldest of the Robert brothers, died in 1911, aged about fifty. The running of the company fell to two other brothers, Georges-Louis and Ivan, following the death of their father, Charles Ivan, in 1912 and their mother, Emma, the next year. Pursuing already successful developments, the brothers further diversified production and embraced new technical challenges such as developing calibers for pocket stopwatches and chronographs and new calibers for wristwatches. Although ads in 1913 were still focusing on pocket watches, five years later they were vaunting Minerva chronographs, stopwatches, and other sports timing devices, as well as tachometers and pulsometers. A new step was taken in the direction of diversification and accuracy when the *manufacture* of chronometric measuring instruments became a powerful feature of the Robert company, marking its difference and complementarity with respect to other watchmakers in Villeret, notably the Blancpain firm that began specializing in small wristwatches. The annual output of the Robert Frères factory then amounted to roughly thirty thousand timepieces per year, yielding annual revenues of five hundred to six hundred thousand francs.[19]

Georges-Louis died in turn in 1918, aged forty-eight. Ivan alone remained at the helm, with no male heir to assist him. As was the practice at the time, he turned to one of his employees, Georges Umiker—the firm's long-time accountant and a close friend of the family—and set up a partnership that same year. The firm then became an incorporated company (*Société Anonyme,* abbreviated S.A.) known as "Fabrique des Faverges, Robert Frères, S.A." The board of directors included Ivan Robert (executive director), Georges-Louis's widow (Lucie Robert-L'Épée), and Umiker, named general manager.

Unstable markets created conditions that were hardly favorable to the new undertaking. Despite these difficulties, two new initiatives were taken that would play a key role in the future of the company. First, the corporate name was changed in 1923 to officially include a reference to Minerva, previously reserved for chronographs and stopwatches; the new name was "Fabrique d'Horlogerie Minerva, Robert Frères, S.A." Next, during these postwar years, the most complicated movements in Minerva's history were developed: a split-seconds stopwatch in 1924 and a wrist-chronograph in 1923. This latter caliber, developed in

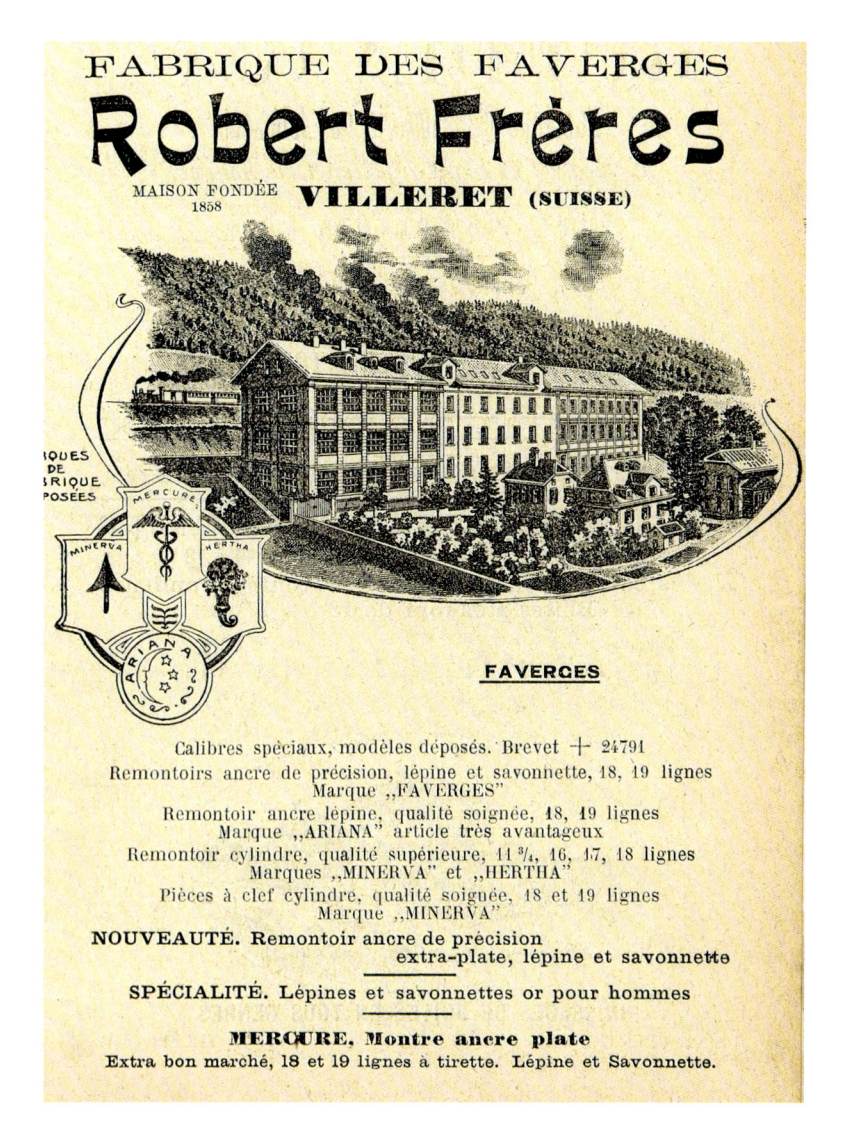

Above

Fabrique des Faverges Robert Frères advertisement, 1906.

Facing page

The assemblers' workshop (1939–1940).

conjunction with the Dubois-Dépraz company from the Joux Valley, remains one of the company's most significant products. It symbolized the level of mastery reached by the firm's horologists and consolidated its reputation in the manufacture of stopwatches and chronographs.

Despite these successes, the partnership between Ivan Robert and Georges Umiker did not produce the desired results. On the family level, Ivan seemed to have a hard time getting over the death of Georges-Louis, and he began making plans to leave the area—especially since other members of the family had already taken this step. In late 1928 the decision was finally made, and Ivan and Lucie handed the management of the company over to a new board of directors composed of Umiker, his own son Georges René, and a Villeret merchant, Paul-Arnold Schmidt. Ivan left the valley for Geneva, where he founded the Jean Richard brand of watches.

With the departure of the Robert family, the company name changed once again. In 1929 it became the "Fabrique d'Horlogerie Minerva, S.A." (Minerva Watchmaking Factory, Inc.). The new management seemed to follow in the footsteps of the earlier one, notably in the realms of technical innovation and diversification. Indeed, the new managers filed several patents: for a hunter watch, for a sports stopwatch, and even for a counting device for billiards. The takeover occurred just prior to the effects of the stock-market crash of 1929. Just then a certain Charles Haussener displayed an interest in the company. Information on Haussener is patchy, but we know he was born in 1888, apparently in the Madretsch neighborhood of Biel, where his family lived and where he spent his teenage years. He received a technical education, probably in mechanics, and in 1919 arrived in Villeret where documents indicate that he managed the production of ébauches.

Since Haussener did not have sufficient funds to acquire the company, he approached one of the firm's employees, Jacques Pelot. Son of François Pelot, a horologist who worked for Blancpain,[20] Jacques was born in Villeret in 1887. He followed in his father's footsteps, and studied at the Saint-Imier school of horology from 1903 to 1906, acquiring an education that, at the time, was reserved for an elite. In 1917 Pelot left Villeret for Turin, where he worked in the weapons industry. He returned to his home village in 1919, the same year as Haussener, and two years later was hired by Robert Frères.

On June 12, 1935, ébauche manager Haussener and horologist Pelot signed a notarial act of purchase of the entire company for the sum of 140,000 francs. The takeover led to yet another change of name: the "Sport" in "Fabrique d'Horlogerie Minerva Sport, S.A.," immediately signaled the direction the new company would take. Share capital of sixty thousand francs was equally divided between the two partners.

Haussener soon emerged as the key player in the firm. He was named chairman of the board of directors and above all handled the commercial side of things, whereas Pelot was active on the technical side.

Above

Charles Haussener and Jacques Pelot in 1935.

Facing page

Fabrique des Faverges Robert Frères advertisement, 1920.

JURA BERNOIS

Horlogerie de Précision
Procédés mécaniques les plus perfectionnés
FABRIQUE DES FAVERGES
Robert Frères

Maison fondée en 1858 — **VILLERET** (Suisse) — Maison fondée en 1858

Marques de Fabrique déposées :

**MINERVA - FAVERGES - MERCURE - ARIANA
BAHNZEIT - HERTHA**

Montres ancre et cylindre, **qualité soignée**, en tous genres
et pour tous pays

Calibres Spéciaux pour Monopoles

Spécialités :

CHRONOGRAPHE COMPTEUR
COMPTEUR OR, Argent Plaqué Niel, Métal DE SPORT
„MINERVA"

Chronographe simple — Cylindre et Ancre
Lépine et Savonnette — 18-20 lignes
- Tachymètres - — - Pulsomètres -

Montres Or 11-22 lignes, Qualité extra-soignée
Réglage de Précision — *Prix très avantageux* — Mouvements négatifs 16 size

Top

Technical office and prototypes with Jacques Pelot in the foreground (1939).

Above

Time measurement at the beginning of the men's downhill ski run. Start time, sector time and finish time were measured very accurately, as the records of the organisation committee of the IV Winter Olympic Games prove.

STABILIZING BUSINESS

The year Haussener and Pelot bought it, the company posted modest profits of three thousand francs. As this figure grew steadily (reaching over 120,000 francs during the Second World War), the firm got back to an even keel. It first made a splash in the athletic sphere by winning the timing contract for the 1936 winter Olympic Games held at Garmisch-Partenkirchen, followed by other competitive sports in the fields of car and horse racing. By then business rested on two pillars: the production of standard watches on the one hand, and on chronographs, stopwatches, and measuring instruments on the other. This strategy would prove highly valuable in the future.

Between 1930 and 1934, even before buying the firm, the highly creative Pelot had explored various directions of research leading to several patents. Jean-Jacques Frey mentions Pelot's development of a clasp system for a hunter watch that rewound the barrel spring, as well as the replacing of flat springs by helical springs, and in 1934 he was also responsible for the design of automatic timers that measured the flying time of an airplane.[21] Pelot continued his research even after becoming head of the company, notably filing a patent for a split-seconds stopwatch in 1937. In 1940 Pelot's nephew, André Frey, became a shareholder in the firm, followed by two of Haussener's sons-in-law, Charles Endters in 1941 (who remained with the company for only a few years) and Maurice Favre in 1945–46. The arrival of these young men reflected a desire to swiftly involve the next generation in the running of the business.

Initially, Frey took over from Pelot in the technical sphere. As reported by Frey's son, Jean-Jacques, he modernized existing calibers (considered to be outmoded) and accelerated the introduction of new technology, which favored interchangeability. He also developed new calibers, some of whose parts and mechanisms were patented.

On the Haussener side, Charles Endters took over the marketing operations and was named a senior executive in 1943, alongside André Frey. Meanwhile, Maurice Favre, who had married Lily Haussener, joined the business as ébauche production manager. Frey and Favre swiftly climbed the ladder of responsibility, being named general managers in 1948 and joining the board of directors four years later. Thus the second generation, after having earned its stripes in the operational sector, increasingly took over senior management.

Although the organization of responsibilities, skills, and succession seemed well established when the war ended in 1945, the retirement of Charles Endters in 1951 and the death of Charles Haussener in 1952 led to a minor upheaval. André Frey, who had been technical director up till then, took over management of the marketing sphere, while the shares of the Haussener family were divided among Charles's widow Alice, his daughter Lily, and his son-in-law Maurice Favre. Research henceforth focused on instruments of measurement, thanks to Favre as technical director, who developed a model of curvometer, a tool used by architects to measure distances on plans.

OPTING FOR QUALITY

Like all businesses at that time, Minerva was obliged to rethink the organization of its means of production. From the early 1950s, Favre's reports to the board of directors reflected this concern. Minerva began a process of steady rationalization from 1950 into the late 1960s—complete renovations were carried out on buildings, production workshops, installations, and machines. Assembly workshops were revamped and jewel-setting equipment was purchased. In 1957, all the lathes were replaced by new, individually controlled machines. A compressed air system and new heating system were also installed.

These renovations were matched on the technical level by a move toward a certain standardization (of dies and bezels) and a reduction in the size of dials, as well as by the quest for constant production improvements (experiments in hot-stamping ébauches, improvement and changes in machine tools, etc.).

These authentic moves toward rationalization, however, did not go so far as automatic, production-line assembly with sophisticated machines. Nor were they designed to succumb to the lure of an apparently insatiable market. "There was never any question of going into mass production," pointed out Monique Beck-Favre. Instead, as André Frey stressed, the goal was "to supply high quality products at a reasonable cost."[22] Minerva opted for a steady process of adaptation and improvement in the quality of its products rather than a complete upheaval of its working methods. The company thereby remained faithful to a measured, moderate spirit of modernization that sought to preserve traditional skills and know-how.

Top

The ébauches workshop (1940–1945).

Above

Minerva celebrates the new company's tenth anniversary in 1945.

Following pages

Formula 1 race at Reims in 1966. Minerva was the official timekeeper of the competition.

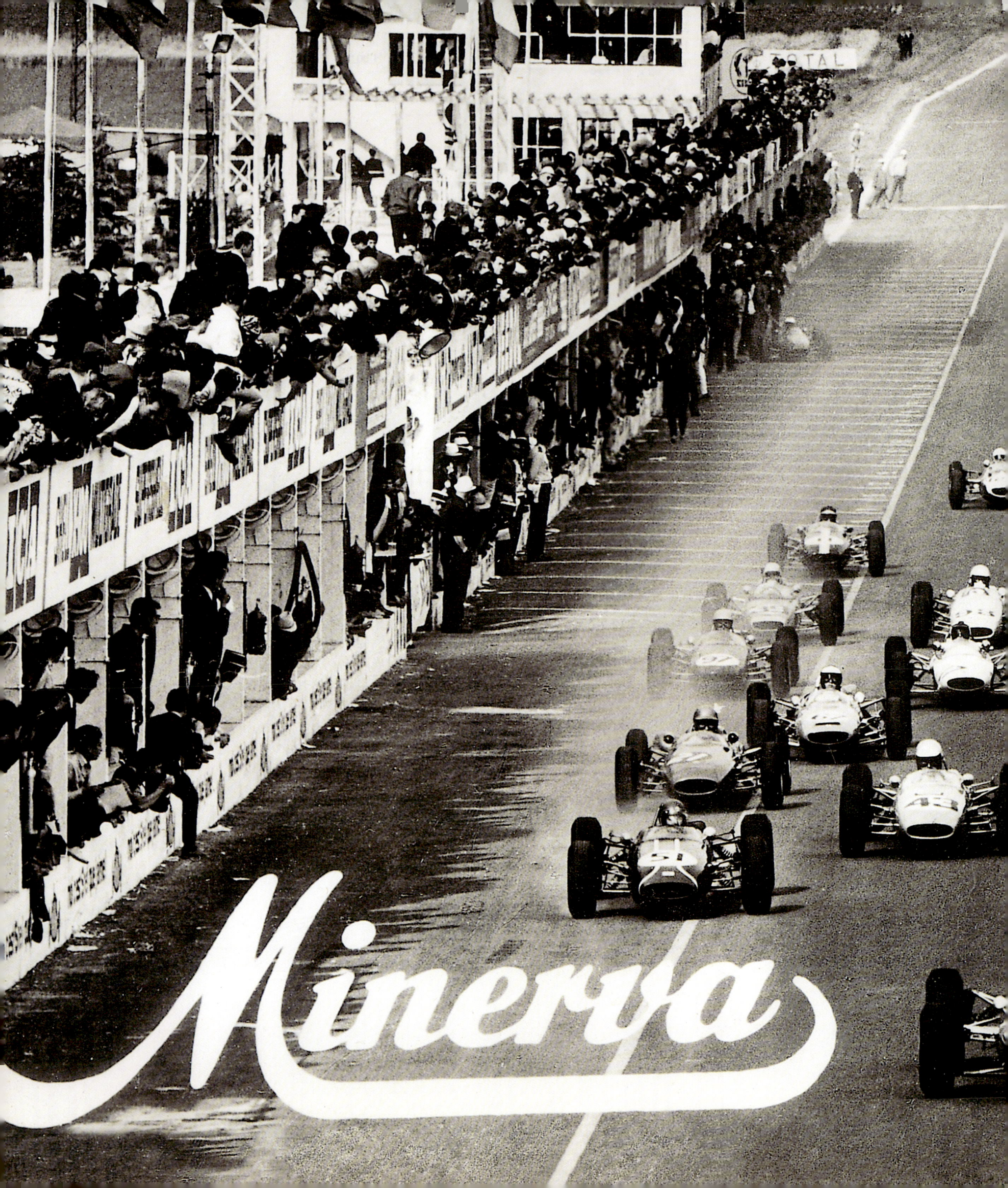
TOTAL
Minerva

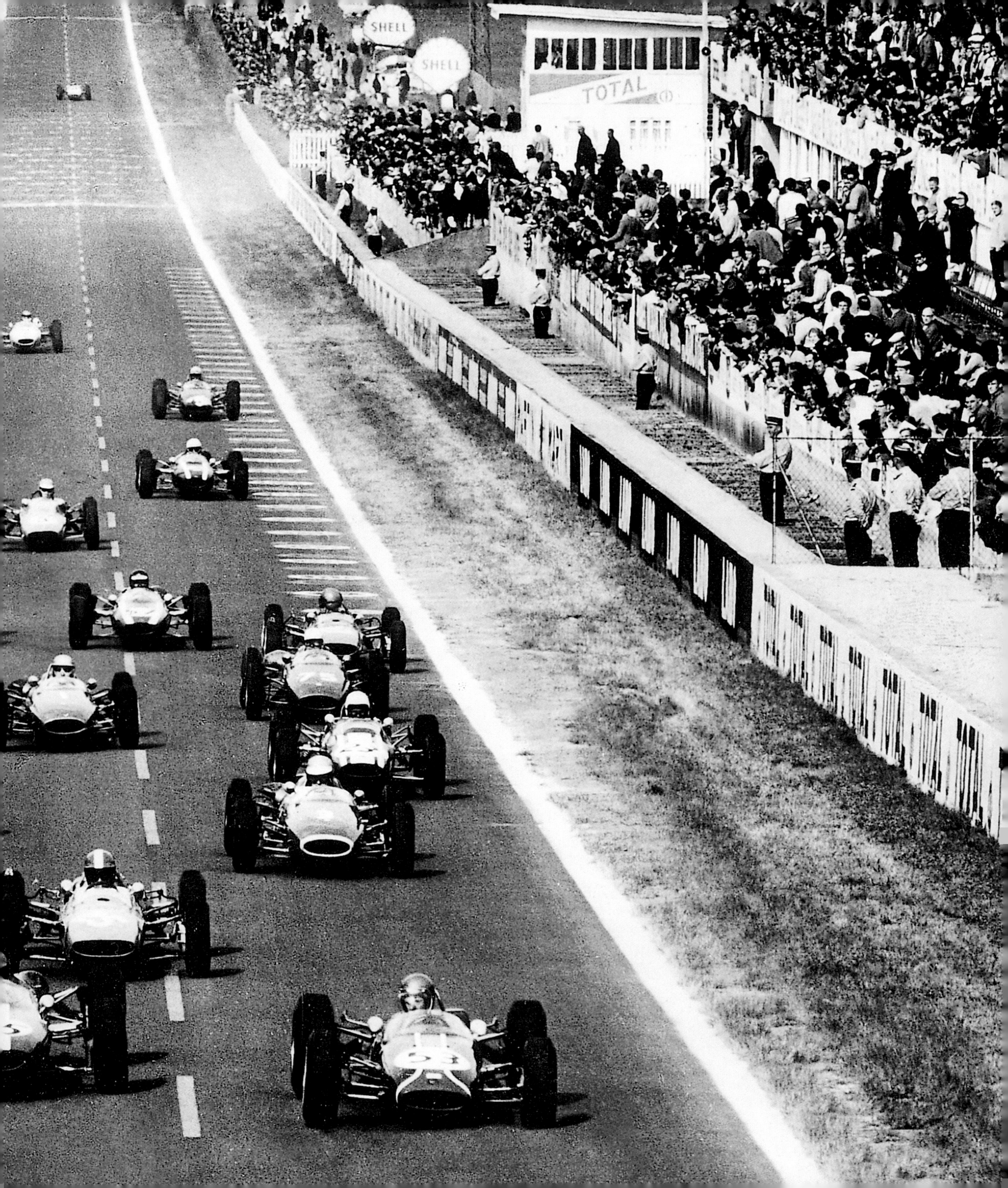
SHELL
SHELL
TOTAL

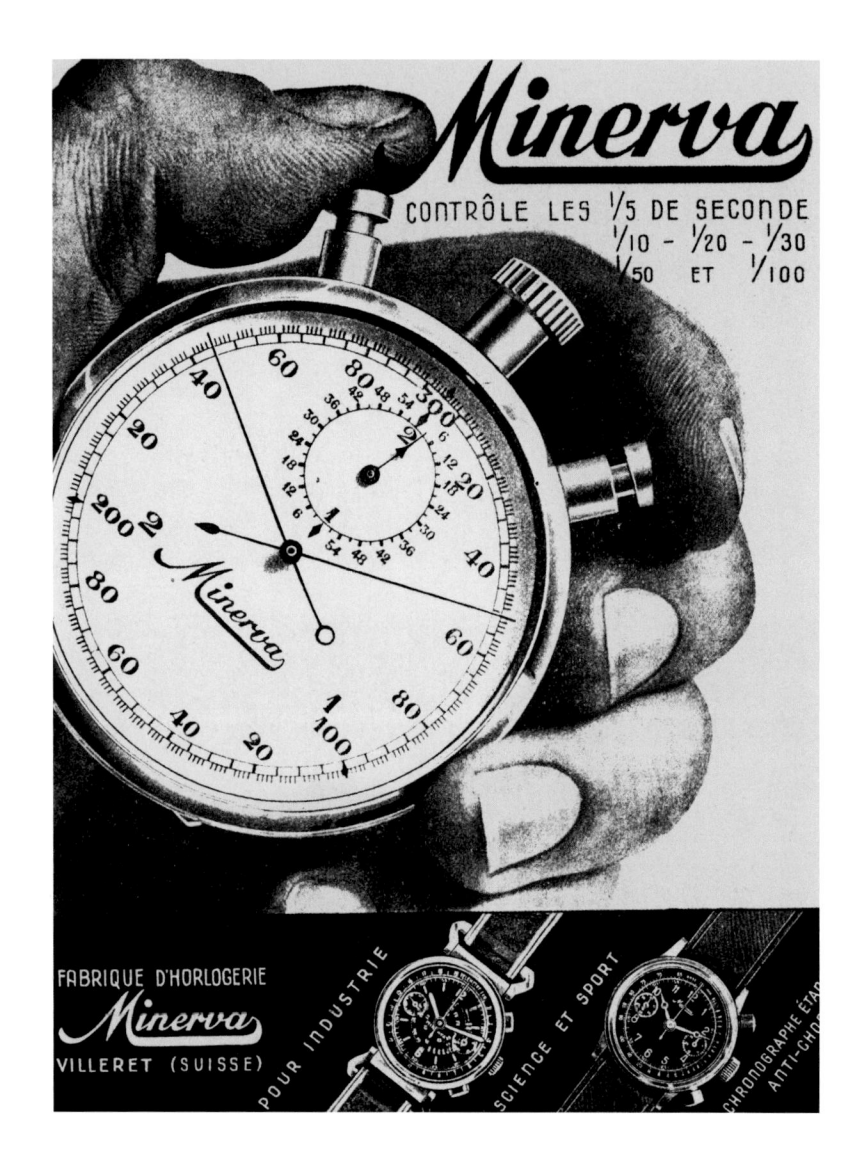

Above
Minerva advertisement, 1964.

GOING IT ALONE

By the late 1950s the Swiss horological industry was showing signs of consolidation, designed to favor expansion and the rationalization of production resources. This trend was also designed to keep costs down, especially salary costs. In Villeret, the Blancpain firm was acquired by a holding company, the Société Suisse pour l'Industrie Horlogère (SSIH), in the early 1960s, while the Lavina (Brack) business was sold to Favre-Leuba. Minerva decided to buck this trend, as recorded in a report to shareholders. "Although a company of modest size, operating in a fashion contrary to all the distinguished economists who advocate consolidation, Minerva, S.A. continues to report favorable end-of-year results with steadily increasing revenues and profits that also increase proportionally."[23] Minerva was thus one of few businesses in the region to retain its independence into the 1990s.

Its corporate structure, financing, shareholding, and management also remained firmly family-based. The constant presence of both families at all levels favored great stability, notably in the handing on of management responsibilities, as well as in the constant monitoring of the evolution of the company and its skills. Even though Minerva was a publicly incorporated company, its shareholders were not concerned primarily with financial considerations—they continued to identify very strongly with a company viewed as a shared asset and heritage that had to be preserved.

These concerns were also reflected in the relationship between management and employees. People referred to "the Minerva family." Senior executives understood the importance of "remaining small," and the firm's success was not measured so much in increasing numbers of workers as in the preservation of a certain quality and continuity of relationships within the existing team. To this end, Minerva placed the emphasis on improving its employees' material conditions.

Although tinged with paternalism, this policy seemed to bear fruit. In 1945, a year for which precise information is available, the company employed roughly fifty people, office staff and factory workers combined. Over ten of them had been with the firm for more than twenty years, and a few had even been with the company from the start, some forty years earlier.

A SINGLE BRAND FOR LOYAL AGENTS

On the marketing level, this period saw Minerva consolidate its reputation through two product lines, watches and stopwatches, based on models developed as late as the 1950s. Some of the best-selling products of the 1960s were wristwatches with 10½-*ligne* movements (calibers 48, 49, and 50, developed in 1945), featuring seconds subdial, central second hand, or date. Two new calibers were launched in 1954 and 1955, yielding a pocket stopwatch with central totalizer and a split-seconds feature. They were followed by several models of curvometer. Minerva's older calibers and products also underwent improvement through higher quality ébauches and the modification of certain mechanisms and manufacturing procedures. The company also produced dies for other makers, thereby maintaining its status of *manufacture*. In contrast to policy at the dawn of the century, all products were henceforth grouped under a single brand name, Minerva.

The management of the day was able to spread this single brand's fame far beyond European borders. Germany and Great Britain, long the firm's leading outlets, were overtaken by the United States, where demand grew steadily. Jean-Jacques Frey has recounted how his father, when attempting to plan production, one day asked his American agent to supply a forecast of future orders, to which he received the reply: "Make as many as wish, you'll never manage to meet demand!"[24] The United States accounted for forty percent of Minerva's sales by 1951, rising to sixty percent in 1966—which sparked concern among senior executives, who sought to diversify their customer base. The watches met with success in Brazil, which led the way for a number of years. But André Frey also prospected the Far East, notably China and Singapore. Thus Minerva was soon exporting its product to roughly twenty countries on five continents, a scope it had not previously attained.

Unlike larger firms such as Longines, Minerva's management decided to adopt a highly discreet profile when it came to advertising and marketing. Monique Beck-Favre recalls that although the company regularly attended the Basel trade show, its most sophisticated products were kept at the back of the stand, away from prying eyes; the horological world of the day was characterized by intense competition between Swiss manufacturers, and attempts at copying had to be thwarted at all costs, leading to great caution when it came to the public presentation of key products.

Minerva nevertheless succeeding in selling its products. Its strength and pride lay in a network of agents, most of whom were exclusive. The major ones included the Ducommun Company in New York, Nisshindo in Tokyo,[25] and Augusto Casanova in Milan. Minerva thereby delegated all non-Swiss marketing, and it never directly participated in foreign trade

Top

André Frey and Jacques Pelot on either side of Augusto Casanova of Milan, brand representative in Italy (1952).

Above

The Nisshindo company from Tokyo, represented the brand in Japan (1955).

shows, appearing in Tokyo or Milan only through its agents. This policy of delegation was not without risks, which Minerva sought to limit by developing extremely faithful relationships with its representatives—one generation succeeded another not only within the firm, but also among its agents.

CAUTION AND THRIFT

An extremely prudent financial policy based on moderate investment—whether such investment concerned technical, material, or labor development—also contributed to the stability of the company. Just when many businesses sought to grow and to replace their production plant, Minerva proceeded in small stages, without radically changing either its premises or its overall infrastructure. It relied solely on its own cashflow to finance investment. The board of directors also opted for a steady-as-you-go policy when it came to shareholders: dividends of ten percent were paid out annually, but this rate only varied during exceptional years, when it would be lowered if profits dropped. To this day both families, reflecting the Protestant work ethic, stress their concern to avoid ostentatious expenditure, whether on themselves or on the company.

The profits of the 1950s and 60s were thus used to build up a reserve. Over the years, thanks to booming business in the late 1960s, this reserve reached a considerable sum. The policy of "squirreling away" some money enabled the company to traverse not only the war years but also periods of economic crisis.

Facing page
A Minerva advertisement from the 1940s, introducing the first wristwatch with a chronograph movement with two push-pieces.

AUTOMATIQUE

CHRONOGRAPHE

COMPTEUR ET RATTRAPANTE

Minerva

vous permet de satisfaire
les goûts et les exigences
les plus variés de votre clientèle

MANUFACTURE D'HORLOGERIE

MINERVA SPORT S.A.
VILLERET (SUISSE)

TOWARD THE NEXT STAGE

Limited production, small size, family management, loyalty of staff and sales network, and strict financial monitoring: those are the bases on which Minerva functioned from 1950 to 1970. The payoff was a steady rise in profits, which increased five hundred percent or more between 1960 and 1974, the firm's record year.

The company faced the difficult years of the 1970s and 80s in the same spirit. In the early stages, its policies proved judicious, allowing the company to avoid the debt trap that was fatal to so many other firms. Its independence and modest size enabled it to react flexibly to fluctuations in demand, and to adapt progressively to the new situation, avoiding major upheavals and layoffs. Although exports of wristwatches collapsed, Minerva could continue to count on its niche market of stopwatches, enabling it to retain an output and skills too specialized to whet the appetite of predators. "This market was too small to interest the major corporations, but sufficed to sustain Minerva," explained Jean-Jacques Frey.[26] Minerva got through the 1970s notably due to the production of measuring instruments, especially curvometers, and even decided not to incorporate quartz technology into its timepieces. Its client base obviously evolved somewhat—it increasingly worked for the automotive and chemical industries as well as television studios and naval shipbuilding (where stopwatches were used to measure the response times of submarine sonar systems). At the same time, its sales to the United States fell considerably.

During these difficult years Minerva was also able to retain a brand image, structure, and skills that dated back to the very founding of the firm. Of the twenty watchmakers doing business in the Saint-Imier Valley in 1950, only two still existed in 1990—Longines and Minerva. Minerva's tradition of high-quality timepieces was reaffirmed by the 1988 launch of a new version of the No. 20 chronograph movement featuring analog calendar and phases of the moon, as well as by a pocket watch dubbed the Tablier.

Yet even though the company managed to preserve its identity and know-how, it lacked the resources to valorize and perpetuate them. And at that very moment the well-oiled mechanism of family succession broke down—as with many similar firms, a struggle erupted between the two controlling families, which led to the permanent withdrawal of the Haussener heirs in 1990. The hard-earned independence of the previous thirty years could not last: the survival of the firm depended on outside support. Jean-Jacques Frey, who had become the main shareholder, began seeking partners, notably in Italy where the brand retained a certain fame. An initial partnership was agreed with the Italian corporation Hopa in 2000, but six years later Minerva joined the Geneva-based Richemont corporation via its Montblanc subsidiary.

This change came just two years short of Minerva's 150th anniversary. Even though top management was no longer based in the Saint-Imier Valley, the better to open new horizons for the company, it was still determined to valorize Minerva's historic heritage. The company is thus now enjoying new growth based on traditional expertise combined with structural, technical, and commercial developments whose ultimate shape and impact are just beginning to emerge.

Facing page

The Montblanc *manufacture* in Villeret following its complete renovation in October 2008.

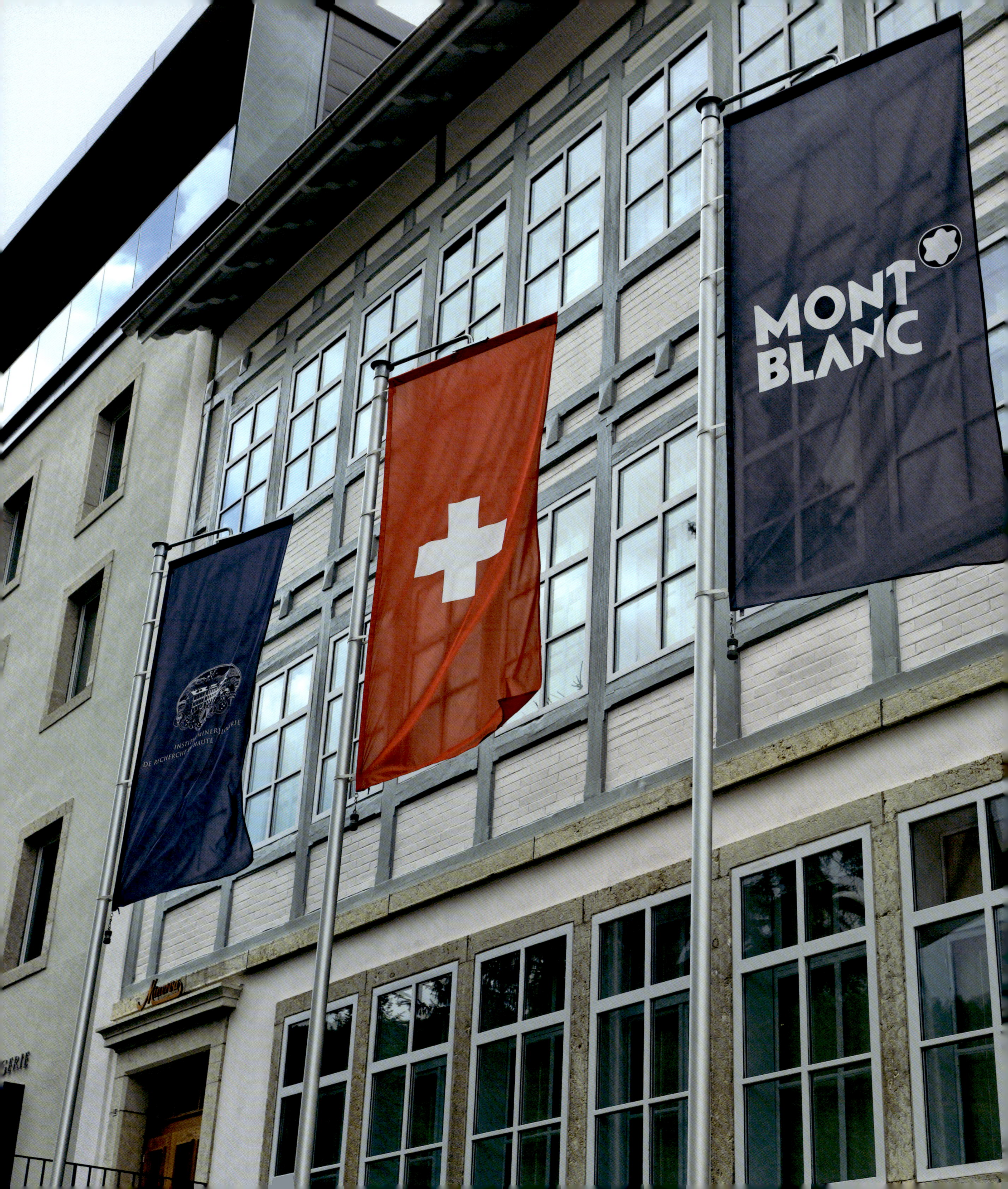
MONT
BLANC

The History of Minerva Watch Movements

Reinhard Meis

III III

The Watchmaking Categorization of Watch Calibers and Watchmaking Equipment 3rd volume, by A.- F. Jobin with the Minerva caliber 19/9CH with a monopusher chronograph movement on the cover page.

La Classification Horlogère

des calibres de montres et des fournitures d'horlogerie suisses

par A.-F. Jobin

Klassifikation der schweizerischen Uhrwerke und Uhrenfurnituren

Clasification de los relojes suizos y de sus piezas de repuesto

Classification of the Swiss Watch Movements and Watchmaterials

Edité par **LA CLASSIFICATION HORLOGÈRE**

GENÈVE - Avenue Blanc, 36
SUISSE

Tous droits réservés - Copyright - Alle Rechte vorbehalten
Imprimé en Suisse - Printed in Switzerland - In der Schweiz gedruckt

Right
Aerial view of the Saint-Imier valley, which starts at La Chaux-de-Fonds and extends to the approaches to Sombeval. nineteenth-century colored lithograph.

Horological Specialties in the Saint-Imier Valley

In the course of the nineteenth and twentieth centuries, many watchmaking companies were established in the Saint-Imier valley, between the Droit and Chasseral mountains. Leonidas Watch & Co. S.A., Saint-Imier 1841; Fabrique Minerva, Robert Frères S.A., Villeret 1858; Excelsior Park, Saint-Imier 1866; Agassiz Watch Co. S.A., Saint-Imier 1876; Longines Watch Co. S.A., Saint-Imier 1867; Berna Watch Co. S.A., Saint-Imier 1864; Moris S.A., Saint-Imier 1893, and Rayville Watch Co. Mfg. Ltd, with the name of Blancpain, Villeret 1815, to name only the most important. Apart from the *manufactures* mentioned above, many small workshops also came into being to supply the "établisseurs"— assemblers—on the cottage-industry principle that was then widespread in Switzerland. At the time, the valley of Saint-Imier enjoyed a flattering reputation in the sector of what were known as three-hand watches: good-quality timepieces for everyday use. However, one shared specialty was common to all these firms: the production of pocket watches equipped with a chronograph function and counters for measuring short intervals of time. Indeed, the progress of industrialization worldwide soon demanded chronographs designed to measure short time lapses, in the form of a complementary mechanism incorporated in a pocket watch or an autonomous timer adapted for sporting or industrial uses.

The gradual transition to wristwatches equipped with the same technology occurred at the beginning of the twentieth century. Though these movements possessed similar characteristics, their dimensions were becoming smaller.

The history of Minerva began in 1858, with the foundation of a "comptoir d'établissage" at Villeret. To start with, it is probable that the company restricted itself to assembling watch movements, but evidence is lacking about this initial stage. In 1887, the "Minerva" brand was registered worldwide. From then on, all the watches produced by the company bore the Minerva name. Their high technical quality and remarkable skill of execution regularly earned them medals and diplomas in international competitions.

Today, Minerva can boast an uninterrupted tradition going right back to the year 1858. Throughout this long period, the company has never ceased producing timepieces designed to meet the most demanding requirements. They were initially equipped with a cylinder escapement, and later with an anchor escapement.

Chronographs and sports timers have always been one of the strong points of Minerva's production. Over the years, they were made in numerous versions, with balance frequencies varying between 18,000 and 360,000 vibrations per hour. In the latter case, the seconds hand made one revolution per second to enable measurements to a hundredth of a second, the dial bearing 100 subdivisions in witness of this extraordinary technical achievement.

Pocket watches equipped with a chronograph, and later with a split-seconds hand, also won fame in the field of sports timekeeping, in particular at the fourth Olympic Winter Sports held at Garmisch Partenkirchen, Germany, in 1936, where Minerva was the official timekeeper. The *manufacture*'s catalog also included monitoring devices for billiard halls, displaying the duration and hire price of the tables.

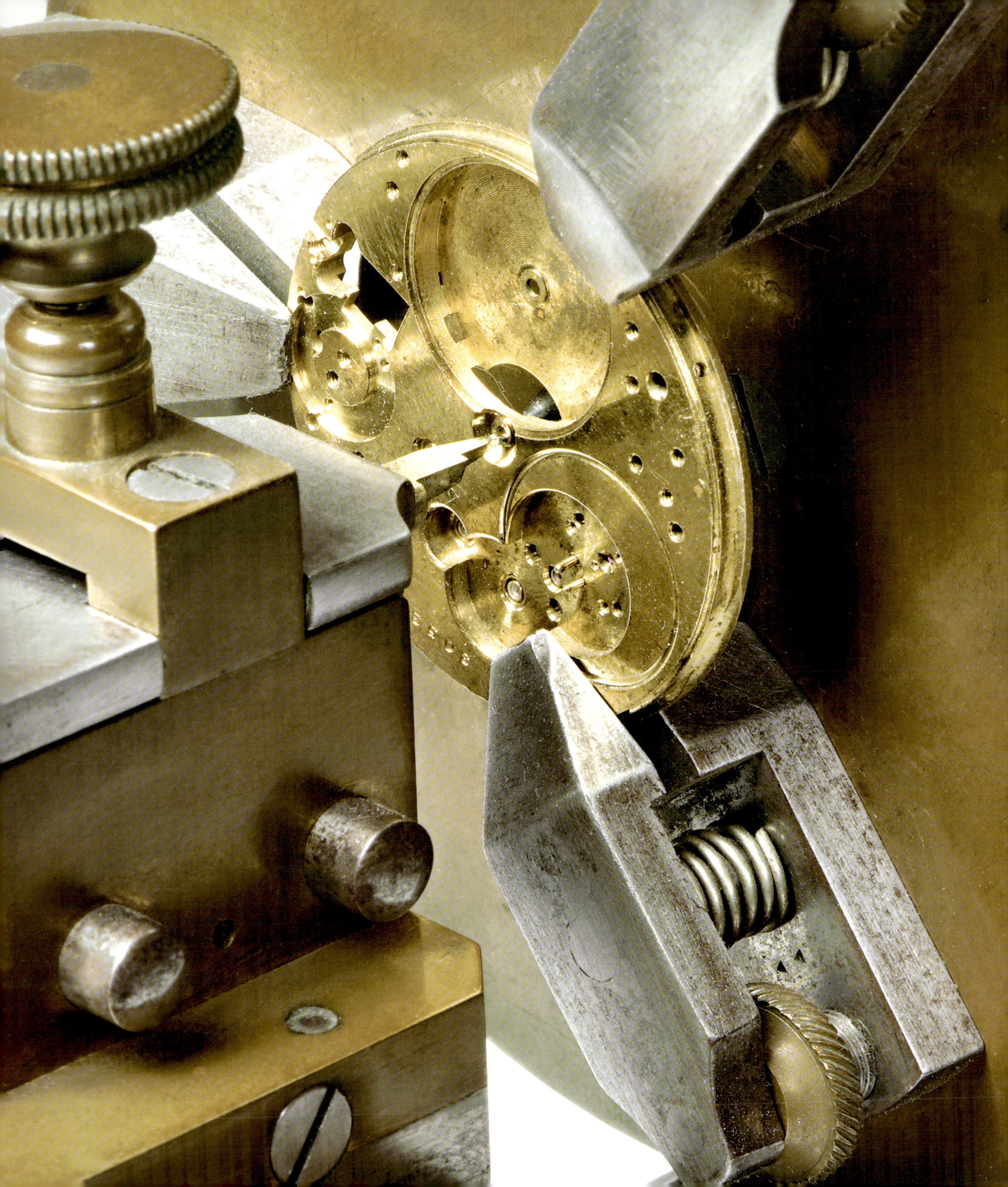

Charles Ivan Robert Starts to Develop Watch Production at Villeret

The era of watches with a verge [1] escapement and an interposed chain and fusee drew to an end in the middle of the nineteenth century. Consisting of an upper plate that covered the gear train and was supported on pillars, this key-wound mechanism, with its balance wheel on its own level, under the chased and pierced verge bridge (ill. 1), no longer met the requirements of the time. Watches with verge escapements were characterized by their excessive depth, while the new movements possessed a novel construction that was considerably thinner. Although key winding survived for a while, the new physiognomy of the movement gradually came to predominate in watchmaking. Henceforth, a movement consisted of a bottom plate fitted with different bridges (ill. 2). Each wheel was fixed under a separate small bridge. The balance wheel was positioned on the same level as the gear train, and new escapements[2] made their appearance in mass-produced watch mechanisms. On some watches, two wheels were still held under a single bridge. Separate bridges were invented by Antoine Lépine, a Paris watchmaker who presented this arrangement in a small series of watches made in about 1760 under the name of "calibre Lépine." While the shapes of the bridges had little in common at the time, this situation changed at the beginning of the nineteenth century with the emergence of the industrial manufacture of watch movements. Bridges then took on the shape of "slices of cake" (ill. 3). In the course of the next few decades, the original star arrangement gradually gave way to a parallel arrangement. These movements were produced in every conceivable size, from small, elegant timepieces for ladies to imposing pocket watches for men. This was the situation in watchmaking at the beginning of the nineteenth century, at a time when the first flat watches were also making their appearance to respond to the new demands of fashion.

1 Verge watch movement no. 79
Key winding by Henry Chanson of Rolle, about 1820. Fire-gilded plate with verge bridge pierced and engraved on top and silver regulating dial. The balance is located on the top plate under the verge bridge.

2 Pocket watch movement by Antoine Lépine, Paris, c. 1840.
New types of movement construction appeared, with the wheels arranged under separate bridges, while the balance was on the same level as the gear train. Cylinder escapement.

3 Flat pocket watch movements, c. 1850.
Typical arrangement of bridges on flat pocket watches with key winding and cylinder escapement. Brass balance wheel with flat hairspring.

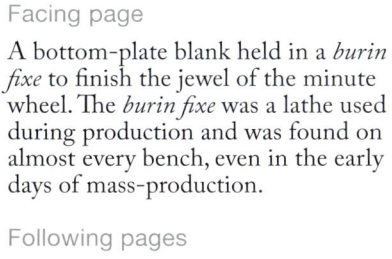

Facing page
A bottom-plate blank held in a *burin fixe* to finish the jewel of the minute wheel. The *burin fixe* was a lathe used during production and was found on almost every bench, even in the early days of mass-production.

Following pages
The Robert family's house and agency (view dating from the early twentieth century).

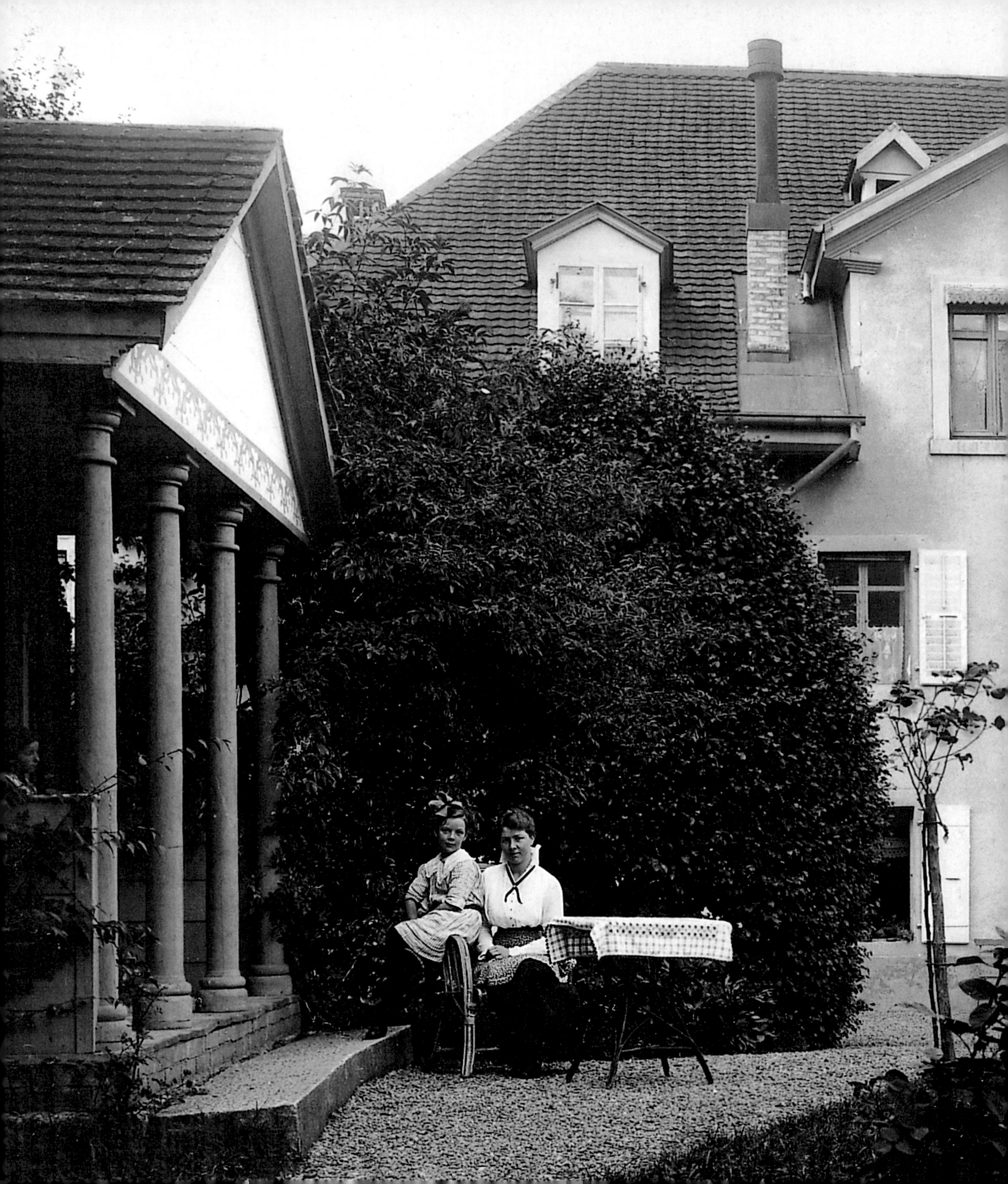

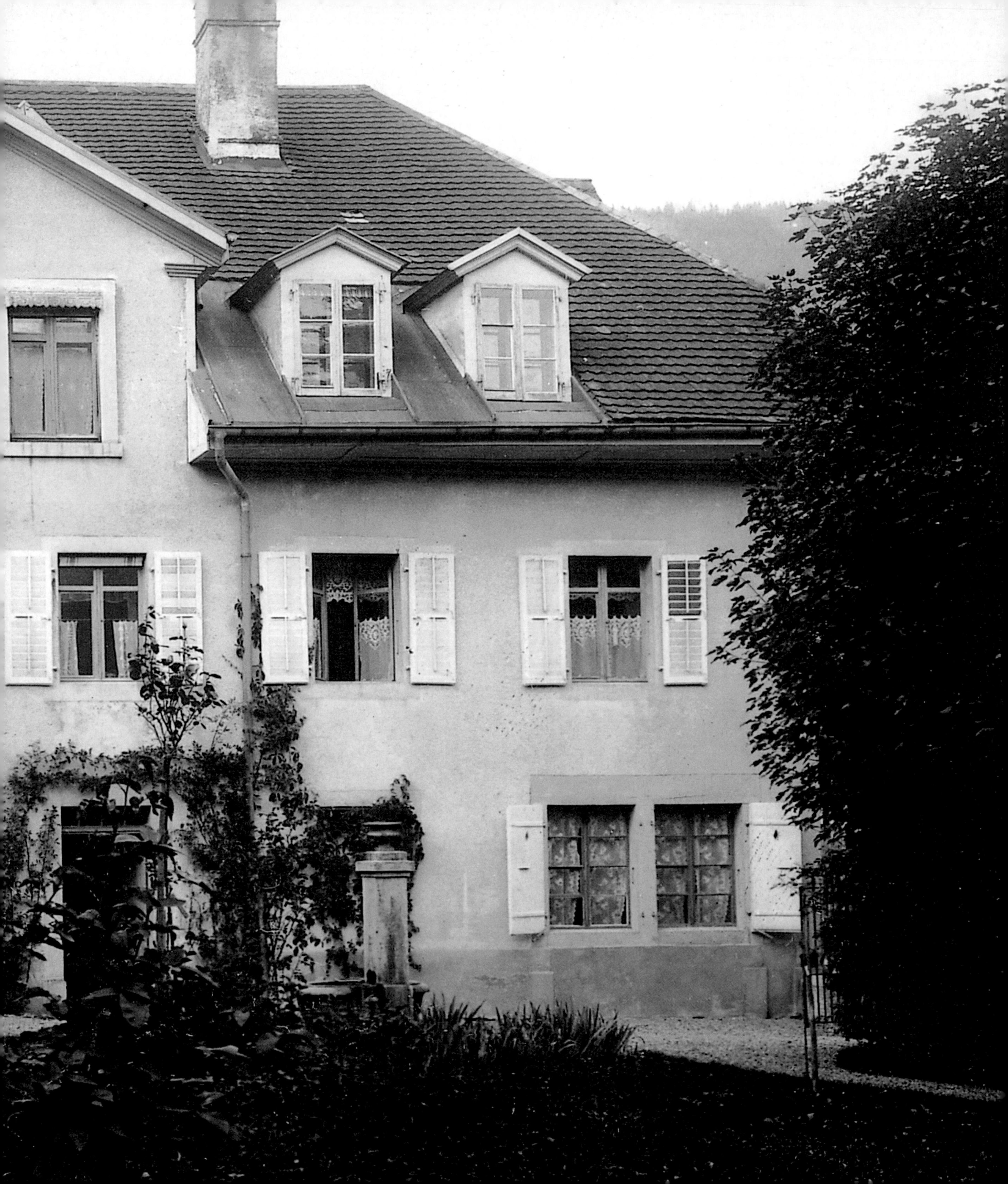

◀ Left
Detailed view of a rounding-up cutter. It used a special milling tool to adapt a gear wheel to the exact distance between centers.

4 Cover of the brochure published for the hundredth anniversary of the "Fabrique d'Horlogerie de Fontainemelon 1825–1925," 48 pages with a wealth of illustrations showing the company and its range of products (watch movements and clocks).

5 Illustration of old pocket watch movements dating from 1850 to 1870. It shows the transition from movements with a complete plate with the cock situated above the wheels to modern movements, with the balance at the same level as the other wheels.

III The History of Minerva Watch Movements

THE FIRST ÉBAUCHES FROM FONTAINEMELON, 1850–1870

To begin with, the Robert factory worked as an "établisseur,"[1] or assembler, buying ébauches from the eponymous firm of Robert established at nearby Fontainemelon (ill. 4). Until the 1870s, ébauches, also known as "blanks" (ill. 5), consisted solely of the bottom plate, the bridges with screw ébauches, the barrel without the spring but with the stop work (most often key-wound), and the regulator. All the other parts, such as the wheels, mainspring, minutes gear-train, the escapement and the balance wheel with its hairspring, were procured from external suppliers, on the cottage-industry[2] principle. Later on, the makers of ébauches also supplied the complete movement, with wheels and minutes gear train.

In the factory workshops, the jewels were bored and set,[3] and the wheels were adapted. These different tasks were always entrusted to specialized workers. It was often necessary to round the pivots and teeth to improve meshing. To carry out these operations, each watchmaker had his own rounding machine on his bench. Then the assemblers assembled the escapement and proceeded to carry out preliminary regulation. These specialists gave life to the watch.

In a system based largely on home-working, with no scope for production control, countless finishing and retouching operations were needed before the watch was ready to work.

The next steps consisted in providing the movements with enameled dials and hands. A serial number was usually stamped onto the mechanism or the dial, sometimes accompanied by a logo or identification symbol. All that remained was to enclose the movements in cases purchased externally, perform the final regulation, and hand over the finished watch to the people in charge of sales.

▲ 4

▼ 5

▲ 6a   ▼ 6b

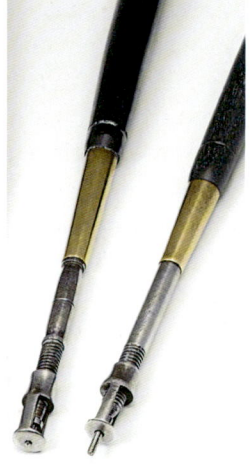

6a Screw shortener, brass, with wooden handle.

6b Detail of a screw shortener with screw inserted.

Left
Machine for polishing the heads of screws in vertical position with ratchet screw ready for final polishing with the wooden disk.

III The History of Minerva Watch Movements

THE FINISHING OF MOVEMENTS

The finishing of movements was a particularly important task, which had to meet demanding requirements. We have already noted the capital importance of technical operations carried out subsequently on ébauches. These were produced in the raw state by the suppliers and delivered in the form of separate parts (ill. 9) in boxes of five toten units. Finishing proper was more concerned with the appearance of the movement, that is to say smoothing, polishing, matt surfacing, and galvanization. In this last field, the choice of color corresponded to a specific standard and the electro-platers carried out gilding, silvering, or nickel-plating of movements, depending on the customer. Wheels were gilded before being riveted onto pinions, which themselves were smoothed and polished before riveting.

The finishing of screws, often delivered in the raw state, was a vital step. The heads were polished by hand or using a machine for polishing screw heads using disks of brass, zinc, or wood and suitable polishing pastes.

One delicate operation consisted in shortening screws, taking care not to damage the already-finished thread. The special instruments for shortening screws (ill. 6a and 6b) could also be used to polish the upper part of the thread, if this was visible from the side of the movement in the plate.

When polishing the winding and stop wheels, it was essential to observe meticulous cleanliness throughout the different stages of the operation so as to keep the surfaces impeccable. The cups of ratchets, unmarked by the tiniest scratch, for example, exert a fascinating effect (ill. 10), as does the perfectly polished central screw of the ratchet (ill. 7). The winding lever, the pawl, the stop springs, and the regulator were given chamfered edges and partly polished. The cock was often engraved or chased (ill. 8). The purpose of all these operations was to enhance the aesthetic appeal of the watch.

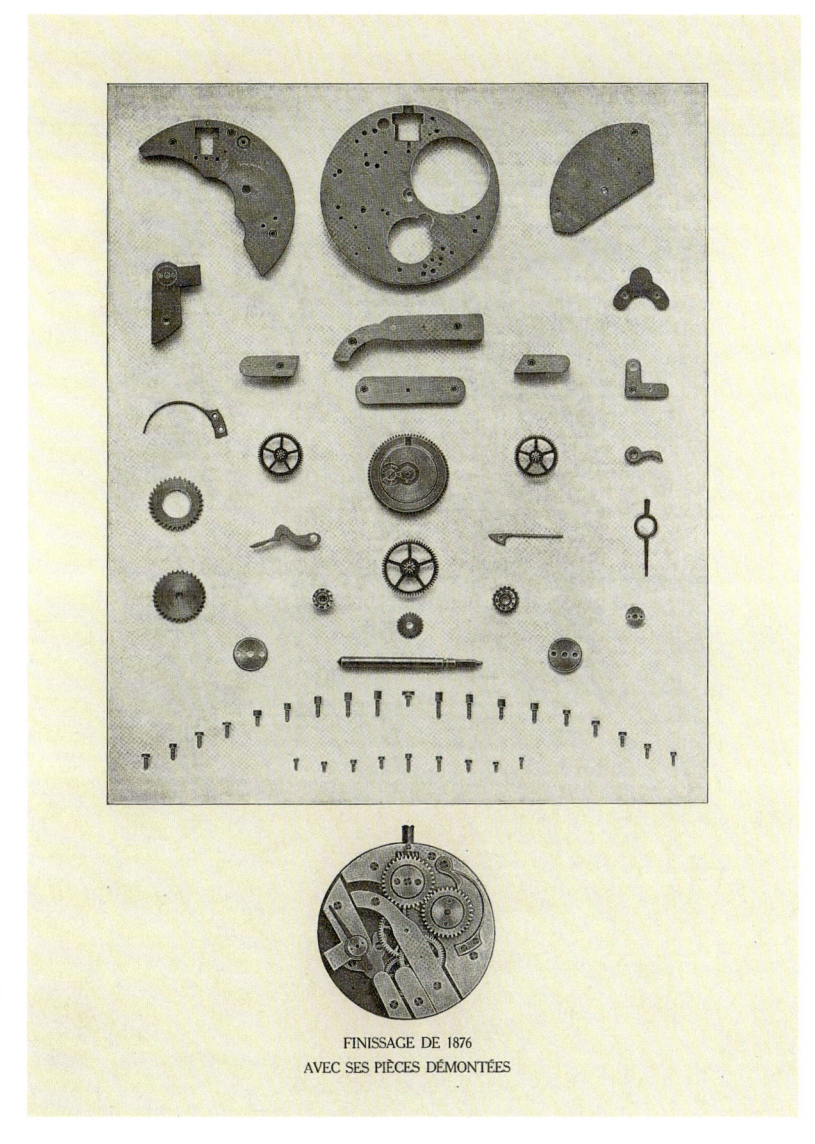

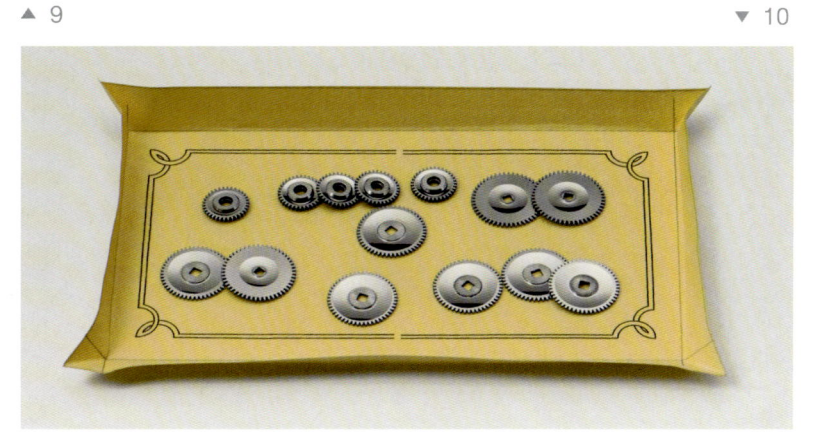

▲ 7   ▼ 8

7 Ratchet screw with completely scratch-free mirror polish.

8 Cock with hand-engraved floral motifs. In the middle, regulation scale:
R = retard (slow);
A = avance (fast).

▲ 9

FINISSAGE DE 1876
AVEC SES PIÈCES DÉMONTÉES

▼ 10

9 Illustration from the book Fontainemelon 1825–1925, showing the different parts of an ébauche supplied to the assemblers about 1876. The mainspring, escapement, balance wheel, and hairspring were bought from other suppliers.

10 Cardboard tray with ratchet covers for different calibers. Before delivery, the ratchets were separated by tissue paper so that they could not scratch each other.

Left
Plate ébauche fixed in an uprighting tool to mark the center hole. The plate is centered with the counterpoint in the lower center hole. With a light tap from a hammer, the upper point marks the position of the center of the jewel on the upper part. Thus the nose pads are positioned exactly one above the other.

11 Winding with a winding system, the winding wheel being visible in relation to the crown wheel and the sliding pinion for the conical drive.

12 Representation of parallel arrangement of bridges, taken from the ébauche manufacturing catalog at Fontainemelon.

13 Pocket watch, key winding. The pendant is small, with a round bow.

14 Pocket watch with winder. The winding crown is incorporated in the pendant. The appearance of the case underwent considerable changes.

III The History of Minerva Watch Movements

FONTAINEMELON ÉBAUCHES OF 1876
(WITH WINDING CROWN)

Toward 1842, J.A. Philippe[1] brought a keyless winding system to watchmaking. This was a highly complex technique in which a right-angle gear wheel was connected to two steel star wheels arranged perpendicularly to each other (ill. 11). A rotating "winding stem" positioned on the side of the case was used to wind the watch. With this invention, which underwent many further developments, the winding key which until then had been provided with each timepiece, became superfluous. It was not until 1870 that the ébauche-making enterprise Robert, in Fontainemelon, started mass production of movements incorporating these new winding systems (ill. 12). On the first models, the hands were set by pressing a corrector situated on the case middle, beside the crown.

To enable the movement to be taken out of the watch after being cased up, the outer end of the winding stem was surmounted with a crown. To this end, the case-maker had to adapt the old pendant (ill. 13) to the new winding crown (ill. 14). This gave an entirely new appearance to the pocket watch, since the crown was now entirely visible in the pendant.

TYPES DE FINISSAGES DÈS 1876

11   ▲ 12   ▼ 13   ▼ 14

193

Left
Third wheel and seconds wheel, inserted in gear train compasses to ensure optimum meshing. The external points could then be used to check or modify the positions of the jewels.

15 Old winding system with winder, with visible ratchets and stop pawl arranged on the upper part.

16 New winding system with winder, with lateral acting ratchet arranged on a lower level.

17 Illustration of winding systems of various designs, from the manufacturing catalog of Fontainemelon, about 1910.

18 New winding mechanism, about 1910, on which the ratchets are arranged on a barrel bridge in two parts.

III   The History of Minerva Watch Movements

FONTAINEMELON ÉBAUCHES OF 1910 (WITH THE NEW WINDING TECHNOLOGY)

Demand for ébauches was very high in Switzerland. As early as 1850, two makers of ébauches—Robert at Fontainemelon, in Switzerland, and Japy[1] at Beaucourt, in France – were producing 500,000 units a year[2]. The industrialization of watch production made giant strides during the second half of the nineteenth century.

Movements took on a new appearance yet again. At Fontainemelon, about 1900, the ratchets visible on the top of the winding crown system of a movement from 1876 (ill. 15) were moved down to a lower level, the winding stops were endowed with springs acting separately (ill. 16), and the ratchets arranged under the barrel bridge, which was most often made in two parts (ill. 17).

While this design of barrel bridge represented a considerable advantage in assembly, it also proved valuable in the case of a repair involving mainspring replacement, as only two screws had to be removed to take out the barrel. The arrangement of the bridges in strict parallel gradually fell out of use, making way for more personalized shapes.

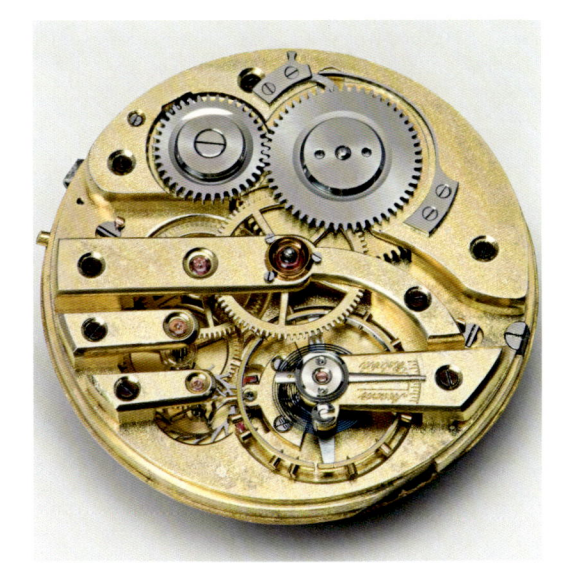

TYPES DE FINISSAGES DÈS 1910

15   16   ▲ 17   ▼ 18

195

19 Books of models published the new registered models of watches.

19a The Usine des Faverges, Robert Frères, Villeret (Switzerland) registered its first five models in 1902. They appeared in Volume II, on page 181.

20 Book of models, volume III, of 1904, with registration of models 6 to 11 of the Fabrique des Faverges Robert Frères, Villeret (Switzerland).

21 Book of models, volume IV, of 1905, page 207, with registration of models 12 and 13.

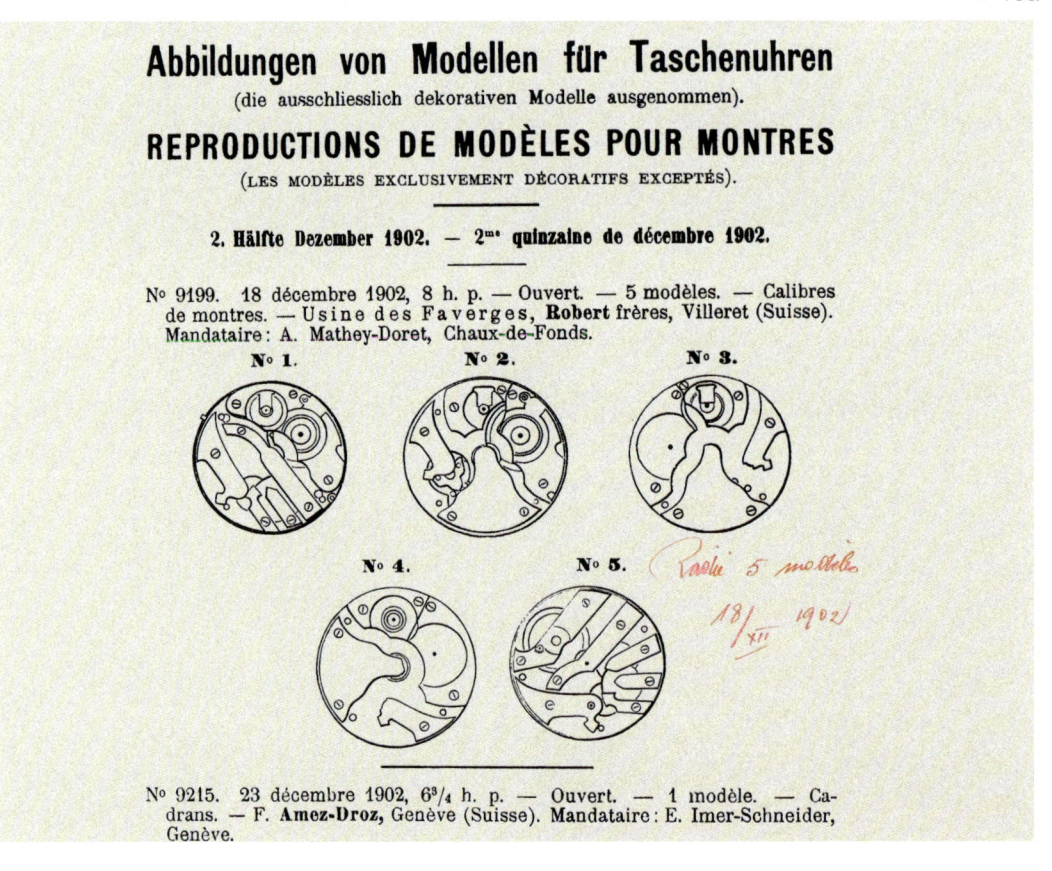

196

The First *manufacture* Movements

ILLUSTRATION OF MODELS, 1902–1921

In 1888, the Federal Office of Intellectual Property (Patent Office) opened its doors in Biel. It included a special department for the deposit of models, and especially samples of watches, which at that time benefited from legal protection for a period of five years, extendable by two further periods of five years. In principle, deposit was solely for purposes of registration. If disputes arose, the parties had to complain to the Court of Justice.

Every year, the Office published books (ill. 19) of reproductions of the models protected in the form of drawings or photographs, showing the official registration number followed by the name of the depositing company together with the date and time of registration. The drawings of the models themselves bore a number specific to the company, beginning with a "1." However, it is not certain that the companies monitored their numbering perfectly. To facilitate the identification of watches that were registered models, their movements were marked with an engraved inscription: "DÉPOSÉ" (registered).

According to company records, Minerva started producing watches, and principally movements, in 1902, in the new premises into which it had just moved. The first five models from the "Usine des Faverges, Robert Frères," Villeret (Switzerland), were registered on December 18, 1902 at 8 a.m. (ill. 19a). They were the first models made by C. Robert at Villeret; two of them had a cylinder escapement and three an anchor escapement. In December 1903, the Manufacture submitted and registered six more models, numbered from 6 to 11, one movement with a cylinder escapement and five with an anchor escapement. Not all these creations, of rather baroque style (ill. 20), went into production.

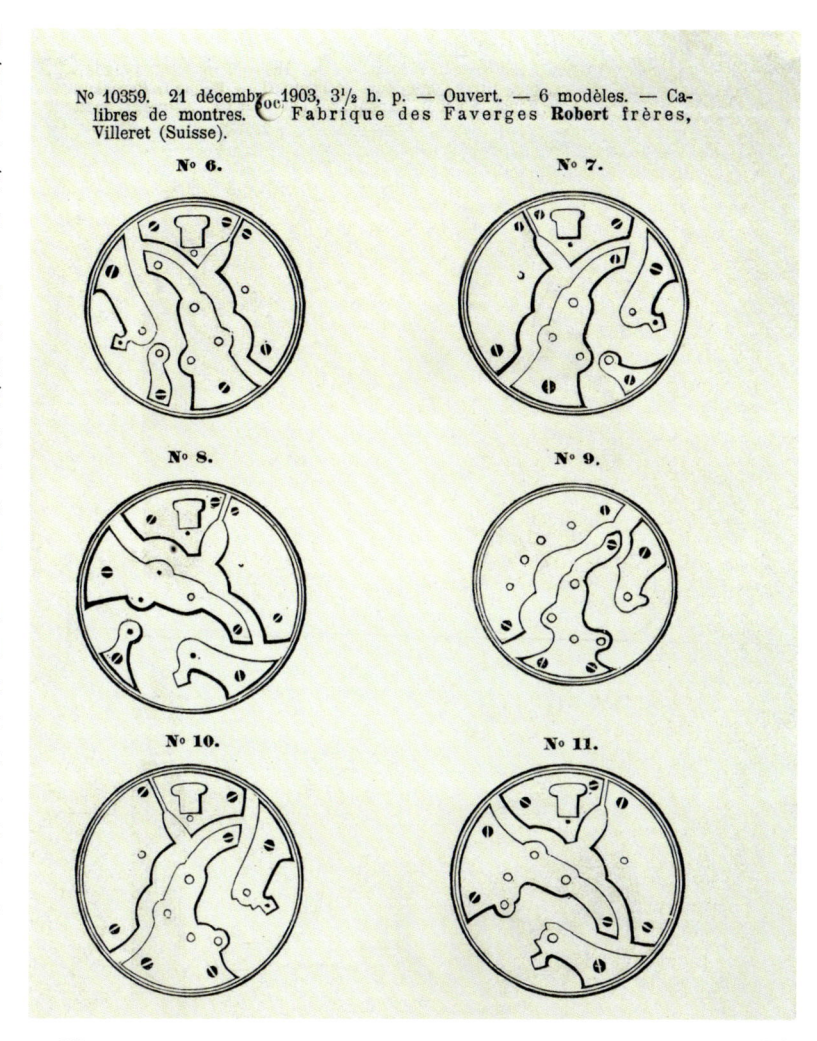

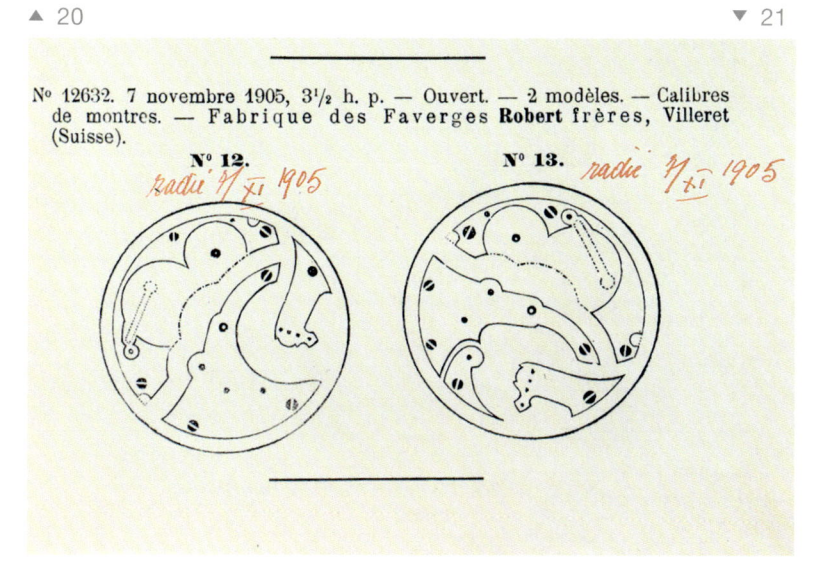

▲ 20   ▼ 21

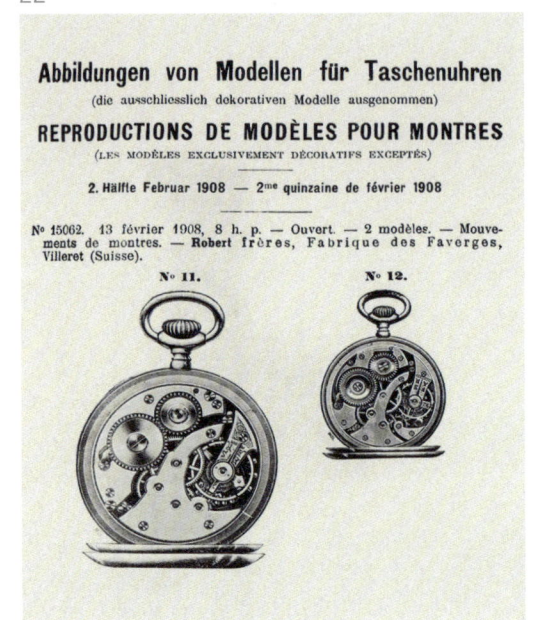

Two years later, in 1905, movements 12 and 13 were registered (ill. 21). Movement no. 13 was already taking on the general form of the present caliber 16/15. Only the ratchet is different today. Over the next few years, Minerva registered various other models, among which figured movements with a full plate (ill. 23). The numbering of the movements still contains some gaps. The highest number that we have found is 109. It is likely that a new numbering series took one hundred as its starting point.

It is apparent that the registration of horological models did not concern movements alone, but also dials (ill. 262), special bridge shapes (ill. 143), and cases. It is easy to follow the trail of the movement models registered by Minerva up to the early 1920s.

22 Book of models, volume V, of 1908, page 37, with registration of models 11 and 12 under the heading Watch Movements, Robert Frères.

23 Book of models, volume VII, of 1911, with registration of models 14 and 65 (so far no explanation has been found for the jump from number 14 to 65).

24 Book of models, volume V, of 1907, with deposit of model 19/10.

25 Book of models, volume X, of 1918, with deposit of models 48 and 72 (so far no explanation has been found for the jump from number 48 to 72).

198

III   The History of Minerva Watch Movements

THE RECORD BOOKS

The movement record books, which begin with number 1, record the movements starting from serial number 313,307. It should be noted that the sequence of numbers from 313,307 is full of gaps (ill. 26). The sequence of numbers is only respected from 500,000 on. The record books then mention the year of manufacture, an indication of the series, the dimensions of the caliber measured in lignes,[1] and a number that does not correspond to the logic of the sequence. Thus, information on the year of manufacture can be obtained with certainty, which is not the case for information on the calibers. The purchaser of the movement (or the watch containing the movement) does not appear in the record books, in contrast to common practice among many other watchmaking companies. There is sometimes a customer number, but most of the commercial registers are lost, so their identification is no longer possible.

The list opposite, of the records in the record books, makes it possible to classify the serial numbers in accordance with year of manufacture, according to the numbering used in the record books. The sequence of numbers begins with the serial numbers recorded on the first page.

Record book 1–32

Seq. no.	serial number	Year	
1	(313,307) 500,001	1902	many gaps
2	600,001	1903	
3	645,001	1904	
4	690,001	1905	
5	733,649	1906	
6	777,743	1907	to following year
7	822,743	1910	
8	867,643	1910	
9	912,655	1911	
10	957,749	1912	to following year
11	1,003,679	1914	
12	1,048,678	1915	
13	1,093,749	1916	to following year
14	1,138,749	1918	to following year
15	1,183,761	1920	
16	1,227,761	1921	to following year
17	1,270,955	1924	
18	1,314,491	1925	to following year
19	1,359,501	1927	to following year
20	1,395,501	1929	to following year
21	1,439,149	1936	to following year
22	1,482,125	1938	to following year
23	1,523,579	1940	to following year
24	1,579,619	1942	to following year
25	1,627,843	1944	
26	1,693,225	1945	
27	1,798,913	1946	to following year
28	1,811,419	1948	
29	1,873,901	1949	to following year
30	1,936,501	1951	
31	1,984,793	1952	to following year
32	2,033,767	1954	
	2,070,297 (end)		

26

26 Record book, number 1, with records of the numbers of movements, showing numerous gaps up to number 500,000. In addition to the movement number, the register also gives a caliber number, for example 19/8, 18/7, and 19/7.

30 The balance wheel rim bears a thin line near the cock attachment. In rest position, it must be at the mid-point of the three points of the plate. The two points to the right and left indicate the end of the lift angle of the balance wheel when the latter is moved manually.

▲ 30   ▼ 31

31 A small pin (at the bottom) is set on the rim of the balance wheel to prevent its inversion. It strikes (top) at right and left a vertical stud inserted in the cock to limit its amplitude of oscillation.

32 Cylinder escapement wheel, with fifteen teeth.

▲ 27

28   29   32

27 Gilded movement of pocket watch (19 lignes) with straight bridges and visible ratchet. Engraved cock with three-armed balance wheel and flat hairspring.

28 The same movement, 17 lignes size.

29 The same movement, 13 lignes size.

200

III The History of Minerva Watch Movements

THE MOVEMENT WITH A CYLINDER ESCAPEMENT

A cylinder movement is a watch movement in which a balance with a cylinder escapement serves as the "standard of time,"[1]. The technology of the cylinder escapement is founded on the principle of the cylinder wheel meshing directly by means of its notches in the cylinder incorporated in the spindle of the balance wheel (ill. 33 and 34) to transmit the impulse to the balance. Due to its very convenient construction, movements fitted with a cylinder escapement could be produced in very large numbers. This is one of the escapements that has seen very wide application in watches for everyday use.

How the escapement works

Illustration 33 explains the events in the different stages of operation of a cylinder escapement. Figure 1 shows the respective positions of the cylinder and the cylinder wheel as well as the motion of the cylinder wheel through the notch.[2] Figure 2 represents the different phases of the motion of the balance wheel. To make this easier to understand, the parts are also shown in perspective in illustration 34. We begin our observations at position A. Let us suppose that the balance wheel is moving toward the right. The tooth of the escapement wheel rests, exerting light pressure, against the outside of the cylinder (black part). The cylinder wheel is motionless. It is only at the moment when the tooth is able to move through the open part of the cylinder and penetrate it that the cylinder wheel starts to move and gives an additional impulse to the balance wheel, through the intermediary of the entry lip on the inclined plane of the top of the tooth (position B). As soon as the entry lip has fallen back from the rear part of the top of the tooth, the point of the tooth makes contact with the inner wall of the cylinder (position C). The balance wheel now swings as far as its point of return; it remains motionless for an instant and changes its direction of movement under the influence of the tension in the hairspring (position D) before swinging back toward the left. All this time, the cylinder wheel has been "at rest," with the tip of a tooth resting against the inside of the cylinder. This is therefore one of the escapements belonging to the "deadbeat" class. When the exit lip slides over the tip of the tooth, it is able to leave the cylinder, thereby giving a new impulse to the balance wheel in the opposite direction through the strong pressure of the head of the tooth on the exit lip (position E). Once the exit lip releases the head of the tooth, the cylinder wheel can turn freely until the next tooth tip is stopped by the outer surface of the cylinder (position F). The process can then begin again from its starting point (position G).

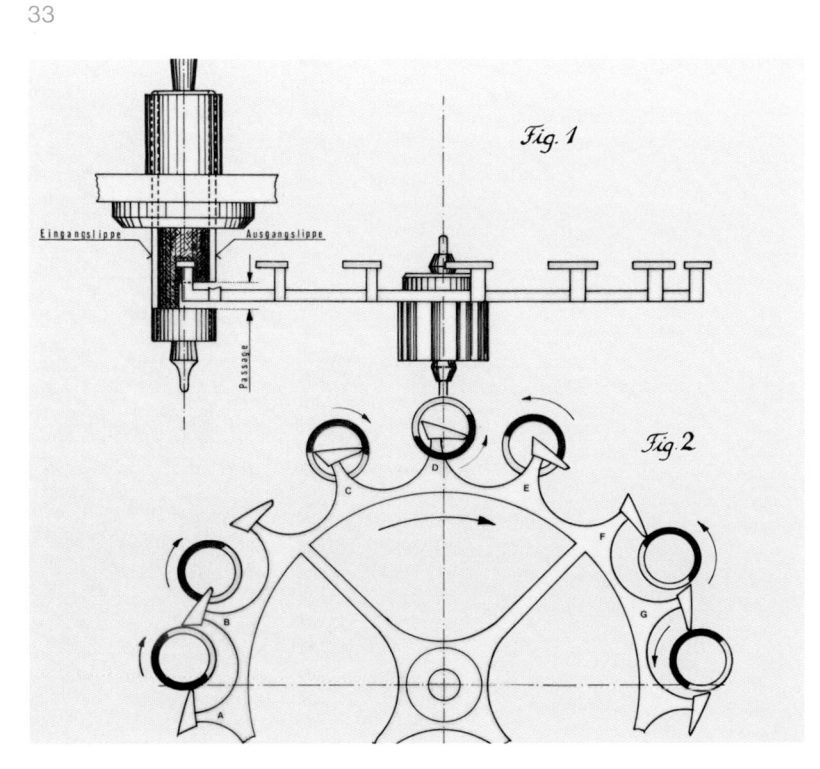

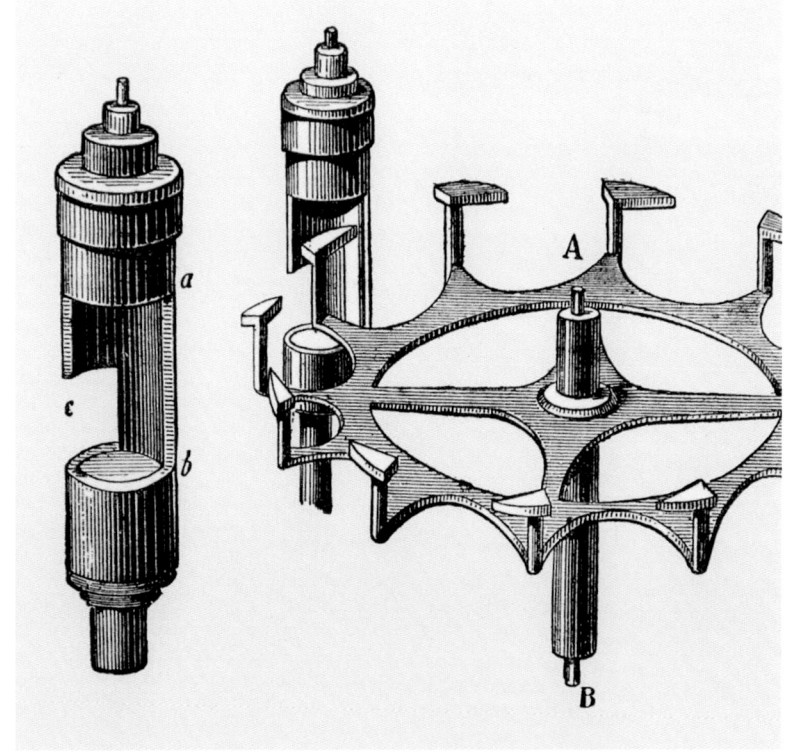

35–36 Pocket watch with crown winding, about 1920, and 18-ligne caliber with cylinder escapement. To start with, cases were made of silver (ill. 35) and, at the time of the first great watchmaking crisis, often only of nickel-silver, a very common nickel alloy. Many specialists established at Saint-Imier made different components of the escapement, such as cylinder wheels or cylinders.

37–38 Lady's pocket watch with silver case for the Hertha brand. Movement punched (13 lignes) on the right on the barrel bridge. White enamel dial with gilt Louis XV hands.

39-40 Man's pocket watch, silver, 17 lignes movement with cylinder escapement. Hertha maker's punch on the barrel bridge, bottom right. Enameled dial with small seconds at 6 o'clock, gilt Louis XV hands.

Following pages
Original design for a traveling clock patented by Minerva in 1931. The clock, in leather cladding with a cover, was wound by repeated opening and closing of the latter.

III The History of Minerva Watch Movements

▲ 37   ▼ 38   ▲ 39   ▼ 40

203

CAL.
IE

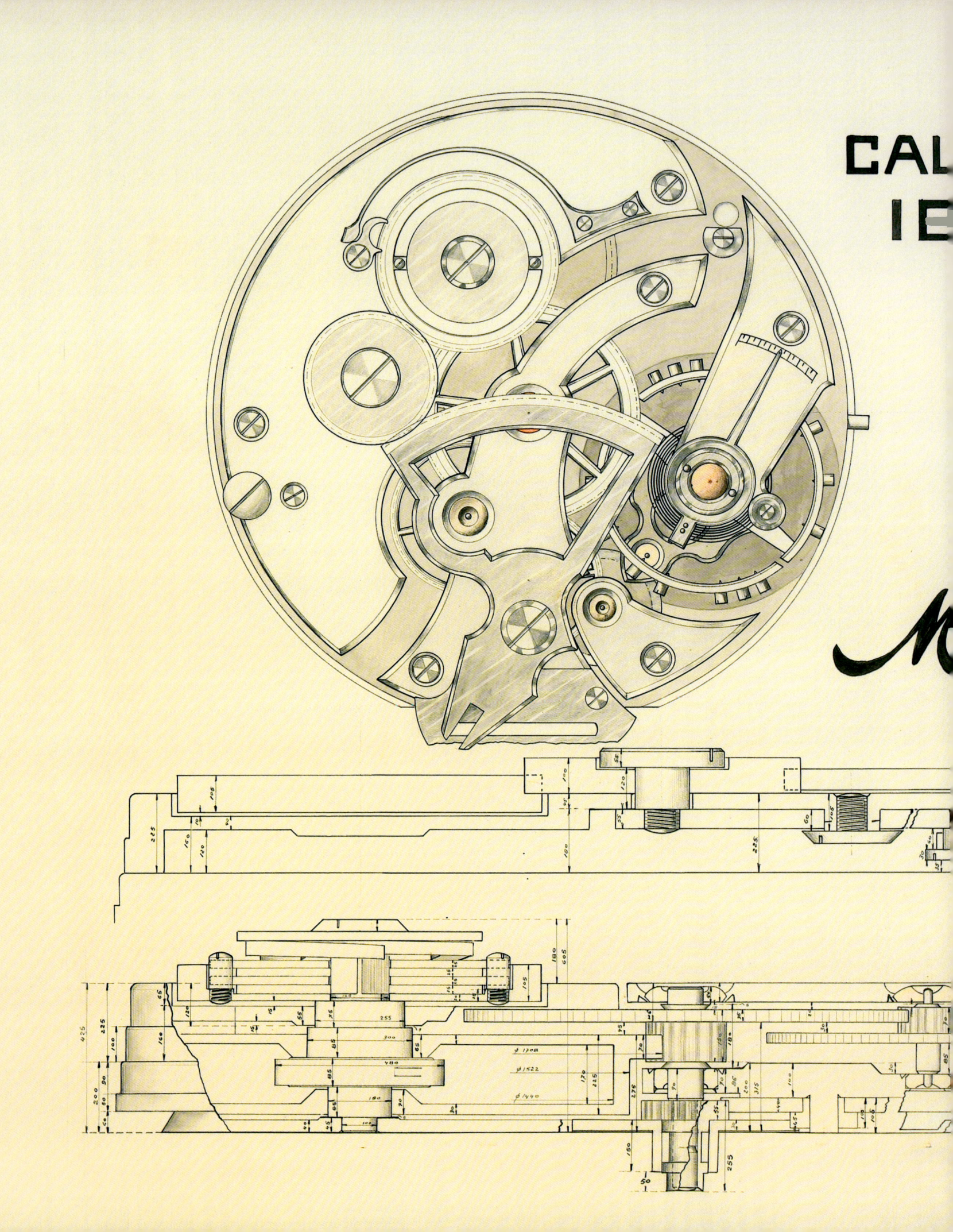

M

BRE
37

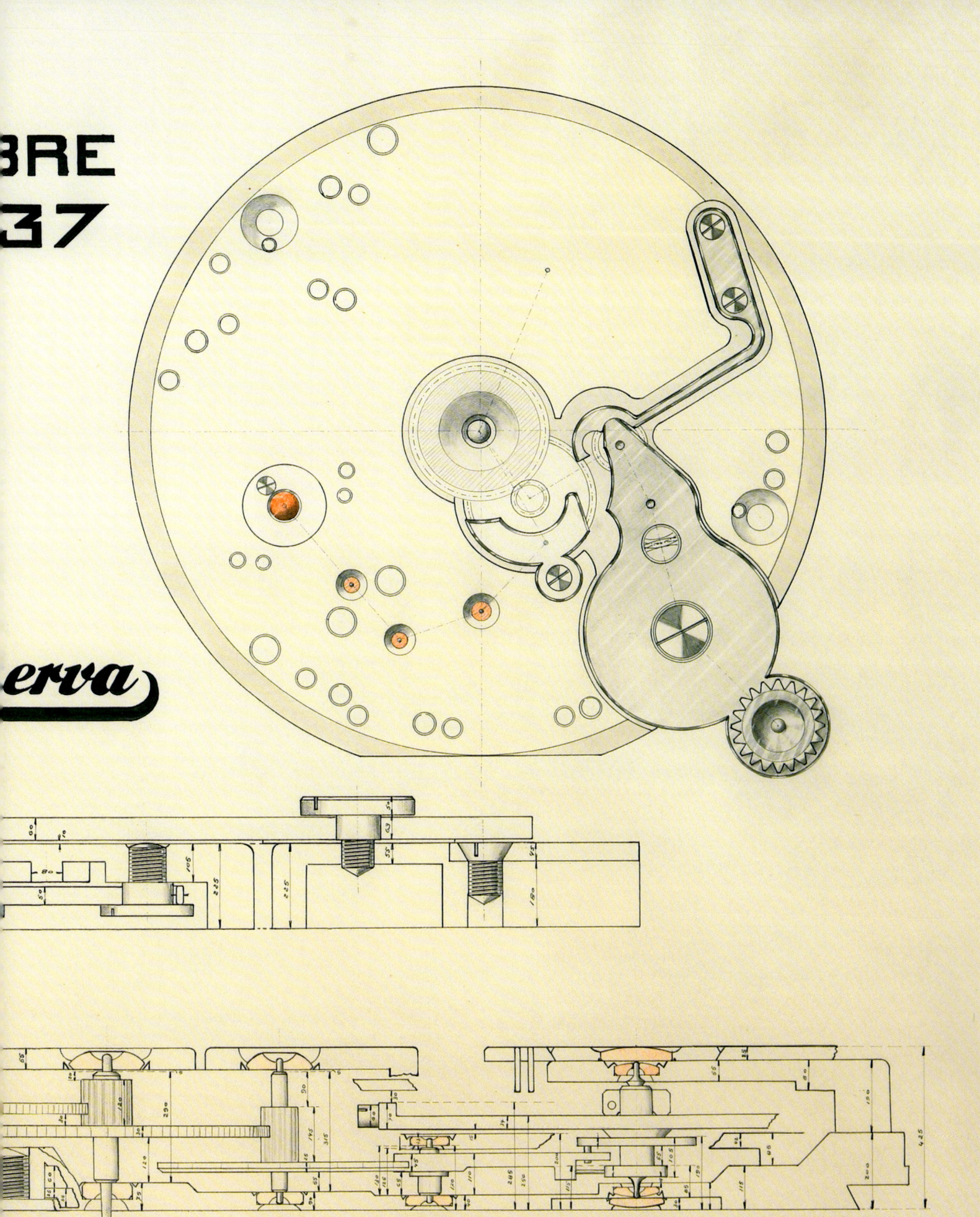

erva

41 Gilded movement (19 lignes) with 15 jewels and winding crown. A single bridge covers all the wheels. Engraved cock with screwed balance wheel and flat hairspring. Anchor escapement.

41a Detail of regulator for flat hairspring with regulator key.

42 Silver-plated movement (19 lignes) with 11 jewels, *"Côtes de Genève"* decoration, and winding crown. A single bridge covers all the wheels. Engraved cock with screwed balance wheel and flat hairspring. Anchor escapement.

43 Rhodium-plated movement (19 lignes) with 15 jewels, fine *"Côtes de Genève"* decoration, and winding crown. One bridge in two parts covers all the wheels. Engraved cock with screwed balance wheel and flat hairspring. Anchor escapement.

44 Detail of the anchor escapement of the movement in illustration 41.

45 Drawing of a Swiss anchor escapement, the principle of which was used by Minerva.

46 Different phases of the rise in a Swiss anchor escapement.

206

III The History of Minerva Watch Movements

MOVEMENT WITH AN ANCHOR ESCAPEMENT

A movement with an anchor escapement is a movement that uses a balance wheel combined with an anchor escapement as standard of time. The movements made by Minerva were divided into three quality classes:
1 simple 7-jewel movements with a "flat hairspring";
2 medium quality movements with up to 15 jewels with a "Breguet hairspring," some of them with a precision regulator;
3 "Extra" movements of superior quality. They included movements that could contain up to 17 jewels, with compensating balance wheel, Breguet hairspring, swan's-neck regulator, and up to 4 screwed settings.

How the escapement works

Illustrations 45 and 46 explain the events in the different stages of operation of an anchor escapement. Note should be taken of the respective arrangement of the balance wheel U, the anchor and the anchor wheel H. The teeth of the anchor wheel are not pointed, but have plane surfaces K, called impulse planes. Let us suppose that the balance wheel is swinging toward the right. The fork of the anchor is resting on its banking pin A, the tooth of the anchor, wheel is at rest on the entry pallet.

Illustration 46 shows the different stages. Position a represents the moment when the tooth meets the pallet. Because of the position of the pallet with respect to the tooth, the pallet penetrates even further into the tooth point circle Z (acceleration of the Pallet, position b) until the fork of the anchor reaches the banking pin A.

The anchor and the balance wheel are now no longer in contact. The balance wheel swings in its complementary arc as far as its point of return, swings back in the other direction propelled by the tension of the hairspring, and takes the anchor in the opposite direction with the ellipse C.

The rise of the anchor (with transmission of the impulse to the balance wheel, illustration 46), begins when the front point of the tooth is able to slide under the pallet (position c).

Then the tooth slides fully under the pallet (position d).

The rise is not yet complete at the moment when the front point of the tooth leaves the pallet (position e).

This is the point of action by the impulse plane (the flat of the tooth) K, which is also arranged at an incline in the circle of teeth. The rise does not end until the moment when the rear point of the tooth has dropped back from the pallet (position f). A low angle is retained throughout the rise between the pallet and the tooth to ensure better retention of the oil (positions c to f).

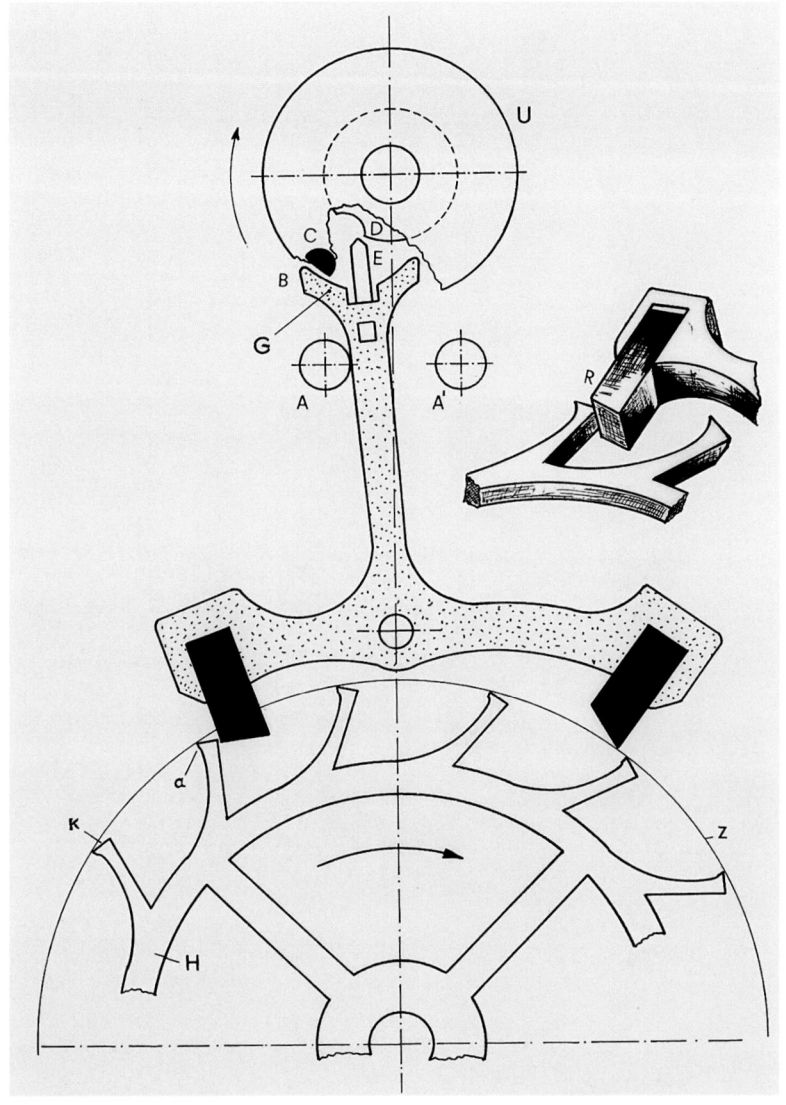

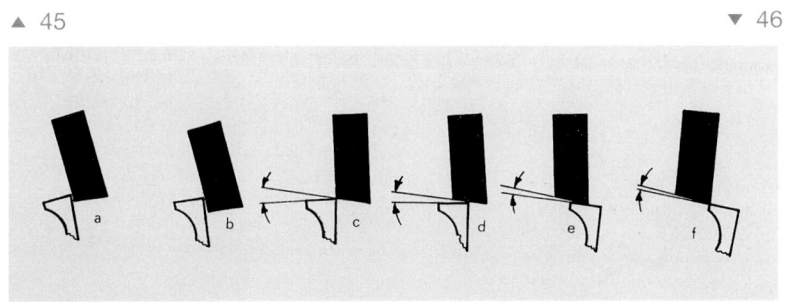

▲ 45   ▼ 46

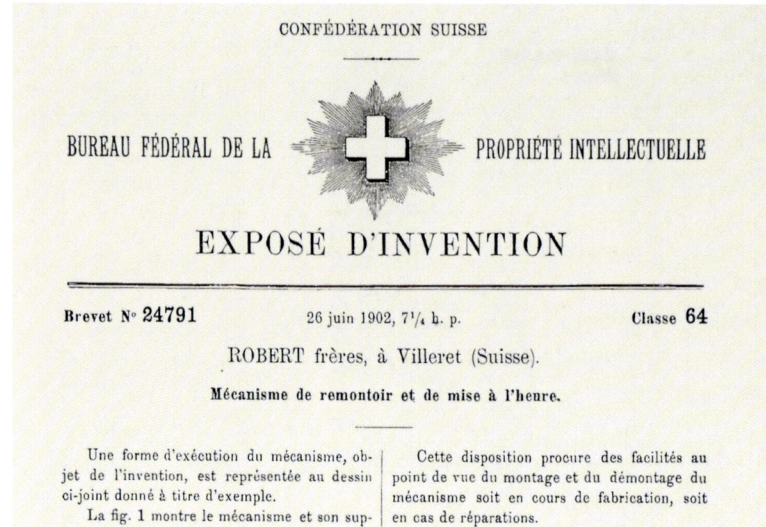

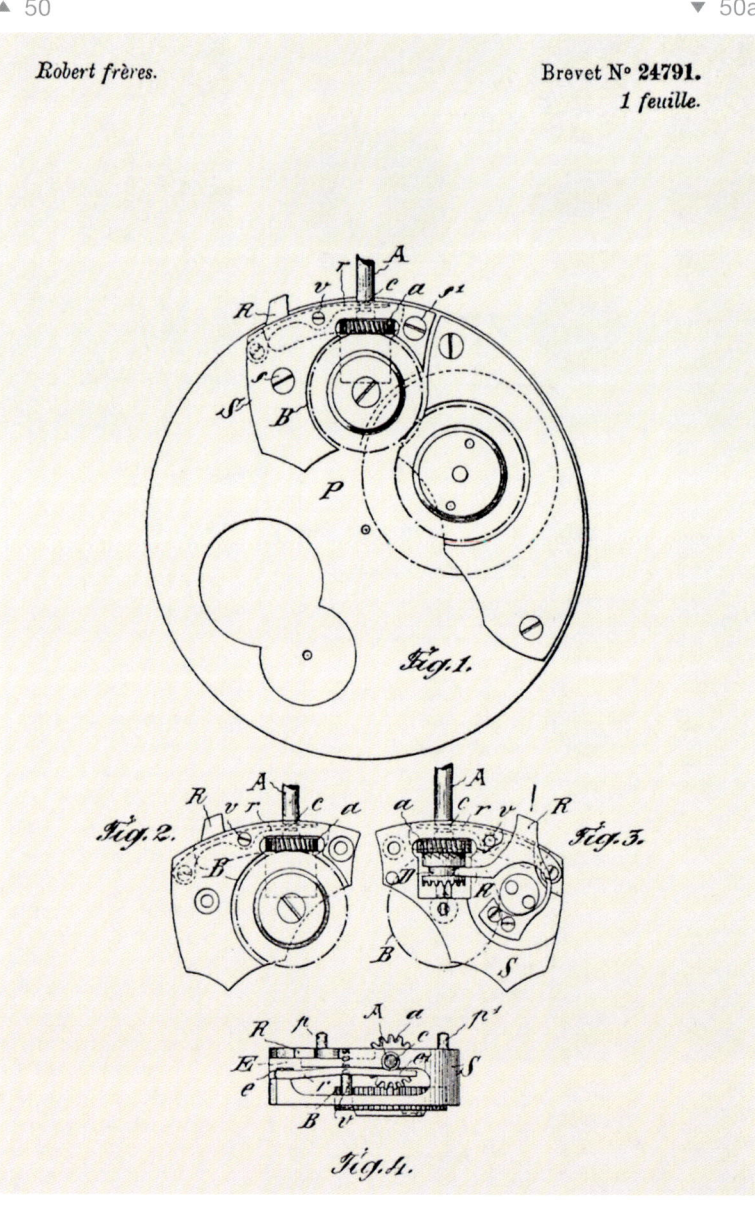

47 Pocket-watch movement with continuous barrel bridge.

48 Pocket-watch movement with separate bridges for the barrel and the winder. The winder is contained entirely inside the winder bridge, and is marked on the movement side with patent no. 24791.

49 Rear of winding bridge with integral winder.

50–50a Swiss patent no. 24791 of 1902 for the new winder.

51 Movement with negative winding. The barrel bridge is withdrawn.

52 Movement with negative winding and winding bridge removed, in time-setting position. The sliding pinion and the winding wheel are engaged by pressing the crown.

53 The sliding pinion and the winding wheel are disengaged when the crown is pulled out to set the time.

54 Dial-side view with right-angle lever and sliding pinion in time-setting position.

208

MINERVA WINDING SYSTEMS

The first series of movements made by Minerva made use of a classical winding system with winder (ill. 47), thus carrying on the customary tradition of Fontainemelon. To improve assembly, a new winding system was developed by Robert Frères in 1902 (ill. 48 and 49), for which a patent was applied for (ill. 50). This invention consisted in fitting the whole winding mechanism in a small, separate bridge which, once it was inserted in the movement, enabled the watch to be wound and the hands to be set.

In the 1920s, another innovation appeared in the shape of "negative winding." This device made it possible to withdraw the whole movement from the case without having to remove the winding stem. This stem was composed of two parts, the inner part having a square on the movement side into which the second part fitted when the movement was put into the case. An extra movable stud in the winding stem actuated a lever which moved the hand setting lever by means of a spring into two positions, winding and setting the time. To make the system easier to understand, illustrations 51 to 54 show and explain the different positions of the mechanism.

▲ 52

▼ 53

51

▼ 54

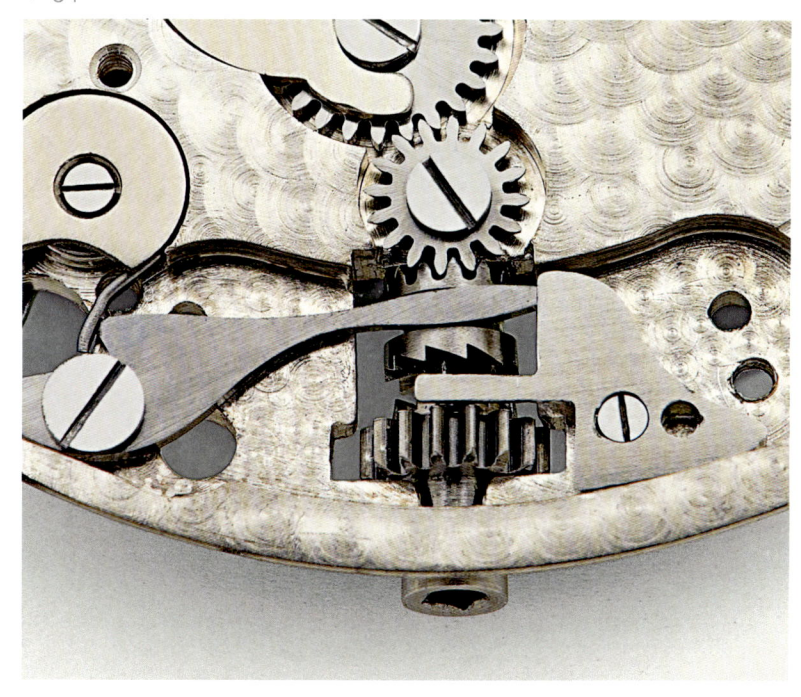

209

▲ 55   ▼ 56   ▲ 55a   ▼ 57

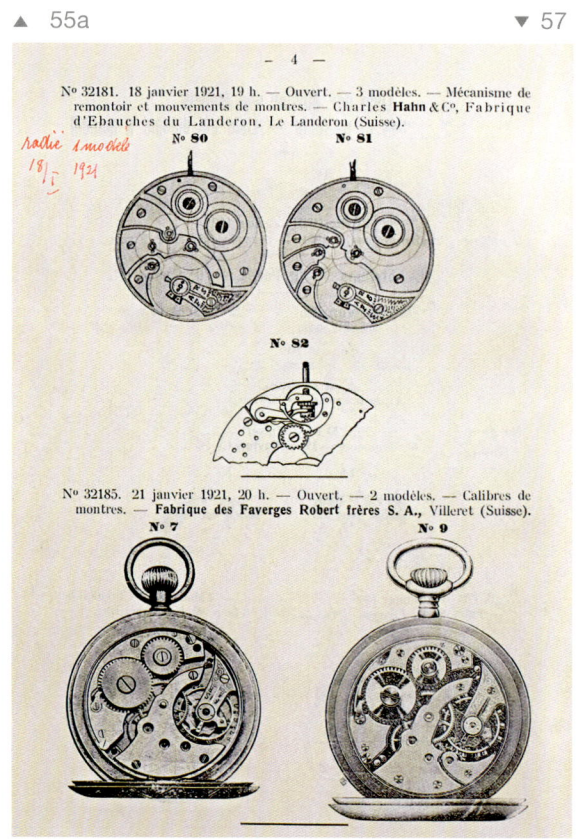

210

III The History of Minerva Watch Movements

ANCHOR MOVEMENTS WITH BREGUET HAIRSPRING

When a flat hairspring is a certain length, the balance wheel oscillates isochronally,[1] but this value is difficult to determine. So in about 1800, Abraham Louis Breguet[2] decided to lift the end of the hairspring to improve its isochronism. This curve, originally defined empirically, was transposed by Édouard Phillips[3] in 1860 into a mathematical formula which is still used today for the end curve of hairsprings. This shape of hairspring, combined with an open, compensated balance wheel and swan's-neck precision adjustment, made it possible to obtain excellent regulation results.

55–56
Two similar high-quality movements, rhodium-plated, of the Lépine caliber (55) and the full hunter (56) with double bridge. Compensating balance wheel with Breguet hairspring under a decorated or engraved cock. Anchor escapement.

55a
Detail of cock with precision regulator, compensating balance wheel, and Breguet hairspring. The banking pins are situated above and inside the outer diameter of the hairspring.

57 Book of models of 1921, with models 7 and 9.

58–59 Two similar high-quality movements, gilded, of the Lépine caliber and the full hunter with integral bridge. Cock with precision regulator, compensating balance wheel, and Breguet hairspring. Anchor escapement.

▲ 58

▼ 59

211

60 Superior quality level for a movement with four screwed settings, decorated bridges, cock with precision regulator, compensating balance wheel with gold screws, and Breguet hairspring. The plate bears the engraved indications: 17 Jewels, 4 Adjustments.

61 High-precision gilded movement with screwed median setting, compensating balance wheel, and Breguet hairspring.

62 Rhodium-plated high-precision movement with compensating balance wheel and Breguet hairspring. The bridge bears the engraved indication: 4 Adjustments.

▼ 63, 64, 65

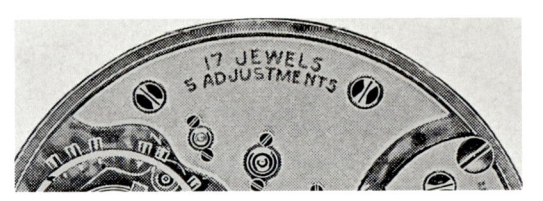

▲ 60   ▼ 61   ▼ 62

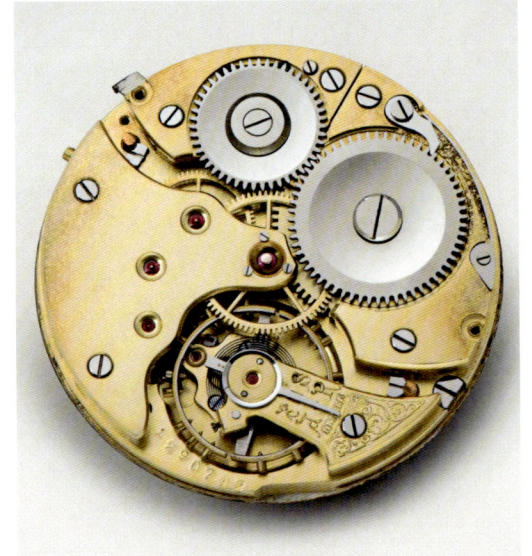

66

212

"Extra Quality" Anchor Escapements

CHRONOMETER

Every manufacture was honor-bound to include an "extra quality" model in its product range. This designation was applicable to pocket watches of outstanding accuracy, regulated in four or five positions and accompanied on request with a "bulletin de marche" (running report) providing official certification of its accuracy. Even if other locations might be mentioned in the *Bulletin de marche de l'observatoire...*, they were generally issued by officials of the municipal Official Bureaux for the observation of watches in Biel or La Chaux-de-Fonds, which had precision pendulum clocks that received a daily time signal from the observatory in Neuchâtel and were thus able to guarantee the uniformity of their measurements.[1]

The test lasted for a period of 15 days for **First Class**:

1 day:	pendant on the left
1 day:	pendant on the right
5 days:	pendant upwards
4 days:	dial upwards

For temperatures:
1 day:	in an oven between 28 and 32°C
1 day:	at room temperature
1 day:	in a cool box between 0 and 4°C
1 day:	at room temperature

The test for **Second Class** lasted 10 days, and did not include the cool box.

In general, watches equipped with a chronograph and small watches of a diameter of less than 30 millimeters were also permitted to undergo the test procedures. At the end of the tests, the bureaux drew up a Bulletin de Marche bearing an official seal. The Bulletin de Marche had to specify the name of the watch, precise details relating to its running and daily timekeeping deviations, and a brief summary of average running as recorded during the period of observation.

The watchmakers often engraved on the upper bridge of tested movements, beside the number of jewels, the indication 3, 4, or even 5 adjustments.

63–65 Tested movements were always marked with the number of jewels and the number of positions (adjustments) in which running had been tested. These tests were performed according to the demands of the customer.

66 Screwed setting as a sign of high quality.

67 Swan's-neck regulation with polished regulator and spring.

68–69 Pocket watch (17 lignes), "extra quality." The dial bears the following indication: Singer Chronometer. Movement with four screwed settings, precision regulator, compensating balance wheel, and Breguet hairspring. Anchor escapement.

213

▲ 70 ▼ 71 ▲ 72 ▼ 73

70–71 Silver pocket watch, Lépine case, enameled dial with Arabic numerals, small seconds at 6 o'clock, and blued steel hands. Silver-plated movement (19 lignes), winding system with winder and double bridge. Ratchet covers finely polished, engraved cock with compensating balance wheel and Breguet hairspring. Anchor escapement.

72–73 Silver pocket watch, Lépine case, enameled dial with Arabic numerals, small seconds at 6 o'clock, and blued steel hands. Silver-plated movement (19 lignes), winding system with winder and double bridge. Ratchet cover with radial polish, simple engraved cock with swan's-neck regulator, compensating balance wheel, and Breguet hairspring. Anchor escapement.

74–75 Gold hunter no. 1290742 by Minerva, Villeret, c. 1927. White enameled dial with Arabic numerals, small seconds at 6 o'clock, and blued steel hands.

75 Gilded movement with screwed median setting and polished screws. Engraved cock with swan's-neck regulator (removed). Compensating balance wheel with Breguet hairspring. Anchor escapement.

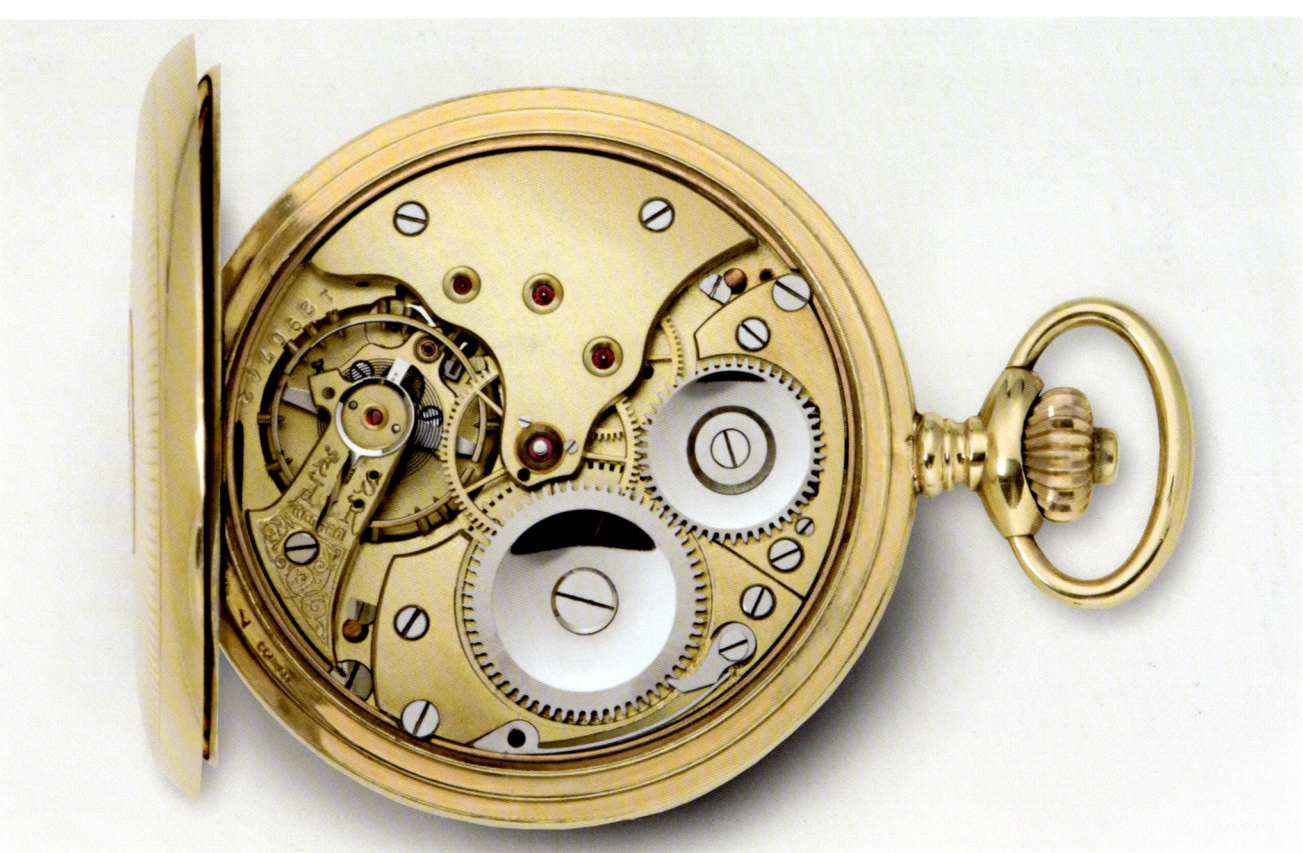

▲ 74

▼ 75

215

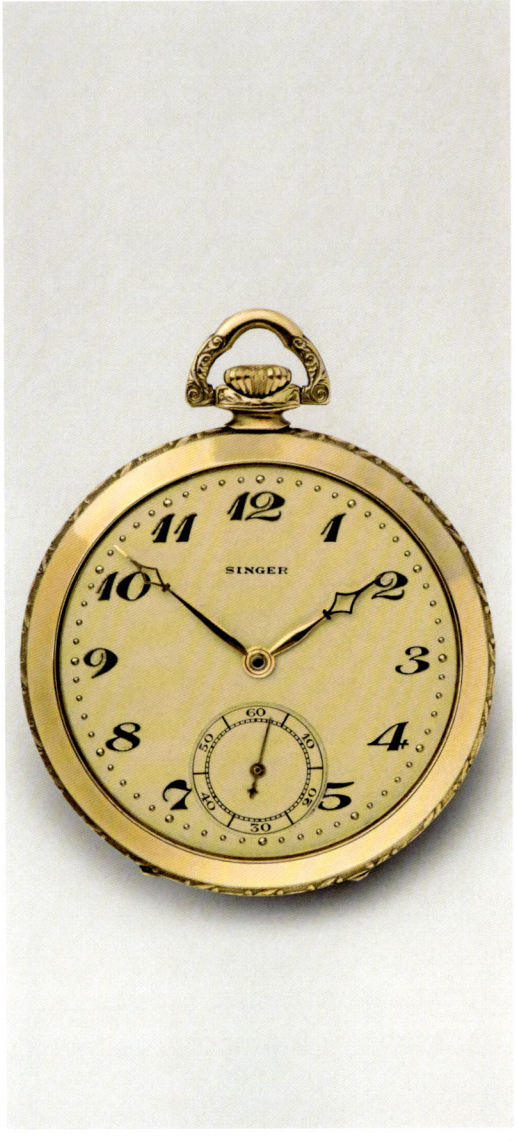

▲ 76 ▼ 77 ▼ 78 ▼ 79 ▲ 80

216

III   The History of Minerva Watch Movements

▲ 81   ▼ 82

76–80 Development of different shapes of bridges for the Minerva 17 lignes caliber, with one bridge covering the entire gear train (78–79), then two bridges (80), then three (76). For special orders, movements and dials bore the name of the customer (76).

81–82 Gold hunter with gilded dial and appliqué numerals. Gilded hands. Gilded bridges with engraved cock. Compensating balance wheel with Breguet hairspring. Anchor escapement.

83–85 Silver hunter with silver-plated dial, Arabic figures, and small seconds. Blued steel hands. Gilded bridges with compensating balance wheel and Breguet hairspring. Anchor escapement. Silver cuvette with the inscription: Minerva, Ancre 15 Rubis, LEVÉES VISIBLES, DOUBLE PLATEAU, Spiral Breguet, Balancier compensé (Minerva, Anchor escapement 15 jewels, VISIBLE ANCHOR RISE, DOUBLE ROLLER, Breguet hairspring, compensating balance wheel.)

217

JOURNAL
Grand-Livre
HORLOGERIE
5

JOURNAL
GRAND-
LIVRE

Grand Livre
1

Grand Livre Horlogerie 2

GRAND-LIVRE Horlogerie 4

Journal 1

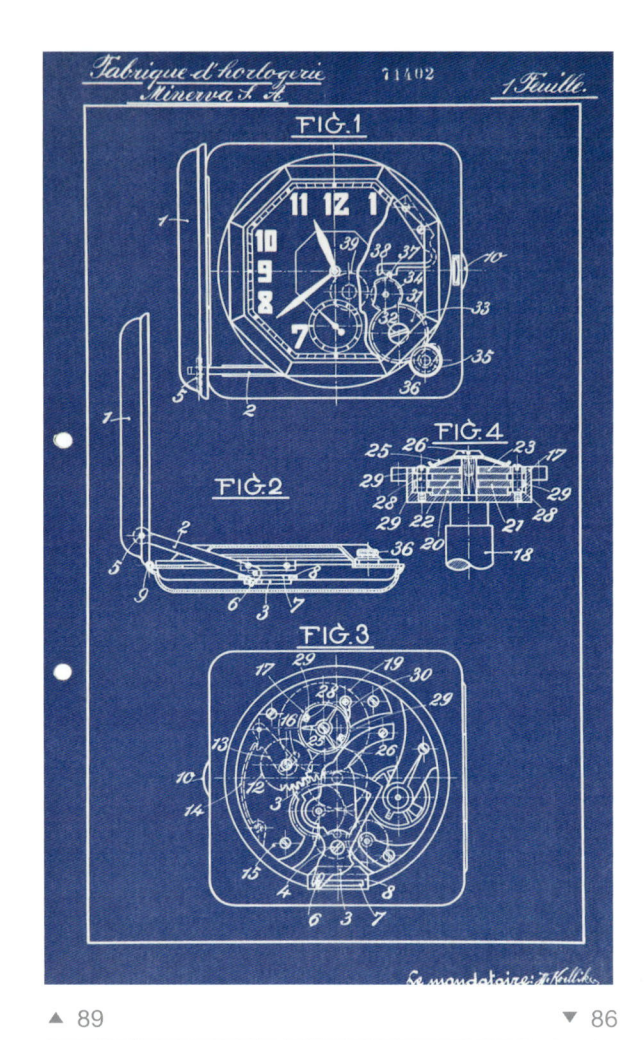

Preceding pages
These large manufacture books date back to the start of the 20th century. They are all carefully preserved in the library on the 4th floor, along with the production registers.

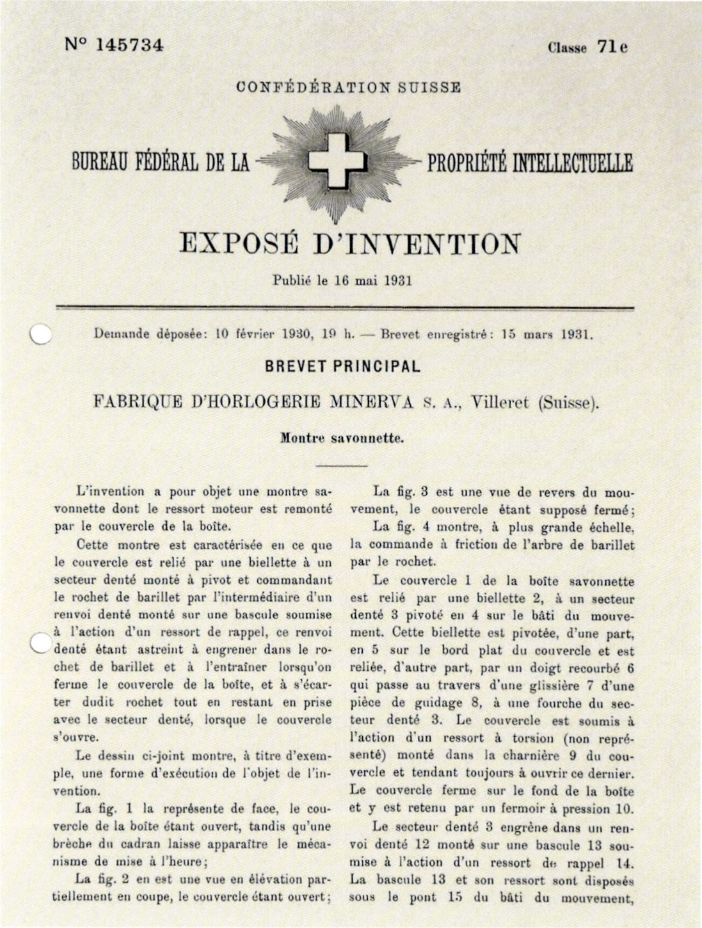

86–87 Traveling watch in leather cladding, wound by the cover. The watch was wound by repeated opening and closing of the cover.

88 Winding by the cover was the subject of a patent in Switzerland in 1931.

89 Original Minerva blueprint for the patent application.

90 Gilded pocket-watch movement with the mark of the Ariana brand.

90a The Ariana brand was registered in 1902 by E. Robert, fabricant, Villeret.

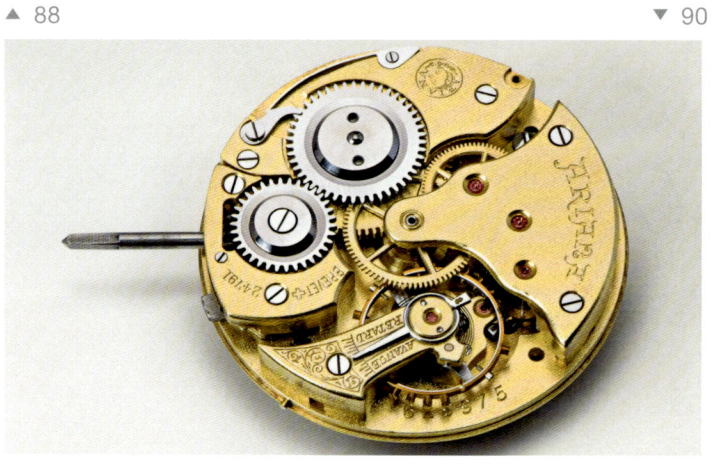

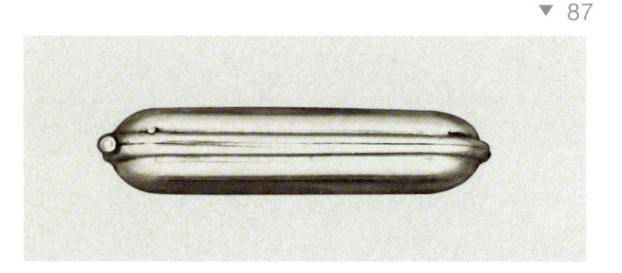

220

ANCHOR MOVEMENTS IN SPECIAL SHAPES

Minerva produced a number of movements in special shapes. The archives contain few documents on this subject, and it is hard to find models.

One incomplete watch has been located, with a 24-ligne movement that would appear to have been made only in limited runs. There also exist a few movements for the Hertha and Ariana brands, bearing the corresponding stamp on the movement. Another very interesting pocket watch is a traveling model, equipped with the caliber 16/37, which was wound by means of the cover and dates from the year 1930. This last function can be clearly recognized from drawings and old photographs.

91 Barrel bridge with the mark of the Hertha brand.

92 The Hertha brand was registered in 1898 by Robert Frères, Villeret.

93 Unfinished 24-ligne Minerva movement. Gilded three-quarter plate with anchor-wheel bridge fitted. Simple cock with ruby endstone. Large compensating balance wheel with 16 counterweights and 4 adjusting screws, with Breguet hairspring. Anchor escapement. Diameter 67.5 mm.

94 Large pocket watch with nickel-silver case. White enameled dial with majestic Arabic numerals and small seconds. Blued steel hands.

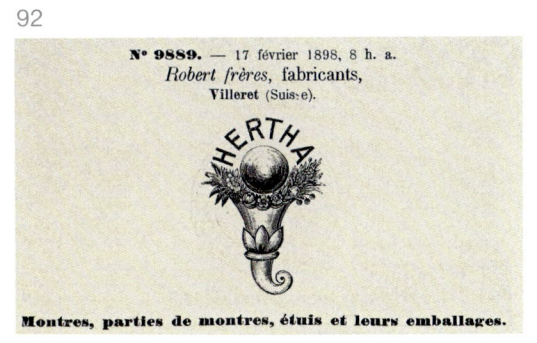

221

▲ 95   ▼ 96   ▲ 97   ▼ 98

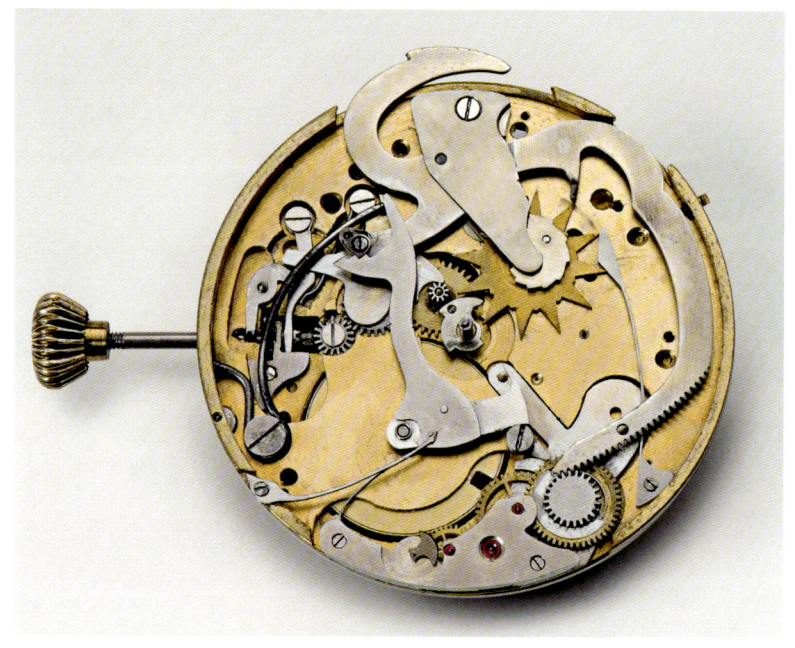

▼ 99

95–99 Pocket watch in niello-silver with quarter-repetition on two notes. Silver case with engraved floral motifs, inlay, and gilt monogram cartouche. Silver cuvette with the inscription: Répétition à Quarts, Ancre de Précision, 15 Rubis [Quarter-hour repeater, precision anchor, 15 jewels].

95 Gilt movement with screwed two-note gong and two hammers at 2 o'clock. Anchor escapement.

96 View of dial with striking train under-dial work. The complete striking mechanism with centrifugal governor is situated at 6 o'clock.

100 Incomplete silver-plated movement for quarter repetition, but without striking mechanism or gongs. Screwed balance wheel with flat hairspring.

101–102 Swiss and German patents for the two Lépine and hunter quarter repeater versions.

222

ANCHOR MOVEMENTS WITH QUARTER-HOUR REPEATER

According to a publication devoted to the history of the manufacture[1], Minerva also marketed watches with quarter-hour and minute repetition. It has proved possible to confirm the existence of a few quarter-hour repeater movements. Production of these movements (ill. 100) was in connection with the patents of Citelli (1905) and Picard & Co. (1907). In all probability, Minerva produced the movements, while the repeater mechanisms were procured from external suppliers. Illustrations 95 to 99 show a complete quarter-repeater watch with the square balance-spring stud characteristic of Minerva. The watch bears no signature. The repeater mechanism was available in two different versions, for the Lépine and hunter calibers. We have no knowledge of a minute-repeater mechanism built by Minerva. To date, no movement of this type has been diskovered in the company's archives.

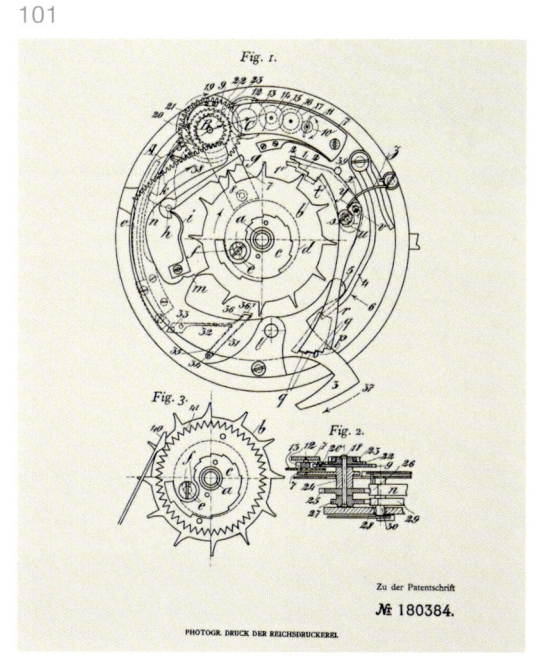

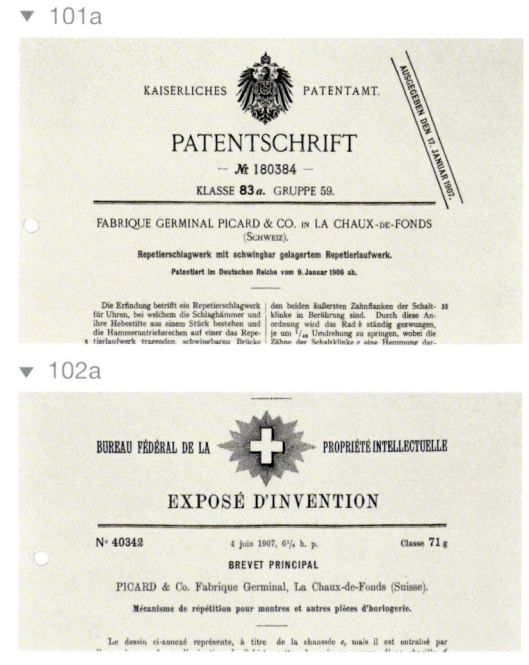

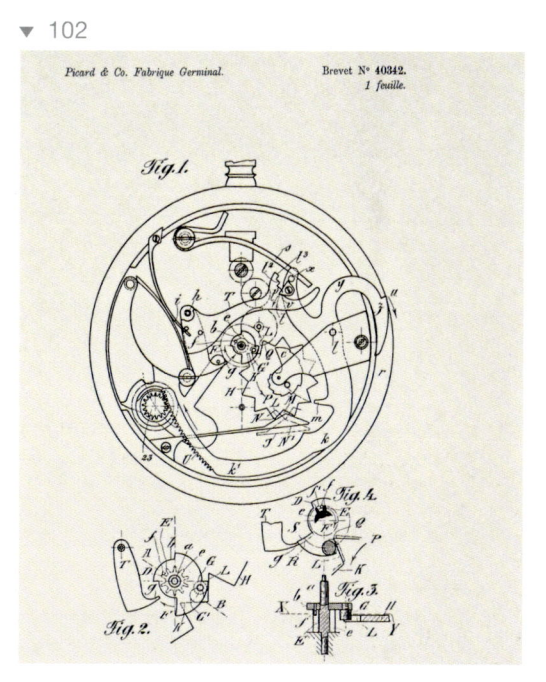

100

101

101a

102

102a

▲ 103

104   105   106   ▼ 107

▲ 108

▲ 109   ▼ 110

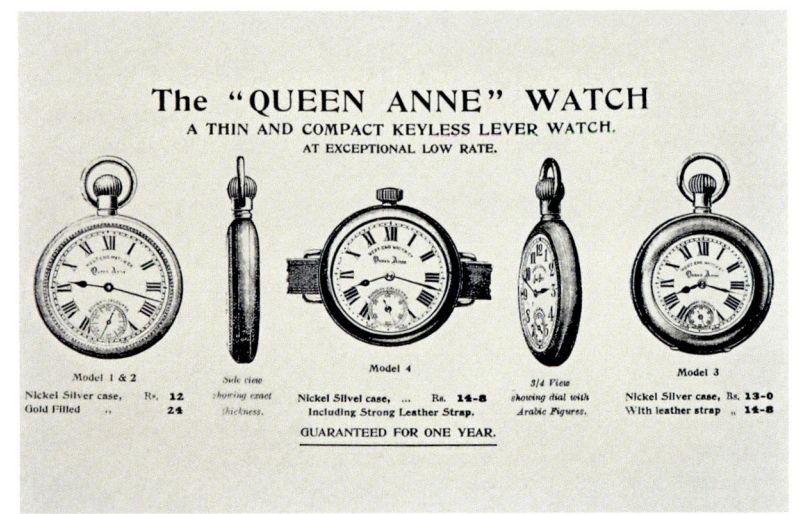

103–106 Hand-written address on an envelope sent to Charles Robert Frères, Villeret, canton Berne, Switzerland. Posted in India, the letter travelled between December 16 and 29, 1905, as shown by the postmarks (ill. 104 to 106).

107 Advertisement by West End Watch S.A., with pocket watches and wristwatches. The movements of these watches were made by Minerva at Villeret.

108 Book of models with registration of the small 15-ligne movement built by La Fabrique des Faverges, Robert Frères, Villeret.

109–110 Gilded, 15-ligne movement with 7 jewels, by Minerva. On the enameled dial, the inscription West End Watch Co. and designation of the model: Secular.

111 Advertisement by West End Watch Co. for small pocket watches which could be worn as wristwatches in a small leather pouch to take military requirements into account.

112–113 Silver pocket watch with chronograph by Minerva. Enameled dial with Roman numerals, small seconds, and 30-minute counter. Gilded movement with chronograph mechanism arranged so as to be visible. Compensating balance wheel with flat hairspring. Anchor escapement.

III The History of Minerva Watch Movements

WEST END WATCH S.A., COMPAGNIE DES MONTRES CO.

Geneva, Bombay, Calcutta, Saint-Imier

This company had numerous branches all over the world, notably in Bombay, in India. The marks and stamps that it placed on its cases and the bridges of its movements were very varied. Minerva supplied the company with simple, seven-jewel watches and chronographs, sold under the name of West End Watch Co. As the letter of 1905 shows, there were regular exchanges of correspondence between India and Villeret, in Switzerland. The watches were destined for the troops based on the sub-continent, and for the staff of the railway companies. Legibility of the dial was therefore of particular importance for these timepieces. Like the model shown in illustration 109, of small size (15 lignes), these movements were encased in wristwatches, which themselves were inserted in leather coverings (ill. 111). Minerva also supplied classical pocket chronographs with thick, easily legible numerals to the West End Watch Co.

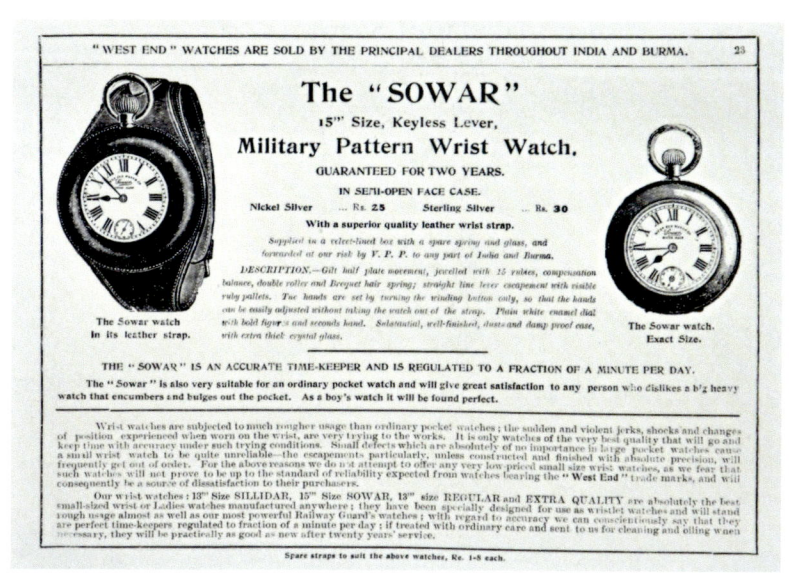

111

112

113

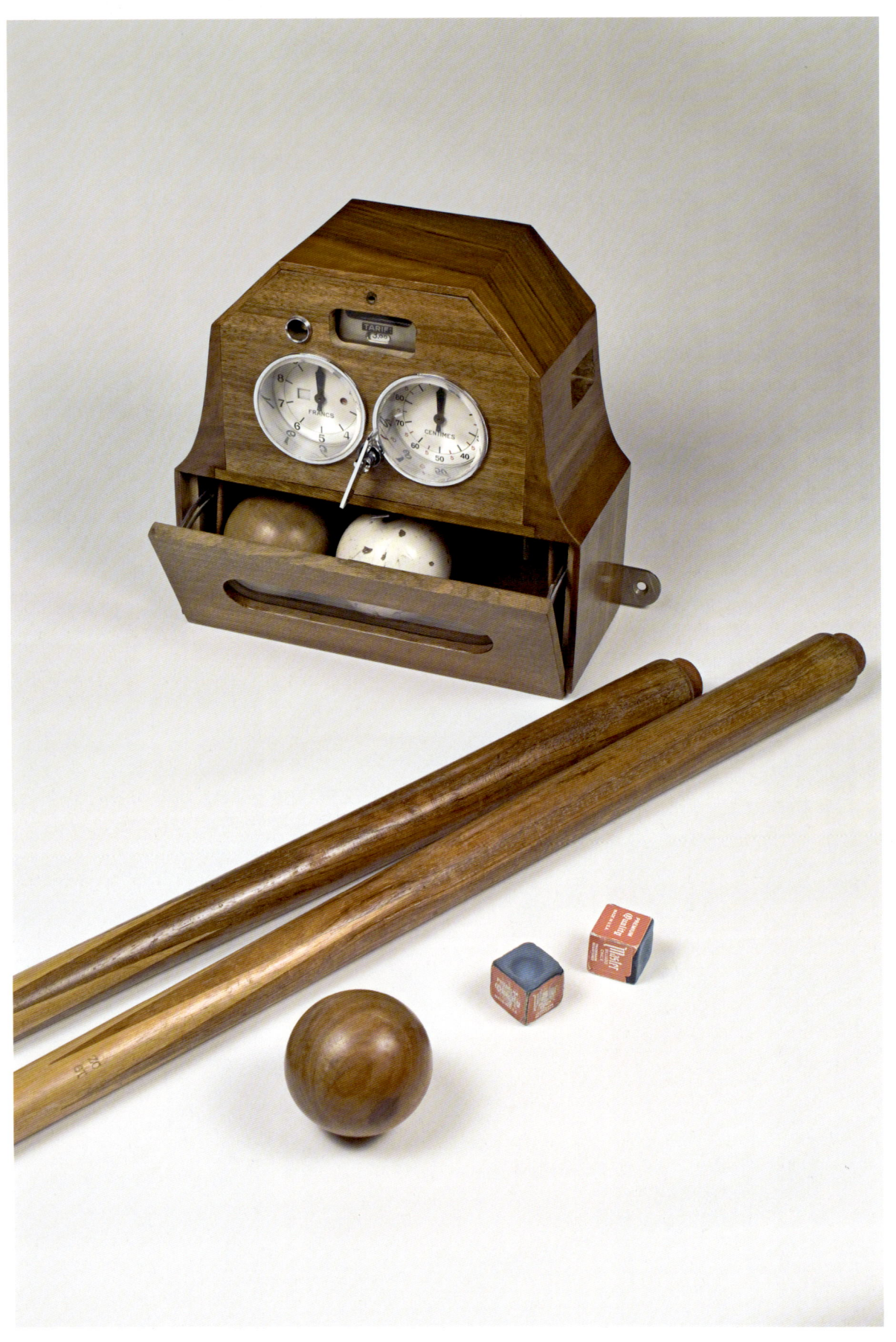

114 Control device for the game of billiards, in walnut cabinet. It does not show the time of day, but the rental price of a billiard table in francs and centimes, and the rental time still remaining. On actuation of the mechanism, the lower drawer opens to allow access to the wooden billiard balls.

114a–114b
This extremely complex product by Minerva was patented in 1932.

N° 163404   Classe **118 d**

CONFÉDÉRATION SUISSE

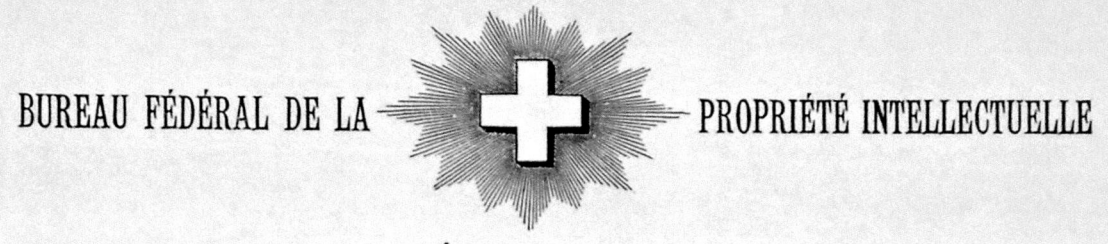

BUREAU FÉDÉRAL DE LA ✚ PROPRIÉTÉ INTELLECTUELLE

EXPOSÉ D'INVENTION

Publié le 1er novembre 1933

Demande déposée: 14 octobre 1932, 19 h. — Brevet enregistré: 15 août 1933.

BREVET PRINCIPAL

FABRIQUE D'HORLOGERIE MINERVA S. A., Villeret (Suisse).

Appareil de contrôle pour jeux de billard.

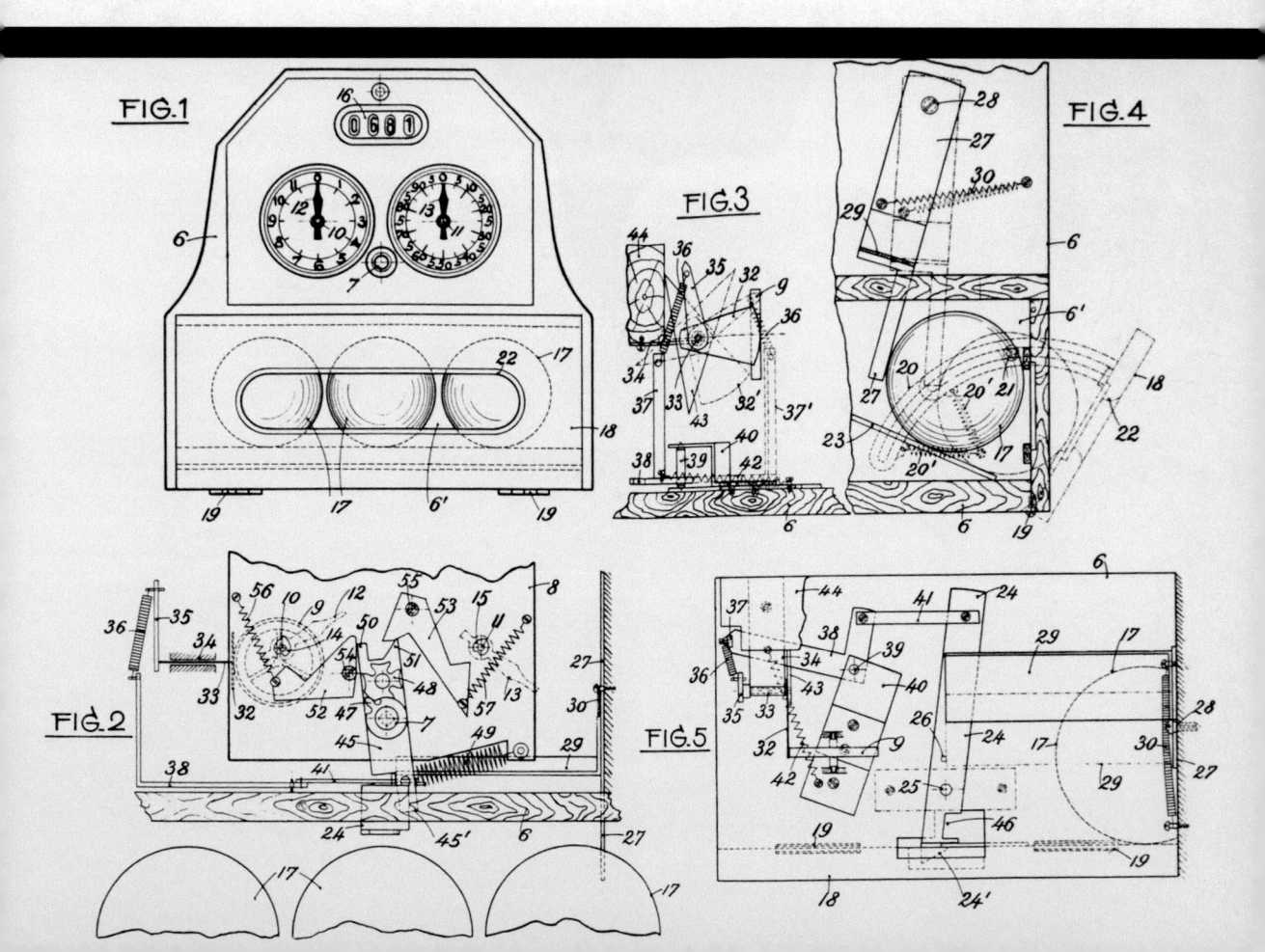

▲ 115   ▼ 116

115 In the background, a simple wooden engraving block with assorted gravers. In the foreground, a guilloche silver case with engraved monogram cartouche.

116 Various models of cases manufactured within the company or procured from external suppliers, with monogram cartouche.

117 Lady's-pocket watch case in .800 silver and niello decorated with stars and monogram cartouche.

118 Lady's-pocket watch case in .800 silver and niello with banded decoration and empty monogram cartouche.

119 Man's-pocket watch case in .800 silver, with engraving and guilloche all over and empty monogram cartouche.

120 Man's-pocket watch case in .800 silver, with engraving and guilloche all over and empty monogram cartouche.

228

III The History of Minerva Watch Movements

CASES DECORATION

From about 1902 onward, Minerva produced its own cases in a specialist department on its new production site. Production ranged from simple models in steel with a monogram cartouche to cases decorated all over with engraving and guilloche. This decoration was done by a machine devised for the purpose and capable of producing the motifs shown in illustration 116.

The engraving, on the other hand, was done almost solely by hand using a graving tool. In more recent periods the motifs, which evolved in accordance with prevailing taste, were predrawn with a guilloche machine and then engraved by hand.

The company also housed movements in niello-silver cases which were not of its own production (ill. 117 and 118). Nevertheless, making cases enabled Minerva to become a fully-fledged manufacture, as it now produced all the essential components of a watch.

117

118

119

120

Numéros	ℋC 13.					
Pivotages						
Remont. finiss.						
Remont. échapp[ts]						
Coupage de balanciers						
Réglages						
Posage de spiraux						
Posage de tirettes						
Mise en boîtes						
Terminage						
Ret. Régl. Visitage						

№		1183173					
TIGES.		57					
COQS.							
ECHAPP.		17	20	20	20	20	23
CHAMP.		~~84~~	77	~~80~~	~~80~~	77	76
P. MOYEN.		86	90	90	92	97	85
G. MOYEN.							

▲ 121   ▼ 121a

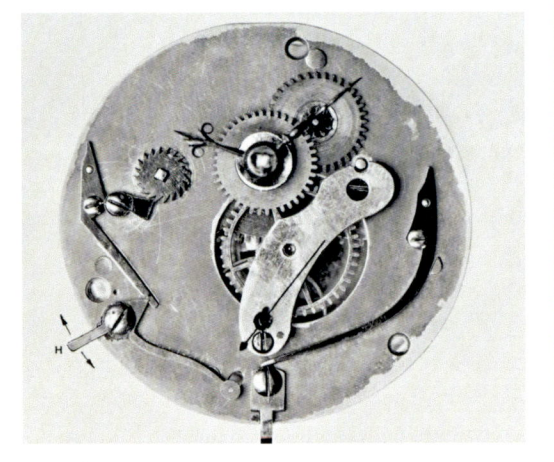

▼ 122

▲ 123   ▼ 122a

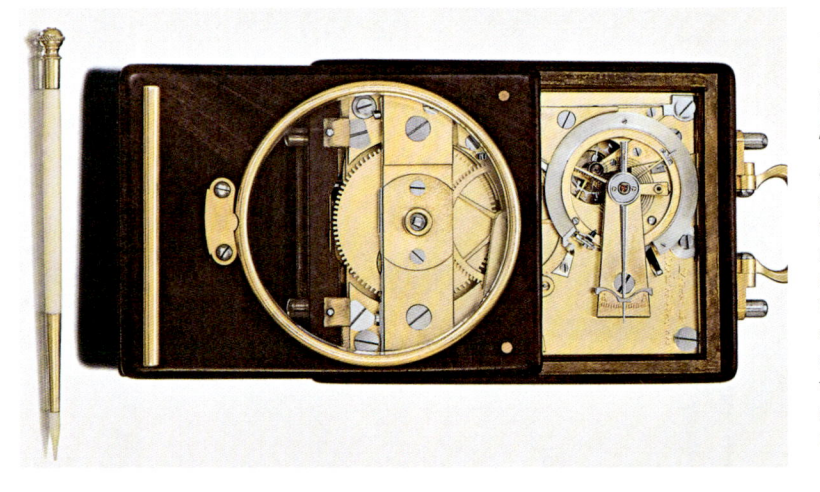

Preceding pages
Cartons enclosing six sets of components for anchor movements with quarter-hour repeater. These cartons were given to watchmakers working from home or in the workshop around 1910. After being assembled and controlled, the movement was dismantled in order to be decorated and gilded or rhodium-plated, before its final assembly.

121–121a
Pocket watch with verge escapement, c. 1790, known as the "Doctor Watch." The seconds hand, arranged on a small separate dial, could be immobilized. A time interval could be measured by stopping the movement with the lever H. However, this action entailed loss of the display of the time of day.

122–122a
Rieussec ink chronograph, c. 1825. Displays: ⅕ second, 60 seconds, 60 minutes and 12 hours on separate dials.

123 The first known model of a recording chronograph by Rieussec, after 1821. The two disks for display of seconds and minutes began to rotate when measurement was started. At the stop, the double index in the center deposited a dot on each disk. The disks with their numbered scales had to be reset to zero by hand.

232

The Birth of the Chronograph

THE "DOCTOR WATCH"

The nineteenth century represented a pivotal epoch for the watchmaking industry, in England and France as well as in Switzerland, where many companies came into being. A large number of inventions of general application simultaneously transformed the appearance of timepieces. With the arrival of the seconds hand on the dials, the smallest unit of time, the second, became visible at all times. To measure the duration of an event that took place in a period of less than a minute, it was necessary to record its beginning and end according to the position of the seconds hand, which was in constant movement. This method was neither convenient nor accurate. In order to offer greater reliability, watchmakers soon equipped watches with a separate counter for the seconds. However, the sciences and medicine soon demanded to be able to immobilise the seconds hand to enable recording of a measurement. The simplest solution was to interrupt the operation of the watch by means of a small lever, and this gave rise to the "Doctor Watch" (ill. 121). But this meant that a consequence of each measurement was the loss of the time display. Astronomers soon had at their disposal a "seconds counter," with its characteristic "tick-tock" mounted on a telescope to measure the duration of celestial phenomena with precision.

NICOLAS MATHIEU RIEUSSEC

In 1821, it occurred to Nicolas Mathieu Rieussec to develop an instrument designed for the measurement of brief intervals of time that would record the duration of the event but would not display the time of day. His invention was used for the first time at a horse race in Paris. With this instrument, it was possible to establish the time, not only of the winner, but also of all the other horses in the competition. To do this, points were marked in ink on two rotating dials, one for minutes and the other for seconds (ill. 123). Rieussec named his instrument the "chronograph," from the Greek *chronos*, time, and *graphos*, writing, in other words a "writer of time." In 1822, he obtained a five-year patent for his seconds chronograph.

Over the years that followed, Rieussec perfected his writing hand by giving it a rotary movement (ill. 125) and provided his dials with marks now ranging from a fifth of a second to 12 hours. In the new arrangement, only the seconds hand in the center retained its marking function.

The drawing nibs of the chronographs were made up of two parts (ill. 130). The lower part, in the form of a spoon, was pierced vertically and filled with a small quantity of thick ink. Through this small orifice, the upper part, in the form of a needle, deposited a spot of ink at each recording on the fixed dial arranged underneath (ill. 129). In this way, it was possible to mark numerous points in succession. A few years later, Rieussec also made ink chronographs in the form of pocket watches.

From 1840 onward, he added a display of the time of day to his chronographs. To do this, he incorporated a second complete movement into his pocket watch, in addition to the chronograph mechanism (ill. 126). This timepiece possessed two balance wheels, one for the chronograph and the other for the watch.

At the same period, Joseph Winnerl, an Austrian watchmaker established in Paris, constructed a pocket watch equipped with a double seconds hand (ill. 131). Simply pressing the button located in the pendant

124

125

124 A racecourse where Rieussec chronographs were used.

125 Pocket watch and recording chronograph by Rieussec, on which the hand turned and the dial remained stationary.

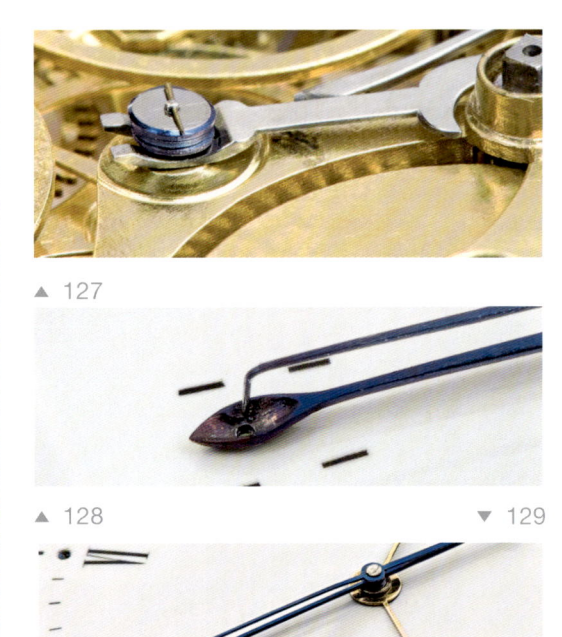

▲ 126

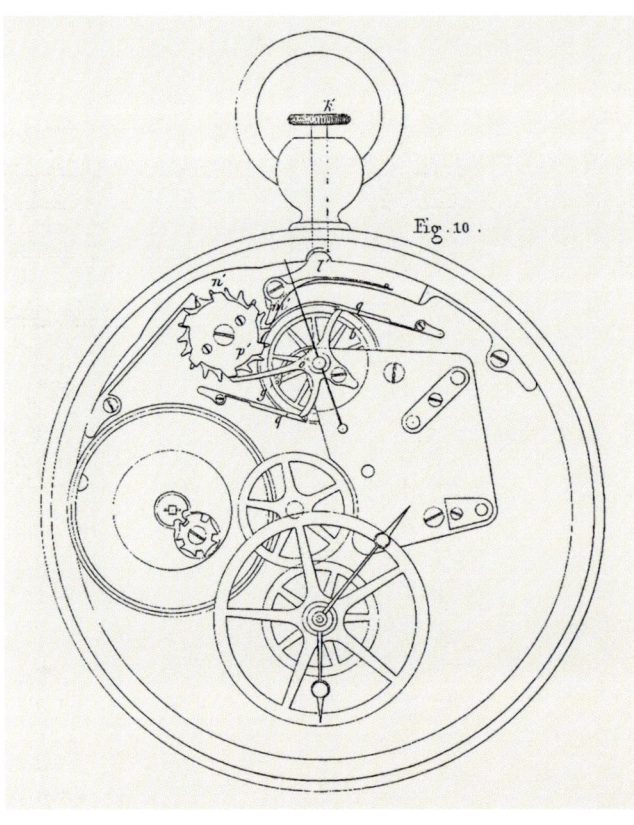

▲ 127

▲ 128 ▼ 129

▼ 130 ▼ 131

126–129
Gold pocket watch with chronograph by Rieussec, c. 1840, with two separate gear trains, one for display of the time and the other for the chronograph. When the chronograph is stopped, the movement for displaying the time of day continues to operate. Illustrations 129 and 130 show the double hand with the little ink reservoir in the shape of a spoon. When timing is stopped, the needle above the spoon passes through the hole, takes a drop of ink and marks a dot on the dial. An unlimited number of dots could be marked on the dial.

234

III The History of Minerva Watch Movements

stopped the gilded lower seconds hand. Pressing the button a second time allowed the gilded hand to catch up with the blue seconds hand, which had continued its progress. In this way, it became possible to measure short intervals by recording the beginning of an event. The principle of this mechanism was the prototype of a split-seconds function, with a clamp for the additional hand and a heart-shaped cam for the flyback function. However, these chronographs with displays or marking lacked one important feature: it was impossible to reset them to zero by simply pressing a push-piece. Imitators were not far behind. Fatton, Breguet (ill. 135) and Perrelet created very similar instruments, equipped with rotating recording hands, in large pocket-watch cases.

ADOLPHE NICOLE AND HENRI FÉRÉOL PIGUET

Another twenty years would pass before Henri Féréol Piguet, of the Joux valley, constructed a heart mechanism with integral zero reset for Adolphe Nicole. Nicole was established in England, and in 1862, at the Universal Exhibition in London, he presented a mechanism under the name of a "chronograph with resetting to zero of the seconds hand." (In 1844, he had already obtained a British patent for a zero reset mechanism employing a heart-shaped cam. There is no evidence of any contact between Nicole and Winnerl, or that Nicole had any knowledge of Winnerl's heart cam.) The new device was patented in London in 1862 and subsequently in Paris. At the end of the period of legal protection, the mechanism was subjected to constant improvements. When the Federal Office of Intellectual Property (Patent Office) opened its doors in Berne in December 1888, patent no. 12 already related to an improvement to a chronograph. In the course of the next five months, it was followed by fifteen other patents in the same field.

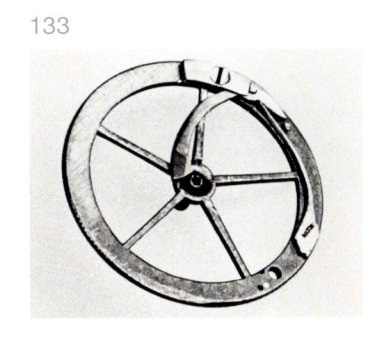

134

130–131
Pocket-chronograph no. 495 by J.T. Winnerl, Paris, about 1840. The two seconds hands move together. Pressing on the pendant once stops one of the hands. When it is pressed a second time, the immobilized hand instantly returns to the position of the hand that has continued its progress. The prototype of a split-seconds mechanism.

132–133
Mechanism with heart cam (133) and jumping wheel (134) by Winnerl. The heart is fixed on the seconds staff, while the jumping wheel is arranged concentrically above it.

134
Chronograph with pen no. 525, by Breguet, Paris, c. 1845.

132   133

235

HOW THE COLUMN-WHEEL CHRONOGRAPH WORKS

As we have just mentioned the genesis of the chronograph, this is a suitable moment to explain its mode of operation, which we shall divide into the different stages that succeed each other after it has been actuated by pressing a push-piece. The chronograph mechanism is mounted on the back of the movement, so that it is entirely visible when the case is opened. To make it easier to understand, illustration 140a only shows the components necessary to the explanation, on the hypothesis that the reader is already familiar with the normal operation of a pocket watch. The parts required for the minute counter have also been removed for the same reason.

The vital control component of a chronograph is the column wheel F, which consists of a lower part, the ratchet with its triangular teeth, and an upper part with vertical columns looking like slices of cake. The columns actuate the clutch W, the heart lever N, and the stopping lever B. Each time the push-piece G is pressed, the column wheel F is moved forward clockwise one tooth of the ratchet by the hook E of the engaging lever D. The position taken up is maintained by the spring of the meshing lever R until the next meshing stage.

Illustration 140a represents the start of a measurement. The drive wheel S is arranged above the bridge on a staff of the seconds wheel and turns continuously with the wheels of the movement that drives the time display. The coupling wheel K is mounted free to rotate in the coupling W. At the moment shown in the illustration, it is engaged with the center chronograph wheel C, to which the large seconds hand is fixed on the dial side. The point of attachment of the coupling W is situated on the eccentric screw T, which forms a straight line with the point of attachment of the drive wheel S and the coupling wheel K. The eccentric screw T is used to adjust the depth of mesh of the drive wheel in the clutch wheel. In the position in which the column wheel is shown, the heart

140 a, 140 b, 140 c ▶

135 Column wheel of a chronograph, constructed on two levels.

136 Engagement hook to advance the column wheel.

137 Center wheel, clutch wheel, and idler wheel of a chronograph.

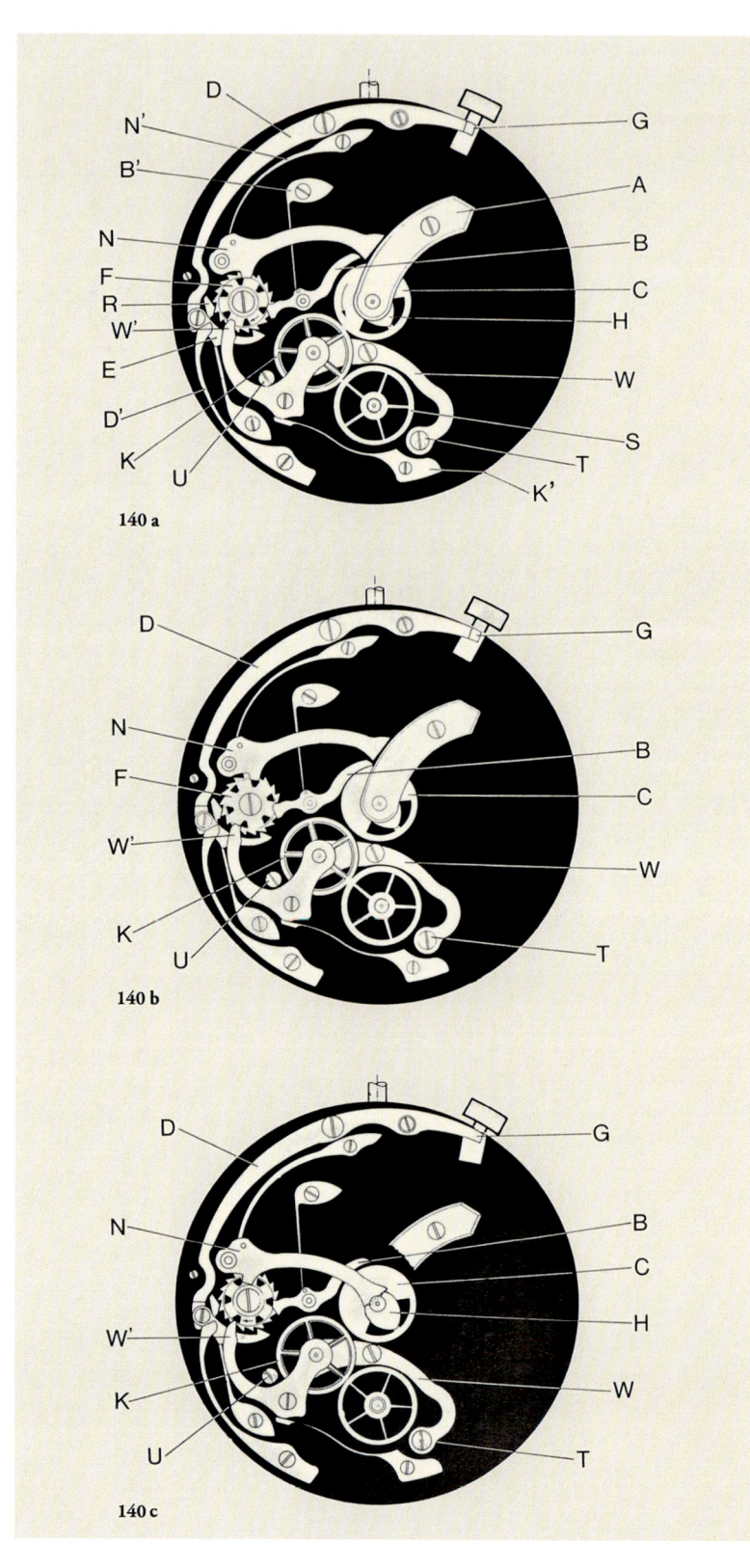

140 a

140 b

140 c

236

lever N is pushed back by the columns as a result of the pressure exerted by the heart lever N, while the stop-lever B is also pushed back by the columns (shown in black) as a result of the pressure exerted by the spring of the stop-lever B. The beak W of the coupling is situated between two columns and can thus effect the meshing of the coupling wheel K with the center chronograph wheel C. The depth to which the beak W penetrates between the columns is determined indirectly by the eccentric screw U. This is used to set the meshing depth of the coupling wheel K with the center chronograph wheel C.

It should also be mentioned that these three wheels always display very fine toothing, and that the teeth are most often triangular in shape. This profile was adopted to meet the need, when the chronograph is actuated, to obtain the smoothest possible start when the coupling wheel K suddenly engages with the center chronograph wheel C, as triangular teeth mesh harmoniously with no jerking. The chronograph center wheel often has twice as many teeth as the other two wheels. This is because fine toothing requires less lateral displacement of the wheels when meshing, which could otherwise result in the dreaded effect of jumping by the seconds hand on the dial.

The next actuation of the push-piece G (ill. 140b) advances the column wheel F one tooth by the movement of the coupling yoke D and its beak E. Simultaneously, one column slides under the beak W of the clutch and disengages the coupling wheel K from the center chronograph wheel C. It is easy to see that the coupling W now no longer rests against the eccentric screw U. In this case, the coupling wheel K remains engaged with the drive wheel S. Simultaneously, the stop-lever B has dropped off "its" column, and the spring of the stop-lever B presses it by its inner curve against the center chronograph wheel in order to maintain it in its present position. By this means, the chronograph hand is also immobilised on the dial. This moment is depicted in illustration 140b.

The next time the push-piece G is pressed, as shown in illustration 140c, the chronograph hand, that is to say the center chronograph wheel C, is reset to zero. The column wheel F is once more advanced by one tooth, the tip of the heart lever N is pressed by its spring N against the seconds heart H on the center chronograph wheel C. The effect of the shape of the seconds heart is to cause the center chronograph wheel instantly to adopt a predetermined position. On the dial, the chronograph hand and that of the minute counter (if any) return respectively to zero and the number 60. However, to make this return to zero possible, the stop-lever B has previously been withdrawn by a column of the column wheel in order to free the center chronograph wheel C, which had been immobilized, as shown in illustration 140b. This completes one cycle of start, stop, and return to zero. Pressing the push-piece once more initiates a fresh measurement.

141 a

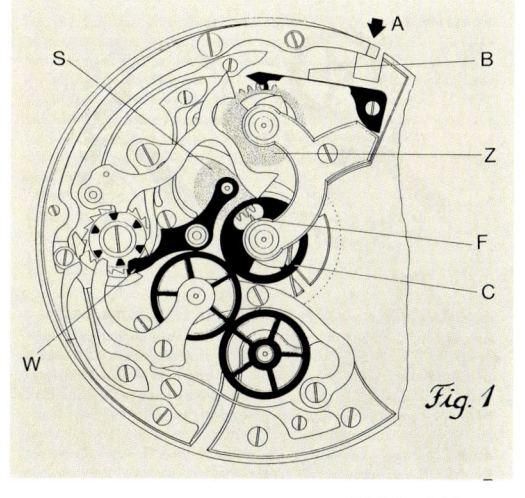

141 b, 141 c ▶

THE SLOW-JUMP MINUTE COUNTER

This system was primarily used in chronographs. It is distinguished by its high reliability and easy consultation of the displays.

Illustration 141 (fig. 1) shows a chronograph with a single push-piece (analogous to the Valjoux 22), which will enable explanation of the different stages in its operation. A finger F is mounted on the chronograph center wheel C. After each complete rotation of the latter, it advances the star wheel S by one tooth. The star wheel is then engaged with the minute-counter wheel Z. On a prolongation of its pivot on the dial side, the hand of the minute counter is fixed. The jumper spring of the minute counter B restrains the wheel Z after each meshing. In detail, the process occurs as follows: figure 1 shows the finger F at the moment when it meshes with the star wheel (the black tooth on the minute-counter wheel is situated to the right of the jumper of the minute counter B). In figure 2, the finger F has turned the star wheel S and the minute counter Z so that the "black tooth" has lifted the jumper B to its highest point. Thus the hand of the minute counter is moved forward one half-division (half a minute). In the next stage, the jumper B advances the minute-counter wheel Z one position to the right and falls back between the teeth. The black tooth is now positioned to the left of the jumper B (fig. 3). This jump by the minute counter Z also advances the star wheel S so that the finger F can continue its rotations unhindered by any meshing. In the "stopped" position, the star wheel S is raised by the column wheel outside the field of action of the finger, so that it can turn freely forward or backward during the zero reset, as it is permanently engaged with the minute-counter wheel Z.

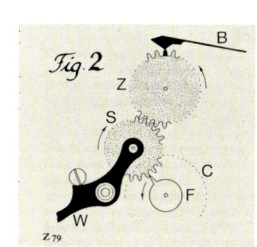

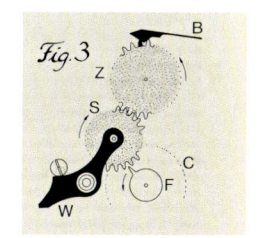

▲ 142 ▼ 143 ▼ 144

Abbildungen von Modellen für Taschenuhren
(die ausschliesslich dekorativen Modelle ausgenommen)
Reproductions de modèles pour montres
(les modèles exclusivement décoratifs exceptés)
Riproduzioni di modelli per orologi
(eccettuati i modelli esclusivamente decorativi)

Erste Hälfte April 1912
Première quinzaine d'avril 1912 — Prima quindicina d'aprile 1912

N° 20735. 10 avril 1912, 8 h. p. — Ouvert. — 1 modèle. — Pont de mouvement de montres. — Fabrique des Faverges **Robert frères**, Villeret (Suisse).

N° 17.

142 Chronograph movement no. 1376750, caliber 19/9CH, c. 1927. Gilded movement with chronograph mechanism arranged so as to be visible. Engraved cock with ruby endstone. Balance wheel with Breguet hairspring. Anchor escapement.

143 The shape of the chronograph bridge was registered as a protected model in 1912.

144 Record book no. 6 of 1908 mentioning the first series of movements of the 19/9CH chronograph.

145 Silver-plated chronograph movement, caliber 19/9CH, in a high quality version with decorative polishing, chronograph levers polished and chamfered. Compensating balance wheel with Breguet hairspring. Anchor escapement.

146 Silver-plated chronograph movement no. 1309313, undecorated, c. 1925. Levers chamfered and polished. Compensating balance wheel with Breguet hairspring. Anchor escapement.

Minerva Chronograph Movements

CALIBER 19/9CH

According to record book no. 6, the first series of chronographs developed by Minerva came into production in 1908: the caliber 19/9CH. This first chronograph movement still bears the imprint of the owners, Robert Frères. The designation 19 of the caliber refers to the size of the 19-ligne[1] movement, /9 to the registration number of the movement in the book of models[2]; CH is the abbreviation of "chronograph." Destined solely for a pocket watch, this movement (ill. 142) had displays for hours and minutes, small seconds, and a separate mechanism fitted on the basic movement for the chronograph. The chronograph functions were controlled by a single push-piece to start, stop, and reset to zero the large center seconds hand and a small minute counter at 12 o'clock or 3 o'clock. Thus it was possible to measure and read off directly short time intervals, from one second to 30 minutes, without losing the time-of-day display. The same movement could be fitted into hunter or Lépine cases at will.

It swiftly became clear that the use of a pocket watch with an additional chronograph function could prove extremely useful in technical occupations, sport, science, and medicine, as well as in leisure activities. The army also displayed a lively interest in the pocket-chronographs, which were equipped with special dials to meet its requirements. Complementary scales designed to enable immediate read-outs were available in great variety: tachometer, spiral tachometer, telemeter, production counter, pulsimeter, or respiration counter.

The quality of manufacture of these movements varied widely. It extended from simple gilded or nickel-plated movements with chamfered levers to superior quality with entirely polished levers and decorated bridges. Minerva primarily, produced three sizes of chronograph: 19, 17, and 13 lignes.

▲ 145

▼ 146

147 Minerva pocket watch with chronograph in a nickel-silver case. Enameled dial with Arabic numerals, 30-minute counter, and small seconds. Colored external spiral scale for tachometer from 20 to 240 km/h. Blued steel hands.

III The History of Minerva Watch Movements

148
Gold pocket watch with chronograph by Minerva. White enameled dial with Arabic numerals, 30-minute counter, and small seconds. Colored external spiral scale for tachometer from 20 to 300 km/h. Blued steel hands.

149 Silver watch with chronograph by Minerva. White enameled dial with 30-minute counter and small seconds.

150 Gilded pocket watch with chronograph by Minerva. White enameled dial with 30-minute counter and small seconds. Blued steel hands.

151 Burnished steel pocket watch with chronograph by Minerva. White enameled dial with Arabic numerals, 30-minute counter, and small seconds. Designation: Ralco. Red hour numerals 13 to 24.

▲ 148   ▼ 149   ▲ 150   ▼ 151

▲ 152

▲ 153   ▼ 154

152–154 Minerva military pocket watch with screwed nickel-silver case. On the back, department number D 571334 H. Black dial with luminous indices and hands and small seconds. Silver-plated 19 lignes movement bridge with special spring attachment.

154 Detail of "Shock Resist" protection. The hole for the jewel is in a flat spring and the endstone under a six-armed spring.

III　The History of Minerva Watch Movements

POCKET WATCHES FOR MILITARY PURPOSES

155 Minerva service watch for the navy with chronograph and nickel-silver case. White enameled dial with Arabic numerals, 30-minute counter, and small seconds. Blued steel hands. Chronograph movement, caliber 19/9CH.

156 Minerva service watch with chronograph and silver case. Black dial with white numerals, 30-minute counter, and small seconds. White painted hands. 17 lignes chronograph movement.

157 Minerva service watch with nickel-silver case. Black dial with luminous numerals, 30-minute counter, and small seconds. Luminous white hands. Chronograph movement, caliber 19/9CH.

Military units were in perpetual need of accurate watches. As a general rule, their suppliers were Swiss companies, such as Minerva, which supplied them with three-hand watches (ill. 152) and chronographs. The manufacture also made special pocket watches for officers and NCOs. These timepieces usually had black dials with luminous numerals and hands, screwed nickel-silver cases, and a movement with shock-protection and a seconds stop function. The department number (ill. 153) and sometimes the name of the officer and the military unit were engraved on the back of the cover.

Minerva also produced chronographs of similar appearance, with a black dial. They were available in two sizes, 19 and 17 lignes. The 19-ligne model (ill. 157) had luminous hands and numerals, while the more refined 17-ligne version, intended for officers, had white hands and numerals.

For naval units, the 19-ligne chronograph (ill. 155) was designed with a white dial and black numerals.

155　　▲ 156　　▼ 157

243

▲ 158 ▼ 159

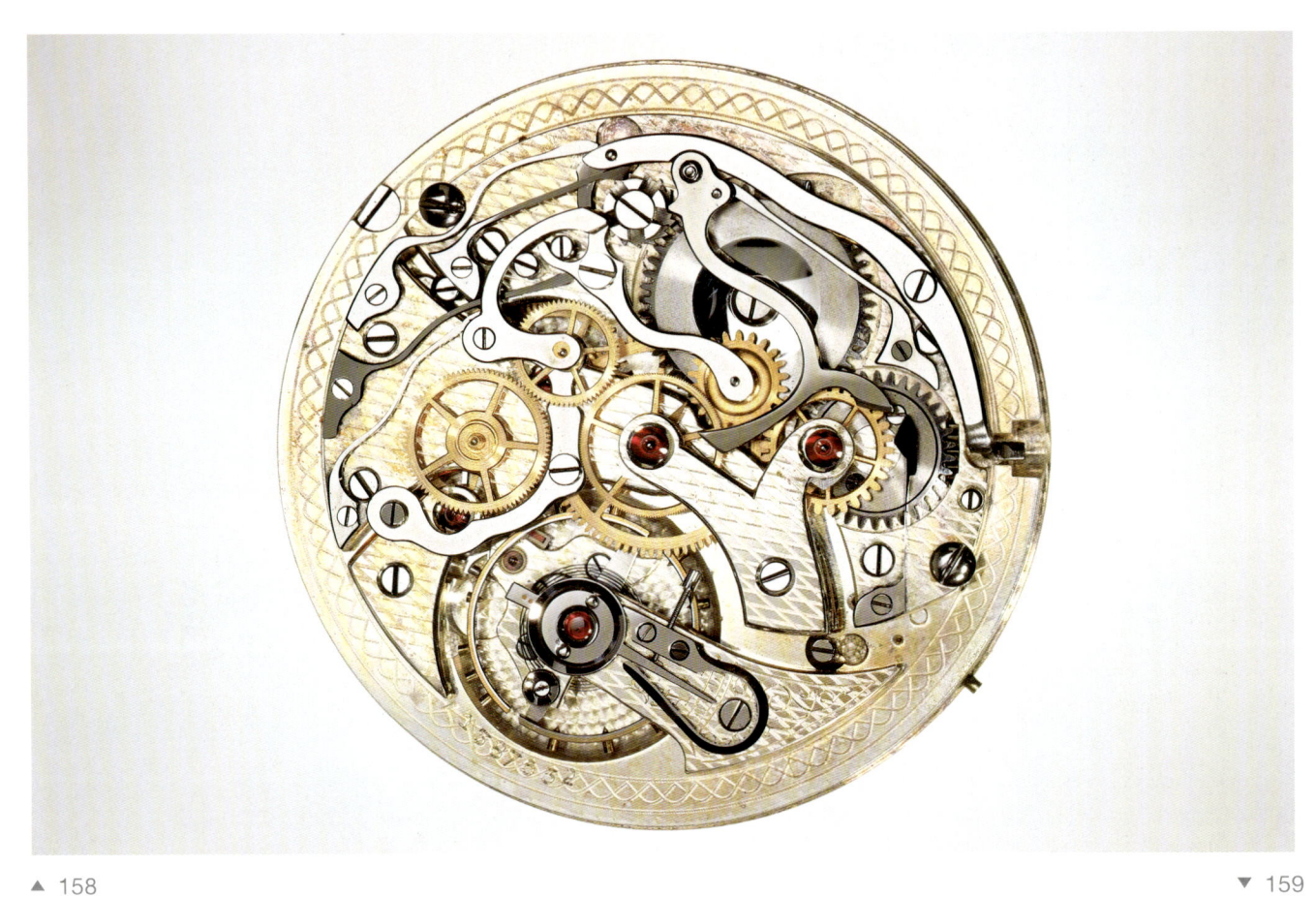

158 Chronograph movement, caliber 17/29, in a high quality version with decorative polishing on the bridges and polished levers. Cock with swan's-neck regulator. Compensating balance wheel with Breguet hairspring. Anchor escapement.

159 Detail drawing of the balance wheel and escapement, produced by Jacques Pelot in 1931 during the development of the movement.

160 Minerva pocket watch with case in white and yellow gold. Enameled dial with Arabic numerals, 30-minute counter, and small seconds. Blued steel hands. Chronograph movement, caliber 17/29.

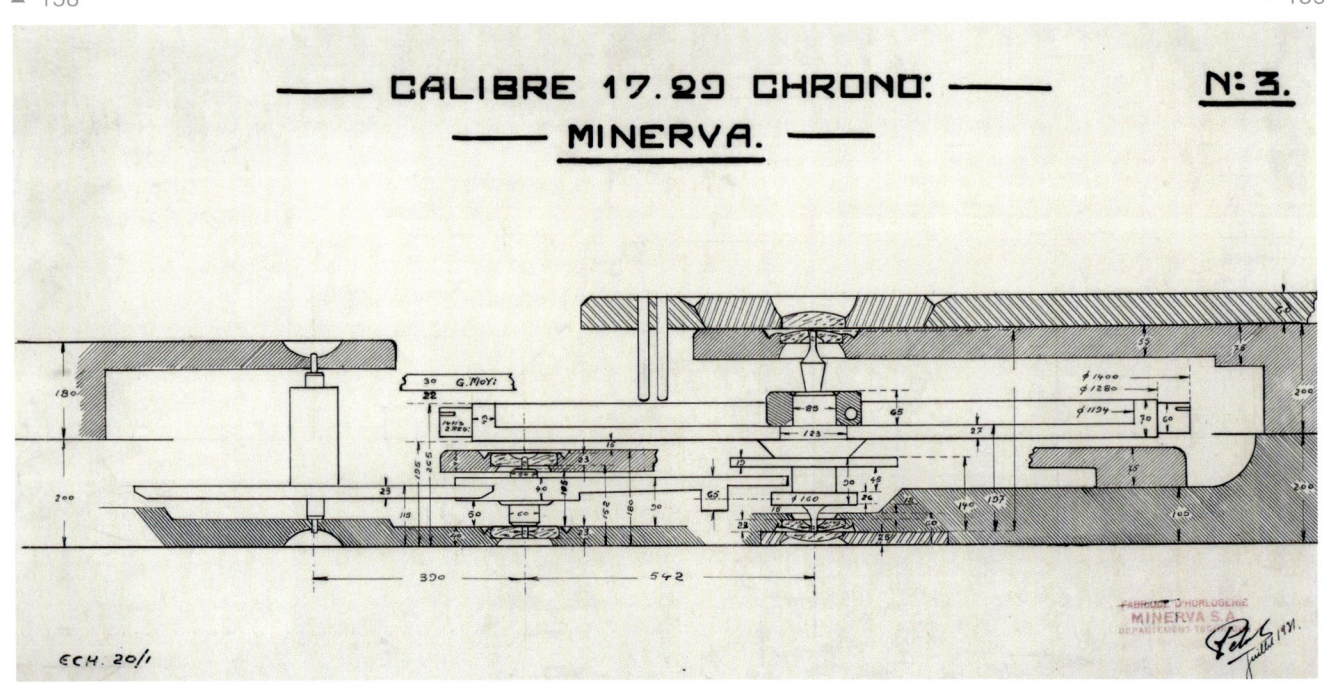

New Chronograph by Minerva

THE CALIBER 17/29

Minerva continued to make the chronograph 19/9CH for more than twenty years without making any changes to it. At that point, however, its size and its thickness of 6.70 millimeters meant that it no longer met the requirements of the time. In 1931, the manufacture decided to produce a flatter, smaller model, the caliber 17/29, no more than 5.60 millimeters thick, which was perfected by Jacques Pelot. Numerous models came into being, with dials in white (ill. 161) or black (ill. 156). In one particularly refined version, the movement was endowed with a swan's-neck precision regulator (ill. 158). This smaller caliber (16¾–17 lignes) is still in production today, in an improved version, in very small editions and with a high level of perfectionist craftsmanship. It is still the basis for new timepieces equipped with innovative technologies or unusual functions.

161–162
Two almost identical pocket chronographs in nickel-silver, differing only in their enameled dials. The model in illustration 161 has upright Arabic numerals, while the one in illustration 162 has italic numerals. Both watches have the same hands. Chronograph movements, caliber 17/29.

▼ 160   ▲ 161   ▼ 162

163

163–167
Pocket chronograph by Minerva with two push-pieces to enable cumulative timing. Chrome-plated case. White enameled dial with Arabic numerals, 45-minute counter, and small seconds. Separate external scale for hundredths of a second. Blued steel hands.

163 Movement with silver-plated bridges, screw balance wheel, and Breguet hairspring. Anchor escapement. Chronograph mechanism modified to operate with two push-pieces, arranged so as to be visible.

164
Repeatedly pressing the push-piece in the crown starts and stops the measurement as many times as necessary. Meanwhile, the heart lever (on the left in the illustration) is retained by a disabling lever. The times measured are then added together.

165 The push-piece at 11 o'clock enables the zero reset by lifting the disabling lever, thereby liberating the heart lever. In the illustration, the heart lever has dropped again.

166 In this sketch, the heart and disabling levers are shown shaded to highlight this innovation. Original drawing by Jacques Pelot, 1955.

Following pages
Horse, chronophotography by Étienne-Jules Marey, c. 1886.

III   The History of Minerva Watch Movements

CHRONOGRAPH FOR ADDING MEASURED TIMES

In about 1935, the caliber 19/9 CH underwent some modifications and a second push-piece appeared on the case. With this, it became possible to read off several times for a given event, and to add them together. To do this, the third function, the zero reset, had to be disabled. With the push-piece at 11 o'clock, the measurement could be started and stopped as many time, as necessary. The crown push-piece freed the heart lever, otherwise kept in disabled position, to actuate the zero reset. At the same time, the heart lever, through a finger, withdrew the star wheel from the field of action of the chronograph center wheel. These two positions are shown in illustrations 164 and 165.

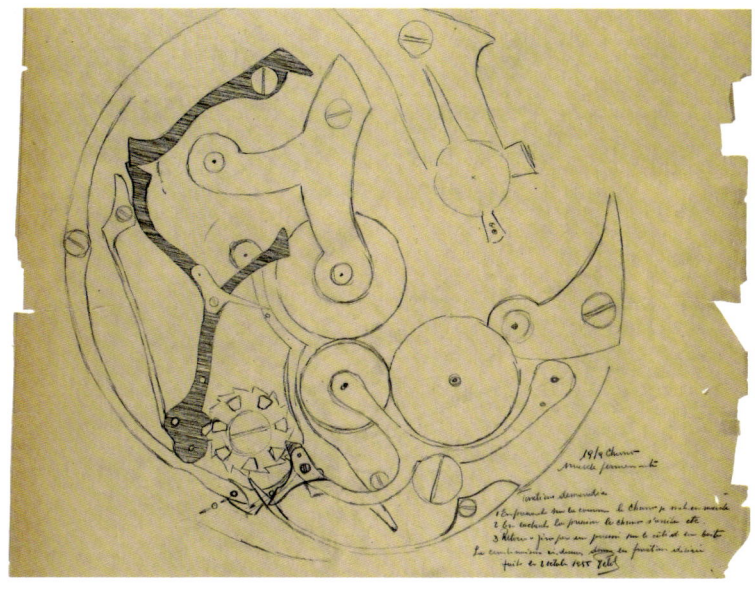

164

165

▲ 166

▼ 167

247

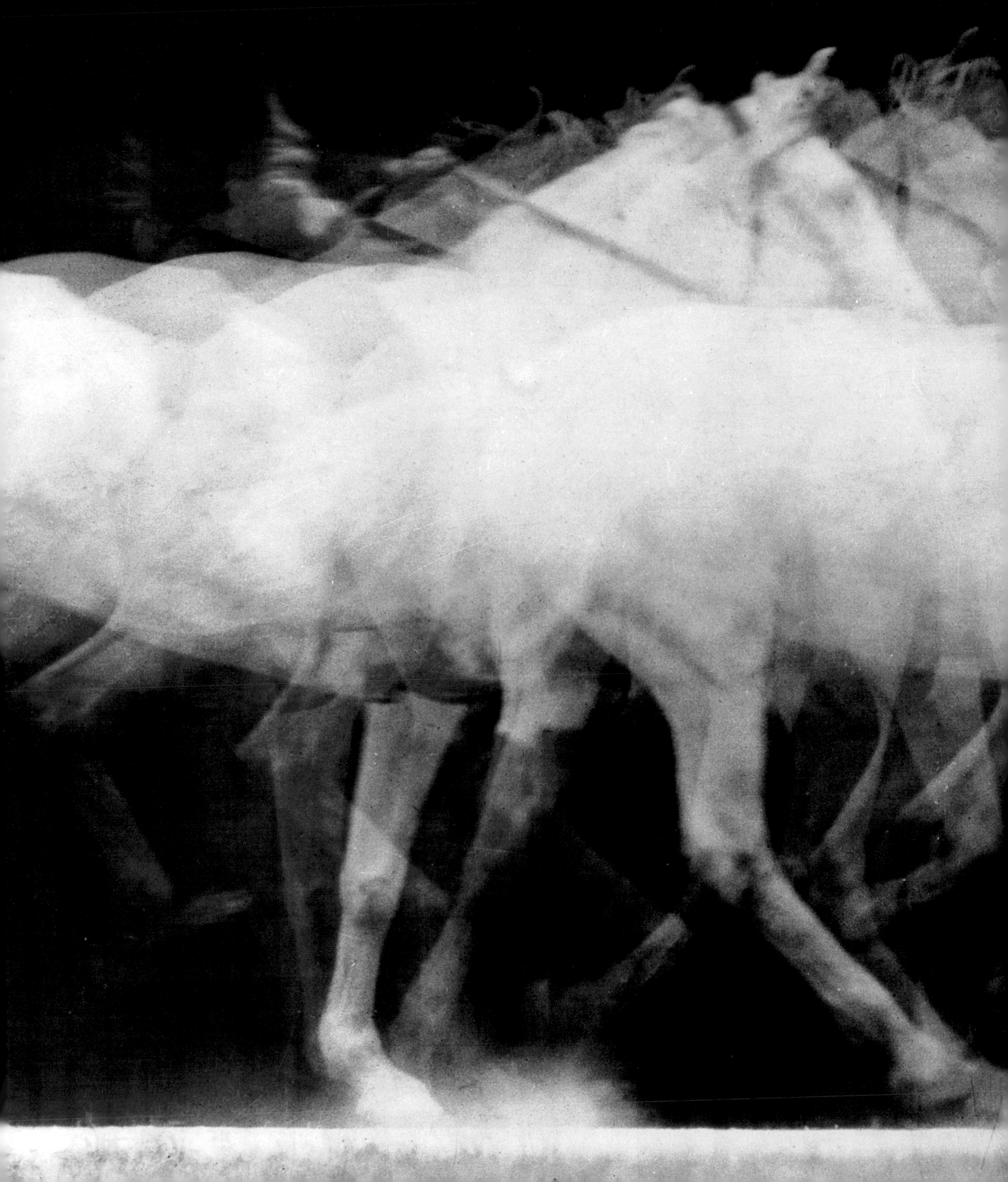

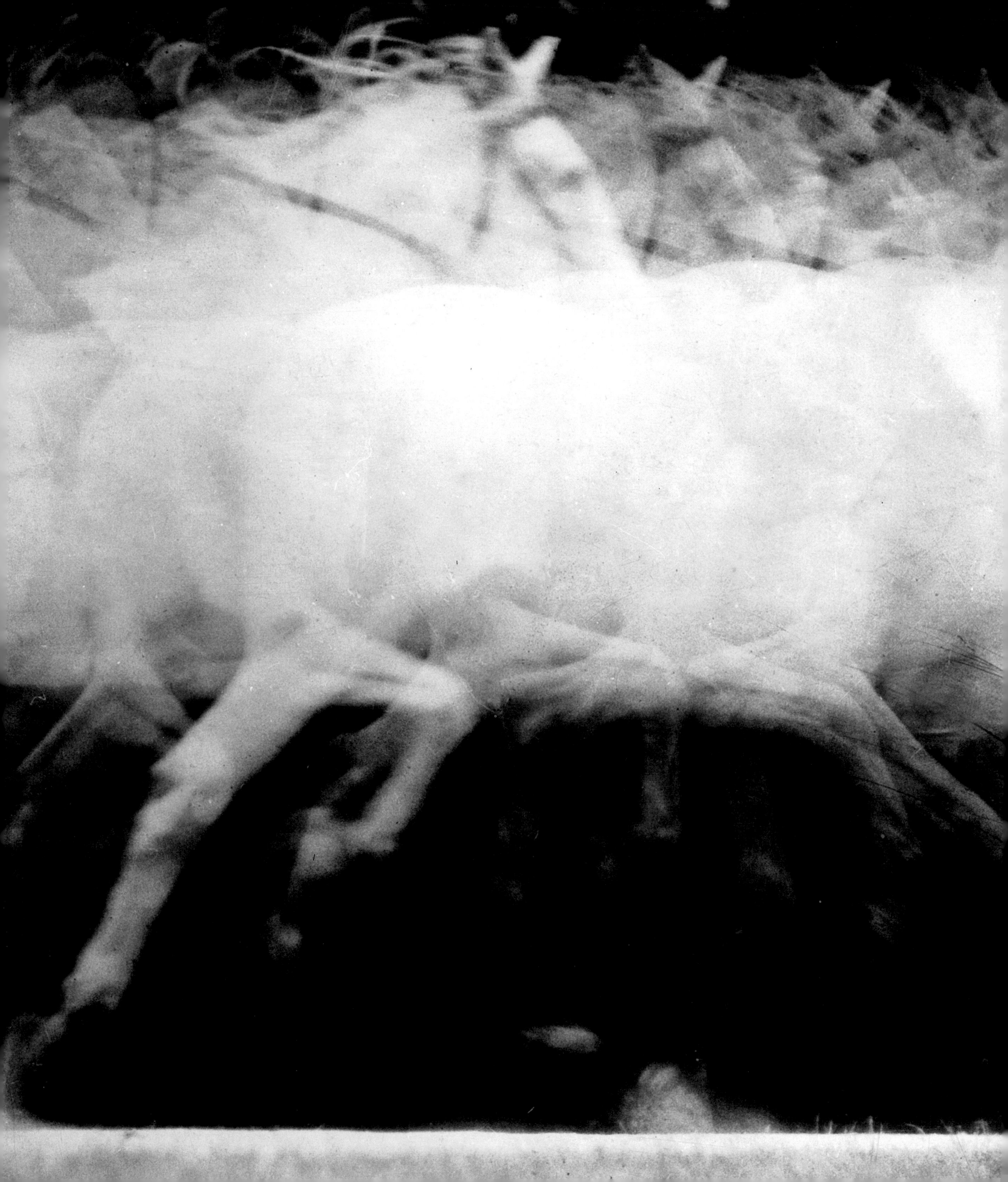

▲ 168 ▼ 169

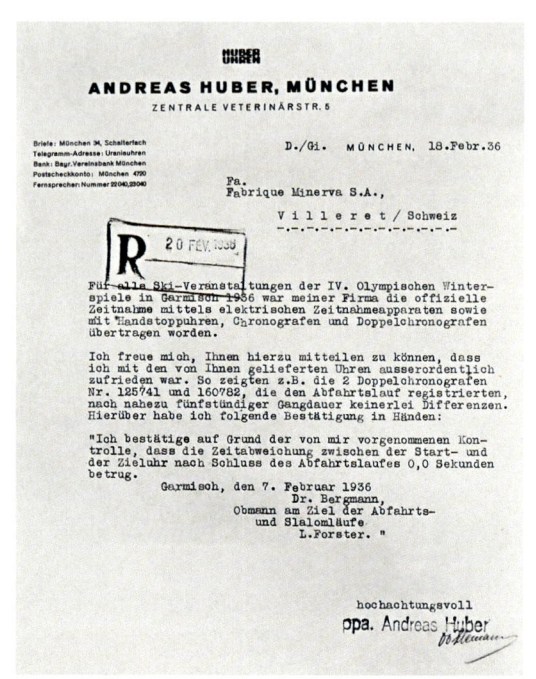

▼ 170 ▲ 171

168–170 and 173 Minerva pocket watch with split-seconds chronograph. Chrome case with two push-pieces. White enameled dial with Arabic numerals, 30-minute counter, and small seconds. Blued steel hands. Nickel-plated movement (caliber 9 Valjoux) with screw balance wheel and Breguet hairspring. Clamp for the flyback hand arranged on the chronograph mechanism.

169 Detail of the clamp of the flyback hand which controls a second column wheel through a second push-piece positioned at 11 o'clock. The flyback hand can also be stopped as often as necessary to measure intermediate times.

250

III The History of Minerva Watch Movements

THE WINTER OLYMPICS OF 1936

The Munich company Andreas Huber took on the functions of official timekeeper at the fourth Winter Olympic Games held in Garmisch Partenkirchen. To carry out this mission successfully, the Huber company used only mechanical timepieces made by the Minerva Manufacture at Villeret, in Switzerland, some of which employed electric actuation (ill. 174). These instruments included sports timers, chronographs for cumulative timing, and double chronographs. As Minerva's production range did not include any double chronograph with time display, the manufacture used specially regulated Valjoux movements (ill. 168). In a letter, (ill. 171), Andreas Huber conveyed his thanks to Minerva for the quality of the timepieces supplied and cites testimony to their irreproachable functioning by the judges.

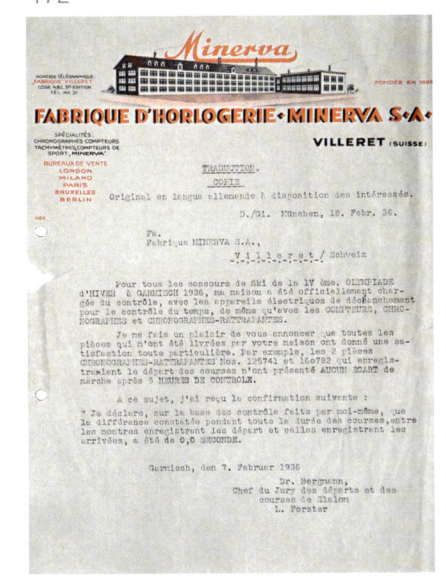

172

▲ 173   ▼ 174

171–172 Letter of thanks from the house of Andreas Huber, Munich, for the good operation of the instruments supplied, and its translation into French.

174 Electric actuation device for the split-time counter, used for timing sports events.

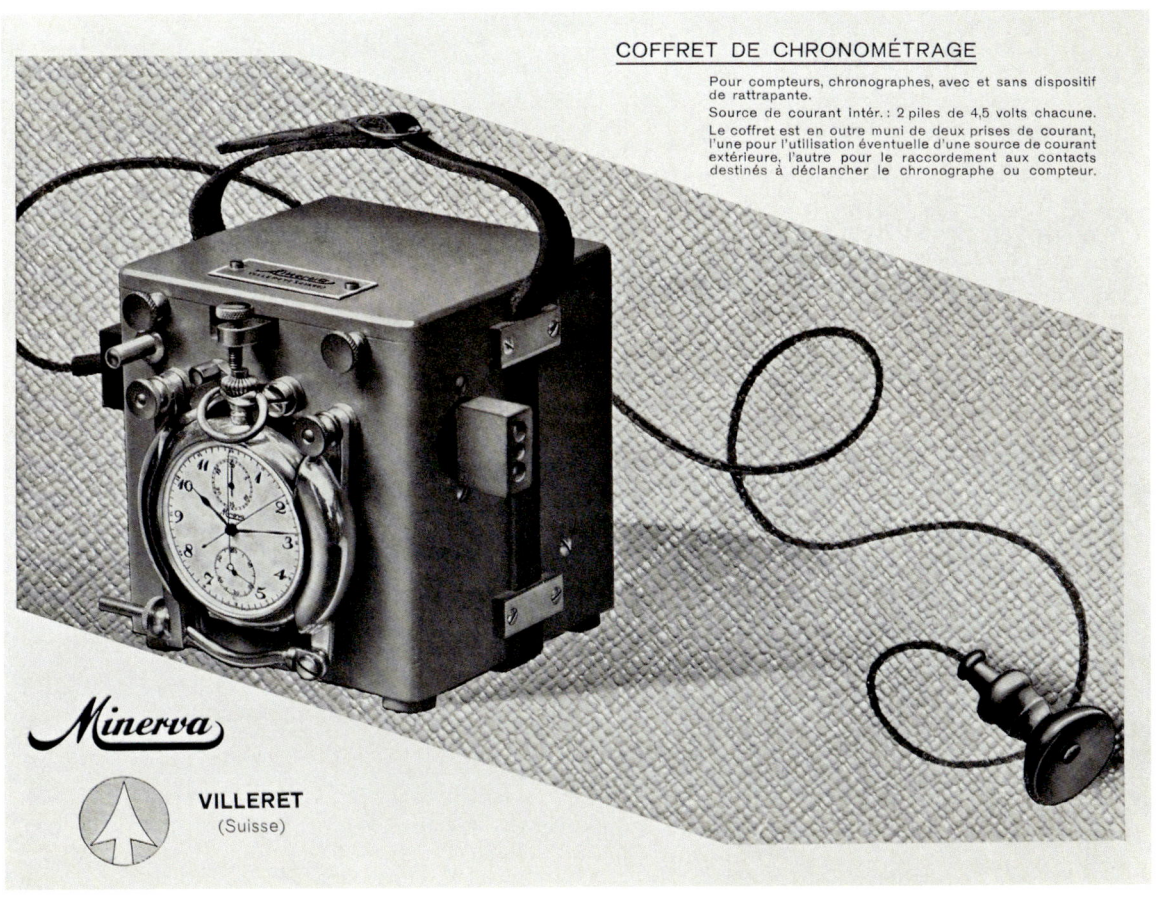

251

▲ 175

▼ 176

175 Large wrist-chronograph with caliber 19/9CH and a push-piece at 2 o'clock on a broad leather strap. Steel case with rotating bezel and red reference mark. Black dial with 30-minute counter and small seconds. External telemeter scale for measuring distances and internal spiral tachometer scale from 20 to 400 km/h. White painted hands.

176 Large wrist-chronograph, caliber 19/9CH like the last example, but with luminous numerals and hands. Spiral tachometer from 20 to 500 km/h.

252

The Wrist-chronograph

CALIBER 19/9CH

177 Large wrist-chronograph, caliber 19/9CH, in steel case without rotating bezel. Black dial with telemeter and spiral tachometer. Massive luminous hands.

178 Minerva chronograph movement, caliber 19/9CH, modified, with push-piece at 2 o'clock.

179 Large wrist-chronograph, equipped with caliber 19/9CH, in double case. White enameled dial with 30-minute counter and small seconds. Blued steel hands. Two external two-color tachometer scales in spiral form, from 30 to 240 km/h.

In the first two decades of the twentieth century, the reign of the pocket watch had not yet drawn to its close, even if a newcomer, the wristwatch, was steadily gaining ground. To start with, the pocket watch was worn on the wrist in a leather outer case (ill. 111). Later, watch manufacturers inserted pocket-watch movements in large cases for wristwatches. The push-piece was initially positioned at 2 o'clock, until a new technique made it possible to house the push-piece in the crown of the wristwatch. Such models figure in Minerva's production catalog in a range of versions and with widely varying dials. During the First World War, the wristwatch developed remarkably fast, as it could be consulted immediately, far more quickly than the time it took to get a pocket watch out of a military uniform pocket. These days, the first Minerva wristwatches are particularly sought after by collectors.

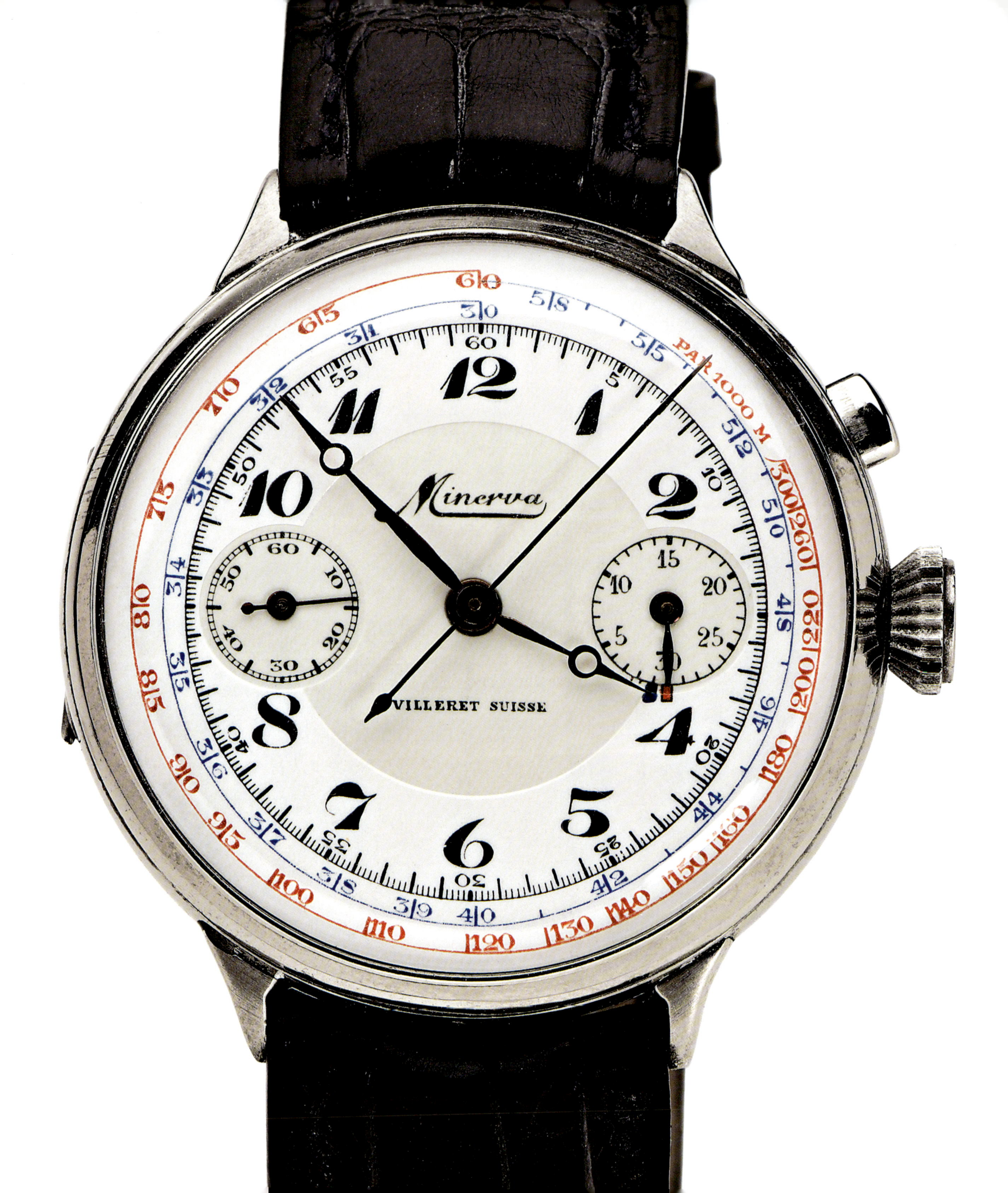
Minerva
VILLERET SUISSE
PAR 1000 M

III The History of Minerva Watch Movements

CALIBER 17/29

180
Wrist-chronograph, caliber 17/29, with steel case. White enameled dial with Arabic numerals, 30-minute counter, and small seconds. Colored external spiral scale for tachometer from 30 to 300 km/h. Blued steel hands.

181
Wrist-chronograph, caliber 17/29, with gilded case. White enameled dial with Arabic numerals, 30-minute counter, and small seconds. Colored external spiral scale for tachometer from 30 to 300 km/h. Blued steel hands.

182 Movement with silver-plated bridges with chronograph caliber 17/29. Engraved cock with ruby endstone. Compensating screwed balance wheel with Breguet hairspring. Anchor escapement. Chronograph mechanism with polished, chamfered levers, mounted visibly on the bridges, with push-piece at 2 o'clock. Gilded chronograph wheels.

183
Wrist-chronograph, caliber 17/29, with steel case, made for Alpina. Black dial with Arabic numerals, 30-minute counter, and small seconds. Colored external tachometer scale from 60 to 500 km/h. Right on the outside ⅕ second divisions for the chronograph. White painted hands.

After launching production of this small caliber, approximate diameter 38 millimeters, used in pocket watches, Minerva developed special cases so that this movement could be worn on the wrist too (ill. 180 to 183). This size gave particularly good legibility even on complicated dials. During the Second World War, there was a considerable increase in demand for wrist-chronographs with black dials and luminous hands and numerals. On these models, the push-piece was located at 2 o'clock.

181   ▲ 182   ▼ 183

CALIBER 13/20

Minerva developed this movement, diameter 28.80 millimeters, exclusively destined for wristwatches, in collaboration with the Dubois-Depraz company, in the Joux valley; it was put on the market in 1923. Designed to meet the demands of a new epoch, it remained in production right up to the 1960s. In many ways, the divisions of the dial resembled those of pocket watches, but the watch as a whole was in slightly reduced form. Very properly, these first wrist-chronographs had a white enameled dial with a large center seconds hand and a small minute counter at 3 o'clock. They looked very modern in design, with little to distinguish them from models produced in our own day.

▲ 184 ▼ 185 ▲ 186 ▼ 187

256

III The History of Minerva Watch Movements

184 Silver-plated movement with chronograph, caliber 13/20. Integral balance wheel with Breguet hairspring. Anchor escapement. Chronograph mechanism with polished levers and gilded chronograph wheels, arranged so as to be visible.

185 Wrist-chronograph from the early years of the caliber 13/20, with silver case. White enameled dial with Arabic numerals, 30-minute counter, and small seconds. $\frac{1}{5}$-second divisions for the chronograph on the circumference. Blued steel hands.

186 Record book 1923: 1st series, December 11, cal. 13/20, chrono, 17 rubies.

187 Wrist-chronograph, caliber 13/20, with gold case. Silver-plated dial with 30-minute counter and small seconds. Blue spiral scale for tachometer from 20 to 1000 km/h and telemeter from 1 to 20 km. Blued steel hands.

188 Chrongraph wrist watch. Silver case, white enameled dial with 30 minutes counter, and small second. Tachymeter indicator on a spiral scale from 300 to 20 km/h. Stainless steel blue hands.

189 Wrist-chronograph, caliber 13/20, with silver case. White enameled dial with 30-minute counter, and small seconds. Colored external spiral scale for tachometer from 20 to 300 km/h. Blued steel hands.

190 Wrist-chronograph, caliber 13/20, with steel case. Two-color metal dial with luminous numerals, 30-minute counter, and small seconds. $\frac{1}{5}$-second divisions for the chronograph on the circumference. Luminous hands.

▲ 188   ▲ 189   ▼ 190

257

191 Silver-plated movement with chronograph, caliber 13/20. Monometal screw balance wheel with Breguet hairspring. Anchor escapement. Chronograph mechanism for two push-pieces for cumulative timing arranged so as to be visible. Gilded chronograph wheels.

192 Wrist-chronograph, caliber 13/20, with two push-pieces, in gold case. Black dial with tachometer scale from 60 to 500 km/h and telemeter from 1 to 20 km. Gilded hands.

193 Wrist-chronograph, caliber 13/20, with two push-pieces, in steel case. Black dial with luminous numerals, tachometer scale from 60 to 700 km/h, and telemeter scale from 1 to 20 km. Luminous hands.

194 Wrist-chronograph, caliber 13/20, with two push-pieces, in chrome-plated case. Silver-plated dial with luminous numerals and 45-minute counter. Tachometer scale and red telemeter scale. Luminous hands.

195 Advertisement for a chronograph with two push-pieces. Dial marked: shock-resistant.

196 Wrist-chronograph with two push-pieces in two-color case. Black dial with luminous numerals and 45-minute counter. Spiral tachometer scale and telemeter scale. Luminous hands.

▲ 191 ▼ 192 ▼ 193

258

III The History of Minerva Watch Movements

THE WRIST-CHRONOGRAPH WITH TWO PUSH-PIECES FOR CUMULATIVE TIMING

At the beginning of the 1930s, Breitling patented separation of the start-stop and zero-reset functions actuated by two push-pieces. This new way of using a chronograph on the wrist swiftly gave rise to imitations. Over the next few years, Minerva also equipped its caliber 12/30 with two push-pieces to enable measured times to be added together. The push-piece at 2 o'clock controlled the start and stop functions, while the zero reset was controlled by the push-piece at 4 o'clock. This function proved extremely useful in the fields of sport and industry. The minute counter was brought up to 45 minutes to meet the new requirements.

While the principle of two push-pieces is still used today, the recent renaissance of Minerva has also led to bringing the chronograph models with a single push-piece back into production.

▼ 194   ▲ 195   ▼ 196

259

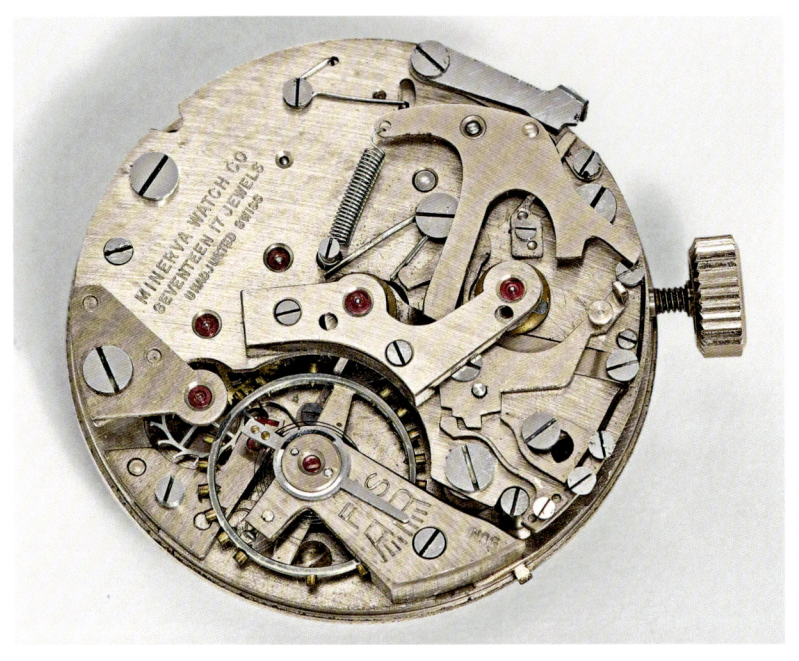

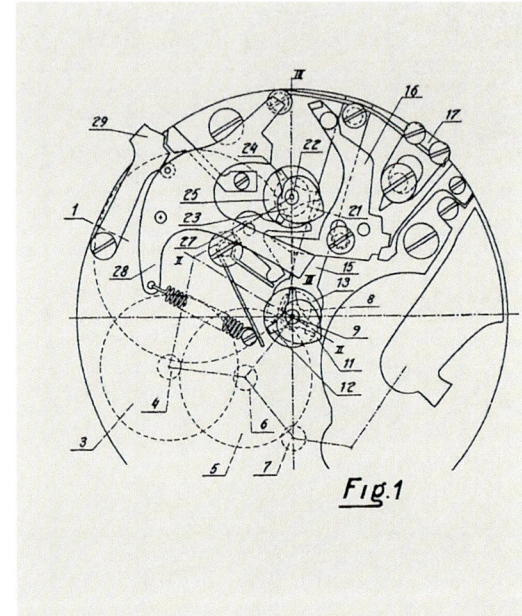

▲ 197

▼ 198a   ▲ 198b   ▼ 198c

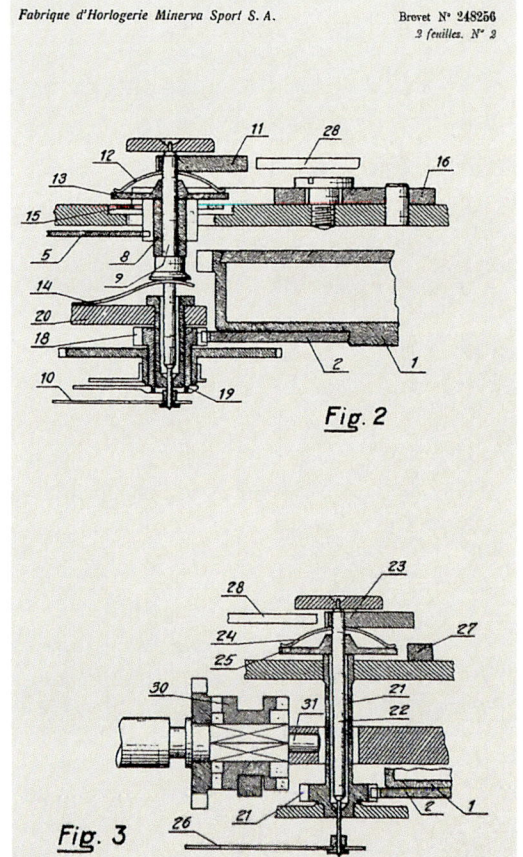

197
Chrome-plated movement, caliber 13/52, with chronograph. Screwed balance wheel with flat hairspring. A mechanism of great simplicity with flat levers made from sheet and wire springs. Vertical clutch for the seconds.

198a–198c
Swiss patent no. 248256 of 1944 for the *Économie* chronograph.

199
Chronograph movement, caliber 13/52, with bridges removed from over the zero-reset hearts. The star-shaped springs for the friction clutches are clearly distinguishable.

200
Wrist-chronograph, with *Économie* movement, in steel case. Silver-plated dial with luminous numerals, 60-minute counter, and small seconds. Blue external tachometer scale from 60 to 1000 km/h. Luminous hands.

III The History of Minerva Watch Movements

THE *ÉCONOMIE* CHRONOGRAPH

In 1944, Minerva presented a perfectly functional chronograph movement with two push-pieces for cumulative timing with a greatly reduced number of components. This mechanism was patented the same year. The simplicity of its design resided in the absence of chronograph wheels in the normal sense of the term. Instead, the movement comprised two pierced pinions in which were fixed the staffs of the hands with a friction clutch and a heart for the seconds counter and the minute counter. The seconds staff was driven by means of a simple vertical clutch (ill. 200). The pinion of the counters was arranged parallel to the hour wheel and meshing with the barrel, while the seconds pinion of the chronograph was mounted parallel to the seconds wheel, with which it meshed.

199

▶ 200

THE FIRST WRISTWATCHES

Minerva had created a first series of small movements for wristwatches as early as 1909. The first of these was a movement of 12 lignes (ill. 202). Models for ladies appeared rapidly in the years preceding the First World War. As they were clearly distinguishable from their masculine equivalents by their dimensions, Minerva developed an even smaller movement, only 10½ lignes in size. The manufacture still possesses one of these watches, with a silver case and enameled dial. The two movements displayed remarkable characteristics: 15 jewels, compensating balance wheel, and Breguet hairspring.

After the war, the Swiss watch industry began to produce movements for wristwatches on a large scale. A complete transformation of the machine-tool base was necessary to respond to this new trend.

▲ 201   ▼ 202   203

262

III The History of Minerva Watch Movements

204

▲ 205

▼ 206

201 The smallest wristwatch movement made by Minerva, 9¾ lignes in size, with compensating balance wheel and Breguet hairspring. Anchor escapement.

202 First wristwatch movement, 12 lignes, series 1, caliber 12/12, made from 1909 on. Compensating balance wheel with Breguet hairspring. Anchor escapement.

203 Extract from record book of 1909, mentioning the first wristwatch movement, caliber 12/12.

204–205 Small lady's wristwatch with silver case and gilded crown. White enameled dial with Arabic numerals and red 12. Blued steel hands.

206 Man's wristwatch with gold case and chased bezels. Silver-plated dial decorated with gilt numerals. Gold hands. Round movement, caliber 12/12.

263

CAD-211
8
CAD-212
9
10
15
16
17
22
23
BLEU
24
29
30
31
36
37
38
CANON
43
CANON
44
BOUCHON
45
50
51
52

12
13
14
19
20
21
26
27
28
33
34
35
40
41
DEFECT
42
47
CHATON
48
CHATON
49
54
55
56

▲ 207   ▼ 208   ▲ 209   ▼ 210

Preceding pages
Storage furniture for enameled dials made during the last century. They allow for antique watches to be restored with original parts.

207
Modern wristwatch, *Pythagoras*, caliber 10½ lignes. Bridge plated in red gold. Monometal balance wheel with flat hairspring. Anchor escapement. This movement was also made with indirect center seconds.

208 Drawing for construction of bridges according to the Golden Ratio.

209 Advertisement for a square man's watch with the *Pythagoras* movement.

210
Shape of baroque case in steel. Silver-plated dial with center minute gear-train. Gilded hands. *Pythagoras* 10½ lignes movement.

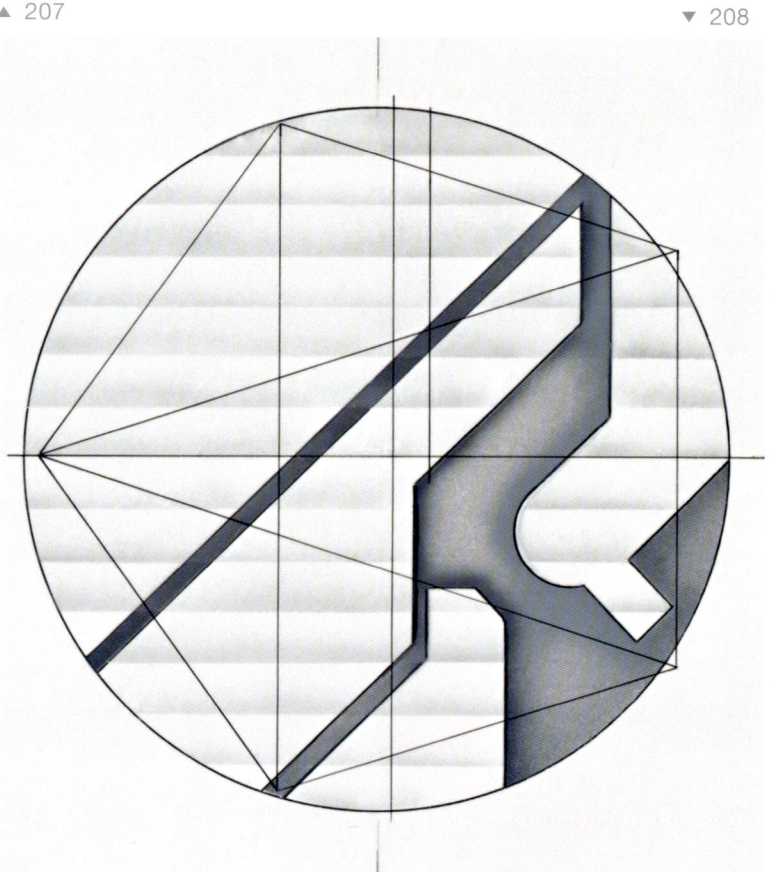

266

The Aesthetics of Mechanisms

PYTHAGORAS

At the beginning of the 1940s, Minerva developed a new caliber of 10½ lignes in accordance with aesthetic criteria. The objective was to apply the Golden Ratio defined by Pythagoras in order to endow the watch movement with a new physiognomy. According to the Golden Ratio, a line can be divided into two parts such that the shorter part A is in the same proportion to the longer part B as the latter is to the whole length of the line C. To put this principle into practice, Minerva inscribed a pentagon in a circle having the diameter of the movement. The ratio of the shorter to the longer radii was identical to the ratio of the longer radii to the diameter – in mathematical terms 1:1.618.

The movement has four bridges, laid out at angles of 0°, 45°, and 90° to each other. It convincingly illustrates a modern movement construction extraordinarily close to the ground plan of the Pantheon.

211 Man's wristwatch with steel case, water-resistant. Black dial with emblems of the imperial navy and luminous numerals. White painted hands. *Pythagoras* movement with center seconds.

212 Man's wristwatch with gilded case and steel back. Silver-plated dial with Roman numerals. Gilded hands. *Pythagoras* 10½ lignes movement with center seconds.

213 Man's wristwatch with steel case. Silver-plated dial with Roman numerals. Gilded hands. *Pythagoras* 10½ lignes movement with center seconds.

267

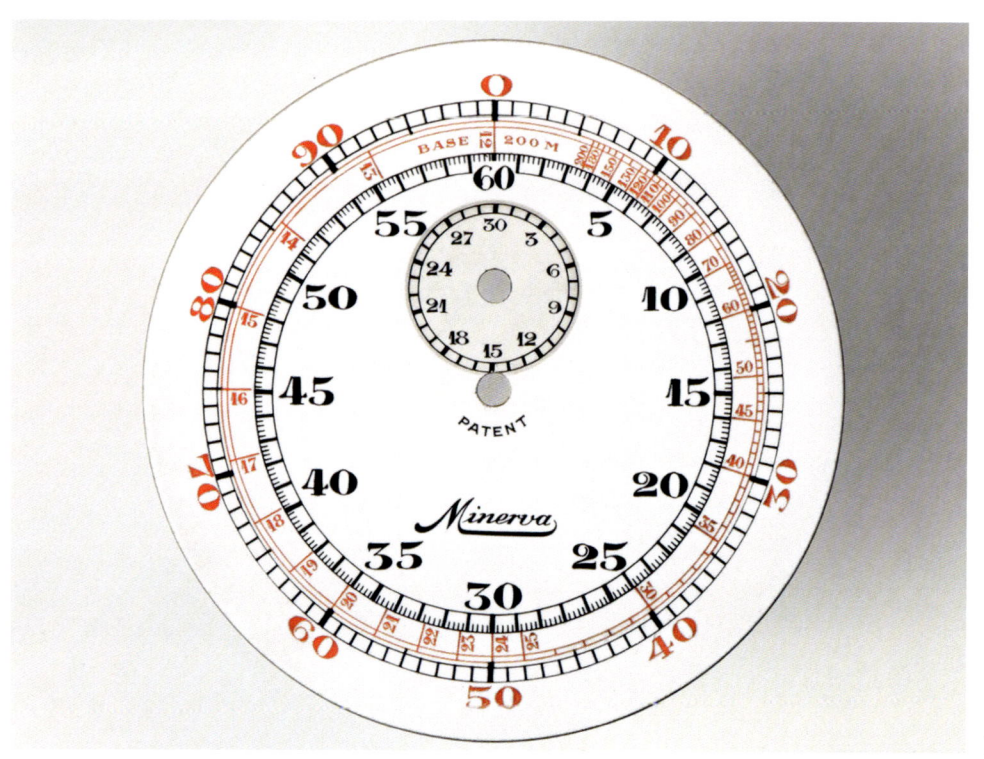

214 Clipboard for recording sports results, equipped with two Minerva timers.

215 Timer dial devised for measuring speed over short distances. Based on a 200-meter course, it comprises divisions of a hundredth of a second.

III The History of Minerva Watch Movements

TIMERS AND THEIR TECHNOLOGIES

216 Records in the book of models of 1911 for the shapes of the upper plate, one for the cylinder escapement (no. 101), the other for the anchor escapement (no 102).

217–218 Gilded sports timer with anchor escapement, 7 jewels. All the levers are polished on the dial side; flat steel springs. Zero reset hearts with friction clutch.

The "Fabrique des Faverges Robert Frères" rediskovered timers in 1911. These pocket instruments did not show the time of day, but just had a large center seconds hand and a small lateral counter for minutes, usually with a scale from 3 to 60 minutes for measuring short time intervals in the domains of industry and sport. However, the fields of application of timers were extremely diverse, so the production range soon included over a hundred dials with different divisions. Two types of escapement were used for these movements of similar design, an economical cylinder escapement and an anchor escapement of superior quality. According to the old tradition of the column wheel, levers and springs controlled the mechanism arranged under the dial. However, the first models were fitted with flat springs which were unable to stand up to hard use, and these soon made way for steel wire springs, which met all expectations.

Over the next few years, Minerva patented a number of inventions in the domain of timers. Some examples of these are shown in the following pages, with their patents and their advantages.

▲ 217

▼ 218

▼ 216

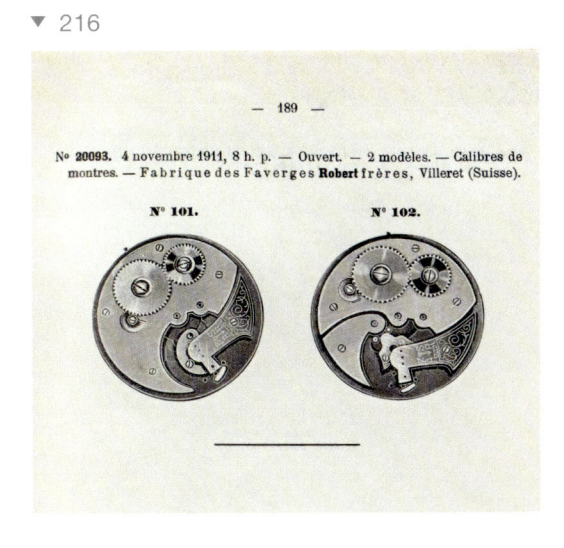

269

▲ 219 ▼ 220 ▲ 221 ▼ 222

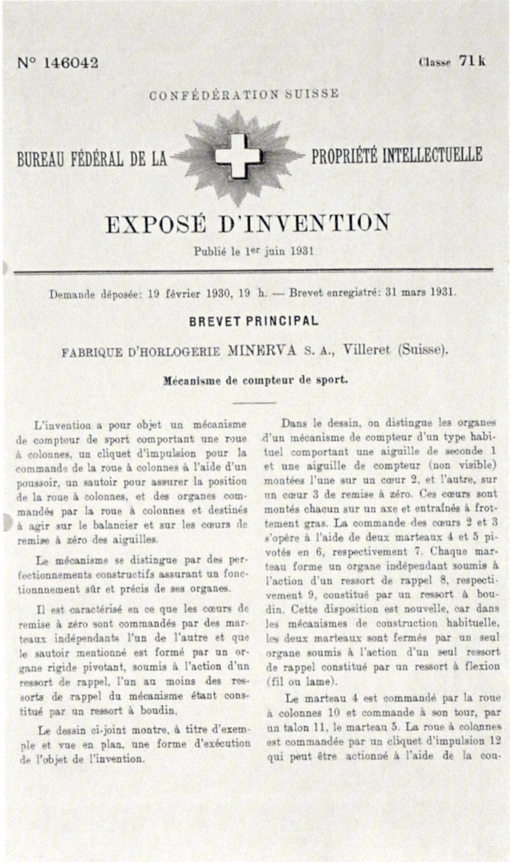

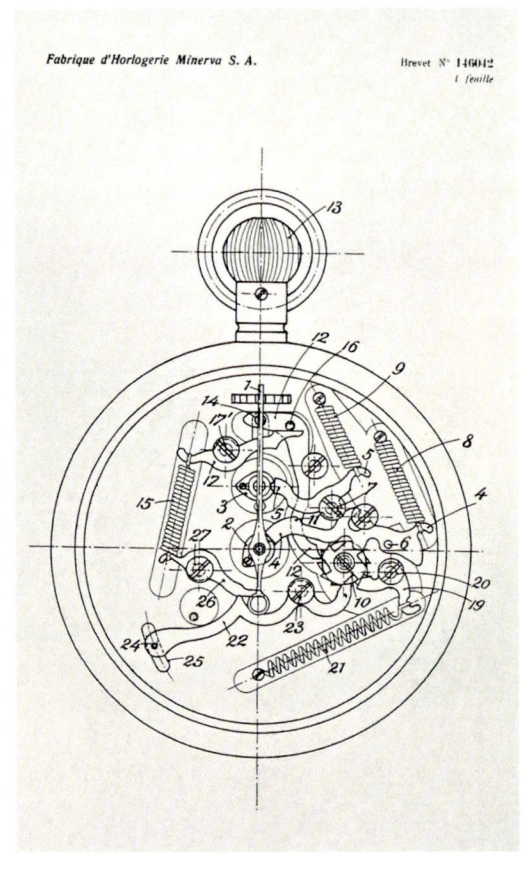

219–220 Improved sports timer movement about 1933. This movement is equipped with shock protection. On the dial side, all the flat steel springs have been replaced with helical springs. Minerva patented this invention in 1933. Practical experience had shown that flat steel springs broke easily when heavily stressed.

221 Cover of Swiss patent no. 146042 of 1930 for Minerva.

222 Drawing of the timer with view under the dial. The new helical springs which are the subject of the patent application are clearly visible.

270

223 Cover of Swiss patent no. 189448 of 1936 for a Minerva split-seconds timer with a friction clutch for the supplementary hand (flyback), which made it necessary to employ a specific shape for the first column wheel and to include a second column wheel.

224 Drawing with view under the dial of the various components required. This movement also has helical springs and wire springs instead of flat steel springs.

225–226 Gilded timer movement with flyback mechanism on the movement side. In the view under the dial, the two column wheels at top and bottom can be distinguished, as well as the flyback clamp in the middle. Helical springs and wire springs are used to control the movement. The balance wheel is shock-protected.

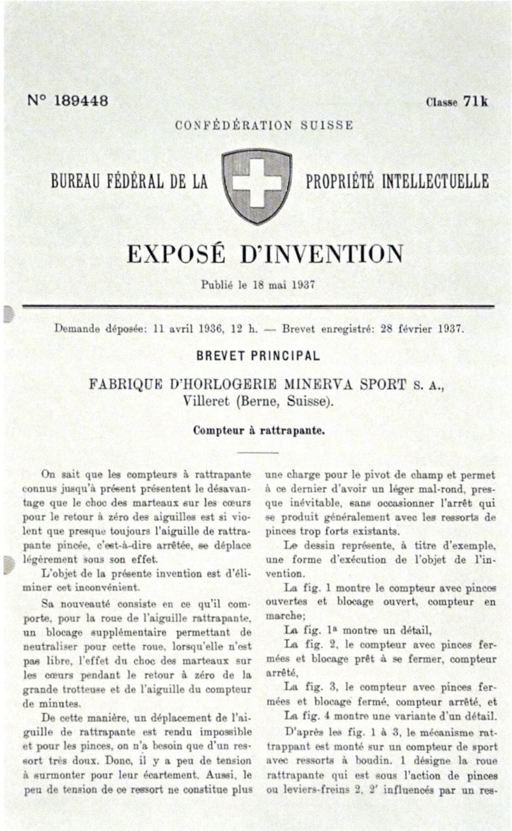

▲ 223   ▼ 224   ▲ 225   ▼ 226

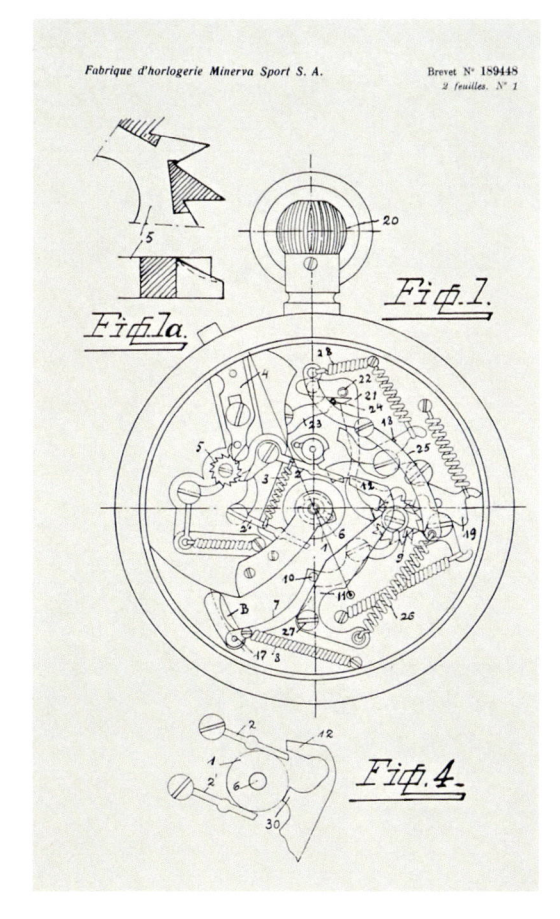

271

▲ 227　　　　　　　　　　▼ 228　　▲ 229　　　　　　　　　　▼ 230

227 Timer in a nickel-silver case with push-piece in the crown. White enameled dial with 15-minute counter. The seconds hand performs one revolution in 30 seconds.

228 Timer with chrome-plated case and two extra push-pieces. White dial with decimal divisions in hundredths of a minute and 30-minute counter. Two center seconds hands for the seconds (blue) and the split-seconds (red).

229 Timer with nickel-silver case, push-piece in the crown, and lateral slide for the zero reset. Enameled dial with divisions for counting production and 30-minute counter. The seconds hand performs one revolution in 60 seconds.

230 Timer with chrome-plated case, push-piece in the crown, and lateral push-piece for the flyback hand. White enameled dial with $\frac{1}{5}$-second divisions and 30-minute counter. Blue seconds hand, red flyback hand.

231 Timer with chrome-plated case and lateral push-piece for the zero reset. White dial with red 60-minute counter in the center.

232 Timer for regattas with chrome-plated case. White dial with center seconds hand and three 5-minute counters for the start phase of a regatta.

233 Timer with chrome-plated case. White dial with ¹⁄₁₀₀-second divisions. The seconds hand performs one revolution in 1 second; 30-seconds counter. The balance wheel oscillates at 360,000 vibrations per hour. The technology for a ¹⁄₁₀₀-second timer was developed by Minerva in the early 1920s.

234 Timer with chrome-plated case and supplementary push-piece for the zero reset. White dial with 60-minute and 12-hour counters for rallies.

235–236 View of the movements of the two sports timers 233 and 234. On the left, it is quite easy to distinguish the balance wheel, oscillating at 360,000 vibrations per hour, significantly smaller than the normal balance wheel, on the right, with a frequency of 18,000 vibrations per hour.

▲ 231   ▼ 232   ▲ 233   ▲ 234   ▼ 235-236

237 Non-stop timer movement based on the 19/9CH chronograph, with off-center minute wheel. Chronograph mechanism of the caliber 19/9CH, arranged so as to be visible.

238 Only the center chronograph wheel is in the center, the minute wheel being displaced.

239 View under the dial with the supplementary hand for split-time, controlled by a second column wheel.

▲ 237   ▼ 238 ▼ 239   ▲ 240

274

III The History of Minerva Watch Movements

NON-STOP TIMER MOVEMENTS

One of the major drawbacks of timers was the irregular acceleration of the balance wheel when it was actuated. As it was immobilized when reset to zero, it started more slowly. This situation obviously had a detrimental effect on accurate measurement. As a solution to this problem, Minerva modified a normal chronograph by moving the center wheel off-center, so that only the chronograph staff passed through the center. As soon as it was wound, the timer worked like an ordinary watch, with a power reserve of about thirty hours. The chronograph mechanism was retained. In this way, the chronograph could be engaged at any moment, with the great advantage that the balance wheel was already performing its oscillations, eliminating the slow-down caused by start-up time.

240–241 Dial of non-stop timer with split-time and 30-minute counter, as well as a non-stop small seconds.

242–243 Non-stop timer movement. View of the movement and, under the dial, the Valjoux 24 caliber with shock protection added by Minerva.

244 Detail view of the flyback clamp, the flyback wheel, and the column wheel controlled by the lateral push-piece on the case.

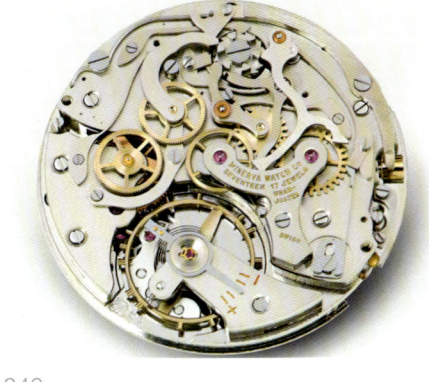

245 *Chronografo a Ritorno* timer movement with two speeds for the seconds hand, twice as fast clockwise as anticlockwise, and jumping 15-minute counter. There are two coupling yokes, engaging alternately.

246 Double gear train for the center chronograph wheel (top right). The coupling yoke for starting is positioned at the top; for reverse operation, the bottom coupling yoke includes a supplementary wheel to reverse the direction of rotation and a slower reduction ratio. The intermediate wheel on the left consists of two superimposed wheels.

247 Detail of the column wheel that controls all the functions.

▲ 245   ▼ 246   ▼ 247

276

III The History of Minerva Watch Movements

THE *CHRONOGRAFO A RITORNO*

Minerva gave this name to a timer with hands that turned clockwise on the first actuation of the push-piece and anti-clockwise on the second actuation of the push-piece. Minerva's contribution to this project is not known. The patent application for this function was submitted to the office concerned in 1927 by G.H. Guinand, Fabrique d'Horlogerie National Park, Les Brenets (Switzerland). However, Minerva made watches and movements of this type, possibly under licence, for various European armed forces. These chronographs are known by professionals as "bomb timers."

Minerva's archives mention three different movements for the Chronografo a Ritorno:
1 Chronograph without counter.
2 Chronograph with counter.
3 Chronograph with counter and split-seconds mechanism under the dial.

The functioning of the chronograph also took on two forms:
1 Forward and backward operation of the chronograph at the same speed, with one revolution round the dial every 60 seconds,
2 Clockwise operation of the chronograph twice as fast as anticlockwise operation, thanks to a supplementary "gear train."

248 On the column wheel specific to the flyback clamp, the columns are "milled" starting here.

249 View under the dial with winding mechanism and flyback clamp.

250 Record in the book of models for 1927 of chronographs with counter (and split-time function).

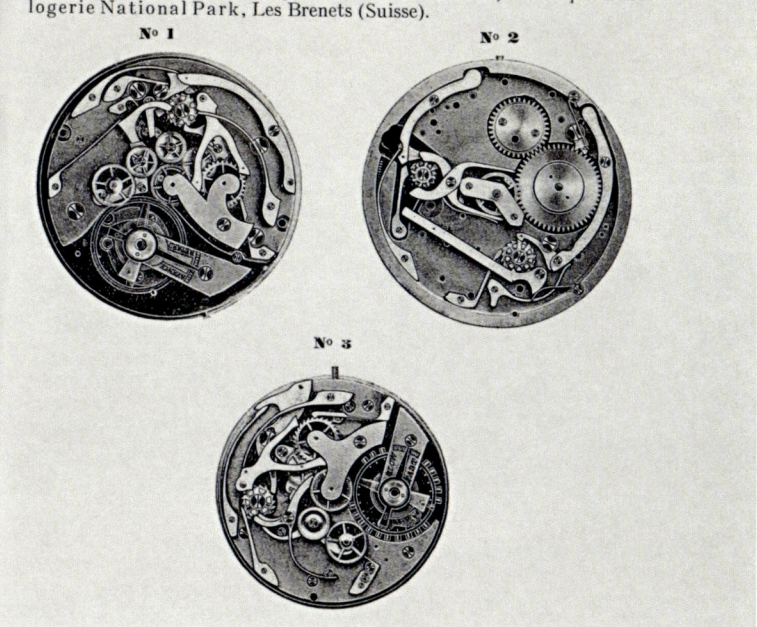

251 ▼ ▲ 253 252 ▲ ▼ 254

251 Same movement construction as in illustration 245, but without split-time and with the same speeds in clockwise and anticlockwise directions.

252 Same movement construction as in illustration 245, but without split-time or minute counter and with two different speeds in clockwise and anticlockwise directions.

253 Large *Chronografo a Ritorno* for the French armed forces, designed to be worn over uniform on the forearm or above the knee, with rotating bezel. 30-seconds scale and altimeter in hectometers, from 500 m to 6 km, as well as 15-minute scale.

254 Same model as in illustration 253, but for the Austrian armed forces, with gilded flyback hand.

255–257 Various versions of the dial in black-painted enamel for the *Chronografo a Ritorno*.

258 Two models of the large chronograph by Minerva to be worn on military equipment.

259 Large wrist-chronograph with altimeter, but without anticlockwise motion of the hand (probably a prototype).

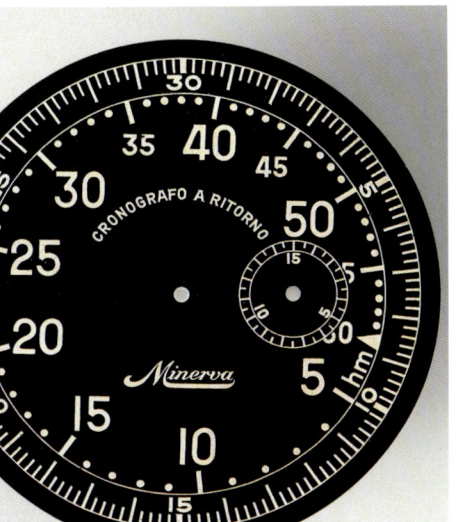

▲ 255

▲ 256   ▼ 257

▲ 258   ▼ 259

279

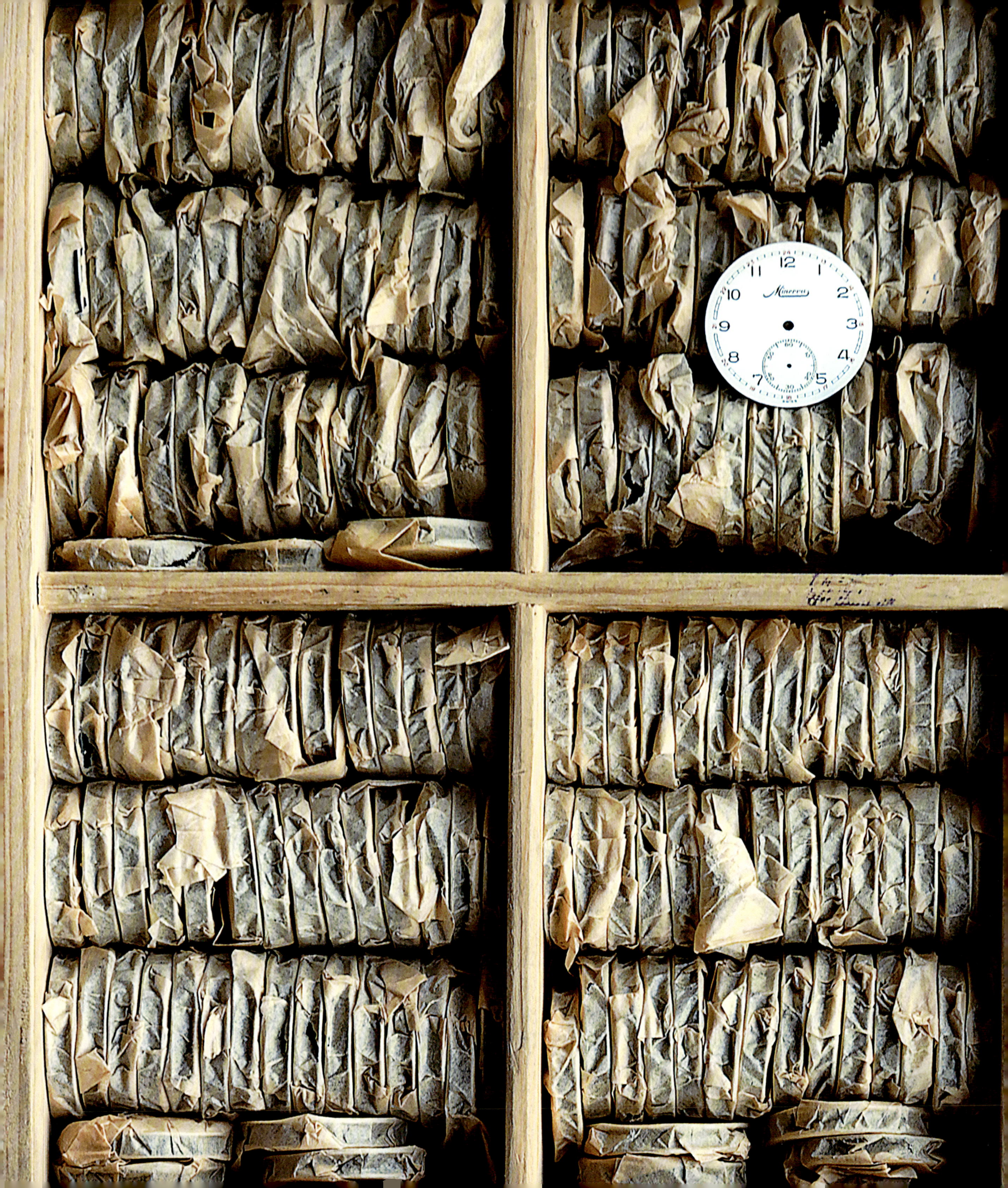
Minerva

Historic enameled dials

TIMERS

50 Timer, $\frac{1}{10}$-second divisions, 1 revolution in 10 seconds, 5-minute counter, for industry.
51 Timer, 1 revolution in 10 seconds, 30-minute counter, for industrial use.
52 Timer, $\frac{1}{20}$-second divisions, 1 revolution in 5 seconds, 150-minute counter, for industry.
53 Timer, $\frac{1}{100}$-hour divisions, 1 revolution in 36 seconds, 30-minute counter, for calculation of the number of pieces.
54 Timer, $\frac{1}{20}$-second divisions, 1 revolution in 15 seconds, 7½-minute counter, for a technical application.
55 Timer, 1 revolution in 30 seconds, 5/100-($\frac{1}{20}$-)minute divisions on the outside based on 1 revolution, 15-minute counter.
56 Timer, 1 revolution in 10 seconds, 15-minute counter, for sport and industry.
57 Timer, 1 revolution in 10 seconds, $\frac{1}{10}$-second divisions, 30-minute counter.
58 Timer, $\frac{1}{50}$-second divisions, 1 revolution in 6 seconds, 3-minute counter, for high-accuracy measurements.
59 Timer, 1 revolution in 60 seconds, 30-minute counter, for sport and industry.
60 Timer, 1 revolution in 60 seconds, 30-minute counter, for sport and industry.
61 Timer, 1 revolution in 60 seconds, 30-minute counter, with small seconds for the non-stop movement.
62 Timer, 1 revolution in 60 seconds, 30-minute counter, with small seconds for the non-stop movement.
63 Timer, 1 revolution in 60 seconds, $\frac{1}{100}$-minute divisions inside, for precision measurements.
64 Timer, 1 revolution in 60 seconds, $\frac{1}{100}$-minute divisions inside, 30-minute counter, for precision measurements.
65 Timer, 1 revolution in 60 seconds, $\frac{1}{100}$-minute divisions inside, 60-minute counter, for precision measurements.
66 Timer, 1 revolution in 60 seconds, center 60-minute counter.
67 Timer, 1 revolution in 60 seconds, $\frac{1}{100}$-minute divisions inside, 30-minute counter.
68 Timer, $\frac{1}{100}$-second divisions, 1 revolution in 60 seconds, 30-minute counter, for monitoring operations in industry.
69 Timer, $\frac{1}{100}$-minute and 1-second divisions, 1 revolution in 60 seconds, 30-minute counter, for purposes of monitoring in industry.
70 Timer, $\frac{1}{100}$-second divisions, 1 revolution in 60 seconds, 60-minute counter, for monitoring operations in industry.
71 Timer, $\frac{1}{100}$-minute and 1-second divisions, 1 revolution in 60 seconds, 30-minute counter, for purposes of monitoring in industry.
72 Timer, $\frac{1}{100}$-minute and 1-second divisions, 1 revolution in 60 seconds, 30-minute counter, for purposes of monitoring in industry.
73 Timer, $\frac{1}{100}$-minute and 1-second divisions, 1 revolution in 60 seconds, 30-minute counter, for purposes of monitoring in industry.
74 Timer with $\frac{1}{100}$-second divisions, 1 revolution in 3 seconds, 1½-minute counter, for high-accuracy measurements.
75 Timer with $\frac{1}{100}$-second divisions, 1 revolution in 3 seconds, 1½-minute counter, for high-accuracy measurements.
76 Timer with quadruple-spiral tachometer 30 to 150 km/h, basis 1,000 m, 30-minute counter, for industry and sport.
77 Timer with triple-spiral tachometer 20 to 300 km/h, basis 1,000 m, 30-minute counter, for industry and sport.
78 Timer with tachometer 12 to 120 km/h, basis 200 m, 30-minute counter, for industry and sport.
79 Timer with tachometer 12 to 120 km/h, basis 200 m, 30-minute counter, for industry and sport.
80 Timer with tachometer 24 to 400 km/h, basis 400 m, 30-minute counter, for industry and sport.
81 Special timer with tachometer scale 60 to 400 km/h and decimal divisions, 30-minute counter.
82 Timer with tachometer 12 to 200 km/h, basis 200 m and decimal divisions, 30-minute counter, for industry and sport.
83 Timer with tachometer 12 to 200 km/h, basis 200 m, 30-minute counter, for industry and sport.
84 Timer, 1 revolution in 60 seconds, decimal divisions on the circumference, 60-minute and 12-hour counters, for rallies.
85 Timer, 1 revolution in 60 seconds, 60-minute and 12-hour counters, for rallies.
86 Timer, 1 revolution in 60 seconds, $\frac{1}{100}$-minute divisions and production timer 60 to 1,800 pieces/minute, 30-minute counter, for industrial use.
87 Timer, 1 revolution in 60 seconds, $\frac{1}{100}$-minute divisions and production timer 30 to 1,800 pieces/2 minutes, 30-minute counter, for industrial use.
88 Timer for football, 1 to 45 minutes on 60-minute counter, 1 revolution in 60 seconds.
89 Timer, $\frac{1}{5}$-second divisions, 1 revolution in 60 seconds, for water polo, 2 x 7 minutes + 3-minute pause in the 30-minute counter.
90 Timer, $\frac{1}{10}$-second divisions, 1 revolution in 30 seconds, for water polo, 2 x 7 minutes + 3-minute pause in the 15-minute counter.
91 Timer with logarithmic divisions in minutes, for a technical application.
92 Timer for regattas with 5-minute counter, 1 revolution in 60 seconds, small diameter.
93 Timer for regattas with 5-minute counter, 1 revolution in 60 seconds, large diameter.
94 Timer for regattas with 5-minute counter, 1 revolution in 60 seconds, large diameter.
95 Timer for regattas with 5-minute counter, 1 revolution in 60 seconds.
96 Timer, 1 revolution in 60 seconds, $\frac{1}{5}$-second divisions, 30-minute counter.
97 Timer with $\frac{1}{100}$-minute and $\frac{1}{5}$-second divisions, 1 revolution in 60 seconds, 30-minute counter, for industry and science.

Historic enameled dials

25 26 27 28
29 30 31 32
33 34 35 36
37 38 39 40
41 42 43 44
45 46 47 48 49

CHRONOGRAPHS

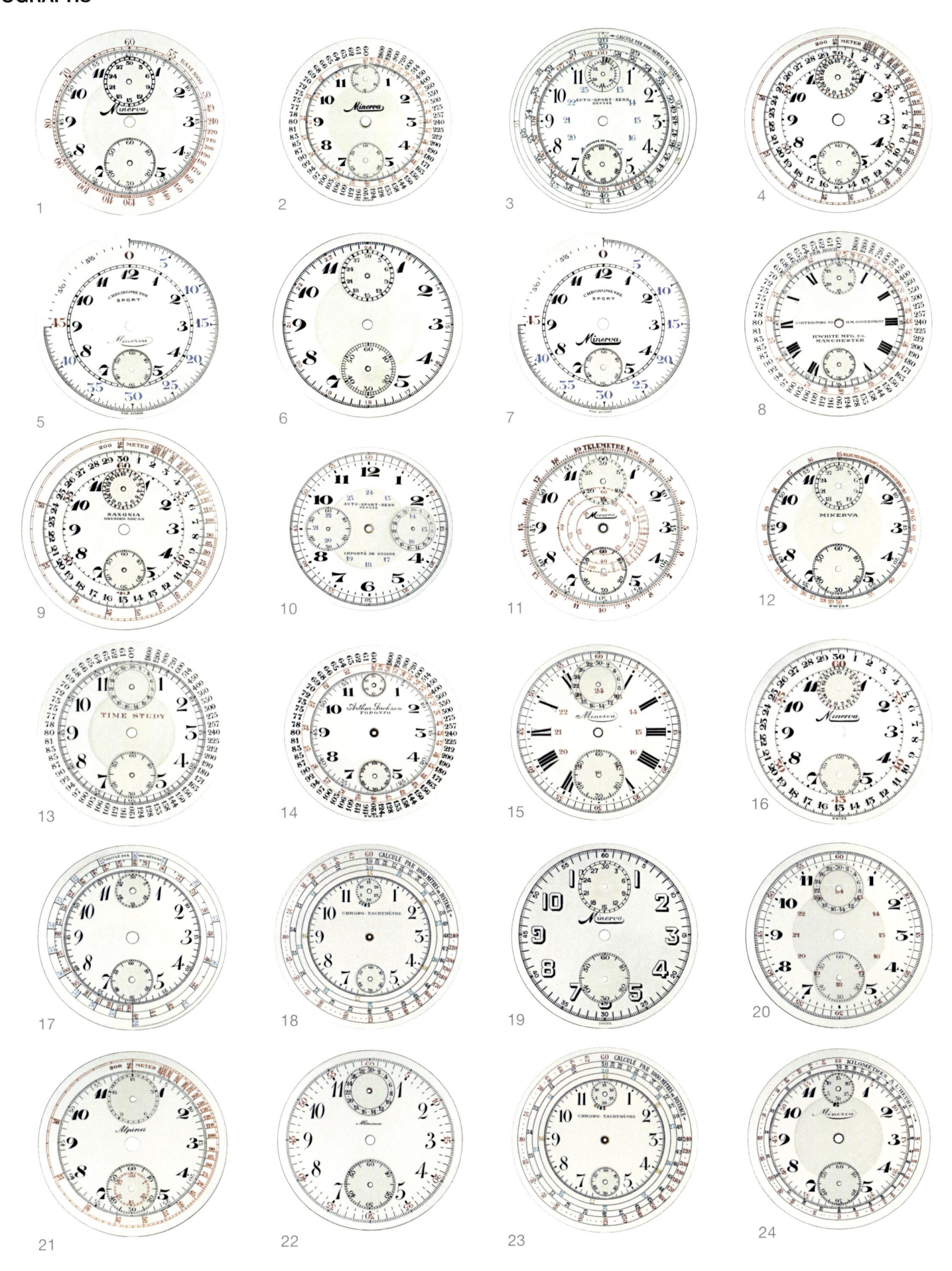

TIMERS

50 Timer, $1/10$-second divisions, 1 revolution in 10 seconds, 5-minute counter, for industry.
51 Timer, 1 revolution in 10 seconds, 30-minute counter, for industrial use.
52 Timer, $1/20$-second divisions, 1 revolution in 5 seconds, 150-minute counter, for industry.
53 Timer, $1/100$-hour divisions, 1 revolution in 36 seconds, 30-minute counter, for calculation of the number of pieces.
54 Timer, $1/20$-second divisions, 1 revolution in 15 seconds, 7½-minute counter, for a technical application.
55 Timer, 1 revolution in 30 seconds, 5/100-($1/20$-)minute divisions on the outside based on 1 revolution, 15-minute counter.
56 Timer, 1 revolution in 10 seconds, 15-minute counter, for sport and industry.
57 Timer, 1 revolution in 10 seconds, $1/10$-second divisions, 30-minute counter.
58 Timer, $1/50$-second divisions, 1 revolution in 6 seconds, 3-minute counter, for high-accuracy measurements.
59 Timer, 1 revolution in 60 seconds, 30-minute counter, for sport and industry.
60 Timer, 1 revolution in 60 seconds, 30-minute counter, for sport and industry.
61 Timer, 1 revolution in 60 seconds, 30-minute counter, with small seconds for the non-stop movement.
62 Timer, 1 revolution in 60 seconds, 30-minute counter, with small seconds for the non-stop movement.
63 Timer, 1 revolution in 60 seconds, $1/100$-minute divisions inside, for precision measurements.
64 Timer, 1 revolution in 60 seconds, $1/100$-minute divisions inside, 30-minute counter, for precision measurements.
65 Timer, 1 revolution in 60 seconds, $1/100$-minute divisions inside, 60-minute counter, for precision measurements.
66 Timer, 1 revolution in 60 seconds, center 60-minute counter.
67 Timer, 1 revolution in 60 seconds, $1/100$-minute divisions inside, 30-minute counter.
68 Timer, $1/100$-second divisions, 1 revolution in 60 seconds, 30-minute counter, for monitoring operations in industry.
69 Timer, $1/100$-minute and 1-second divisions, 1 revolution in 60 seconds, 30-minute counter, for purposes of monitoring in industry.
70 Timer, $1/100$-second divisions, 1 revolution in 60 seconds, 60-minute counter, for monitoring operations in industry.
71 Timer, $1/100$-minute and 1-second divisions, 1 revolution in 60 seconds, 30-minute counter, for purposes of monitoring in industry.
72 Timer, $1/100$-minute and 1-second divisions, 1 revolution in 60 seconds, 30-minute counter, for purposes of monitoring in industry.
73 Timer, $1/100$-minute and 1-second divisions, 1 revolution in 60 seconds, 30-minute counter, for purposes of monitoring in industry.
74 Timer with $1/100$-second divisions, 1 revolution in 3 seconds, 1½-minute counter, for high-accuracy measurements.
75 Timer with $1/100$-second divisions, 1 revolution in 3 seconds, 1½-minute counter, for high-accuracy measurements.
76 Timer with quadruple-spiral tachometer 30 to 150 km/h, basis 1,000 m, 30-minute counter, for industry and sport.
77 Timer with triple-spiral tachometer 20 to 300 km/h, basis 1,000 m, 30-minute counter, for industry and sport.
78 Timer with tachometer 12 to 120 km/h, basis 200 m, 30-minute counter, for industry and sport.
79 Timer with tachometer 12 to 120 km/h, basis 200 m, 30-minute counter, for industry and sport.
80 Timer with tachometer 24 to 400 km/h, basis 400 m, 30-minute counter, for industry and sport.
81 Special timer with tachometer scale 60 to 400 km/h and decimal divisions, 30-minute counter.
82 Timer with tachometer 12 to 200 km/h, basis 200 m and decimal divisions, 30-minute counter, for industry and sport.
83 Timer with tachometer 12 to 200 km/h, basis 200 m, 30-minute counter, for industry and sport.
84 Timer, 1 revolution in 60 seconds, decimal divisions on the circumference, 60-minute and 12-hour counters, for rallies.
85 Timer, 1 revolution in 60 seconds, 60-minute and 12-hour counters, for rallies.
86 Timer, 1 revolution in 60 seconds, $1/100$-minute divisions and production timer 60 to 1,800 pieces/minute, 30-minute counter, for industrial use.
87 Timer, 1 revolution in 60 seconds, $1/100$-minute divisions and production timer 30 to 1,800 pieces/2 minutes, 30-minute counter, for industrial use.
88 Timer for football, 1 to 45 minutes on 60-minute counter, 1 revolution in 60 seconds.
89 Timer, $1/5$-second divisions, 1 revolution in 60 seconds, for water polo, 2 x 7 minutes + 3-minute pause in the 30-minute counter.
90 Timer, $1/10$-second divisions, 1 revolution in 30 seconds, for water polo, 2 x 7 minutes + 3-minute pause in the 15-minute counter.
91 Timer with logarithmic divisions in minutes, for a technical application.
92 Timer for regattas with 5-minute counter, 1 revolution in 60 seconds, small diameter.
93 Timer for regattas with 5-minute counter, 1 revolution in 60 seconds, large diameter.
94 Timer for regattas with 5-minute counter, 1 revolution in 60 seconds, large diameter.
95 Timer for regattas with 5-minute counter, 1 revolution in 60 seconds.
96 Timer, 1 revolution in 60 seconds, $1/5$-second divisions, 30-minute counter.
97 Timer with $1/100$-minute and $1/5$-second divisions, 1 revolution in 60 seconds, 30-minute counter, for industry and science.

CHRONOGRAPHS

1 Chronograph, 1/5-second divisions, 30-minute counter, tachometer 49 to 240 km/h, basis 1,000 m.
2 Chronograph, 1/10-second divisions, 30-minute counter, production timer 30 to 1,800 units/2 minutes.
3 Chronograph, 1/5-second divisions, 30-minute counter, quadruple spiral tachometer 13 to 150 km/h, basis 1,000 m.
4 Chronograph, 1/10-second divisions, 15-minute counter, tachometer 24 to 400 km/h, basis 200 m.
5 Chronograph, 10-second divisions, specially designed for football: 45-minute counter/divisions, new Minerva logo.
6 Chronograph, 1/5-second divisions, 30-minute counter, classic.
7 Chronograph, 10-second divisions, specially designed for football: 45-minute counter/divisions, old Minerva logo.
8 Chronograph, 1/10-second divisions, 30-minute counter, production timer 30 to 1,800 pieces/2 minutes.
9 Chronograph, 1/10-second divisions, 15-minute counter, tachometer 24 to 400 km/h, basis 200 m.
10 Full hunter chronograph, 12/24-hour display, 1/5-second divisions, 30-minute counter, square.
11 Chronograph, 30-minute counter, triple-spiral tachometer 20 to 360 km/h, basis 1,000 m, telemeter 1 to 20 km.
12 Chronograph, 30-minute counter, tachometer 15 to 100 mph, basis 1/2 mile.
13 Chronograph, 1/5-second divisions, 30-minute counter, production timer 60 to 1,800 pieces/minute.
14 Chronograph, 1/5-second divisions, 30-minute counter, production timer 30 to 1,800 units/2 minutes.
15 Chronograph, 12/24-hour display, 1/5 second divisions, 30-minute counter, Roman numerals.
16 Chronograph, 1/10-second divisions, 15-minute counter, classic.
17 Chronograph, 1/5-second divisions, 30-minute counter, double spiral tachometer 24 to 120 km/h, basis 1,000 m.
18 Chronograph, 1/5-second divisions, 15-minute counter, quadruple spiral tachometer 15 to 240 km/h, basis 1,000 m.
19 Chronograph, 1/5-second divisions, 30-minute counter, classic with luminous numerals.
20 Chronograph, 1/5-second divisions, 30-minute counter, 12/24-hour display.
21 Chronograph, 1/10-second divisions, 15-minute counter, tachometer 24 to 400 km/h, basis 200 m, two seconds hands, from 1 to 30 and from 1 to 60.
22 Chronograph, 1/5-second divisions, 30-minute counter, classic with Arabic numerals.
23 Chronograph, 1/5-second divisions, 15-minute counter, quadruple spiral tachometer 15 to 240 km/h, basis 1,000 m.
24 Chronograph, 1/5-second divisions, double spiral tachometer 30 to 240 km/h, basis 1,000 m.
25 Chronograph, 1/5-second divisions, 30-minute counter, quadruple spiral tachometer 15 to 300 km/h, basis 1,000 m.
26 Chronograph, 1/5-second divisions, 30-minute counter, pulsimeter 40 to 200 beats/minute.
27 Chronograph, 1/5-second divisions, 30-minute counter, tachometer 200 to 42 km/h, basis 200 m.
28 Chronograph, 1/5-second divisions, 30-minute counter, classic.
29 Full hunter chronograph, 1/5-second divisions, 30-minute counter, production timer 30 to 1,800 pieces/2 minutes.
30 Chronograph, 1/5-second divisions, 30-minute counter, pulsimeter 40 to 180 beats/minute.
31 Chronograph, Arabic numerals, 1/5-second divisions, 30-minute counter, quadruple spiral tachometer 15 to 150 km/h, basis 1,000 m.
32 Chronograph, Roman numerals, 1/5-second divisions, 30-minute counter, quadruple spiral tachometer 15 to 150 km/h, basis 1 000 m.
33 Chronograph, 1/5-second divisions, 30-minute counter, pulsimeter 40 to 200 vibrations/minute.
34 Chronograph, 1/5-second divisions, 30-minute counter, quadruple spiral tachometer 15 to 300 km/h, basis 1,000 m.
35 Wrist-chronograph, 1/5-second divisions, 30-minute counter, classic.
36 Chronograph, Roman numerals, 1/5-second divisions, 30-minute counter, classic.
37 Wristwatch with chronograph, 1/5-second divisions, 15-minute counter, triple-spiral tachometer 20 to 300 km/h, basis 1,000 m.
38 Full hunter chronograph, 1/5-second divisions, 15-minute counter, triple-spiral tachometer 20 to 300 km/h, basis 1,000 m.
39 Wrist-chronograph, 1/5-second divisions, 30-minute counter, classic.
40 Full hunter chronograph, 1/5-second divisions, 15-minute counter, quadruple spiral tachometer 15 to 240 km/h, basis 1,000 m.
41 Chronograph, Roman numerals, 1/5-second divisions, 30-minute counter, classic.
42 Chronograph, 1/5-second divisions, 30-minute counter, classic.
43 Chronograph, 1/100- and 1/60-minute divisions, 30-minute counter, classic.
44 Full hunter chronograph, 1/5-second divisions, 15-minute counter, triple-spiral tachometer 20 to 300 km/h, basis 1,000 m.
45 Chronograph with luminous numerals, 1/5-second divisions, 30-minute counter, double spiral tachometer 30 to 300 km/h, basis 1,000 m.
46 Full hunter chronograph, 1/5-second divisions, 30-minute counter, pulsimeter 40 to 200 beats/minute.
47 Wrist-chronograph, 1/5-second divisions, 30-minute counter, tachometer 49 to 240 km/h, basis 1,000 m.
48 Wrist-chronograph, 1/5-second divisions, 30-minute counter, classic.
49 Wrist-chronograph, 1/5-second divisions, 30-minute counter, tachometer 49 to 240 km/h, basis 1,000 m.

268

269

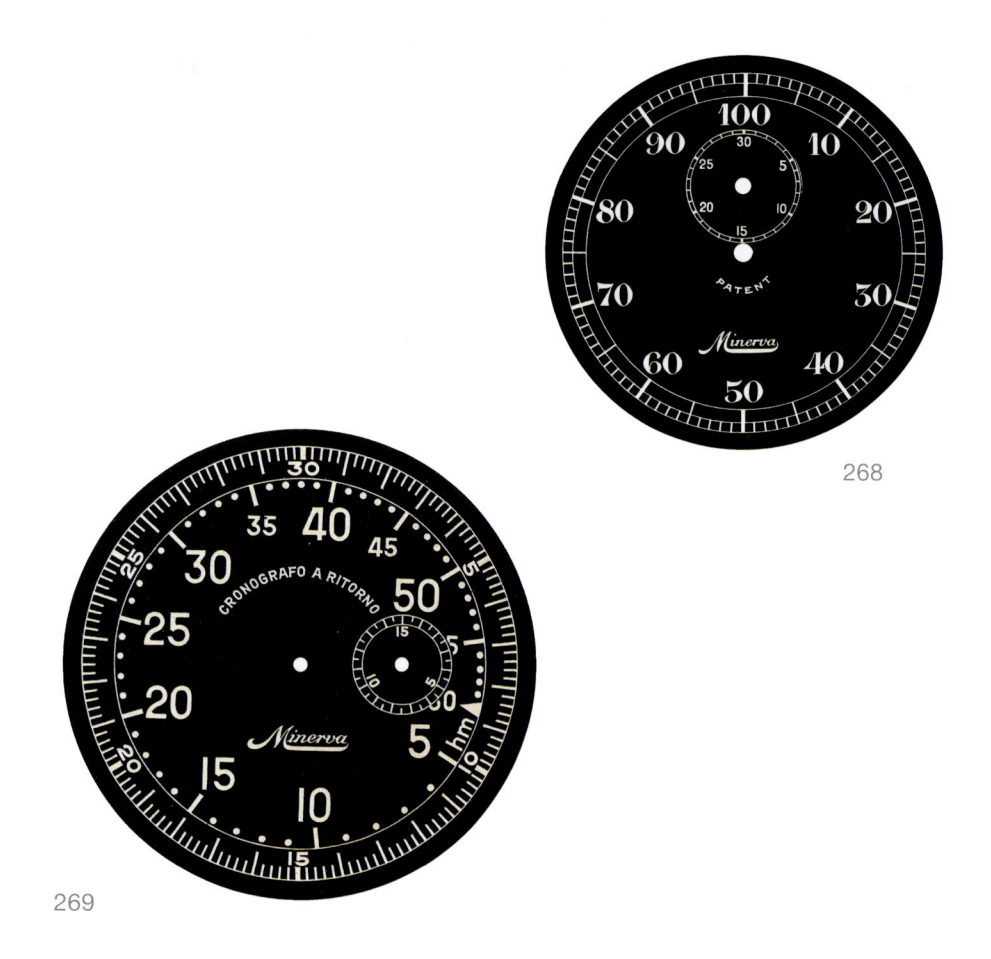

HISTORIC ENAMELED DIALS

The collection of historic enameled dials for Minerva's timers and chronograph watches, conserved in the Minerva Museum in Villeret, provides an excellent demonstration of watchmaking's responses to the various technical and social needs of the early twentieth century. Indeed, mechanical chronographs expanded rapidly at this time due to the increasing demand from physicians, engineers, the army and sportsmen to measure short time intervals. Minerva developed dials and mechanisms adapted to each use, until the invention of electronic time measurement in the 1970s.

267-269
Black timer dials for military applications with special divisions.

CHRONOGRAPHS

1 Chronograph, $\frac{1}{5}$-second divisions, 30-minute counter, tachometer 49 to 240 km/h, basis 1,000 m.
2 Chronograph, $\frac{1}{10}$-second divisions, 30-minute counter, production timer 30 to 1,800 units/2 minutes.
3 Chronograph, $\frac{1}{5}$-second divisions, 30-minute counter, quadruple spiral tachometer 13 to 150 km/h, basis 1,000 m.
4 Chronograph, $\frac{1}{10}$-second divisions, 15-minute counter, tachometer 24 to 400 km/h, basis 200 m.
5 Chronograph, 10-second divisions, specially designed for football: 45-minute counter/divisions, new Minerva logo.
6 Chronograph, $\frac{1}{5}$-second divisions, 30-minute counter, classic.
7 Chronograph, 10-second divisions, specially designed for football: 45-minute counter/divisions, old Minerva logo.
8 Chronograph, $\frac{1}{10}$-second divisions, 30-minute counter, production timer 30 to 1,800 pieces/2 minutes.
9 Chronograph, $\frac{1}{10}$-second divisions, 15-minute counter, tachometer 24 to 400 km/h, basis 200 m.
10 Full hunter chronograph, 12/24-hour display, $\frac{1}{5}$-second divisions, 30-minute counter, square.
11 Chronograph, 30-minute counter, triple-spiral tachometer 20 to 360 km/h, basis 1,000 m, telemeter 1 to 20 km.
12 Chronograph, 30-minute counter, tachometer 15 to 100 mph, basis ½ mile.
13 Chronograph, $\frac{1}{5}$-second divisions, 30-minute counter, production timer 60 to 1,800 pieces/minute.
14 Chronograph, $\frac{1}{5}$-second divisions, 30-minute counter, production timer 30 to 1,800 units/2 minutes.
15 Chronograph, 12/24-hour display, $\frac{1}{5}$ second divisions, 30-minute counter, Roman numerals.
16 Chronograph, $\frac{1}{10}$-second divisions, 15-minute counter, classic.
17 Chronograph, $\frac{1}{5}$-second divisions, 30-minute counter, double spiral tachometer 24 to 120 km/h, basis 1,000 m.
18 Chronograph, $\frac{1}{5}$-second divisions, 15-minute counter, quadruple spiral tachometer 15 to 240 km/h, basis 1,000 m.
19 Chronograph, $\frac{1}{5}$-second divisions, 30-minute counter, classic with luminous numerals.
20 Chronograph, $\frac{1}{5}$-second divisions, 30-minute counter, 12/24-hour display.
21 Chronograph, $\frac{1}{10}$-second divisions, 15-minute counter, tachometer 24 to 400 km/h, basis 200 m, two seconds hands, from 1 to 30 and from 1 to 60.
22 Chronograph, $\frac{1}{5}$-second divisions, 30-minute counter, classic with Arabic numerals.
23 Chronograph, $\frac{1}{5}$-second divisions, 15-minute counter, quadruple spiral tachometer 15 to 240 km/h, basis 1,000 m.
24 Chronograph, $\frac{1}{5}$-second divisions, double spiral tachometer 30 to 240 km/h, basis 1,000 m.
25 Chronograph, $\frac{1}{5}$-second divisions, 30-minute counter, quadruple spiral tachometer 15 to 300 km/h, basis 1,000 m.

26 Chronograph, $\frac{1}{5}$-second divisions, 30-minute counter, pulsimeter 40 to 200 beats/minute.
27 Chronograph, $\frac{1}{5}$-second divisions, 30-minute counter, tachometer 200 to 42 km/h, basis 200 m.
28 Chronograph, $\frac{1}{5}$-second divisions, 30-minute counter, classic.
29 Full hunter chronograph, $\frac{1}{5}$-second divisions, 30-minute counter, production timer 30 to 1,800 pieces/2 minutes.
30 Chronograph, $\frac{1}{5}$-second divisions, 30-minute counter, pulsimeter 40 to 180 beats/minute.
31 Chronograph, Arabic numerals, $\frac{1}{5}$-second divisions, 30-minute counter, quadruple spiral tachometer 15 to 150 km/h, basis 1,000 m.
32 Chronograph, Roman numerals, $\frac{1}{5}$-second divisions, 30-minute counter, quadruple spiral tachometer 15 to 150 km/h, basis 1 000 m.
33 Chronograph, $\frac{1}{5}$-second divisions, 30-minute counter, pulsimeter 40 to 200 vibrations/minute.
34 Chronograph, $\frac{1}{5}$-second divisions, 30-minute counter, quadruple spiral tachometer 15 to 300 km/h, basis 1,000 m.
35 Wrist-chronograph, $\frac{1}{5}$-second divisions, 30-minute counter, classic.
36 Chronograph, Roman numerals, $\frac{1}{5}$-second divisions, 30-minute counter, classic.
37 Wristwatch with chronograph, $\frac{1}{5}$-second divisions, 15-minute counter, triple-spiral tachometer 20 to 300 km/h, basis 1,000 m.
38 Full hunter chronograph, $\frac{1}{5}$-second divisions, 15-minute counter, triple-spiral tachometer 20 to 300 km/h, basis 1,000 m.
39 Wrist-chronograph, $\frac{1}{5}$-second divisions, 30-minute counter, classic.
40 Full hunter chronograph, $\frac{1}{5}$-second divisions, 15-minute counter, quadruple spiral tachometer 15 to 240 km/h, basis 1,000 m.
41 Chronograph, Roman numerals, $\frac{1}{5}$-second divisions, 30-minute counter, classic.
42 Chronograph, $\frac{1}{5}$-second divisions, 30-minute counter, classic.
43 Chronograph, $\frac{1}{100}$- and $\frac{1}{60}$-minute divisions, 30-minute counter, classic.
44 Full hunter chronograph, $\frac{1}{5}$-second divisions, 15-minute counter, triple-spiral tachometer 20 to 300 km/h, basis 1,000 m.
45 Chronograph with luminous numerals, $\frac{1}{5}$-second divisions, 30-minute counter, double spiral tachometer 30 to 300 km/h, basis 1,000 m.
46 Full hunter chronograph, $\frac{1}{5}$-second divisions, 30-minute counter, pulsimeter 40 to 200 beats/minute.
47 Wrist-chronograph, $\frac{1}{5}$-second divisions, 30-minute counter, tachometer 49 to 240 km/h, basis 1,000 m.
48 Wrist-chronograph, $\frac{1}{5}$-second divisions, 30-minute counter, classic.
49 Wrist-chronograph, $\frac{1}{5}$-second divisions, 30-minute counter, tachometer 49 to 240 km/h, basis 1,000 m.

74 75 76 77
78 79 80 81
82 83 84 85
86 87 88 89
90 91 92 93
94 95 96 97

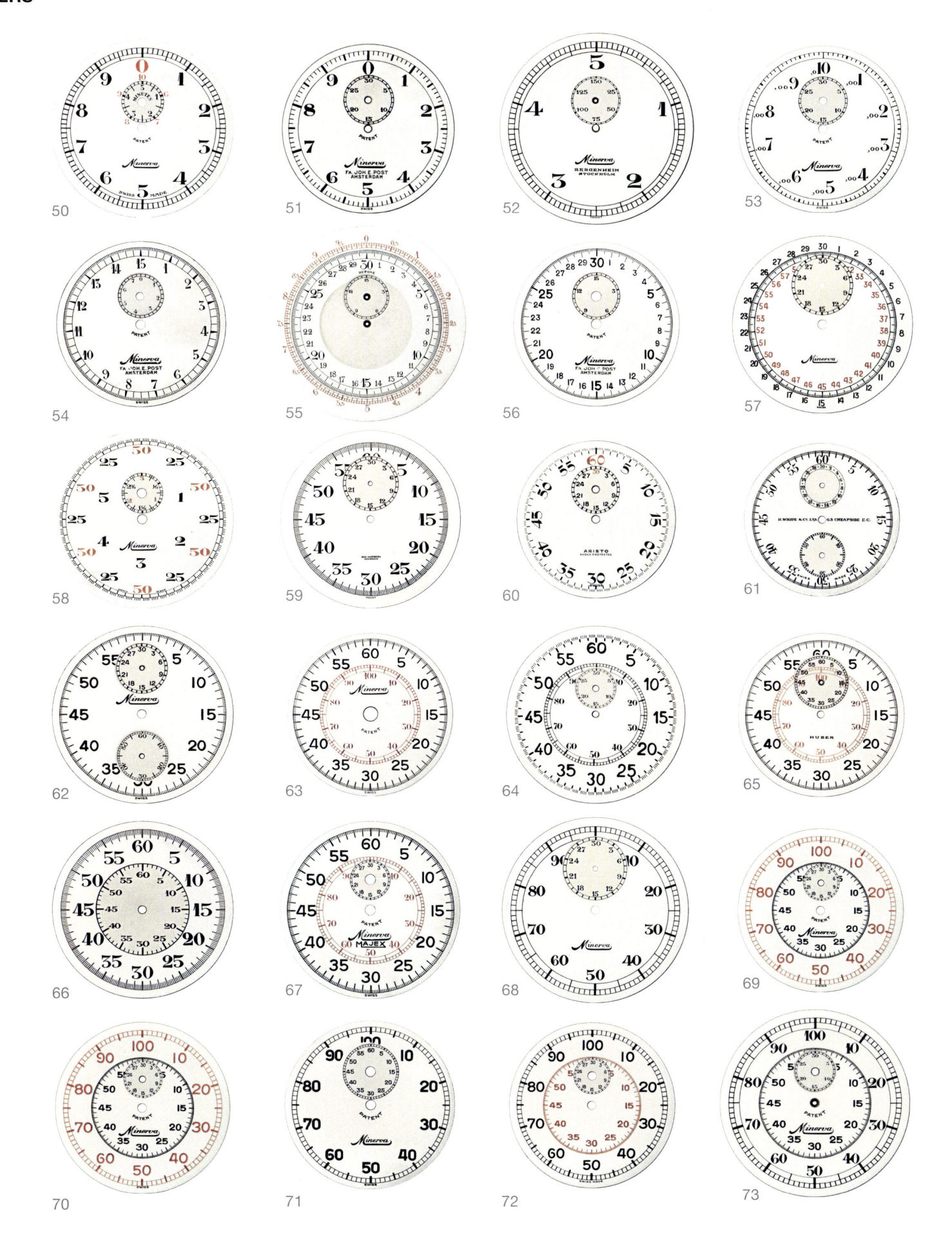

TIMERS

268

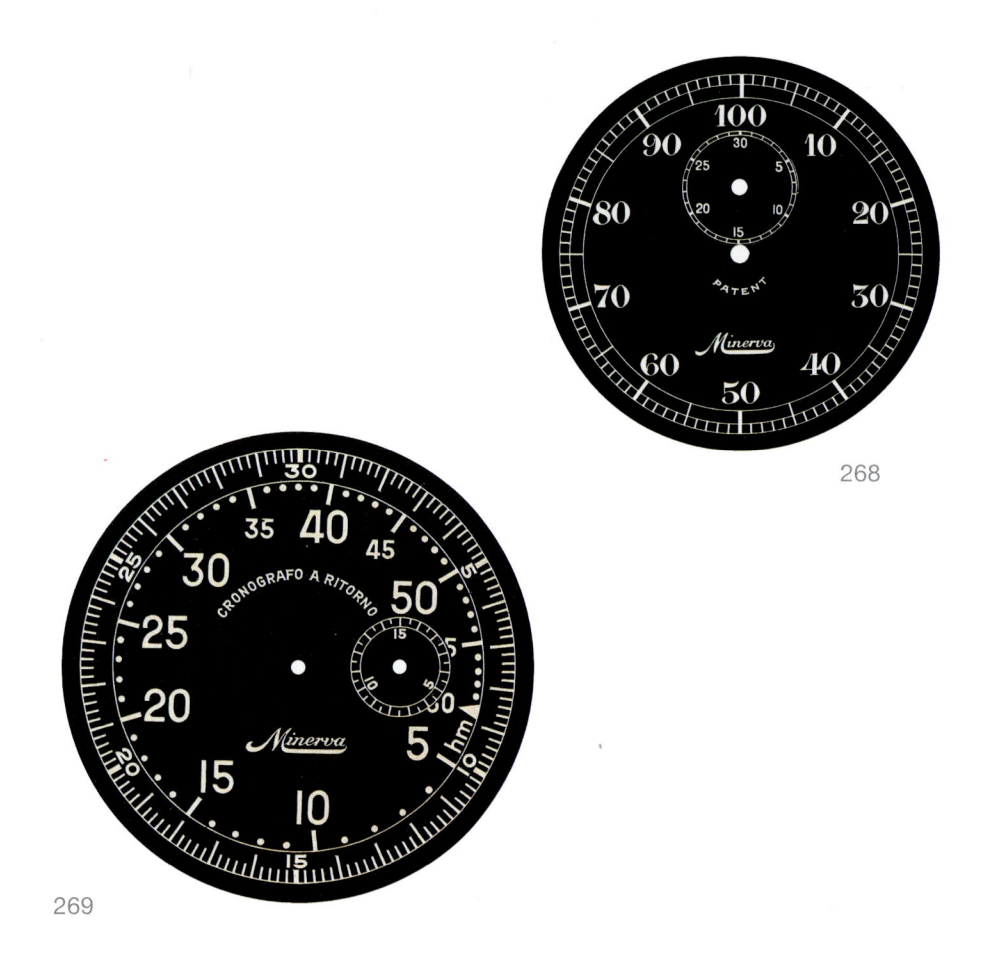

269

Historic enameled dials

The collection of historic enameled dials for Minerva's timers and chronograph watches, conserved in the Minerva Museum in Villeret, provides an excellent demonstration of watchmaking's responses to the various technical and social needs of the early twentieth century. Indeed, mechanical chronographs expanded rapidly at this time due to the increasing demand from physicians, engineers, the army and sportsmen to measure short time intervals. Minerva developed dials and mechanisms adapted to each use, until the invention of electronic time measurement in the 1970s.

267-269
Black timer dials for military applications with special divisions.

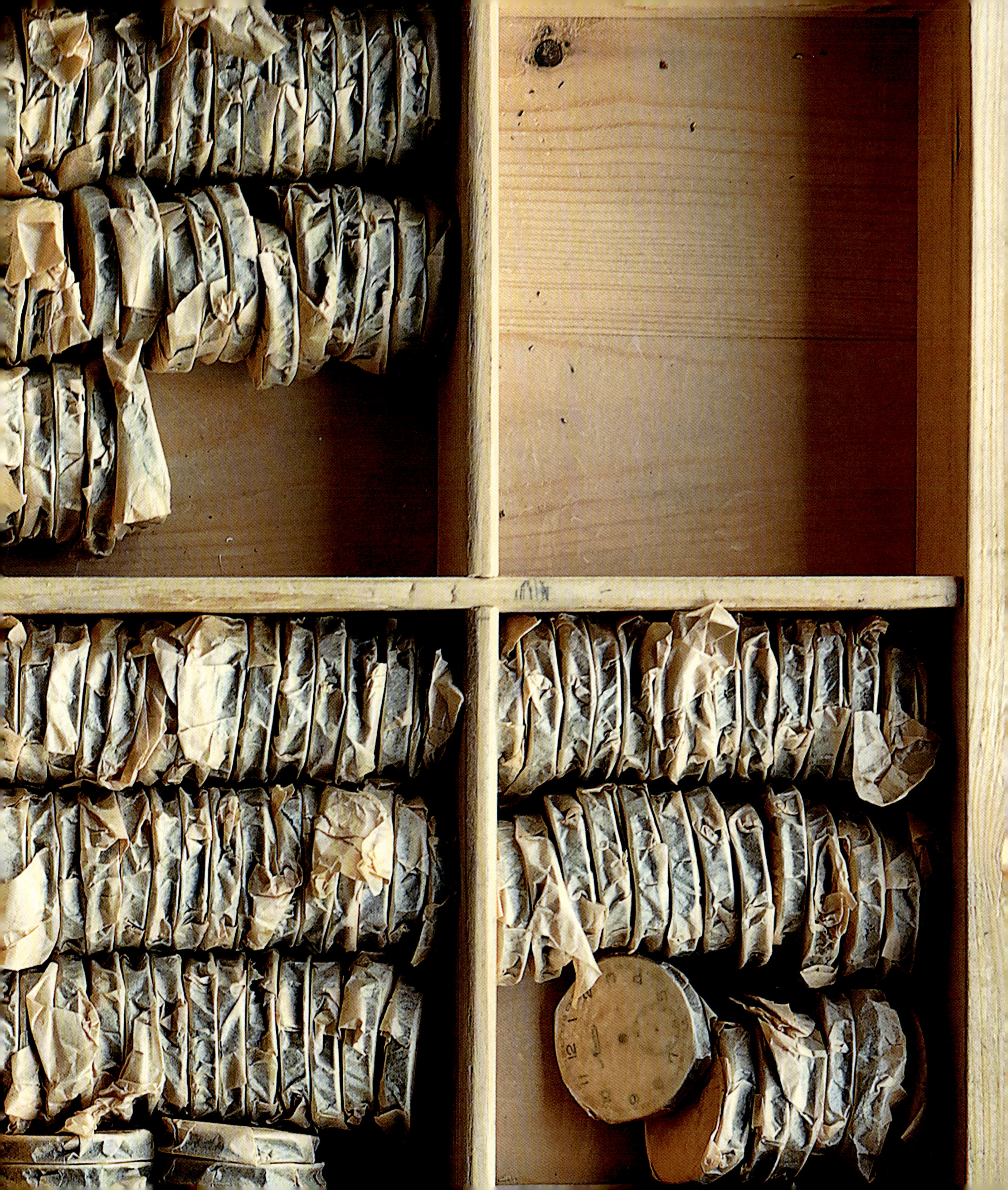

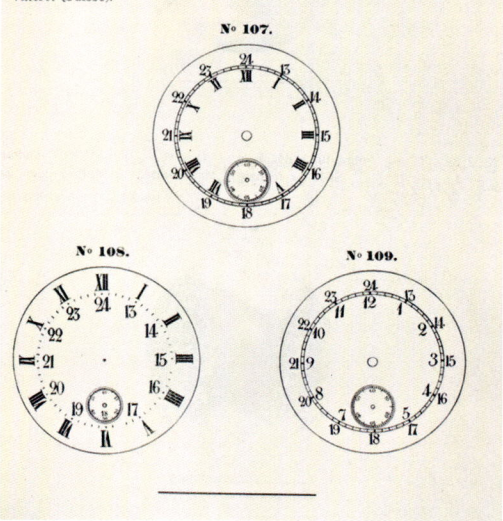

▲ 265 ▼ 266

282

Making an enamel dial

Enamel is a coating as hard as glass, resistant to oxidation and temperature variations, white or colored, deposited by melting or sintering on metal surfaces. The techniques of enameling were already known in the Middle Ages and were used up to the seventeenth century for cases, and later for dials as well. Until the early decades of the twentieth century, the art of enameling was much favoured for its creative potential and the printing technique that was perfected for dials.

Both on watch cases and on dials, the enamel powder is always applied to both sides of the metal substrate (which is usually copper, though occasionally gold for particularly prestigious cases). The material deposited on the inside of the case or the underneath of the dial is called the counter-enamel. The inside of a case was often painted. On high-quality pieces, secondary dials, for small seconds for example, were inserted in the main dial and soldered onto the metal base from behind.

The inscription (logo) and numerals are also made of enamel—formerly by hand with the aid of fine paint-brushes, these days by pattern plate using the stamping technique followed by melting in a second firing. For this purpose, the use of the colors red and blue used to be systematic.

Even today, the production of an enamel dial is still primarily a work of craftsmanship, and every dial is unique. The principal stages of the work are these:

1 The base material (0.20 mm) consists of a disk of copper in the shape of a shallow dish.
2 The feet of the dial are placed in predetermined positions.
3 Each foot is soldered using a wire previously positioned under each one.
4 The first firing generally melts the counter-enamel deposited on the dial in powder form.
5 A first coat of white enamel is spread over the face of the dial and melted at a temperature of about 830 to 850°C. The process is repeated with successive layers until a thickness of 0.8 to 0.9 mm is attained.
6 After each firing, as the dial tends to bulge under the effect of the heat, it needs to be flattened with a carbon pad while the enamel is still hot (and therefore soft).
7 It is then possible to apply the logo and numerals in black enamel (powder and oil) by stamping, and carry out a second firing.
8 Each new colour requires separate application and another firing.
9 Using an eyeglass, the dial is centred according to the indications on it and the centre hole is bored with a diamond drill to respect the minimum tolerances between the centre hole and the displays on the dial.
10 The centre of the seconds hand is positioned with respect to the centre hole and predrilled.
11 The hole is enlarged to the size of the seconds dial with a file and a special polishing stone.
12 The enamel on the feet is removed down to the level of the dial with a special diamond file.
13 The small seconds dial, made meanwhile by the same process and not quite as thick as the main dial, is matched to its destined location by grinding, put in place and soldered on the line between 12 o'clock and 6 o'clock.
14 The dial is polished to the exact diameter, with a small facet each side.
15 The exact length of the feet is determined using a template.
16 Due to the different coefficients of expansion of the copper, lengthwise and widthwise, depending on the direction in which it was rolled, the position of the feet alters during cooling. These inevitable changes must be taken into account when deciding on their position. The deviation cannot be calculated but can be estimated intuitively with experience – quite an achievement, when one considers the close tolerances employed in the watch industry.

Preceding pages
Wooden drawers used to store enameled dials made during the last century. A valuable treasure for the after-sale service.

264 Dial with luminous numerals. The luminescent substance formerly used was radium, which emitted harmful radiation.

265 Enameled dial with large hand-painted numerals.

266 Division of the dial and inscriptions: record in the book of models of 1912, Fabrique des Faverges, Robert Frères, Villeret.

Following pages
A racecourse where Rieussec chronographs were used.

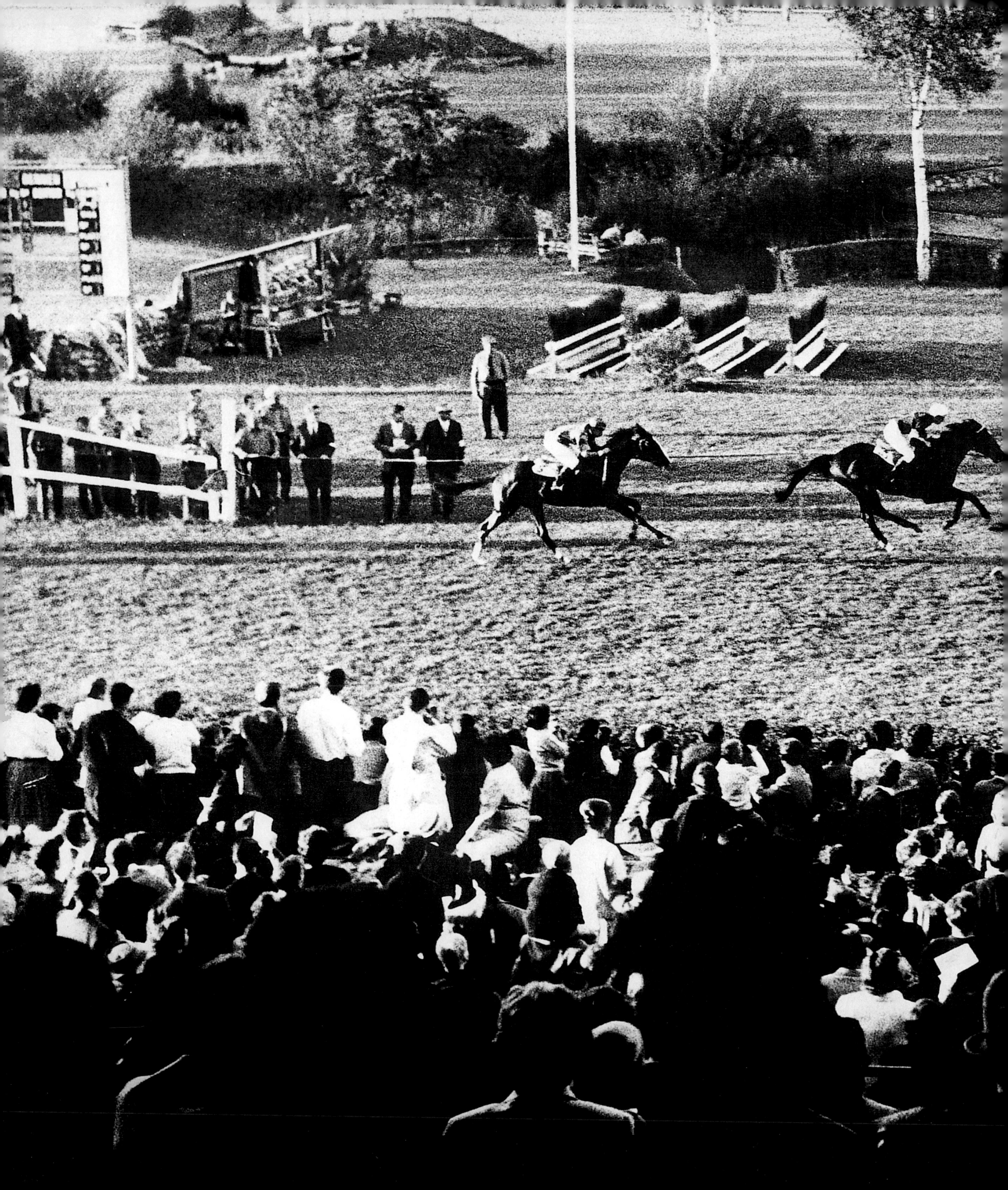

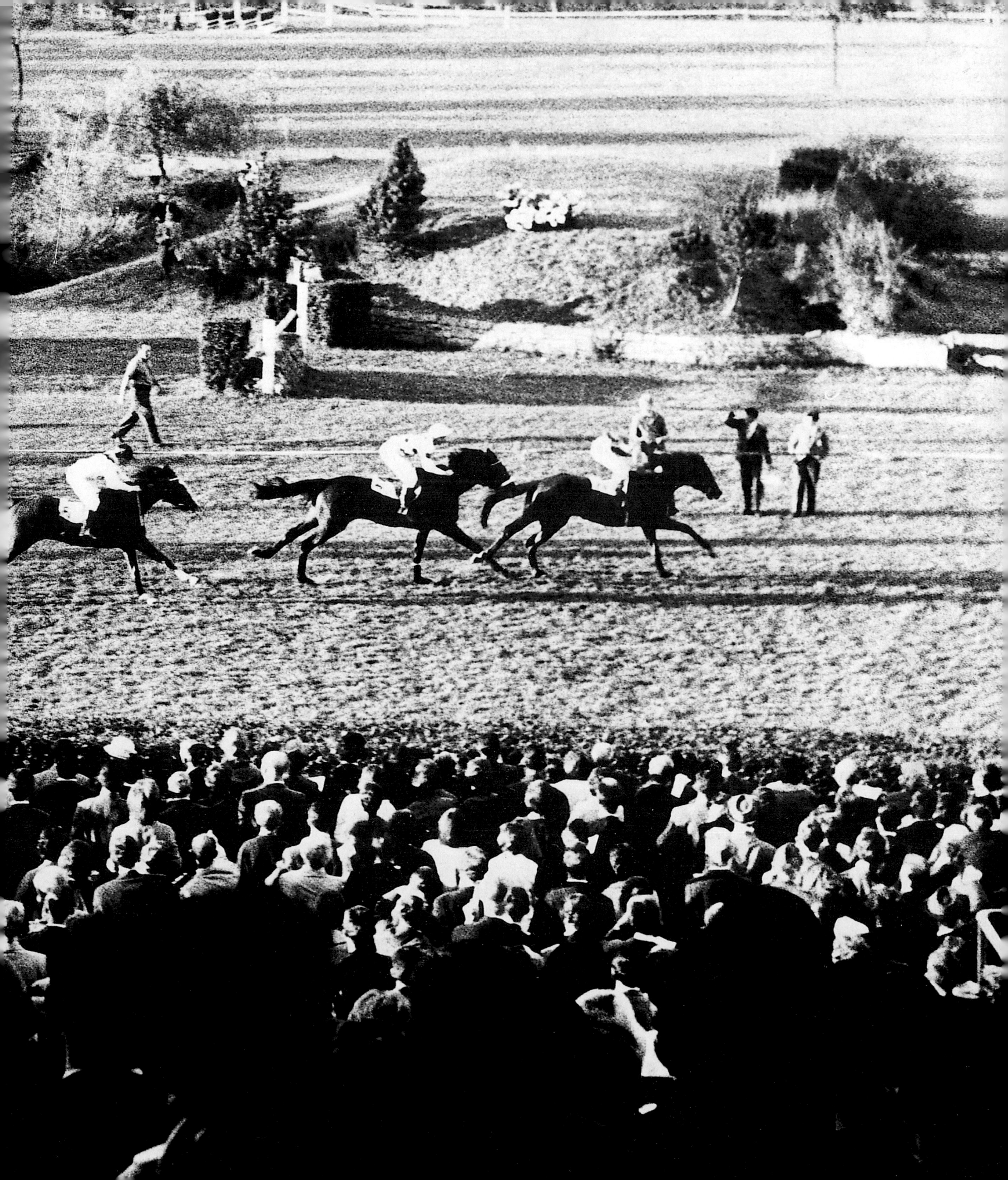

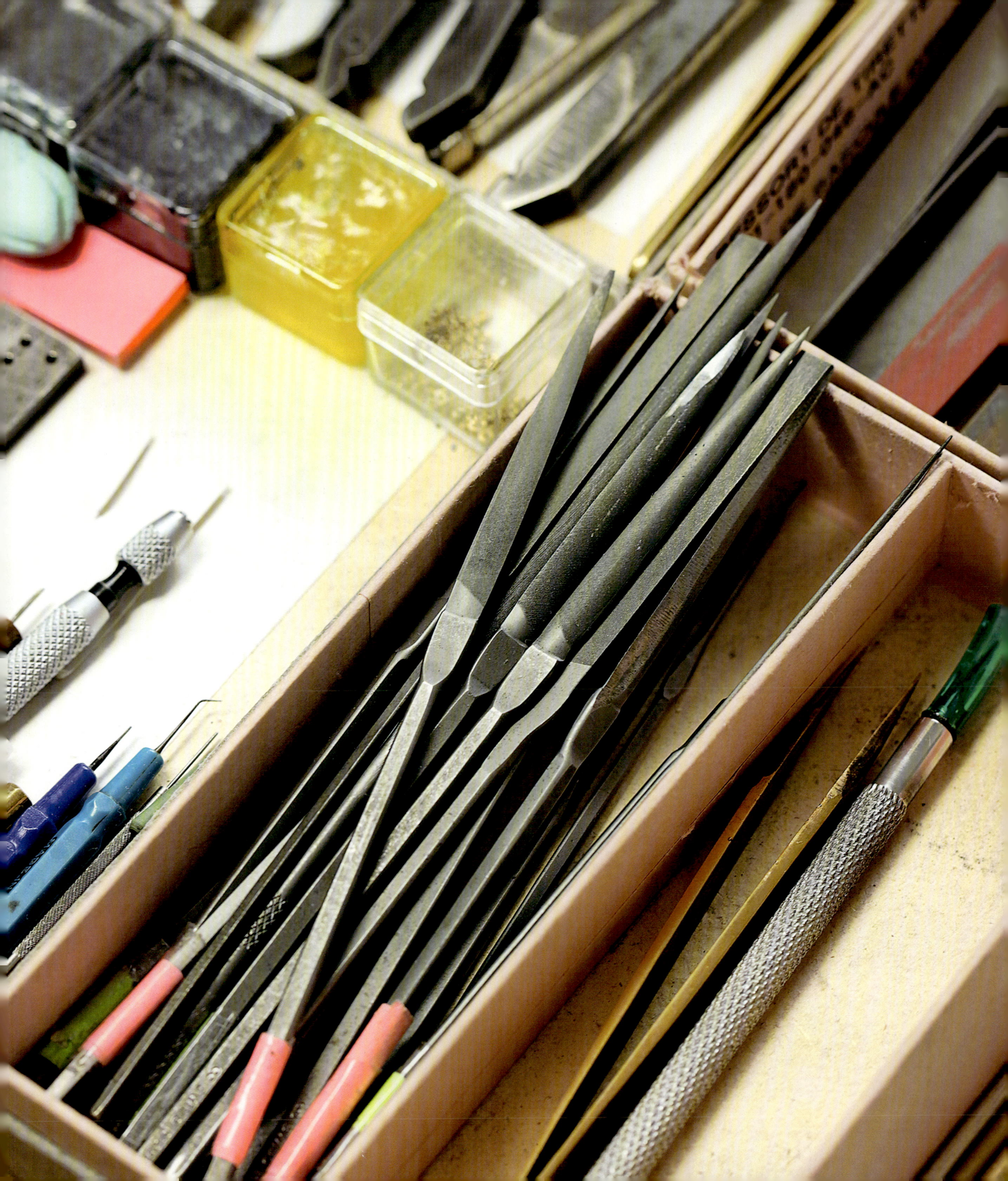

Notes

II. 150 YEARS OF WATCHMAKING TRADITION IN VILLERET

1 Saint-Imier Valley was part of France from 1797 to 1814, then returned to Switzerland (the canton of Bern) in 1815.
2 Marx Karl, *Capital: A Critique of Political Economy*, translated by Edward Aveling (Chicago: Charles H. Kerr & Co, 1906), vol I, part IV, chap. 14, section 3; Jean-François Gravier, *Economie et organisations régionales* (Paris: Masson, 1971), p. 37.
3 Claude Blancpain, *La famille Blancpain* (Nonan-sur-Matran/Fribourg: privately printed, 1994) pp. 52–53.
4 Jean-Jacques Frey, *L'histoire Minerva* (Villeret: Minerva, SA, 1993).
5 Blancpain, *La famille Blancpain*, p. 353.
6 "Histoire de l'horlogerie dans le Jura bernois," *Communications de la Chambre cantonale bernoise du Commerce et de l'Industrie* 2 (April 10, 1920) p. 67.
7 Jacqueline Henry Bédat, *Une région, une passion: l'horlogerie. Une entreprise: Longines* (Saint-Imier: Compagnie des montres Longines Francillon, 1992), p. 70.
8 The new system eliminated the need for a winding key; winding was done via a knob located beneath the pendant ring of the case.
9 Official Swiss Trade records, 1883, no. 42, p. 319.
10 *Catalogue de l'Exposition universelle d'Anvers,* Section 21 (Antwerp: Imprimerie E. Stockmans & Cie, 1885).
11 *Rapport de César Brandt de Bienne*, member of the Horology jury, Class 26, for the 1889 Universal Exposition in Paris (Neuchâtel: Imprimerie Delachaux et Niestlé, 1890), p. 18.
12 *Catalogue officiel des sections suisses*, 1889 Universal Exposition in Paris (Zurich: Orell Füssli), pp. 37 and 110.
13 A.-H. Rhodanet, *Exposition universelle d'Anvers 1885*, *Rapport du jury international des récompenses*, Group II, Class 21, p. 169.
14 Les Faverges was the name of a local area near the factory.
15 Jacques Pelot, *Discours prononcé à l'occasion du centenaire de l'entreprise*, typescript, Minerva archives, Villeret, 1958.
16 *Indicateur Suisse de l'Horlogerie*, 1913.
17 For a more detailed discussion of technical developments, see the second half of this book.
18 Kathleen H. Pritschard, *Swiss Timepiece Makers, 1775–1975* (Phoenix Publishing, 1997), vol. 2, p. M-76.
19 See the more precise figures cited in Frey, *L'histoire Minvera*, p. 11.
20 This information was supplied by Jean-Jacques Frey, Jacques Pelot's grand-nephew, on April 30, 2008.
21 Frey, *L'Histoire Minerva*; and *Feuille Officielle Suisse du Commerce*.
22 Minutes of the shareholders' Annual General Meeting, November 29, 1958. Minerva, S.A. archives, Villeret.
23 André Frey, report to shareholders' Annual General Meeting, December 12, 1968. Minerva, S.A. archives, Villeret.
24 Entretien avec Jean-Jacques Frey du 30 avril 2008 à Saint-Imier.
25 Today Nisshindo sells the best Swiss brands in its shop in the Ginza district of Tokyo.
26 Interview with Jean-Jacques Frey, April 30, 2008, Saint-Imier.

Left
A watchmaker's tool set used in the after-sales service to restore antique watches.

III. THE HISTORY OF MINERVA WATCH MOVEMENTS

CHARLES IVAN ROBERT STARTS TO DEVELOP WATCH PRODUCTION AT VILLERET
1 Watches equipped with movements employing a verge escapement required considerable depth.
2 The new escapements were usually cylinder or anchor escapements, arranged on the same level as the gear train.

THE FIRST ÉBAUCHES FROM FONTAINEMELON, 1850–1870
1 The *établisseurs* were watchmakers who bought all the parts of a watch from external suppliers (the local specialised industry) and assembled the timepieces in their own workshops.
2 In Switzerland, cottage industry was a special mode of division of labour, in which the many components of a watch were made to orders placed by middlemen. Pay was on a piecework basis.
3 Until the early decades of the twentieth century, the jewels were set into the plate from the back. This operation was performed using a *burin fixe*. Today, the rubies are just pressed into the holes, an operation made possible by the reduced tolerances achieved through technical progress.

FONTAINEMELON ÉBAUCHES OF 1876 (WITH WINDING CROWN)
1 Jean Adrien Philippe (1815-1898), co-founder with A.N. de Patek of the *manufacture* of Patek, Philippe & Co., in Geneva, in 1848. In 1842, Philippe invented the crown winding system for pocket watches.
Cf. *LesMontres sans clef ou se remontant et se mettant à l'heure sans clef*, Geneva, 1863.

FONTAINEMELON ÉBAUCHES OF 1910 (WITH THE NEW WINDING TECHNOLOGY)
1 Frédéric Japy, (1749-1813), in Beaucourt, invented a range of tools and machines for making ébauches in 1776. With his sons, he founded the ébauche factory of Japy frères in 1810.
2 Cf. Jean-Jacques Frey; *L'Histoire, Minerva*, p. 3.

THE RECORD BOOKS
1 Old French measure of length formerly used in watchmaking.
1 line = 2.252 mm.

THE MOVEMENT WITH A CYLINDER ESCAPEMENT
1 The term "standard of time" relates to an oscillating system, a pendulum or balance wheel with hairspring, which oscillates at a given frequency. For pocket watches, for example, the usual frequency is 18,000 vibrations per hour.
2 The open part is the cut-out C (ill. 34), or the part left open in the cylinder to allow the balance wheel to oscillate with sufficient amplitude.

ANCHOR MOVEMENTS WITH BREGUET HAIRSPRING
1 Oscillation is said to be "isochronal" when large and small oscillations of the balance wheel are of equal duration, an essential precondition for accurate regulation.
2 Abraham Louis Breguet (1747-1823) went to Paris in 1762 and worked with different watchmakers of the time before setting up on his own account in 1782. The many mechanisms and devices of which he is the author include two inventions, the tourbillon (1802) and the end curve that bears his name in the "Breguet hairspring."
3 Édouard Phillips (1821-1890), a well known mathematician who, at the request of Ferdinand Berthoud, studied the properties of the hairspring and provided a mathematical basis for the curves discovered by Arnold.

"EXTRA QUALITY" ANCHOR ESCAPEMENTS
1 Cf. E. James, *Leitfaden der Präzisionsreglage*, 53 sqq.

ANCHOR MOVEMENTS WITH QUARTER-HOUR REPEATER
1 Cf. Jean-Jacques Frey, L'Histoire, Minerva, op. cit., p. 9.

MINERVA CHRONOGRAPH MOVEMENTS
1 Old French designation of the diameter of a movement. 1 line = 2.252 mm.
2 In the books of models, the movements were registered under successive numbers.

Photographic credits

All photographs in this book were taken by Francis Hammond and Éric Sauvage except:

Actes de la Société jurassienne d'émulation: 174 / Archives Christian Pfeiffer-Belli, Munich: 57, 230 (122, 122a, 123), 231 (125), 232 (130, 131), 233 (134) / Archives de l'Ancien Evêché de Bâle, Porrentruy: 145 / Archives de la famille Blancpain, Nonan-s/Matran: 157, 158-159 / Archives de la famille Robert, Genève: 148 (top), 149 (bottom), 156, 160, 161, 164-165, 186-187 / Archives Montblanc: 7, 17, 20, 21, 22, 23, 24, 25, 26, 27, 34, 35, 45, 49, 54, 55, 108, 111, 118, 125, 126, 141, 142, 143, 153 (right), 166, 168, 170, 171, 172, 173, 175, 180, 189, 191 (9), 193 (12), 195 (17), 204-205, 208 (50, 50a), 210 (57), 218 (86, 87, 88, 89, 90a), 219 (92), 221 (101, 101a, 102, 102a), 222 (107, 108), 223 (111), 225, 226 (116), 231 (124), 236 (143, 144), 242(159), 245 (166), 248 (171), 249 (172, 174), 254 (186), 258 (198a, 198c), 260 (203), 266 (214), 267 (216, 217, 218), 268 (221, 222), 269 (223, 224), 275 (250), 277 (258), 282 (266), 284-285 / Archives Nationales de France/ Guillaume Picon: 56, 58 / Exposition universelle de Paris (1889), *Catalogue officiel des sections suisses*, Zurich: Orell Füssli: 153 (left) / Frey, Jean-Jacques (1993), *L'histoire Minerva*, Villeret: Minerva SA: 149 (top) / Indicateur suisse de l'horlogerie: 167, 169 / Journal suisse de l'horlogerie : 177 / La Cinémathèque française / Etienne Jules Marey: 246-247 / Mémoires d'Ici, Centre de recherche et de documentation du Jura bernois, Saint-Imier: 150-151, 154-155, 163 / Nils Hermann: 15, 28, 29, 30, 38, 39 / Reinhard Meis: 179, 184, 185, 188, 190, 191 (left, 6a, 6b, 7, 8, 10), 192 (left, 11, 13, 14), 193, 194, 195 (left, 15, 16, 18), 196, 197, 198, 199, 200, 201, 202, 203, 206, 207, 208, 209, 210, 211, 212, 213, 214, 215, 216, 217, 218 (90), 219 (91, 93, 94), 220, 221 (100), 222 (103, 104, 105, 106, 109, 110), 223 (112, 113), 224, 226 (115), 227, 230 (121, 121a), 232 (126, 127, 128, 129), 233 (132, 133), 234, 235, 236 (142), 237 (145, 146), 238, 239, 240, 241, 242 (158), 243, 244, 245 (164, 165, 167), 248 (168, 169, 170), 249 (173), 250, 251, 252, 253, 254 (184, 185, 187), 255, 256, 257, 258 (197), 259 (199, 200), 260 (201, 202), 261, 264, 265, 266 (215), 268 (219, 220), 269 (225, 226), 270, 271, 272, 273, 274, 275 (248, 249), 276, 277 (255, 256, 257, 259), 280, 281, 282 (264, 265), gatefold: *Historic Enameled Dials* / Stern Creations/ Archives Montblanc: 93 / Villars Graphic, Neuchâtel: 148 (bottom).

The trademarks Glucydur, Nivarox and Pfinodal are not owned by Montblanc.